Practice and Principles
of Compiler Building with C

Practice and Principles of Compiler Building with C

Henk Alblas and Albert Nymeyer

Prentice Hall

London New York Toronto Sydney Tokyo Singapore
Madrid Mexico City Munich

First published 1996 by
Prentice Hall Europe
Campus 400, Maylands Avenue
Hemel Hempstead
Hertfordshire, HP2 7EZ
A division of
Simon & Schuster International Group

Printed and bound in Great Britain by
Hartnolls Limited, Bodmin, Cornwall

Library of Congress Cataloging-in-Publication Data

Alblas, H.
    Practice and principles of compiler building with C / Henk Alblas
and Albert Nymeyer.
        p.   cm.
    Includes bibliographical references and index.
    ISBN 0-13-349267-2
    1. Compilers (Computer programs)   2. C (Computer program language)
I. Nymeyer, Albert.   II. Title.
QA76.76.C65A39   1996
005.4'53–dc20   96–2515
                                                                    CIP

British Library Cataloguing in Publication Data

A catalogue record for this book is available from
the British Library

ISBN 0-13-349267-2

---

1 2 3 4 5   00 99 98 97 96

Trademark information

Intel is a trademark of the Intel Corporation
Turbo Pascal is a trademark of Borland International, Inc.
UNIX is a trademark of AT&T Bell Laboratories

Contents

Preface

This book is about building a compiler. The approach that is used attempts to strike a balance between the high level and the low level, the concepts and the code. The underlying philosophy is that practical experience motivates the study of principles. The study of the practice and principles of compiler building embodies many important computer-science concepts such as software engineering, algorithms, computer architecture, data structures, and the theory of languages and grammars. Compiler construction lies at the core of computer science—it is computer science in a microcosm.

Synopsis

In Chapter 1 we introduce the concepts of syntax and semantics, analysis and synthesis, and the role of a compiler. In Part I we outline the practice of building a compiler. This involves both writing a compiler by hand, and using a generator tool. The principles behind the compiler generator are explained in Part II.

Part I—Practice This part consists of 5 chapters. In Chapter 2 we define a simple imperative language, and a virtual machine and its interpreter. We show how language constructs can be mapped onto this machine. A step-wise process is then used in Chapter 3 to write a compiler for this language. The first step is to develop a scanner and a context-free parser. The parser is then extended with actions to check context-constraints, and finally, actions are added to emit code for the virtual machine. This process is very systematic. It is straightforward to convert the regular expressions that define the tokens of a language into a scanner. Similarly, it is possible to convert a context-free grammar into a top-down parser. In Chapter 4 we show that a context-free grammar can be extended to an attribute grammar. This allows us to specify the context-sensitive syntax and translation of the given language. We then introduce a compiler generator that is based on attribute grammars, and specify and generate the compiler that we wrote by hand in Chapter 3. The reader is now ready for more complicated language features. In Chapter 5, we extend the source language by adding arrays and procedure parameters to the language, and we generate a compiler for this new language. Because we have generated code for a virtual machine, we need to use an interpreter to execute the code. An interpreter can be very slow, however. To reduce the execution time, we build in Chapter 6 code generators that translate the code for the virtual machine into C-code and assembly code. When compiled and linked, this code executes much faster than the interpreter.

Part II—Principles The 3 chapters in this part are concerned with the theory of scanning, parsing and attribute evaluation. In Chapter 7 we show how a lexical analyser can be generated from a specification, and in Chapter 8, how a top-down parser can be generated from a context-free grammar. We also briefly explain bottom-up parsing. In the last chapter, we reconsider attribute grammars and their evaluation. As in Chapter 4, we begin with a 1-pass scheme, but we also consider a multi-pass and multi-visit scheme.

We use the ANSI-C language throughout this book. Note, however, that our aim is not to write a compiler using C, but to specify and generate a compiler. The programming language that is used is therefore to a large extent incidental.

This book is particularly suited to an undergraduate course. Readers of the book are expected to be familiar with at least one programming language, and to understand basic concepts like variables, stacks, lists and trees. It is our experience that building a compiler can only really be understood by doing it. The student is therefore invited to design and specify his or her own language, and generate a compiler for it. Laboratory assignments in Chapters 4 and 5 suggest a number of languages that are supported by our compiler generator.

Availability

The compiler generator that is developed is a version of a system that is available by *ftp* from the Faculty of Computer Science at the University of Twente. The address is: `ftp.cs.utwente.nl`. The directory *pub/tcgs* contains the compressed tar files *sun.tar.Z* and *pc.tar.Z*, corresponding to versions of the system that run on a SUN workstation (Solaris) and a PC386/486. Each version contains a user interface, a scanner generator (called *scangen*), a parser generator (*parsgen*), an interpreter (*interpr*) and 2 code generators (*v2c* and *v2a*).

Acknowledgements

This book is the culmination of years of work by scores of people. Some people deserve special mention for their substantial contribution to the material presented: many thanks to Joos Schaap-Kruseman for countless discussions, her insight, ideas and software skills. We are indebted to Wim Schepers and Han Groen for their dedication and programming expertise: Wim and Han have done a fine job making the compiler-generator system robust and flexible. Also thanks to Rieks op den Akker for contributing to the text, and to Frans Faase for his work on the software. Part of this book is based on the text for a course on compiler construction written by Henk Alblas, Hans van Berne, Arie Duijvestijn, Theo van der Genugten, Gerry Kamsteeg-Kemper and Joos Schaap-Kruseman. The work of students in the evolution of a course text often goes unsung. Top marks go to Aad Droppert for his work on the attributed parser generator; Theo Ruijs, Ric Klaren and Tsjeard de Boer for their work on the code generator; and Albert Hofkamp for helping with the illustrations.

Twente   Henk Alblas
February 1996   Albert Nymeyer

Chapter 1

Introduction

1.1 Why compilers?

Every computer system has a machine language. Programs in the machine language can be executed by the hardware of the computer system, i.e. the hardware is able to decode the instructions of the machine language and can perform actions according to their meaning. Unless a program is written in the machine language of the computer system, it cannot be executed by the hardware of the system. For programs written in a language that is not the machine language, software tools are needed to help execute such programs. For example, assume we have some high-level language (like C or Pascal). We will call this language SLANG. If a computer must directly execute a program written in SLANG, then it must have SLANG as its machine language. Unfortunately, a machine with such a machine language does not exist.

A solution is to develop an interpreter program that reads and interprets the statements of the program written in SLANG, i.e. it recognises each statement and performs associated actions. In fact, the interpreter program simulates a SLANG computer. Another solution is to first transform (translate) the SLANG program into an equivalent program in a language for which the interpretation process is much simpler, and next to let another interpreter program for this language execute the instructions of the translated program. The machine language is the easiest language to interpret, because for this language no software tools are needed.

The design problem of a translator for the language SLANG is to express the meaning of every SLANG program in machine instructions. Because SLANG is a high-level language, the "distance" between SLANG and machine languages is rather large. Therefore, an *intermediate language* is often used in the translation process (see Figure 1.1). Such an intermediate language allows us to perform the translation not in 1 large step, but in 2 smaller steps.

A good choice of the intermediate language allows a large part of the translation, i.e. the translation of SLANG to the intermediate language, to be machine-

1

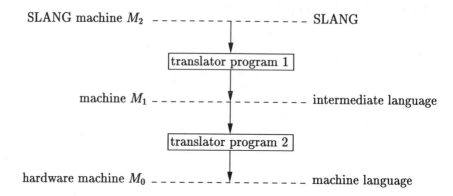

Figure 1.1   Design of a translator from SLANG into machine language in 2 steps.

independent. There are 2 methods to execute the program in the intermediate language:

1. The program is translated into a program in machine language.
2. An interpreter program interprets the program.

1.1.1   Method 1

First, the SLANG program is translated into a program in the language of a hypothetical machine M_1. Next, the program in the language of machine M_1 is translated into a program in the language of machine M_0 (the real or physical machine). Finally, the program in the machine language of M_0 is interpreted by the hardware of M_0. We say that machine M_2 is first mapped onto machine M_1, which in its turn is mapped onto M_0.

The hypothetical machine M_1 is selected such that the meaning of any SLANG program can easily be expressed in the language of machine M_1. When mapping machine M_2 onto machine M_1 we ignore the machine-dependent details of the language of machine M_0. We want to express the meaning of SLANG programs in the language of machine M_1. Therefore, machine M_1 must be structured such that this mapping can be realised without too many problems (the structure of M_1 should, however, not result in a complicated mapping from M_1 onto M_0). The features of M_0 play a role in the mapping of machine M_1 onto machine M_0.

By introducing the hypothetical machine M_1, the translation is split into a machine-independent part $M_2 \rightarrow M_1$ and a machine-dependent part $M_1 \rightarrow M_0$. As a result, the translator for SLANG can rather easily be brought (ported) to another physical machine. Only the mapping $M_1 \rightarrow M_0$ has to be rewritten. This makes the translator portable, which is a valuable asset as the number and variety of computers is large.

1.1.2 Method 2

A different method of executing a SLANG program is depicted in Figure 1.2. The SLANG program is translated into a program in the language of the hypothetical machine M_1. The program in the language of machine M_1 is interpreted by an interpreter program. As before, the language of machine M_1 is considered an intermediate language, in the sense that the language is situated somewhere in between SLANG and the machine language. On the one hand, the intermediate language is selected so that the meaning of any SLANG program can easily be expressed in this language. On the other hand, the intermediate language must be structured so that it can easily be interpreted.

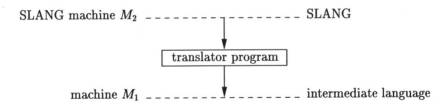

Figure 1.2 Design of a translator from SLANG into an intermediate language, which can be interpreted by an interpreter program.

1.1.3 Analysis-synthesis model

Consider again Figure 1.1 where a program in a high-level source language is translated into a low-level target (machine) language. Translator program 1 is usually called the *front-end*, while translator program 2 is called the *back-end*. The front-end is the source-language-dependent and the target-language-independent part, whereas the back-end is the target-language-dependent and the source-language-independent part.

A related view of translation is the *analysis-synthesis model*. The *analysis phase* recognises the structure and the meaning of the source program, while the *synthesis phase* constructs the desired target program. We will further develop analysis and synthesis in subsequent sections of this chapter.

1.1.4   Compilers

A translator which performs the translation of a high-level language into an intermediate language or a machine language is called a *compiler*. The term compiler was invented in the early 1950s. Translation was then viewed as the "compilation" of a sequence of subprograms selected from a library.

Generally speaking, a compiler is a program that reads a program written in a source language and translates it into an equivalent program in a target language. In Figure 1.1, for example, SLANG is the source language and the machine language is the target language. But compilers have a broader application area than just translating programming languages into machine-languages. Text formatters that translate text and formatting commands into typesetter commands are in fact compilers. Another example of a translator that transforms a high-level source language into a low-level target language is the silicon compiler that translates VLSI design rules into a composition of signals in a switching circuit.

The target program of a compiler generally needs further processing before it can be executed. Figure 1.3 shows a typical language-processing system. The compiler generates assembly code that is translated by an assembler into relocatable machine code. The linker/loader links this relocatable machine code with files of relocatable code from libraries and adjusts addresses, so that the final code can actually run on the machine.

1.2   Language definition

Both the programmer and the compiler writer need a strict definition of the programming language they are dealing with. The programmer who wants to express his or her algorithms in the language will consult the language definition in order to find out what the possible language constructs are, and what their meanings are. The compiler writer has to provide for every language construct a translation according to its meaning.

Every language has a vocabulary, a list of words. Sentences can be formed by combining words into sequences. It is characteristic of languages that some sequences of words are correct, well-formed sentences, and others are incorrect or ill-formed. The *grammar* or *syntax* of the language defines which sequences are correct. The syntax, however, is more than just a means to define which sentences are correct. The syntax is a set of rules that defines how words can be arranged to form sentences. These rules provide every sentence with a structure, i.e. they can be used as an instrument to recognise the structure of the sentences.

The *semantics* defines the meaning of the well-formed sentences. Syntax and semantics are connected in the sense that the semantics give the meaning of every language structure recognised by the syntax.

Every implementation of a language has its restrictions, e.g. a limit on the

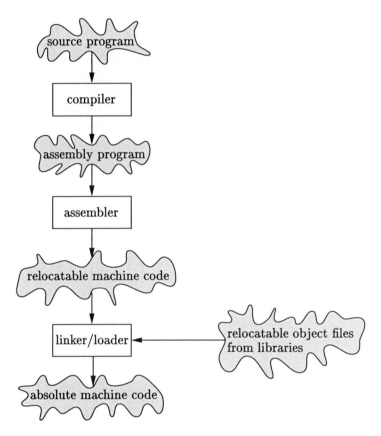

Figure 1.3 Structure of a language processing system.

number of identifiers that can be used or a bound on the depth of recursion. These characteristics of a specific implementation are named its *pragmatics*.

We first describe a formalism for the (context-free) syntax and explain it by means of examples. We also briefly discuss context constraints, semantics and pragmatics.

1.2.1 Syntax

Consider a syntax for simple English sentences, which consist of a subject, followed by a verb, and an object. We restrict ourselves to a subset of the simple sentences, where the subject and the object consist of an article followed by a noun.

The notions *sentence, subject, verb, object, article* and *noun* are not meant to be words in the language. Such notions merely play a role in the language description;

in particular, they denote parts of sentences. They are therefore called *syntactic categories*.

In formal languages, the words are often called *tokens*. Together, the sets of syntactic categories and tokens form the vocabulary of *grammar symbols*. In some manner, the syntactic categories have to be distinguished from the tokens. We will adopt the convention that an italicised name is a syntactic category and any non-italicised name or symbol may be assumed to be a token.

The syntactic categories are defined by means of *rewriting rules*, which we demonstrate by way of the following definition for simple English sentences:

sentence	→	*subject verb object*
subject	→	*article noun*
verb	→	bites
object	→	*article noun*
article	→	a	the
noun	→	man	dog

The syntactic category *sentence* denotes a notion that can be defined as the set of all strings of tokens that satisfy the definition of *sentence*. The rewriting rule

   sentence → *subject verb object*

has the meaning: the syntactic category *sentence* is defined as the set of all strings that can be formed by concatenating an element from the set *subject*, an element from the set *verb*, and an element from the set *object*. This should be read as: a *sentence* is defined as a *subject*, followed by a *verb*, followed by an *object*. The rewriting rule

   article → a | the

leaves one to choose from 2 possibilities. These possibilities are separated by a vertical bar.

The language definition described is a generation scheme, in the sense that any well-formed sentence can be generated by starting at the syntactic category *sentence* and successively applying rewriting rules. This can be explained by considering the creation of the sentence "the dog bites a man", as illustrated in the tree structure in Figure 1.4. Each node in the tree is labelled by a grammar symbol. An interior node and its children correspond to a rewriting rule; the interior node corresponds to the left-hand side of the rewriting rule, the children to the right-hand side.

The tokens, such as "a", "the", "dog", "man" and "bites" are called *terminal symbols* or *terminals*, because they appear at the end of the generation process. The syntactic categories *sentence*, *subject*, *verb*, *object*, *article* and *noun* are called *nonterminal symbols* or *nonterminals*. The rewriting rules, such as

   sentence → *subject verb object*

are called *production rules* or *productions*, because they produce the sentences of

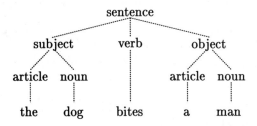

Figure 1.4 Syntactic tree of the sentence "the dog bites a man".

the language. The nonterminal *sentence* is called the *start symbol*, because it is the distinguished nonterminal where the generation process of every sentence starts, i.e. from which all sentences are derived.

A grammar, as described above, is called a *context-free grammar* because its productions can be applied in any context in which the nonterminals occur. A language is called context-free if it can be defined by means of a context-free grammar. Summing up, a context-free grammar consists of:

- A set of terminals or tokens. Representations of tokens occur in sentences of the language.
- A set of nonterminals which do not occur in the language, but merely play a role in the language description.
- A start symbol, a distinguished nonterminal from which all sentences are derived.
- A set of productions (syntax rules). Every production consists of a left-hand side and a right-hand side, separated by a right-arrow. The left-hand side consists of a single nonterminal. The right-hand side is empty or consists of 1 or more alternatives, separated by vertical bars. Every alternative consists of a string of nonterminals and terminals. The string containing zero tokens, written as ϵ, is called the empty string.

A grammar *generates* (or *derives*) a sentence by beginning with the start symbol and repeatedly applying a production. The application of a production consists of the replacement of the left-hand side by one of its alternatives in the right-hand side (which may be empty). The token strings that can be derived from the start symbol form the *language* defined by the grammar.

We have ignored the semantics of our simple English sentences, because one may assume that the meaning of the words "a", "the", "man", "dog" and "bites" are well known in their context. In a programming language like C or Pascal, however, we need the semantics of every language structure recognised by the syntax. Take, for example, the evaluation of arithmetic expressions. With respect to the operators one could simply say that they have the "usual meaning", but their precedence has to be defined, either in the syntax or in the semantics. For every operator one should also define the result type for every combination of operand types.

Parse trees. The syntax tree in Figure 1.4 is called a *parse tree*. A parse tree depicts how a string in the language can be derived from the start symbol. Formally, a parse tree for a context-free grammar has the following properties:

1. The root is labelled by the start symbol.
2. Each leaf is labelled by a token or ϵ.
3. Each interior node is labelled by a nonterminal. If X_0 is the nonterminal labelling this node and $X_1, X_2, \ldots, X_n$ are the labels of its children from left to right, then there must be a production $X_0 \to X_1 X_2 \ldots X_n$, where each $X_1, X_2, \ldots, X_n$ is either a terminal or a nonterminal. If the node has a single child labelled ϵ, then there must be a production $X_0 \to \epsilon$.

In the parse tree, shown in Figure 1.4, the root is labelled *sentence*, the start symbol of our grammar for simple English sentences. The children of the root, from left to right, are labelled *subject*, *verb* and *object*, respectively. Note that the production

$$sentence \quad \to \quad subject \; verb \; object$$

is applied at the root.

The leaves of a parse tree, spelled out from left to right, form the *yield* of the tree. We say that the string that forms the yield is *generated* or *derived* from the start symbol at the root of the tree. In Figure 1.4, the string "the dog bites a man" is generated.

We have already defined a language generated by a grammar as the result of a rewrite process, i.e. the token strings that can be derived from the start symbol by repeatedly applying a production of the grammar. A parse tree is a pictorial representation of such a derivation. Another definition of a language is therefore the set of yields of the possible parse trees. The process of constructing a parse tree for a string of tokens is called *parsing* that string.

Ambiguity. The parse tree of a token string is a hierarchical description of that string according to a given grammar. It is, however, not always possible to talk about *the* parse tree of a string according to a grammar as the string can have more than 1 parse tree. Such a string is said to be *ambiguous*. A grammar is ambiguous if it can derive token strings that are ambiguous. Hence, to show that a grammar is ambiguous, we simply need to find a token string that has more than 1 parse tree. As a string with more than 1 parse tree often has more than 1 meaning, we want to avoid ambiguous grammars. This means that we will use unambiguous grammars, or ambiguous grammars with *disambiguating rules* that select 1 specific tree as valid, and discard the others.

We illustrate ambiguity by means of a grammar that describes expressions of digits and plus and minus signs. The productions are:

$$expr \quad \rightarrow \quad expr + expr \mid expr - expr \mid digit$$
$$digit \quad \rightarrow \quad 0 \mid 1 \mid 2 \mid 3 \mid 4 \mid 5 \mid 6 \mid 7 \mid 8 \mid 9$$

Figure 1.5 shows 2 parse trees for the expression $3-2+1$. The 2 trees correspond to the 2 possible ways in which parentheses can be used in this expression, i.e. $(3-2)+1$ and $3-(2+1)$. The second parenthesisation results in the value 0 rather than the customary value 2.

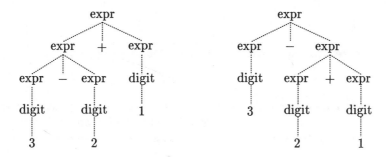

Figure 1.5 Parse trees for the expression $3-2+1$.

Associativity of operators. Consider again the expression $3-2+1$. As the operand 2 has operators to its left and right, a disambiguating rule is needed to decide which operator takes that operand. By convention $3-2+1$ is equivalent to $(3-2)+1$. Since an operand between plus and minus signs is taken by the operator to its left, we say that the operators $+$ and $-$ are *left-associative*. In most programming languages the arithmetic operations addition, subtraction, multiplication and division are left-associative, whereas exponentiation and assignment are right-associative.

To resolve the ambiguity of the previous grammar for expressions we change the productions as follows:

$$expr \quad \rightarrow \quad expr + digit \mid expr - digit \mid digit$$
$$digit \quad \rightarrow \quad 0 \mid 1 \mid 2 \mid 3 \mid 4 \mid 5 \mid 6 \mid 7 \mid 8 \mid 9$$

Right-associativity of the exponentiation operator can be expressed by the following grammar (where exponentiation is the only operator):

$$expr \quad \rightarrow \quad digit \uparrow expr \mid digit$$
$$digit \quad \rightarrow \quad 0 \mid 1 \mid 2 \mid 3 \mid 4 \mid 5 \mid 6 \mid 7 \mid 8 \mid 9$$

The difference between parse trees for left-associative and right-associative operators is shown in Figure 1.6. The parse tree for $3-2+1$ grows down towards the left, whereas the parse tree for $3 \uparrow 2 \uparrow 1$ grows down towards the right.

Precedence of operators. We next consider the combination of addition and

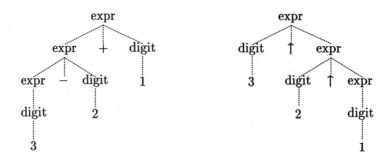

Figure 1.6 Parse trees for left- and right-associative operators.

multiplication in an expression. The expression $3 + 2 * 1$ has 2 possible interpretations, i.e. $(3 + 2) * 1$ and $3 + (2 * 1)$. The associativity of $+$ and $*$ does not resolve this kind of ambiguity. We therefore need to know the relative precedence of the operators $+$ and $*$ when they have the same operand.

By convention, the operator $*$ takes its operands before the operator $+$ does. We therefore say that $*$ has *higher precedence* than $+$. The expression $3 + 2 * 1$ is thus equivalent to $3 + (2 * 1)$.

A grammar for arithmetic expressions. We will construct a grammar for arithmetic expressions from the table below, which shows the associativity and precedence of operators. The meaning of each of these operators is self-explanatory. The operators are presented in order of decreasing precedence, and operators on the same line have the same precedence level.

operator	associativity
$\uparrow$	right
$* \div$	left
$+ -$	left

We introduce nonterminals *expr*, *term* and *factor* for the 3 levels of precedence, and nonterminals *primary*, *natnum* and *digit* to define natural numbers and expressions between parentheses. A natural number is a list of digits.

$$\begin{aligned}
\textit{primary} &\;\rightarrow\; \textit{natnum} \mid (\textit{expr}) \\
\textit{natnum} &\;\rightarrow\; \textit{natnum digit} \mid \textit{digit} \\
\textit{digit} &\;\rightarrow\; 0 \mid 1 \mid 2 \mid 3 \mid 4 \mid 5 \mid 6 \mid 7 \mid 8 \mid 9
\end{aligned}$$

The binary operator $\uparrow$ has the highest precedence, and associates to the right. Its production is therefore

$$\textit{factor} \;\rightarrow\; \textit{primary} \uparrow \textit{factor} \mid \textit{primary}$$

The binary operators $*$ and $\div$ have the next highest precedence. As these operators associate to the left, their productions are

$$term \quad \rightarrow \quad term * factor \mid term \div factor \mid factor$$

Similarly, the productions for $+$ and $-$, which have the lowest precedence, are

$$expr \quad \rightarrow \quad expr + term \mid expr - term \mid term$$

The resulting grammar is therefore

$$
\begin{array}{lcl}
expr & \rightarrow & expr + term \mid expr - term \mid term \\
term & \rightarrow & term * factor \mid term \div factor \mid factor \\
factor & \rightarrow & primary \uparrow factor \mid primary \\
primary & \rightarrow & natnum \mid (expr) \\
natnum & \rightarrow & natnum\ digit \mid digit \\
digit & \rightarrow & 0 \mid 1 \mid 2 \mid 3 \mid 4 \mid 5 \mid 6 \mid 7 \mid 8 \mid 9
\end{array}
$$

This grammar defines an expression as a sequence of terms chained by either $+$ or $-$ operators, a term as a sequence of factors chained by $*$ or $\div$ operators, and a factor as a sequence of primaries chained by $\uparrow$ operators. An expression enclosed between parentheses is a primary, so with parentheses we can write nested expressions of any depth.

1.2.2   Context constraints

Thus far we have seen that a language can be defined by means of a context-free grammar. In many programming languages, however, context-sensitive aspects, e.g. scope and type rules, also play an important role. Scope rules determine the scope of each declaration and allow the declaration of each identifier to be located. Type rules make it possible to infer the type of each expression and thus to ensure that each operator is supplied with operands of the correct type. The term "context constraints" is used because not only the context-free syntax of an expression, but also the declarations of its constituents in the context, determine whether the expression is well-formed. Context constraints are often called *static semantics*.

1.2.3   Semantics

We will very briefly discuss the semantics of the arithmetic expressions defined using the syntax presented above.

An arithmetic expression is a rule for computing an integer value. This value is obtained by executing the indicated arithmetic operations on the values of the natural numbers of the expression. The value of a natural number is obvious. A

token	example	informal description
add_operator	+	+
assignment_operator	:=	:=
relational_operator	$<, <=, =, <>, >=, >$	$<$ or $\leq$ or $=$ or $\neq$ or $>$ or $\geq$
identifier	sum, ys15hp	letter followed by a, possibly empty, sequence of letters and digits
integer	13, 1993	sequence of digits
begin	**begin**	keyword **begin**

Figure 1.7 Examples of single and multi-character tokens.

natural number is a special case of an integer number. The operators $+, -, *, \div$ and $\uparrow$ are defined for integer numbers and have the conventional meanings.

The precedence and associativity of the operators are expressed by the grammar. The expression between a left parenthesis and the matching right parenthesis is evaluated independently and this value is used in subsequent calculations. Consequently, the desired order of execution of operations within an expression can always be arranged by appropriate positioning of parentheses.

1.2.4   Pragmatics

Some aspects of a language depend on the characteristics of the implementation (of the compiler). Examples are the maximum number of characters of an identifier, and the largest integer value that that can be expressed. These restrictions are usually described in the compiler documentation.

1.3   Analysis of the source program

In Section 1.2 we presented arithmetic expressions consisting of digits, operators and parentheses. Each input character forms a single token. In most programming languages, the tokens are composed of more than 1 character. Examples of some single and multi-character tokens are presented in the table shown in Figure 1.7.

The task of recognising the tokens is given to a special program, the token recogniser. The recognition of tokens is called *lexical* (i.e. *lexicographic*) *analysis*. The parsing process is now simplified because it is relieved of analysing a lot of details. The tokens are, in fact, at a higher abstraction level than the single characters from which the tokens are built.

The border between lexical and syntax analyses is somewhat arbitrary. The main reason for the separation is the simplification of the analysis phase. The inclusion of *recursion* in a grammar turns out to severely complicate the parsing process. The recognition of tokens does not require recursion, whereas the recognition of syntactic constructs often does. One criterion in determining the separation is therefore whether a language construct is inherently recursive or not. Although identifiers can be defined by means of a left-recursive definition, for example

$$identifier \quad \rightarrow \quad letter \mid identifier\ letter \mid identifier\ digit$$

we can also define an identifier without recursion. We do this by simply scanning the input stream, starting with a letter, and reading letters and digits, until a character that is neither a letter nor a digit is found. Lexical analysis is therefore often called *scanning*.

Such a linear scan is not powerful enough to analyse expressions or statements however. For example, it is impossible to properly match parentheses in expressions without a recursive (i.e. nesting) structure. Expressions are thus inherently recursive, and in Section 1.2 we have therefore used the productions

$$
\begin{aligned}
expr &\quad\rightarrow\quad expr + term \mid expr - term \mid term \\
term &\quad\rightarrow\quad term * factor \mid term \div factor \mid factor \\
factor &\quad\rightarrow\quad primary \uparrow factor \mid primary \\
primary &\quad\rightarrow\quad (expr)
\end{aligned}
$$

In the language definition in Section 1.2 we have distinguished between (context-free) syntax and context constraints. Above we have distinguished between lexical constructs (i.e. tokens) and syntax constructs (e.g. declarations, statements and expressions). Analysis now consists of the following 3 phases:

1. *Lexical analysis*, in which the character stream of the source program is read and subdivided into substrings that represent *tokens*.
2. *Syntax analysis*, in which a hierarchical description of the program is obtained, i.e. a derivation of the token string from the start symbol (usually in the form of a parse tree).
3. *Context analysis*, in which context constraints are checked to ensure that the program is a coherent whole.

In the following sections we discuss each of these phases in turn.

1.3.1   Lexical analysis

The lexical analyser translates the character string of a source program into a series of tokens in which each token corresponds to a substring. The character sequence forming a token is called the *lexeme* for the token.

For example, the sequence of characters in the assignment statement

```
fahrenheit  :=  32 + celsius * 1.8
```

would be translated into the following sequence of tokens:

- The identifier `fahrenheit`.
- The assignment operator `:=`.
- The integer `32`.
- The addition operator `+`.
- The identifier `celsius`.
- The multiplication operator `*`.
- The real `1.8`.

Blanks between the tokens are usually eliminated by the lexical analyser, so that the parser will not have to consider them. Comments can also be treated as white space, and eliminated by the lexical analyser.

Strings of characters that correspond to an integer or real are usually collected by the lexical analyser and converted into a token. The lexical analyser will then pass both the token *integer* or *real* and its associated value to the parser. The parser can then treat numbers as single units.

Compilers also usually treat an identifier as a token. When the scanner recognises an identifier in the input, some mechanism is needed to determine whether the corresponding character string has been seen before. The string is therefore stored in a symbol table, if it is not already there. The token *identifier* with the associated pointer to the table entry is passed to the parser.

Almost all languages use *keywords* such as **begin, end, if, then** and **else**, to mark the beginning and the end of certain constructs, and as punctuation marks. These keywords are generally *reserved* identifiers. Reserved identifiers are often included in the symbol table and marked as keywords.

Observe that the lexical analyser acts as an interface between the parser and the stream of input characters. It recognises tokens in the input stream. These tokens (and in some cases an associated value) are then passed to the parser, which uses them to verify the syntax.

We return to the example at the beginning of this section and look how the lexical analyser processes the string

```
fahrenheit  :=  32 + celsius * 1.8
```

We shall use the notation id_i, where id denotes the token *identifier*, and i the index in the symbol table, to emphasise that the internal representation differs from the lexeme forming the identifier. We shall use the notation int_{32}, where `int` denotes the token *integer*, and 32 the associated value, as the internal representation of the digit string 32. Similarly, we use the notation $real_{1.8}$, where `real` denotes the token *real*, and 1.8 the associated value, as the internal representation of the string 1.8. Figure 1.8(a,b) shows the representations before and after lexical analysis.

Earlier in this section, we introduced the symbol table. When an identifier in the source program is detected by the lexical analyser, its lexeme is entered into the symbol table. More information about the identifier cannot normally be determined during lexical analysis. Subsequent compiler phases will add information

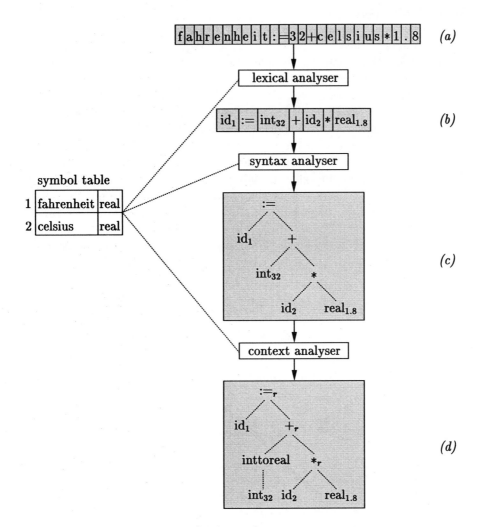

Figure 1.8 Analysis of a source program.

about identifiers to the symbol table. The context analyser, for example, will determine the types of the identifiers, and add this information to the symbol table. During code generation, this type information will be used to generate proper operations.

1.3.2   Syntax analysis

Given a string of tokens and a grammar, parsing is the process of determining if and how the token string can be generated by the grammar. Although a compiler may not actually construct a parse tree, it is often helpful to imagine that a parse tree is being constructed.

Most parsing methods work *top-down* or *bottom-up*. These terms refer to the order in which new nodes are added to the parse tree during its construction. A top-down parser works from the top (the root) towards the bottom (the leaves), while a bottom-up parser starts from the leaves and works up towards the root. In Section 1.5 we will see how efficient and understandable top-down parsers can be easily constructed by hand. Top-down parsers are therefore very popular, although bottom-up parsers are more powerful (i.e. they can parse a greater variety of languages).

We will now explain top-down parsing by means of a simplified version of the expression grammar in Section 1.2.

$$
\begin{aligned}
\textit{assignment} \quad &\rightarrow \quad \textit{identifier} := \textit{expr} \\
\textit{expr} \quad &\rightarrow \quad \textit{expr} + \textit{term} \mid \textit{term} \\
\textit{term} \quad &\rightarrow \quad \textit{term} * \textit{factor} \mid \textit{factor} \\
\textit{factor} \quad &\rightarrow \quad (\textit{expr}) \mid \textit{identifier} \mid \textit{integer} \mid \textit{real}
\end{aligned}
$$

The top-down construction of a parse tree starts by constructing the root node, and labelling it with the start symbol. The following steps are then repeatedly performed:

1. Select a node (labelled with a nonterminal) that has not previously been selected.
2. Let the selected node be n_0, and be labelled with nonterminal X_0. Select a production $X_0 \rightarrow X_1 X_2 \ldots X_k$ and construct at n_0 the children $n_1, n_2, \ldots, n_k$ with labels $X_1, X_2, \ldots, X_k$, respectively.

If the grammar obeys certain restrictions, the above steps can be implemented during a single left-to-right scan of the input string. The token that has just been scanned and given to the parser is called the *look-ahead* symbol. Initially, the look-ahead symbol is the first, i.e. leftmost, token of the input string. At each iteration in the procedure above, we select a node and construct a parse tree at that node. Initially, the node labelled with the start symbol is selected. The objective is to construct a parse tree whose yield matches the complete input string.

When we select a node labelled with a nonterminal, we choose a production for that nonterminal that can derive a string that starts with the look-ahead symbol. Application of the production implies the construction of child nodes labelled with symbols on the right-hand side of the production. After the expansion of the tree we select the leftmost child of the children that have just been constructed. When a node labelled with a terminal is selected, and the terminal matches the look-ahead symbol, then the next child in the parse tree (immediately to the right of the terminal that has just been matched) will be selected. The next token in the input becomes the new look-ahead symbol. For example, in Figure 1.9 we depict the top-down construction of the sentence

```
fahrenheit  :=  32 + celsius * 1.8
```

Initially, the token *identifier* is the look-ahead symbol, and the parse tree consists of a single node labelled with the start symbol, *assignment*. There is only 1 production corresponding to *assignment*, namely

assignment $\rightarrow$ *identifier* := *expr*

Application of this production results in the second parse tree in Figure 1.9. Now the leftmost child, which has label *identifier*, matches the look-ahead symbol. The second left child, which has label :=, matches the next look-ahead symbol. After the nodes with labels *identifier* and := we have the node with label *expr*, and the current look-ahead is *integer*. We continue parsing by selecting the production(s) corresponding to *expr*.

Notice that every nonterminal, except *assignment*, has 2 or 3 productions. This means that from now on, whenever a nonterminal is selected, we must choose between different productions. By making correct choices, we stepwise build the parse tree, as depicted in Figure 1.9. It is, however, unrealistic to expect that we will always make the correct choice. If a correct choice cannot always be predicted, then we must follow a *trial-and-error* approach. That is, at each step where more than 1 production might apply, we arbitrarily choose a production. If eventually our choice turns out to be incorrect, that is, a parse tree that matches the input string cannot be constructed, then we *backtrack* and choose another production. Not surprisingly, such a non-predictive parsing scheme, which requires undoing incorrect decisions, should be avoided for reasons of performance. To avoid making incorrect decisions, we make use of the look-ahead symbol. A parser that always chooses correctly is called *predictive*. We will come back to predictive parsing in Section 1.5.

Often, a special kind of tree is used in which each node represents an operator and the children of the node represent the operands. This kind of tree is a compressed representation of the parse tree, in the sense that nonterminals (which are, in fact, unimportant for translation) are left out, and operators are lifted to a higher level. The parse tree is often called the *concrete syntax tree*, and the compressed version is called the *abstract syntax tree*. For example, the abstract syntax tree for the assignment-statement

```
fahrenheit  :=  32 + celsius * 1.8
```

is shown in Figure 1.8(c). Note that this tree is derived from the complete parse tree in Figure 1.9 by removing the nonterminals, and lifting the operator := to the position of *assignment*, + to the position of *expr* and * to the position of *term*.

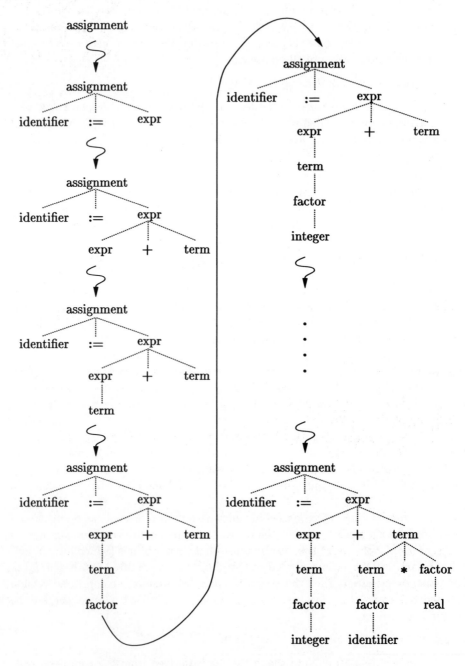

Figure 1.9 Top-down construction of a parse tree.

1.3.3 Context analysis

The context analyser checks if the source program meets the context constraints and collects type information for the synthesis phase of compilation. It uses the abstract syntax tree determined by the syntax analyser, which shows the relation between the operators and operands in expressions.

An important task of a context analyser is type checking, i.e. checking if operands have the correct type according to the language definition. For example, the index of an array must be of type integer, and the operands of a Boolean operator must be of type Boolean. In some cases, however, the compiler will automatically insert coercion operators. If, for instance, a binary arithmetic operator is applied to an integer and a real operand, then the compiler may insert an operator to convert the integer representation to a real representation. Note that the internal representations for integers and reals, even if they have the same value (e.g. 32 and 32.0), are different. Suppose, for example, that the variables `fahrenheit` and `celsius` in the statement

```
fahrenheit  :=  32 + celsius * 1.8
```

have been declared to be of type real. By its denotation, the number 1.8 has been recognised as a real, whereas the number 32 has been recognised as an integer. Type calculation in Figure 1.8(c) reveals that + is applied to a number, 32, of type integer, and a subexpression, `celsius * 1.8`, of type real. This type conflict in the abstract syntax tree can be resolved by inserting an extra node for the operator `inttoreal` that explicitly converts an integer into a real. Figure 1.8(d) shows the extended abstract syntax tree after context analysis. Note that we know now that the operators +, *, and := operate on real operands. These operators are therefore denoted by $+_r$, $*_r$ and $:=_r$.

1.3.4 Analysis tools

Programming environments offer software tools that assist in manipulating, e.g. editing, checking and printing, source programs. Some tools are:

1. *Static checkers.* A static checker is a tool that analyses a source program, and is therefore similar to a compiler front-end. A static checker, however, does not generate any code, but it may analyse (i.e. without running the program) the control flow of the source program. In this way it may not only detect the usual lexical, syntax and context errors, but also that a variable might be used before being assigned, and that certain parts of the source program can never be executed (called dead code).
2. *Syntax-directed editors.* A syntax-directed editor is a combination of an editor and an analyser. The editor assists the programmer in creating and modifying the source program, whereas the analyser performs the lexical,

syntax and context analysis of the thus far created program. Often a distinction is made between a structure-oriented and a text-oriented syntax-directed editor. A structure-oriented editor keeps the phrase structure of the source program correct. In fact, it only allows the creation of a syntactically correct program. If the user selects "While" then the editor sets up the skeleton of a while-statement with the keywords **while** and **do**, and "placeholders" for the Boolean expression between **while** and **do** and the statement after **do**. A text-oriented syntax-directed editor is an extension of a normal text editor. In text mode, the user may create (syntactically incorrect) source programs. In analysis mode, the editor performs lexical, syntax and context checks. A hybrid editor has characteristics of both a structure-oriented and a text-oriented syntax-directed editor.

3. *Pretty printers.* A pretty printer analyses a source program, improves the lay-out, and then prints it. An important aspect of the lay-out of a source program is the indentation of nested declarations and statements.

1.4   Synthesis of the target program

Conceptually, synthesis may consist of 3 phases:

1. Intermediate code generation.
2. Code optimisation.
3. Code generation.

Intermediate code generation involves translating the original source program into an intermediate representation (see Figure 1.1). This intermediate code is first optimised, and then machine code is generated. Figure 1.10(a,b,c,d) shows an example of the application of these phases to the statement

```
fahrenheit   :=   32 + celsius * 1.8
```

Note that synthesis starts from the extended abstract syntax tree of Figure 1.8(d). We will now briefly describe each of the phases.

1.4.1   Intermediate code generation

In Section 1.1 we motivated the use of an intermediate language to simplify the compilation process. The intermediate program must be easy to produce during the analysis phase and easy to translate to target (machine) code during the synthesis phase.

An intermediate language can have a variety of forms, e.g. graphs, trees, stack code, or 2- or 3-address code. The source program

```
fahrenheit   :=   32 + celsius * 1.8
```

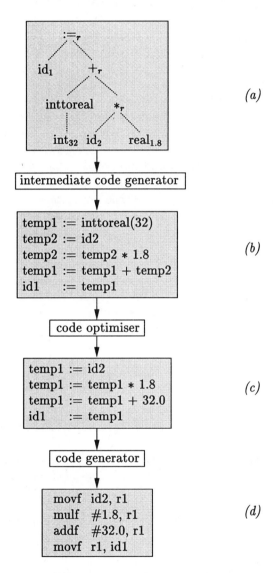

(a)

(b)

(c)

(d)

Figure 1.10 Synthesis of a target program.

might be translated, for example, into the sequence of 2-address instructions in Figure 1.10(b).

Each 2-address instruction has at most 1 operator in addition to the assignment, and at most 2 operand addresses, one of which is also the result address. The order in which the instructions appear is the order in which the operators are found during a postorder traversal of the abstract syntax tree (which is produced by the context-analysis phase). The compiler generates the temporary variables `temp1` and `temp2` to hold the intermediate values computed by the instructions.

1.4.2   Code optimisation

The code optimiser tries to modify the intermediate code in order to obtain a shorter and/or faster-running code sequence. The code generated in the previous section can be improved by using the 4 instructions in Figure 1.10(c).

When it analyses the intermediate code, the optimiser finds that a coercion operator (`inttoreal`) is applied to a number (32). This conversion could be done at compile time, so that the `inttoreal` operation can be deleted. Moreover, the copying of this real number into a temporary variable can be postponed until the multiplication has been applied. After some renaming, the resulting code becomes the 4 instructions in Figure 1.10(c).

Some "optimising compilers" spend a large fraction of their time on optimisation. An investment in compilation pays back if the program runs long and often. In a student compiler, however, this is generally not the case as student programs are usually discarded after they have been completed. Improvement of code may be time-consuming. There are, however, simple optimisations that significantly improve the target program without taking too much compilation time.

1.4.3   Code generation

During the code-generation phase, assembly code or relocatable machine code is generated. Important aspects of code generation are instruction selection and the assignment of registers and memory locations to variables. In particular register allocation is complicated because most machines have only a few registers. In our example register allocation is trivial because only 1 temporary variable is used.

Using register `r1` instead of `temp1` the improved intermediate code might be translated into the assembly code shown in Figure 1.10(d). The assembly instructions consist of an operator name, a source and a destination, respectively. The instruction `movf` moves the source operand to the destination location. The instruction `mulf` multiplies the source and destination operands and stores the result at the destination address. The instruction `addf` adds the source operand to the destination operand and stores the result at the destination address. The `f` suffix of each operator name indicates that the instruction operates on floating-point numbers. The first 2 instructions copy the contents of the storage address `id2` into register `r1`, and multiply it with the real number `1.8`. The `#` indicates that `1.8` is not used as a reference to an operand, but is itself an operand. The third instruction adds the value `32.0` to the contents of register `r1`. Finally, the value in register `r1` is copied into the storage location with address `id1`.

1.5 A simple 1-pass translator

We explained in Sections 1.3 and 1.4, and showed in Figures 1.8 and 1.10, that a compiler operates in phases, each of which may transform the source program from one representation to another. In practice, however, several phases may be combined into 1 *pass*. This pass (usually) consists of a left-to-right examination of the source program. For example, lexical analysis, syntax analysis, context analysis and intermediate code generation could be performed during a single pass, as shown in Figure 1.11. We may think of the syntax analyser being the master program, and the lexical analyser its slave (i.e. subroutine). Every time the syntax analyser needs a token, the lexical analyser is activated. Context analysis is performed during syntax analysis, and every time a language construct is recognised and checked, the corresponding intermediate code is generated.

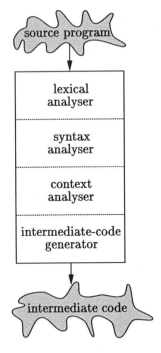

Figure 1.11 Phases of a 1-pass compiler.

In this section, we describe the implementation of a translator that uses this scheme. Consider the following grammar:

$$
\begin{aligned}
const\_expr &\rightarrow expr \\
expr &\rightarrow expr + term \mid term \\
term &\rightarrow term * factor \mid factor \\
factor &\rightarrow (expr) \mid digit \\
digit &\rightarrow 0 \mid 1 \mid 2 \mid 3 \mid 4 \mid 5 \mid 6 \mid 7 \mid 8 \mid 9
\end{aligned}
$$

The language described by this grammar consists of constant arithmetic expressions in *infix* form. Let us assume that we wish to translate these infix expressions into *postfix* form, and output the result. We begin by first considering the implementation of the scanner and parser for infix expressions. Following this we will extend the parser with actions that emit the required postfix form.

The scanner and the parser communicate via the variable *look_ahead*. This variable contains the current, just scanned, input token. We will assume that the routine *next_token* reads the next (i.e. the first unread) token from the input and places it into the variable *look_ahead*. The routine *next_token*, in fact, is the lexical scanner.

We will now develop a predictive recursive-descent parser for the above grammar. *Recursive descent* is a top-down parsing method that takes its name from the fact that it is implemented by means of a set of possibly recursive routines that descend through the parse tree as they recognise the source program. The basic idea is that a parsing procedure or function is associated with each nonterminal of the grammar. In its general form, a recursive-descent parser is *non-predictive* in the sense that the parsing function associated with a nonterminal will try the first alternative of the right-hand side, and if this fails, it will try the second alternative, and so on. Each function returns the value true or false depending on whether it has recognised a substring generated by the associated nonterminal. Such a non-predictive parser, based on trial-and-error, needs backtracking and is inefficient. We will therefore consider a *predictive* recursive-descent parser that uses the look-ahead to select the correct alternative of the right-hand side of the production. Note that a parse tree need not be built, but that it is implicitly defined by the calling sequence of the syntax procedures.

Parsing begins with a call of the procedure for the start symbol, i.e. the procedure *const_expr*, which is shown below.

```
void const_expr(void)
{
    next_token();
    expr();
}
```

In the procedure for *factor* we select *digit* as the second alternative if the look-ahead is not a left parenthesis.

```
void factor(void)
{
    if (look_ahead == '(') {
```

```
    next_token();
    expr();
    if (look_ahead == ')')
      next_token();
  } else
    digit();
}
```

The body of procedure *digit* contains a call to a function *is_digit*, which checks if the look-ahead is a digit.

```
void digit(void)
{
  if (is_digit(look_ahead))
    next_token();
}
```

Note that in parsing right-hand sides, each terminal is directly matched with the look-ahead symbol, whereas the recognition of each nonterminal is delegated (by means of a call) to its associated procedure.

The look-ahead symbols guide the selection of the alternatives to be applied. If an alternative starts with a token, and the look-ahead symbol matches that token, then the alternative is clearly applicable. This is not so simple if 2 alternatives start with a nonterminal, as in

$$expr \;\rightarrow\; expr + term \mid term$$

In this case we need to know which symbols (or strings) can be generated by *expr* and *term*. We define FIRST(X) as the set of tokens that can begin a string derivable from X. The function *in_set* checks if the look-ahead is in the first set. The procedure for *expr*[1] is:

```
void expr(void)
{
  if (in_set(look_ahead, FIRST("expr"))) {
    expr();
    if (look_ahead == '+')
      next_token();
    term();
  } else if (in_set(look_ahead, FIRST("term")))
    term();
}
```

It is possible for a recursive-descent parser to loop forever. In fact, this will happen with our grammar for constant expressions. In that case, we find that FIRST(*expr*) is equal to FIRST(*term*), so that it is impossible to make a choice

---

[1]In programs we sometimes need to distinguish between a nonterminal name and its associated procedure name, which appear the same. The nonterminal name will then be enclosed by quotes.

between the 2 right-hand sides of *expr*. This is caused by the *left recursion* in the production

$$expr \;\to\; expr + term$$

Our implementation of the procedure *expr* will always select the first alternative, i.e. *expr*. This will be repeated in the next invocation of the procedure *expr*, which will result in an infinite repetition of the same procedure call. Note that exchanging the alternatives, i.e. first trying *term*, does not help either, as the parser will then only recognise the head of the input string, and neglect the tail.

To resolve this problem, the productions for *expr* can be replaced by

$$
\begin{aligned}
expr \quad &\to\quad term\ more\_terms \\
more\_terms \quad &\to\quad + term\ more\_terms \mid \epsilon
\end{aligned}
$$

Here *more_terms* is a new nonterminal. The production

$$more\_terms \;\to\; + term\ more\_terms$$

is *right recursive*. During its construction, a tree for a right-recursive production will grow downwards and to the right. For trees that grow to the right it is generally harder to translate expressions that contain left-associative operators, such as minus, although in our case, this will not be a problem. The complete right-recursive grammar is:

$$
\begin{aligned}
const\_expr \quad &\to\quad expr \\
expr \quad &\to\quad term\ more\_terms \\
more\_terms \quad &\to\quad + term\ more\_terms \mid \epsilon \\
term \quad &\to\quad factor\ more\_factors \\
more\_factors \quad &\to\quad * factor\ more\_factors \mid \epsilon \\
factor \quad &\to\quad (\,expr\,) \mid digit \\
digit \quad &\to\quad 0 \mid 1 \mid 2 \mid 3 \mid 4 \mid 5 \mid 6 \mid 7 \mid 8 \mid 9
\end{aligned}
$$

The procedures for the right-recursive nonterminals are shown below.

```
void  more_terms(void);
void  term(void);
void  more_factors(void);

void  expr(void)
{
  term();
  more_terms();
}

void  more_terms(void)
{
  if (look_ahead == '+') {
    next_token();
    term();
```

```
      more_terms();
    }
}

void term(void)
{
  factor();
  more_factors();
}

void more_factors(void)
{
  if (look_ahead == '*') {
    next_token();
    factor();
    more_factors();
  }
}
```

We have seen that a recursive-descent parser associates with each nonterminal a recursive procedure. The body of the procedure contains a syntactic action for each grammar symbol in the right-hand side of the production for that nonterminal. For each terminal, there is an associated matching statement, and for each nonterminal there is an associated procedure call. The position of the grammar symbol in the right-hand side determines when the syntactic action takes place.

To specify a translation (e.g. from infix to postfix form) we extend a context-free grammar to a *translation scheme*. A translation scheme is a context-free grammar with *semantic actions* in the right-hand sides of the productions. We will write a semantic action as a program fragment in bold fount. Every semantic action in the right-hand side of a production will be literally copied into the associated procedure. As in the case of grammar symbols, the position of the action determines when it will be executed. Take, for example, the extended production

more_terms   →   + *term* **print('+')** *more_terms*

Note that the action **print('+')** will be performed after *term* is parsed, but before *more_terms* is parsed. Other examples are the extended productions

digit   →   0 **print('0')**
| 1 **print('1')**
| 2 **print('2')**

which execute print actions for digits.

We now add semantic actions to the context-free grammar for constant arithmetic expressions to specify a translation from infix to postfix form. The complete translation scheme is shown below.

$$
\begin{array}{lcl}
const\_expr & \rightarrow & expr \\
expr & \rightarrow & term\ more\_terms \\
more\_terms & \rightarrow & +\ term\ \mathbf{print('+')}\ more\_terms \mid \epsilon \\
term & \rightarrow & factor\ more\_factors \\
more\_factors & \rightarrow & *\ factor\ \mathbf{print('*')}\ more\_factors \mid \epsilon \\
factor & \rightarrow & (\ expr\ ) \mid digit \\
digit & \rightarrow & 0\ \mathbf{print('0')} \\
& \mid & 1\ \mathbf{print('1')} \\
& \mid & 2\ \mathbf{print('2')} \\
& \mid & 3\ \mathbf{print('3')} \\
& \mid & 4\ \mathbf{print('4')} \\
& \mid & 5\ \mathbf{print('5')} \\
& \mid & 6\ \mathbf{print('6')} \\
& \mid & 7\ \mathbf{print('7')} \\
& \mid & 8\ \mathbf{print('8')} \\
& \mid & 9\ \mathbf{print('9')}
\end{array}
$$

The complete compiler is listed below. Note that the call *print(look_ahead)* in the body of *digit* must occur before the next token is read.

```
void expr(void);
void more_terms(void);
void term(void);
void more_factors(void);
void factor(void);
void digit(void);

void const_expr(void)
{
    next_token();
    expr();
}

void expr(void)
{
    term();
    more_terms();
}

void more_terms(void)
{
    if (look_ahead == '+') {
        next_token();
        term();
        print('+');
        more_terms();
    }
}
```

```
void  term(void)
{
    factor();
    more_factors();
}

void  more_factors(void)
{
    if (look_ahead == '*') {
        next_token();
        factor();
        print('*');
        more_factors();
    }
}

void  factor(void)
{
    if (look_ahead == '(') {
        next_token();
        expr();
        if (look_ahead == ')')
            next_token();
    } else
        digit();
}

void  digit(void)
{
    if (is_digit(look_ahead)) {
        print(look_ahead);
        next_token();
    }
}
```

We have already mentioned that right-recursive productions sometimes make it hard to handle left-associative operators, which are normally expressed using left-recursive productions. To overcome this problem, we use *syntactic operators* to remove left recursion from the grammar. An example of a syntactic operator is the *closure* operator "*", which means zero or more instances of a grammar symbol. If a number of grammar symbols are involved, then we use braces (i.e. { and }). We can apply this syntactic operator to the grammar for constant arithmetic expressions to express the left-associativity of the + and * arithmetic operator, as shown below:

$$
\begin{aligned}
const\_expr &\rightarrow expr \\
expr &\rightarrow term \; \{+ \; term\}^* \\
term &\rightarrow factor \; \{* \; factor\}^* \\
factor &\rightarrow (expr\,) \mid digit \\
digit &\rightarrow 0 \mid 1 \mid 2 \mid 3 \mid 4 \mid 5 \mid 6 \mid 7 \mid 8 \mid 9
\end{aligned}
$$

This grammar is said to be an *extended context-free grammar*. The new procedure for *expr* is:

```
void expr(void)
{
  term();
  while (look_ahead == '+') {
    next_token();
    term();
  }
}
```

1.6   Compiler-construction tools

As compiler writing is a very systematic process, it is natural that systems have been developed that support compiler construction. In the literature, these systems are often referred to as *compiler-compilers, compiler generators* or *translator-writing systems*. There are also tools available for helping implement various phases of compilers. The following list classifies some of these tools:

1. *Parser Generators*. These automatically generate parsers from a grammar. The system TCGS (Twente Compiler-Generator System) includes a parser generator that produces top-down parsers from extended context-free grammars. YACC (Yet Another Compiler Compiler) produces bottom-up parsers from context-free grammars. Parsers and parser generators are discussed in Chapter 8.

2. *Scanner Generators*. As every parser needs a scanner, most parser generators come with an associated scanner generator. TCGS contains a scanner generator, and *Lex* is a scanner generator associated with YACC. Scanner generators produce a lexical analyser from a specification called a *regular definition*. Regular definitions, scanners and scanner generators are discussed in Chapter 7.

3. *Context-analyser Generators*. These are usually based on attribute grammars. Attribute grammars form an extension of the context-free grammar framework in the sense that information is associated with programming-language constructs by attaching attributes to the nonterminals representing these constructs. Attribute grammars form a suitable means to describe type checking, intermediate-code generation, code optimisation and code generation. Several attribute-based tools are available, which usually are a part of a larger system. TCGS and YACC are examples of systems that support the use of attributes.

4. *Code-generator Generators*. These are often based on "template matching". Intermediate code is translated into "templates" that represent machine instructions, in such a way that these templates fit together, i.e. a common

variable of 2 neighbouring templates must be mapped onto the same register or storage location. The main phases of a code generator are *instruction selection* and *storage allocation*, which mutually depend on each other. This *phase-ordering problem* is the reason that code generation is still a topic of research.

5. *Syntax-directed Editor Generators.* These generate syntax-directed editors and are a combination of a parser/scanner generator, a context analyser (type checker) generator and a transformer generator. A transformer generator supports the replacement of a language construct by another language construct, with the restriction that the new construct must fit into the old environment. The generated editor is usually *incremental*, which means that the consistency checks are done with as little effort as possible. An example of a system based on attribute grammars is the *Synthesizer Generator*.

6. *Compiler Generators.* These are compiler-construction environments of integrated tools with which an (almost) complete compiler can be specified. These environments may include preprocessors to set up specifications, modules to generate scanners, parsers, abstract syntax-tree builders, attribute evaluators, tree transformers, code generators and optimisers.

1.7   Exercises

1. Consider the following production rule for an if-statement:

$$if\_statement \quad \rightarrow \quad \textbf{if } relation \textbf{ then } statement \textbf{ else } statement$$
$$| \quad \textbf{if } relation \textbf{ then } statement$$

where the if-statement is 1 of the possible statements. Show that the grammar that contains this if-statement is ambiguous.

2. Consider the following extended context-free grammar for constant arithmetic expressions:

$$
\begin{array}{lcl}
const\_expr & \rightarrow & expr \\
expr & \rightarrow & term \ \{+ \ term\}^* \\
term & \rightarrow & factor \ \{* \ factor\}^* \\
factor & \rightarrow & (\,expr\,) \mid digit \\
digit & \rightarrow & 0 \mid 1 \mid 2 \mid 3 \mid 4 \mid 5 \mid 6 \mid 7 \mid 8 \mid 9
\end{array}
$$

Extend this grammar to a translation scheme that specifies the translation from infix to postfix: in other words, add semantic actions to print operators and digits. Construct a recursive-descent compiler based on this translation scheme.

1.8   Bibliographic notes

The idea of subdividing a compiler into a front-end and back-end, with an intermediate language as interface, dates back to 1958, when a committee report by Strong *et al.* [131, 132] proposed a universal intermediate language, named UNCOL (UNiversal Compiler Oriented Language). The benefit of such a language is, given n languages and m computers, only $n+m$ compilers are needed (n front-ends and m back-ends), instead of $n*m$ compilers. For many different combinations of languages and machines the idea has been found to be optimistic, and today it still remains an ideal. However, in a restricted sense, there are "universal" intermediate languages in use today. Consider, for example, the Pascal-P compiler, which produces intermediate code (P-code) for a simple machine-independent stack computer (P-machine). For a description we refer to Nori *et al.* [104] in [20]. Partitioning a compiler into a front-end and back-end makes it possible to retarget a compiler, i.e. the same front-end can be combined with different back-ends.

The concept of context-free grammars was introduced in the 1950s by Chomsky [31, 32] in a formal treatment of natural languages. The first use of context-free grammars to define programming languages was in 1963 by Naur [38], who used a context-free grammar as a grammatical model to define ALGOL 60.

The use of syntax as the basis for compiler construction started with Irons [83], who developed a syntax-directed compiler for ALGOL 60.

It is not clear who first came up with the idea of recursive-descent parsing. Several authors seem to have invented the idea independently. The recursive-descent scheme has been used since the early 1960s and is still popular.

Part I

Practice

Chapter 2

A source language and virtual machine

In this chapter we present a small, simple programming language and a virtual machine. The language is called SLANG, which is an abbreviation for Source LANGuage. We want to translate programs written in SLANG into code that will run on an "imaginary", or VIrtual Machine, which we call VIM. Because VIM does not really exist, we execute VIM code by using an interpreter. The definition of SLANG is presented in Section 2.1. The virtual machine VIM, its memory organisation, instruction set and interpreter are developed in Sections 2.2, 2.4 and 2.6. The translation from SLANG to VIM is discussed in Section 2.3 and 2.5. A complete compiler for SLANG will be developed in Chapter 3.

2.1 The source language SLANG

SLANG is a simple high-level language. The design of SLANG is the result of 2 competing aims. First, the language needed to be complex enough to properly illustrate the compilation process. This is why we have included procedures, for example. Second, the language also needed to be small and simple. This is why the procedures do not have parameters, and why there is only 1 data type (namely integer). The language is, however, defined in such a way that it is easy to add new constructs, which we will make use of in Chapter 5 to explain manipulation of structured data and parameter passing. In this section, we briefly characterise SLANG and explain the selection of its language structures.

The language provides arithmetic expressions that have constants, variables and expressions between parentheses as operands. The only data type is integer. The priorities of the operators in arithmetic expressions and relations are as follows. The unary operators negation (represented by NEG) and absolute value (ABS) have the highest priority, the multiply operators multiplication ($*$), division ($/$) and modulo ($|$) the next highest, then the add operators addition ($+$) and subtraction ($-$), and finally the relational operators, represented by $=$, $<>$, $<$, $<=$, $>$ and $>=$.

35

We do not consider Boolean expressions because their translation is analogous to arithmetic expressions. An arithmetic relation is included in the language because we need a selection mechanism in conditional and repetitive statements.

As SLANG is an imperative language, it has an assignment statement. There are also statements that allow selection, repetition, the calling of procedures and input/output. The language has a conditional statement, namely the if-statement, and a repetitive statement, namely the while-statement. A case-statement, for-statement and repeat-statement are not included in SLANG as they are variations of the if-statement and while-statement.

The first version of SLANG is kept as small and simple as possible. Procedures do not have parameters as they are only used to demonstrate the scope of identifiers and the control flow inherent to a procedure call. Parameter mechanisms will be added in Chapter 5. Input/output statements are defined only for reading from the keyboard and for writing to the screen.

The if-statement requires an arithmetic relation between IF and THEN. Furthermore, this statement has a closing symbol FI. This makes it possible to include a sequence of statements between THEN and ELSE, and between ELSE and FI, without being obliged to join them in a compound statement. Because the while-statement also provides the delimiters DO and OD, there is no need to have a compound statement as a separate language structure in SLANG.

SLANG does not provide a goto-statement. The reason is not only that the application of goto-statements easily leads to ill-structured programs, more importantly, it is because the goto-statement is difficult to deal with from a compiler-construction point of view. The goto-statement is not just a statement to interrupt the normal order of execution of statements, and to indicate where to continue the execution of the program, it is also a statement that requires rather involved memory management. In particular, this is the case when procedures are nested, i.e. when a procedure contains in its declaration section the declaration of other procedures. If the execution of a goto-statement results in the exit from a procedure, then the existence of the variables, declared in the associated block, has to terminate. The exit from a function is even more complicated, as this interrupts the evaluation of the expression of which the function call is a part of. These problems are considered too complicated for an introductory course in compiler construction.

2.1.1 Formalisms and notation

We will first make some general remarks about data and actions on data, and then explain how the syntax, context constraints, semantics and pragmatics can be specified.

Data and actions. A program consists of declarations and statements. Declarations are used to describe data, and statements are used to describe actions on data.

Data can be denotations of (whole) numbers, constants, variables and procedures. The association of a denotation with a number is implicit and need not be declared. A declaration, however, is needed to associate, or *bind*, an identifier with a constant, variable or procedure. Note that the binding between a denotation and a number is fixed, whereas the binding between an identifier and a constant, variable or procedure can be changed by a declaration. A statement, of course, cannot change the binding of an identifier.

The part of a program where the binding of an identifier to an object (a constant, variable or procedure) holds is called its *scope*. The scope of a binding is the block of the procedure in which the declaration occurs. Procedures can be nested, and so can blocks and scopes. A procedure that is (recursively) declared in the block of a procedure is called a *subordinate procedure*.

A binding that holds in the block of a procedure holds throughout the procedure, i.e. in the block of the procedure and (recursively) in the blocks of its subordinate procedures. An identifier may be bound to different objects in different blocks, as long as an identifier is not declared (bound) twice in the same block. This means that the binding of an identifier to an object holds throughout the entire block containing its declaration, and also in its subordinate blocks, unless the identifier is redefined in a subordinate block.

Example 2.1
Consider the program shown in Figure 2.1. The values and scopes of the identifiers used in this program are shown in Figure 2.2. ◇

A constant declaration binds an identifier to a number. This binding implies that the number is directly bound to the identifier. A constant cannot be assigned. The value of a constant, therefore, cannot be changed.

A variable declaration binds an identifier to a variable. To explain the binding of an identifier to a variable we introduce the concept of a *memory* or *store*. A store consists of *cells* in which values can be held. Each cell resides at a particular *location*. The binding of an identifier to a variable implies that a location is bound to an identifier. As integer is the only type, the only storable values are internal representations of numbers. A value can be written to a location by means of an assignment statement or a read-statement. An assignment statement computes the value of an expression and assigns the value to a variable (i.e. the value is written to the location associated to the variable). A read-statement reads a sequence of values from the input and assigns them to variables (i.e. the values are written to the locations associated to the variables).

Notice that there are also values that cannot be named. These are numbers and truth values that occur as intermediate values of (sub)expressions and relations. The value of an expression is used as an operand in a larger expression, or assigned to a variable, or sent to the output. The truth value of a relation is used to control the execution of an if-statement or a while-statement.

```
BEGIN INT a=1, b=2, c=3;
    ⋮
    PROC p1
    BEGIN INT b=4, d=5, e=6;
        ⋮
    END
    ⋮
    PROC p2
    BEGIN INT c=7, d=8, f=9;
        ⋮
    END
    ⋮
END.
```

Figure 2.1 Nesting of scopes.

constant	value	scope
a	1	entire program
b	2	entire program, excluding p1
b	4	p1
c	3	entire program, excluding p2
c	7	p2
d	5	p1
d	8	p2
e	6	p1
f	9	p2

Figure 2.2 Values and scopes of identifiers.

A procedure declaration binds an identifier to a procedure. The binding of an identifier to a procedure implies that a block is bound to an identifier. The procedure may be invoked (i.e. the block may be activated) in a call-statement. To explain the effect of a procedure call we introduce the concept of an *environment*. An environment models the binding of identifiers during the execution of the program. We mentioned earlier that the binding between an identifier and an object holds throughout the entire block containing its declaration, and also in its subordinate blocks, unless the identifier is overwritten in a subordinate block. This implies that environments usually change at scope boundaries. When we call an identifier that is bound to a procedure, the block bound to the identifier is executed in an environment identical to the environment in which the identifier was declared.

Syntax. For the specification of the syntax of SLANG we will use the concept of an *extended context-free grammar*. Such a grammar allows the application of *syntactic operators* to represent some number of instances of a (number of) grammar symbol(s). We mentioned extended context-free grammars earlier in Section 1.5, where the syntactic operator "*" was applied to remove left recursion from a grammar for constant expressions. For example, recall that in the production

$$expr \ \rightarrow \ term \{+ \ term\}^*$$

the closure operator "*" means that zero or more instances of the part between the braces may occur.

The extended context-free grammar that we use to specify SLANG will use a different notation, however. Instead of the right-arrow "→" we will write a colon ":", the end of a production will be marked by a dot, and the closure operator "*" will be written as "**clos**".

Until now we have used a representation for the tokens, e.g. "+" for the plus operator. In future, we will use names with the suffix "token", e.g. plus_token for the plus operator. This leaves the implementer of the compiler free in the choice of the representations for the tokens. A list of representations for the tokens will be given in Figure 2.4. As this list is only used by the scanner, the parser remains independent of the selected representations.

Using the new notation, the production above can be rewritten as

$$expr \ : \ term \ \{plus\_token \ term\} \ \textbf{clos}.$$

The operator **clos** is not enough to specify SLANG. To keep the specification concise and readable, we define a number of operators. These are shown, and described, in Figure 2.3. Not shown in this table is the concatenation operator, which is implicit. For example, in the previous production, there is an implicit concatenation operator between plus_token and *term*.

The operators **option**, **seq**, **chain**, **list** and **pack** can also be expressed in terms of other operators, as shown below:

$$
\begin{array}{lll}
a \ \textbf{option} & : & a \mid \epsilon. \\
a \ \textbf{seq} & : & a \ a \ \textbf{clos}. \\
a \ \textbf{chain} \ b & : & a \ \{b \ a\} \ \textbf{clos}. \\
a \ \textbf{list} & : & a \ \textbf{chain} \ list\_token. \\
a \ \textbf{pack} & : & open\_token \ a \ close\_token.
\end{array}
$$

The tokens list_token, open_token and close_token are usually represented by ",", "(" and ")", respectively. To delete unnecessary braces in productions we stipulate that all operators are left-associative, and that:

operator	meaning
|	choose between 2 phrases
option	0 or 1 instance of a phrase
clos	0 or more instances of a phrase
seq	1 or more instances of a phrase
chain	a sequence of instances of a phrase
	separated by occurrences of a certain other phrase
list	a sequence of instances of a phrase
	separated by commas
pack	a phrase between parentheses

Figure 2.3 Definition of syntactic operators.

1. the unary operators **option**, **seq**, **clos**, **list** and **pack** have the highest precedence;
2. the binary operator **chain** has the second highest precedence;
3. concatenation has the third highest precedence;
4. choice ("|") has the lowest precedence.

Productions may be spread over different lines and spaces may be used to enhance readability.

In the following example we show a part of the syntax specification of SLANG, and in particular, explain the role of the syntactic operators. The entire specification will be given in Section 2.1.2.

Example 2.2

block	:	begin_token *declaration_part statement_part* end_token.
declaration_part	:	{*constant_declaration* | *variable_declaration*} **clos**
		procedure_declaration **clos**
	.	
variable_declaration	:	var_token *type_declarer identifier* **list** separator_token.
statement_part	:	*statement* **chain** separator_token.

In this specification, a block consists of a declaration-part and a statement-part, enclosed by a begin-token and an end-token. A declaration-part consists of zero or more constant declarations or variable declarations, followed by zero or more procedure declarations. A variable declaration begins with a var-token and ends with a separator-token, and in between these tokens are a type declarer and a sequence (list) of identifiers (which are separated by list-tokens). A statement-part is a sequence of statements, separated by separator-tokens.

The following productions specify an operand as an identifier, a number or an expression between parentheses. An identifier must begin with a letter, which may be followed by any combination and number of letters and digits. A number may consist of any number of digits.

$$operand \quad : \quad identifier$$
$$| \quad number$$
$$| \quad expression \textbf{ pack}$$

$$identifier \quad : \quad \text{letter } \{\text{letter} \mid \text{digit}\} \textbf{ clos}.$$
$$number \quad : \quad \text{digit } \textbf{seq}.$$

Finally, in the following production, we show the combination of 2 syntactic operators. A read-statement consists of a read-token, followed by a list of identifiers (i.e. a sequence of identifiers, separated by list-tokens) that is surrounded by parentheses.

$$read\_statement \quad : \quad \text{read\_token } identifier \textbf{ list pack}. \qquad\qquad \diamond$$

Context constraints. The context-sensitive part of the syntax of SLANG will be specified informally. One of the context constraints is that every applied occurrence of an identifier must be uniquely associated with a defining occurrence. The defining occurrence of an identifier (i.e. its declaration) determines its scope (the block), its kind (constant, variable or procedure) and its type (integer). An identifier may not be declared twice in the same block. Every applied occurrence of an identifier must be in the scope of a defining occurrence of the right kind and type. This implies, for instance, that an identifier in an expression must be in the scope of the declaration of the identifier.

Semantics. In the semantics of SLANG we need to describe the meaning of each program construct. This involves the following aspects:

- the order of execution of declarations and statements;
- the evaluation of expressions;
- the changes to the store, input and output;
- the changes to the environment.

Pragmatics. The compiler may have restrictions on the number and length of identifiers, the magnitude of numbers and the depth of recursion, for example. This is usually documented in the compiler documentation.

2.1.2   Language definition

In this section we present the language definition of SLANG. We will refer to this definition in subsequent chapters.

Special symbols

open_token	:	(.	plus_token	:	+ .
close_token	:	) .	minus_token	:	− .
			times_token	:	* .
list_token	:	, .	over_token	:	/ .
period_token	:	. .	modulo_token	:	| .
separator_token	:	; .	equal_token	:	= .
			not_equal_token	:	<> .
becomes_token	:	:= .	less_than_token	:	< .
			less_or_equal_token	:	<= .
open_comment_token	:	{ .	greater_than_token	:	> .
close_comment_token	:	} .	greater_or_equal_token	:	>= .

Keywords

begin_token	:	BEGIN .	if_token	:	IF .
end_token	:	END .	then_token	:	THEN .
			else_token	:	ELSE .
int_token	:	INT .	fi_token	:	FI .
var_token	:	VAR .			
procedure_token	:	PROC .	while_token	:	WHILE .
			do_token	:	DO .
call_token	:	CALL .	od_token	:	OD .
read_token	:	READ .	negate_token	:	NEG .
write_token	:	WRITE .	absolute_token	:	ABS .

Figure 2.4 The representation of special symbols and keywords in SLANG.

The vocabulary of SLANG consists of letters, digits, special symbols and keywords. Letters and digits can be simply defined using the following rules:

letter → a|b|c|d|e|f|g|h|i|j|k|l|m|n|o|p|q|r|s|t|u|v|w|x|y|z.
digit → 0|1|2|3|4|5|6|7|8|9.

Note that we exclude upper-case letters in our definition of *letter*. Identifiers and numbers can be constructed from letters and digits.

Special symbols include punctuation marks and operators. A program also contains keywords that are used to identify certain constructs, or as punctuation. The special symbols and keywords in SLANG are defined in the tables in Figure 2.4.

We will now consider each language construct in SLANG. The language constructs are specified by the productions in the context-free grammar. For each construct, we will describe the context constraints (if any) and the semantics.

Programs

>*program_declaration*   :   *block* period_token.

Semantics: A new environment is created. The block is then executed, and finally the environment is deleted. Deleting the environment involves undoing the bindings of identifiers that have been created during the execution of the block.

Blocks

>*block*   :   begin_token *declaration_part statement_part* end_token.

Semantics: The declaration-part is executed, followed by the statement-part.

Declarations

>*declaration_part*   :   {*constant_declaration* | *variable_declaration*} **clos**
>*procedure_declaration* **clos**

Semantics: The declarations are processed in the order in which they occur.

Constant declarations

>*constant_declaration*   :   *type_declarer*
>{*identifier* equal_token *number*} **list**
>separator_token

>*type_declarer*   :   int_token.

Context constraints: Every identifier in the constant declaration denotes a number. The scope of a constant is the block in which the declaration occurs. An identifier may not be declared twice in the same block.

Semantics: Every identifier in the list in the constant declaration is bound to its associated number.

Variable declarations

>*variable_declaration*   :   var_token *type_declarer identifier* **list** separator_token.

Context constraints: Every identifier in the variable declaration denotes a variable. The scope of a variable is the block in which the declaration occurs. An identifier may not be declared twice in the same block.

Semantics: For each identifier in the list, a new location, *loc* (say), is obtained in the store, and *loc* is bound to the identifier.

Procedure declarations

>*procedure_declaration*   :   procedure_token *identifier block* separator_token.

Context constraints: The identifier in the procedure declaration denotes a procedure. The scope of a procedure is the block in which the declaration occurs. An
identifier may not be declared twice in the same block.

Semantics: The block is bound to the identifier.

Statements

    statement_part : *statement* **chain** *separator_token.*
    statement   : *assignment_statement*
                  | *if_statement*
                  | *while_statement*
                  | *call_statement*
                  | *read_statement*
                  | *write_statement*
                  .

Semantics: The statements are processed in the order in which they occur.

Assignment statements

    assignment_statement : *left_part* becomes_token *expression.*
    left_part   : *identifier.*

Context constraints: The assignment statement must occur in the scope of the
identifier in the left part, and the identifier must denote a variable.

Semantics: The expression is evaluated, and its value is written to the location
bound to the identifier.

If-statements

    if_statement : if_token *relation* then_token *statement_part*
                   {else_token *statement_part*} **option**
                   fi_token

Semantics: The relation is evaluated. If its value is true then the statement-part
following the then-token is executed. If the value of the relation is false then,
if present, the statement-part following the else-token is executed, otherwise no
action is taken.

While-statements

    while_statement : while_token *relation* do_token *statement_part* od_token.

Semantics: The relation is evaluated. If its value is true then first the statement-
part is executed, and next the while-statement is again executed. If the value of
the relation is false no action is taken.

Call-statements

> *call_statement*   :   call_token *identifier*.

Context constraints: The call-statement must occur in the scope of the identifier, and the identifier must denote a procedure. The call-statement must also occur after the identifier of the declaration of the procedure.[1]

Semantics: The block bound to the identifier is executed in the environment in which the identifier was declared. When the execution of the call-statement is finished, the execution of the statement-part (of which the call-statement forms a part) is resumed at the point it was interrupted.

Read-statements

> *read_statement*   :   read_token *identifier* **list pack**.

Context constraints: The read-statement must occur in the scope of every identifier in the list, and every identifier must denote a variable.

Semantics: For each identifier in the list, and in the order of occurrence, the first number of the input is written to the location, bound to the identifier, and then removed from the input.

Write-statements

> *write_statement*   :   write_token *expression* **list pack**.

Semantics: For each expression in the list, and in the order of occurrence, the expression is evaluated, and the number that corresponds to the value of the expression is added to the output.

Expressions

expression	:	*term* **chain** *add_operator*.
term	:	*factor* **chain** *multiply_operator*.
factor	:	*unary_operator* **option** *operand*.
operand	:	*identifier*
	|	*number*
	|	*expression* **pack**
	.	
add_operator	:	plus_token | minus_token.
multiply_operator	:	times_token | over_token | modulo_token.
unary_operator	:	negate_token | absolute_token.

---

[1]This means that a procedure may be freely called from the block in which is declared. Calls from subordinate procedures in this block are, however, restricted. A procedure may be recursively called from its own block, and from blocks of procedures that are declared after the declaration of the procedure that is called, but not from blocks of procedures that are declared before this procedure.

Context constraints: The expression must occur in the scope of every identifier that occurs as an operand in the expression, and every identifier must denote a variable or a constant.

Semantics: An expression is a rule for computing a numerical value of type integer. The value is obtained by applying the arithmetic operators on the actual values of the operands of the expression. The actual value of an operand is obvious in the case of a denotation of a number, or an identifier that denotes a constant. For an identifier that denotes a variable it is the current value at its location (i.e. the last value assigned during the execution of the program).

The arithmetic operators plus, minus, times, over (division with truncation), modulo, negate and absolute have the conventional meanings. The syntax specifies the following precedence rules:

> **highest priority:** negate, absolute
> **next highest priority:** times, over, modulo
> **lowest priority:** plus, minus

An expression enclosed between left and right parentheses is first evaluated and this value is used in subsequent calculations. Consequently, the order of application of operators within an expression can always be arranged by appropriate positioning of parentheses.

Relations

relation	:	*expression relational_operator expression.*
relational_operator	:	equal_token | not_equal_token
	|	less_than_token | less_or_equal_token
	|	greater_than_token | greater_or_equal_token
	.	

Semantics: A relation is a rule for computing a truth value. The value is obtained by applying the relational operator on the actual values of the left expression and the right expression in the relation.

The relational operators equal, not equal, less than, less or equal, greater than and greater or equal have the conventional meanings.

Identifiers and numbers

identifier	:	letter {letter | digit} **clos.**
number	:	digit **seq.**

Context constraints: Identifiers serve to denote constants, variables and procedures. The same identifier must not be defined twice in the declaration-part of a block.

Semantics: Numbers are denoted using the usual decimal notation, and have the conventional meanings.

Comments and spaces

comment	:	open_comment_token
		any text not containing the close_comment_token
		close_comment_token

white_space	:	{newline | tab | space} **seq**.

Semantics: Comments, new-lines, tabs and spaces may occur everywhere in the program. They have no meaning, and act as separators between tokens.

To complete this section, we give 2 examples of SLANG programs.

Example 2.3
The following SLANG program reads numbers from the keyboard until a zero is encountered, adds these numbers, and writes the result to the screen.

```
BEGIN  VAR INT number, sum;
       sum := 0;
       READ (number);
       WHILE number <> 0 DO
           sum := sum + number;
           READ (number)
       OD;
       WRITE (sum)
END.
```

◇

Example 2.4
The following program reads numbers from the keyboard until a zero is encountered, and writes these numbers to the screen with the digits of each number in reverse order.[2]

```
BEGIN  VAR INT number;
       PROC reverse
       BEGIN WRITE (number | 10);
             IF number >= 10 THEN
                 number := number / 10;
                 CALL reverse
             FI
       END;
       READ (number);
       WHILE number <> 0 DO
           CALL reverse;
```

---

[2]Note that because SLANG cannot write spaces and new-lines, the numbers will simply be concatenated.

```
          READ (number)
      OD
  END.
```
                                                                    ◇

2.2   A simple version of the virtual machine VIM

In this section, we will develop a simple version of the virtual machine VIM. VIM consists of an architecture, instruction set and interpreter. The virtual machine is designed in such a way that the semantics of the language constructs of SLANG can easily be expressed in the instructions of VIM. This version of VIM does not include any special provisions for the handling of procedures.

Before proceeding, we give the reader an impression of the kind of instructions that we need in VIM by considering 2 examples of the translation of statements in SLANG. In these examples, we assume that every variable has a cell in the memory (store) of the virtual machine. The cell holds the value of the variable (if it is assigned). Every cell has a *location*, called its *address*, which is a natural number. Hence, every variable is represented by its memory address. A SLANG program is mapped as a series of machine instructions onto the memory of SLANG. Since every instruction resides in a cell, every instruction has an address. Successive instructions of a program therefore reside in cells with increasing addresses.

Example 2.5
Consider the statement

```
  a := b + c
```

where a and b are variables, and c is a constant. The semantics of assignment statements and expressions in the language definition require that:

- the expression b+c in the right part of the assignment statement a:=b+c must be evaluated, and its value must be written to the location bound to a in the environment;
- the value of the expression b+c be obtained by applying the operator + to the actual values of the operands b and c;
- the value of the variable b be read from its location in the store;
- the value of the constant c is its synonym, i.e. the value from its declaration.

In VIM, the execution of the above-mentioned assignment statement involves the following steps:

1. The value of the variable b, **val_b** (say), is read from its address, **addr_b** (say), in memory.

2. The value of the constant c, val_c (say), is directly available.
3. The values val_b and val_c are added.
4. The result of the computation is written to the address, addr_a (say), of the variable a in memory.

◇

Example 2.6

Now let's consider the statements

```
IF cond THEN stats1 ELSE stats2 FI; stats3
```

where cond is a relation, and stats1, stats2 and stats3 are statement-parts. The semantics of if-statements and statement-parts in the language definition require that:

1. the relation cond be evaluated, i.e. the resulting value will be true or false;
2. if the value is true then statement-part stats1 will be executed, otherwise statement-part stats2 will be executed;
3. statement-part stats3 will be executed.

In VIM, the execution of the above-mentioned statements involves the following steps:

1. The address of the first instruction of cond is determined, and cond is evaluated (i.e. the instructions of cond are executed). The resulting value will be true or false.
2. If the value is true then the address of the first instruction of stats1 is determined, and the instructions of stats1 are executed. Otherwise, the address of the first instruction of stats2 is determined, and the instructions of stats2 are executed.
3. The address of the first instruction of stats3 is determined, and the instructions of stats3 are executed.

◇

2.2.1 The architecture

The virtual machine VIM has separate program and data memories. Every instruction occupies 1 cell in the *program memory*. The addresses of the cells in the program memory are natural numbers. An instruction pointer contains the address of the instruction in the program memory that is about to be executed. Every number occupies 1 cell in the *data memory*. The addresses of the cells in the data memory are also natural numbers.

Instructions consist of an operator and at most 1 argument, which may be a number or an address in the program or data memory.

Arithmetic and relational operators have implicit arguments. They operate on 1 or 2 values (operands) on top of the *arithmetic stack* (*stack*, for short). These operands are replaced by the result obtained by applying the operator to the operands.

Load and store, input and output and jump instructions have 1 argument. The load instruction copies the value of a variable from the data memory to the top of the stack, whereas the store instruction removes the top value from the stack and stores it in the data memory. The input instruction reads a value from the keyboard and stores it on the stack, whereas the output instruction removes the top value from the stack and writes it to the screen.

For the implementation of the conditional and while-statement we need jump instructions. The unconditional jump instruction transfers control to its argument (i.e. the address of an instruction in the program memory). A conditional jump instruction also transfers control to its argument (i.e. an address in the program memory) depending on the truth value on top of the stack.

Finally, there is a halt instruction, which has no arguments. This instruction stops the execution of the program.

We now consider the VIM instruction set in more detail, and then the execution of a VIM program by an interpreter.

2.2.2   The instruction set

The VIM instructions are divided into 10 classes: unary arithmetic, binary arithmetic, comparison, load and store, unconditional jump, conditional jumps, call and return, input and output, storage management and halt. Call and return instructions and instructions for storage management will be introduced in Section 2.4.1 when we handle procedures. A definition of the other classes of instructions is given in Figure 2.5.

We now return to Examples 2.5 and 2.6 at the beginning of this section. In these examples we informally described the translation of SLANG statements. In the following examples we show the actual translations.

Example 2.7
The translation of the assignment statement shown in Example 2.5, namely

```
a := b + c
```

in VIM instructions is as follows:

```
ldvar   b
ldcon   c
add
stvar   a
```

Unary arithmetic

These instructions first remove the top (integer) value, `intval` (say), from the stack, and perform for each instruction the following actions:

instruction	meaning
neg	stores the integer value $-$`intval` on the stack
abs	stores the absolute value of `intval` on the stack

Binary arithmetic

These instructions first remove the 2 top (integer) values, `intval2` and `intval1` (say), in this order from the stack, and perform for each instruction the following actions:

instruction	meaning
add	stores the integer value `intval1` $+$ `intval2` on the stack
sub	stores the integer value `intval1` $-$ `intval2` on the stack
mul	stores the integer value `intval1` $*$ `intval2` on the stack
dvi	stores the integer value `intval1` $\div$ `intval2` on the stack
mdl	stores the integer value `intval1` $\mid$ `intval2` on the stack

Note that, for every pair of integers a and b ($b \neq 0$), unique integers q and r exist, such that $a = q * b + r$ for $0 \leq r < b$. The integer q is called the quotient and r the residue. We define $a \div b = q$ and $a \mid b = r$.

Comparison

These instructions first remove the 2 top (integer) values, `intval2` and `intval1` (say), in this order from the stack, and perform for each instruction the following actions:

instruction	meaning
eq	stores the truth value `intval1` $=$ `intval2` on the stack
ne	stores the truth value `intval1` $\neq$ `intval2` on the stack
lt	stores the truth value `intval1` $<$ `intval2` on the stack
le	stores the truth value `intval1` $\leq$ `intval2` on the stack
gt	stores the truth value `intval1` $>$ `intval2` on the stack
ge	stores the truth value `intval1` $\geq$ `intval2` on the stack

Figure 2.5 Instructions of the virtual machine VIM.

Load and store

instruction	meaning
ldcon intval	stores the (integer) value **intval** on the stack
ldvar address	copies the (integer) value from memory address **address** to the stack
stvar address	removes the top (integer) value from the stack and writes it to memory address **address**

Unconditional jump

instruction	meaning
jump address	continues execution at the instruction with address **address** in the program memory

Conditional jumps

instruction	meaning
jift address	removes the top (truth) value, **truthval** (say), from the stack; if the value of **truthval** is true then execution is continued at the instruction with address **address** in the program memory, otherwise the next instruction is executed
jiff address	removes the top (truth) value, **truthval** (say), from the stack; if the value of **truthval** is false then execution is continued at the instruction with address **address** in the program memory, otherwise the next instruction is executed

Input and output

instruction	meaning
rdint	reads an integer value from the keyboard and stores it on the stack
wrint	removes the top value from the stack and writes it to the screen

Halt

instruction	meaning
halt	stops execution

Figure 2.5 (continued) Instructions of the virtual machine VIM.

Notice that we have used the variables a and b, and constant c, from the SLANG statement as representations for the corresponding addresses and value in the VIM instructions. Snapshots of the stack during the execution of the VIM instructions are shown in Figure 2.6. The figure begins with an empty stack, and shows the stack configuration after the execution of each instruction. We have let the variable b have value 37, and the constant c be a synonym for value 2.   ◇

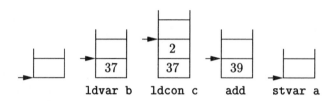

Figure 2.6   Snapshots of the stack during the execution of the assignment statement of Example 2.7.

Example 2.8
Consider the statements

    IF a < b THEN a := b+2 ELSE b := a-2 FI; c := a

where a, b and c are variables. These statements form a concrete version of the statements shown in Example 2.6. The translation of the if-statement requires jump instructions. The arguments of these jump instructions (which are addresses in the program memory) will be denoted by the labels `else` and `fi`. The label `else` is the location immediately after the then-part, and is used if the relation yields false. The label `fi` is the location immediately after the else-part, and is used if the relation yields true and the then-part is executed.

The VIM instructions are shown below. Snapshots of the stack during the execution of the if-statement are shown in Figure 2.7. We have let the initial value of the variables a and b be 87 and 37, respectively.

```
ldvar   a
ldvar   b
lt
jiff    else
ldvar   b
ldcon   2
add
stvar   a
```

```
        jump   fi
else:   ldvar  a
        ldcon  2
        sub
        stvar  b
fi:     ldvar  a
        stvar  c
```

◇

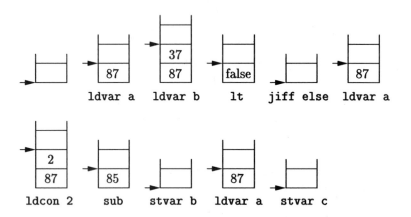

Figure 2.7   Snapshots of the stack during the execution of the if-statement and the assignment statement of Example 2.8.

2.2.3   The interpreter

VIM has a separate program memory and data memory. The program memory is represented by an array *prog* of type *instruction*. Each instruction consists of an operation, and for some instructions an operand, which may be a value or an address. The instruction counter *ic* points to the instruction that is about to be executed. The data memory is represented by an array *data* of type integer.

The interpreter contains a procedure *read_code*, which reads the VIM program from a file, and writes it to the array *prog*.

Arithmetic and relational operations are performed on a stack. The stack is also involved in input and output operations. The stack is represented by an array *stack* of type integer. The procedures *push* and *pop* are used to store a value on, or remove a value from, the stack, and manipulate the stack pointer *sp*. The truth values true and false are represented on the stack by 1 and 0, respectively.

The interpreter consists of a case-statement with a case-list element for every kind of instruction. Arithmetic, relational, load and store and input and output instructions operate on the stack. Jump instructions manipulate the instruction counter *ic*. The program runs as long as the Boolean value *stop* is false. The interpreter is shown below.[3]

```
#define max_prog          1000      /* length of program memory */
#define max_data          100       /* length of data memory */
#define max_stack         100       /* maximum depth of stack */


typedef enum {
  true = 1,  false = 0
} boolean;

typedef enum {
  neg, abs_, add, sub, mul, dvi, mdl, eq, ne, lt, le, gt, ge,
  ldcon, ldvar, stvar, jump, jift, jiff, rdint, wrint, halt
} operation;

typedef struct {
  operation  code;
  union {
    /* no operands for:    neg, abs_, add, sub, mul, dvi, mdl, eq,
                           ne, lt, le, gt, ge, rdint, wrint, halt */
    int value;            /* for: ldcon */
    int address;          /* for: ldvar, stvar, jump, jift, jiff */
  } u;
} instruction;


instruction       prog[max_prog];
int               data[max_data];
int               stack[max_stack];
int               sp;


void read_code(void)
{
  /* reads the VIM program from a file and writes it to the array prog */
}


void push(int x)
{
  stack[sp++] = x;
}
```

---

[3]In the interpreter program we use *abs_* instead of *abs*, because *abs* is a reserved word in the standard ANSI-C library.

```
void pop(int *x)
{
  *x = stack[--sp];
}

void read_int(int *x)
{
  /* reads an integer value from the keyboard and assigns it to parameter x */
}

void write_int(int x)
{
  /* writes the integer value of parameter x to the screen */
}


void main(void)
{
  instruction    *instr;
  int            ic, next, left_operand, right_operand, operand, result;
  boolean        truthval, stop;

  read_code();
  ic    = 0;
  sp    = 0;
  stop  = false;

  while (!stop) {
    next = ic + 1;
    instr = &prog[ic];
    switch (instr->code) {

    case neg:
    case abs_:
      pop(&operand);
      switch (instr->code) {

      case neg:
        result = -operand;
        break;

      case abs_:
        if (operand < 0)
          result = -operand;
        else
          result = operand;
        break;

      }
      push(result);
      break;
```

```
case add:
case sub:
case mul:
case dvi:
case mdl:
  pop(&right_operand);
  pop(&left_operand);
  switch (instr->code) {

  case add:
    result = left_operand + right_operand;
    break;

  case sub:
    result = left_operand − right_operand;
    break;

  case mul:
    result = left_operand * right_operand;
    break;

  case dvi:
    result = left_operand / right_operand;
    break;

  case mdl:
    result = left_operand % right_operand;
    break;

  }
  push(result);
  break;


case eq:
case ne:
case lt:
case le:
case gt:
case ge:
  pop(&right_operand);
  pop(&left_operand);
  switch (instr->code) {

  case eq:
    truthval = (left_operand == right_operand);
    break;

  case ne:
    truthval = (left_operand != right_operand);
    break;
```

```
  case lt:
    truthval = (left_operand < right_operand);
    break;

  case le:
    truthval = (left_operand <= right_operand);
    break;

  case gt:
    truthval = (left_operand > right_operand);
    break;

  case ge:
    truthval = (left_operand >= right_operand);
    break;

  }
  if (truthval)
    result = 1;
  else
    result = 0;
  push(result);
  break;

case ldcon:
  push(instr->u.value);
  break;

case ldvar:
  push(data[instr->u.address]);
  break;

case stvar:
  pop(&data[instr->u.address]);
  break;

case jump:
  next = instr->u.address;
  break;

case jift:
  pop(&operand);
  if (operand == 1)
    next = instr->u.address;
  break;

case jiff:
  pop(&operand);
  if (operand == 0)
    next = instr->u.address;
  break;
```

```
    case rdint:
      read_int(& operand);
      push(operand);
      break;

    case wrint:
      pop(& operand);
      write_int(operand);
      break;

    case halt:
      stop = true;
      break;
    }
    ic = next;
  }
}
```

The interpreter above does not provide error detection. If the VIM program that is executed is correct, then the only error that can occur is stack overflow. By adding a check to the routine *push*, stack overflow can easily be detected.

2.3   Translation from SLANG to simple VIM

In Section 2.3.1 through 2.3.5 we more formally specify the translations into VIM code of expressions, relations and statements, but not of procedures. The translation of procedures is postponed until Section 2.5.1 because procedures require special instructions and more involved memory management.

2.3.1   Expressions and relations

In Section 2.2.1 we mentioned that all arithmetic and relational operations in VIM are performed using a stack. If, instead of *infix notation*, we had expressions in *postfix notation*, then it is quite a simple matter to generate stack instructions. We illustrate this in the next 2 examples.

Example 2.9
The postfix form of the relation a < b is a b <. Assuming a and b denote variables, this corresponds to the following stack instructions:

```
    ldvar   a
    ldvar   b
    lt
```

Example 2.10

Consider the infix expression (a + b) ∗ c + d + e ∗ f. The postfix form of this expression is a b + c ∗ d + e f ∗ +, and the corresponding stack instructions are (assuming all identifiers denote variables):

```
ldvar   a
ldvar   b
add
ldvar   c
mul
ldvar   d
add
ldvar   e
ldvar   f
mul
add
```

Observe that in both examples, the resulting value remains on the stack.

Given postfix notation, therefore, we can directly generate stack code. The task of the compiler, therefore, is to translate infix notation into postfix. This translation can be specified using the same context-free grammar formalism that we use to specify the syntax of SLANG. We begin by considering the translation of expressions and relations into postfix.

In the language definition (Section 2.1.2) we defined the nonterminal *expression* as follows:

   expression : *term* **chain** *add_operator*.

However, it is easier to explain the translation to VIM code if we express the **chain** operator in this production in terms of the **clos** operator, as follows:

   expression : *term* {*add_operator term*} **clos**.

This production specifies an add operator in infix notation. We can specify the translation of an infix expression to postfix form by rewriting the production in the following way:

   <expression> : *<term>* {*<term>* *<add_operator>*} **clos**.

Here we use the angular brackets to denote "the translation of". We can read this production then in the following way: the translation of *expression* consists of the translation of *term* followed by zero or more repetitions of the translation of *term* followed by the translation of *add_operator*.

We can, in fact, specify the translation of every SLANG language construction using this technique. We use the convention that if "*X*" is a nonterminal in the SLANG grammar, then "*<X>*" denotes the translation of this nonterminal. A more complete specification of the translation of expressions is shown below.

<expression>	:	*<term>* {*<term>* *<add_operator>*} **clos.**
<term>	:	*<factor>* {*<factor>* *<multiply_operator>*} **clos.**
<factor>	:	*<operand>* *<unary_operator>* **option.**
<operand>	:	**ldvar** *identifier*
	|	**ldcon** *identifier*
	|	**ldcon** *number*
	|	*<expression>*
	.	
<add_operator>	:	**add** | **sub.**
<multiply_operator>	:	**mul** | **dvi** | **mdl.**
<unary_operator>	:	**neg** | **abs.**

Note that "**ldvar** *identifier*" is the translation of an identifier that denotes a variable, "**ldcon** *identifier*" the translation of an identifier that denotes a constant, and "**ldcon** *number*" the translation of (the denotation of) a number.

Relations also need to be translated from infix to postfix. The specification is shown below.

<relation>	:	*<expression>* *<expression>* *<relational_operator>.*
<relational_operator>	:	**eq** | **ne**
	|	**lt** | **le**
	|	**gt** | **ge**
	.	

2.3.2　Assignment

The syntax of assignment statements is:

assignment_statement	:	*left_part* becomes_token *expression.*
left_part	:	*identifier.*

The semantics requires that first the expression be evaluated, and next, that its value be written to the location bound to the identifier. The translation is therefore:

<assignment_statement>	:	*<expression>* *<left_part>.*
<left_part>	:	**stvar** *identifier.*

An example of the translation of an assignment statement is shown in Example 2.7.

2.3.3　Selection and repetition

If-statements in SLANG may or may not have an else-part. The following syntax makes this clearly visible:

if_statement :   if_token *relation* then_token *statement_part* fi_token
         | if_token *relation* then_token *statement_part*
             else_token *statement_part* fi_token

.

In the translation we will use the labels `else` and `fi`. The label `else` denotes the address of the first instruction of the else-part, and the label `fi` the address of the first instruction after the if-statement. From the semantics it follows immediately that the translation should be:

```
<if_statement>  :           <relation>
                            jiff fi
                            <statement_part>
                    fi:
                |           <relation>
                            jiff else
                            <statement_part>
                            jump fi
                    else:   <statement_part>
                    fi:
```

.

Notice that the result of the execution of the relation is a truth value that is put onto the stack. The `jiff` instruction will remove this value from the stack. An example of the translation of an if-statement can be found in Example 2.8.

The translation of the while-statement is straightforward. Let the label `while` denote the address of the first instruction of the relation, and the label od the address of the first instruction after the while-statement. We can then write the translation as:

```
<while_statement>  :  while:  <relation>
                              jiff od
                              <statement_part>
                              jump while:
                      od:
```

.

Example 2.11
Consider the translation of the while-statement

```
    WHILE a >= b DO a := b-1 OD
```

which results in the following sequence of VIM instructions:

```
while: ldvar  a
       ldvar  b
       ge
```

```
    jiff    od
    ldvar   b
    ldcon   1
    sub
    stvar   a
    jump    while
od:
```

Observe that the label **while** is used to return to the beginning of the while-statement, and that the label **od** is used to jump over the statement-part if the relation yields false.   ◇

2.3.4   Input and output

We recall the syntax of the read-statement:

   read_statement   :   read_token *identifier* **list pack**.

The semantics of the read-statement requires that numbers be read from the input and assigned to identifiers in a list. This can be realised by means of an **rdint** instruction, which reads an integer from the keyboard and stores it on the stack, followed by an **stvar** instruction, which removes this value from the stack and assigns it to the variable denoted by the identifier. A **seq** operator allows for any number (at least one) of integers to be read and assigned:

   <*read_statement*>   :   { **rdint**
                            stvar *identifier*
                        } **seq**

The syntax of the write-statement is:

   write_statement   :   write_token *expression* **list pack**.

The semantics of the write-statement requires that each expression be evaluated, and each result, which is left on the stack, be added to the output. This can be realised by means of a **wrint** instruction, which moves an integer from the stack to the screen. The translation of the write-statement is therefore as follows:

   <*write_statement*>   :   { <*expression*>
                             wrint
                         } **seq**

2.3.5   Statements

The translation of statement-parts and statements is straightforward:

$$
\begin{array}{lll}
<statement\_part> & : & <statement> \ \textbf{seq}. \\
<statement> & : & <assignment\_statement> \\
& | & <if\_statement> \\
& | & <while\_statement> \\
& | & <call\_statement> \\
& | & <read\_statement> \\
& | & <write\_statement>
\end{array}
$$

The translation of the call-statement is discussed in Section 2.5.1.

2.4   The virtual machine VIM

In the previous section we have developed a simple version of the virtual machine VIM. This version has no special provisions for procedures. In this section we will redefine the storage organisation in such a way that recursive procedures can be handled, and we will define special instructions for the calling of procedures.

2.4.1   The architecture

During execution of a SLANG program, space in the data memory must be allocated for the variables of the program. For a program without recursive procedures, the total amount of data memory needed by the program can be determined during the compilation of the program as every variable uses 1 cell (the only data type is integer). Each variable can therefore be associated with an index in the array *data*. For example, the variable **number** in Example 2.5 could be associated with index 0, and the variable **sum** with index 1. However, this solution is not possible for a program that contains recursive procedures with local variables, as in that case different memory cells must be allocated for the local variables for each recursive call of the procedure. This means that it is impossible to determine the space needed for variables before the program is executed, i.e. at compile time.

A solution to this problem is to create a separate memory array each time a procedure is called. Local variables in procedures are addressed by a 2-tuple that consists of the address of the memory array itself, and an index (displacement) in that array. We will call such a memory array a *segment* (also referred to as an *activation record* or *frame*), and we will map these segments in some way on the array *data*. As the procedure that is called last is the first to be terminated, the set of segments can be visualised as a last-in-first-out stack, i.e. the segment created last will be the first to be deleted.

This approach ensures that each variable has a unique address. However, we have not solved the problem of how to determine the segment addresses at compile time. We need those addresses at that time, because every variable must be bound to its corresponding 2-tuple when its declaration is parsed. Notice that it is impossible to assign a unique number to every segment because at compile time it is not known how many times a procedure will be called. To put it another way, the depth of the recursion is not known, and this implies that it is not known how many instances of every procedure segment are needed.

Note, however, that we do not need to address all the segments at the same time, because the only segments used during execution of a procedure is the segment corresponding to the called procedure, the segments of those nested procedures that contain the declaration of the called procedure, and the program segment. We call this set of segments the *current segment group*, as this forms the collection of segments (and thus of the variables) that can be addressed during the execution of the called procedure.

Example 2.12
Consider the SLANG program in Figure 2.8 and its corresponding structure tree in Figure 2.9. The possible *segment groups* in the example are:

- {program }
- {program, p1 }
- {program, p1, p3 }
- {program, p1, p4 }
- {program, p2 }
- {program, p2, p5 }
- {program, p2, p5, p6 }

Several copies of (parts of) these groups can exist at the same time, but only the group that contains the segment created last is the current group. For instance, consider the invocation of p1 in the body of p6. Just before the call, the current group was { program, p2, p5, p6 }. After the call the current group will be { program, p1 }. ◇

The order of the segments in a group is always the same, independent of the order in which procedures are called and segments created. Furthermore, every segment always has the same position in every group it belongs to.

As both the possible segment groups and the order of segments in a group can be determined during compilation, we can assign a *segment number* (sn) to each segment. This number corresponds to the nesting level of the procedure. In Example 2.12 the segments of procedures p1 and p2 have number 2, the segments of p3, p4 and p5 have number 3, and the segment of p6 has number 4. The segment of the program always has number 1.

These segment numbers are used as indices in an array *Current Segment Group* (CSG) (also called a *display*). Array CSG contains the addresses of the segments of

```
BEGIN PROC p1
      BEGIN PROC p3 BEGIN ...END;
            PROC p4 BEGIN VAR INT x; ...END;
            ⋮
      END;
      PROC p2
      BEGIN PROC p5
            BEGIN PROC p6 BEGIN ...; CALL p1; ...END;
                  ⋮
                  CALL p6;
                  ⋮
            END;
            ⋮
            CALL p5;
            ⋮
      END;
      ⋮
      CALL p2;
      ⋮
END.
```

Figure 2.8 Nesting of procedures.

the current segment group. The index of a variable in a segment will be called its *displacement* (dpl). The address of a variable x with displacement dpl_x in procedure p4 with segment number sn_{p4} is therefore $CSG[sn_{p4}] + dpl_x$.

Now that we have introduced the concepts of segment and segment group, the next problem to solve is when to create a new segment group, and when to terminate a segment group, i.e. when to restore the previous group. We will first discuss the creation of a new group, and consider whether the invocation of a procedure and the corresponding creation of a segment implies the creation of a new group.

In Example 2.12 we saw that the call of p2 in the program block results in the segment of p2 being added to the current segment group, which up to that time consisted of the program segment only. The call of p5 in the procedure block of p2 and the call of p6 in the block of p5 results in the segments of p5 and p6 being added to the current segment group. Up to this point a new segment group is not needed. A general rule then is: a segment group can be extended as long as procedures are called that are on a single path starting at the root of the structure

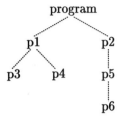

Figure 2.9 Structure tree that shows the nesting of procedures.

tree and descending to a leaf.

The situation is different for the call of procedure p1 in the procedure block of p6. In this case a new group must be created because p1 is on a different path from the root. The new group is not completely different from the previous one, because both groups contain the segment of the program at the first position. A second general rule then is: the new group and the previous group have a part in common—this part begins at the root and ends at the point where the paths in the structure tree diverge. At that point the newly created segment is added to form the new current segment group.

In summary, the general rules for creating and restoring segment groups are:

- If the called procedure has a nesting level that is 1 higher than that of the caller, then the new segment is added to the current segment group. When the called procedure returns, the last created segment is deleted.
- If the called procedure has a nesting level that is lower than or equal to that of the caller, then a new segment group is created. The new segment group consists of the old group up to the segment of the procedure with nesting level one lower than that of the called procedure. The segment of the called procedure is added to this new group. When the called procedure returns, the last created segment is deleted and the previous segment group is restored.

An implementation question is where to save the information of the previous segment group when a new group is created. A possible solution could be to save it in the segment of the called procedure. But as the length of the segment groups of the various callers can be different, the space needed cannot be determined beforehand.

An often-used method of storing segment information involves the concept of a *static* and *dynamic link*. In this method, the address of both the segment of the caller (the *dynamic link*) and that of the block in which the procedure is defined (the *static link*) are stored in the segment of the called procedure. The static and the dynamic links, found in the segment of the caller, are used to restore the previous segment group.

```
BEGIN PROC p1                                              1
      BEGIN VAR ...;                                       2
              PROC p3 BEGIN ......END;                     3
              PROC p4 BEGIN ...; CALL p3; ...END;          4
              ⋮
              CALL p3;                                     5
              CALL p4;                                     6
              ⋮
      END;                                                 7
      PROC p2                                              8
      BEGIN VAR ...;                                       9
              PROC p5                                     10
              BEGIN VAR ...;                              11
                      PROC p6 BEGIN ......END;            12
                      ⋮
                      CALL p6;                            13
                      ⋮
              END;                                        14
              ⋮
              CALL p5;                                    15
              CALL p1;                                    16
              ⋮
      END;                                                17
      ⋮
      CALL p1;                                            18
      CALL p2;                                            19
      ⋮
END.                                                      20
```

Figure 2.10 Procedure calls.

Example 2.13

Consider the program in Figure 2.10. The execution of the program starts with the creation of the program segment S0 (say). The address of S0 is stored in CSG[1], and the value 1 is assigned to the *current segment number* csn. The static and dynamic links of the program are 0 as the program is the outermost block. The only segment group is {S0}.

We now observe what happens when p1 and p2 are called at lines 18 and 19 in the program. We first consider the call of **p1** at line 18:

- Create the segment S1 of **p1** and store the address of S1 in CSG[2]. The current segment number (csn) is 2, and the static and dynamic links of S1 receive the value of CSG[1], i.e. the address of the program segment S0.
- Call of **p3** at line 5. Create the segment S3, and add this to the current segment group. The only and current segment group is {S0, S1, S3}. The static and dynamic links of S3 point to S1, and csn is incremented to 3.
- Termination of **p3**. The segment S3 is removed from the current segment group, and csn is decremented to 2.
- Call of **p4** at line 6. Create the segment S4. The only and current segment group is {S0, S1, S4}. The static and dynamic links of S4 point to S1, and csn is incremented to 3.
- Call of **p3** at line 4. Now a new segment group must be created, as the segment number of **p3** is the same as that of **p4**. The new group is {S0, S1, S3}. The value of CSG[3] is assigned the address of S3 (was the address of S4). The static link of S3 points to S1 and the dynamic link to S4.

The present configuration of CSG and the segment stack is depicted in Figure 2.11. Notice that a segment consists of an administration part and a data part. The administration part contains the segment number, the data length, and the static and dynamic links. The data part contains the variables of the procedure block. The address of the data part is used as the address of the segment. The reason for this is that we want to make the computation of the address of a variable as fast as possible. The address of a variable with segment number sn and displacement dpl is CSG[sn]+dpl. If the address of the beginning of the segment would have been used as the address of the segment, then the address would have been CSG[sn]+dpl+4. The extra factor 4 makes the computation slower. Continuing where we left off:

- Termination of **p3** at line 4. The segment S3 is removed, and CSG[3] is restored by means of the dynamic link of S3. The segment group {S0, S1, S3} is removed, and {S0, S1, S4} becomes the current segment group.
- Termination of **p4** at line 6. The segment S3 is deleted and csn becomes 2.
- Termination of **p1** at line 18. The segment S1 is deleted and csn becomes 1.

Note that CSG and the segment stack have the same configuration as before the call of **p1** at line 18. Furthermore, the only segment group is again {S0}.

We next consider the call of **p2** at line 19:

- Create the segment S2 of **p2**, and csn becomes 2.
- Call of **p5** at line 15. Create the segment S5, and csn becomes 3.
- Call of **p6** at line 13. Create the segment S6, and csn becomes 4.

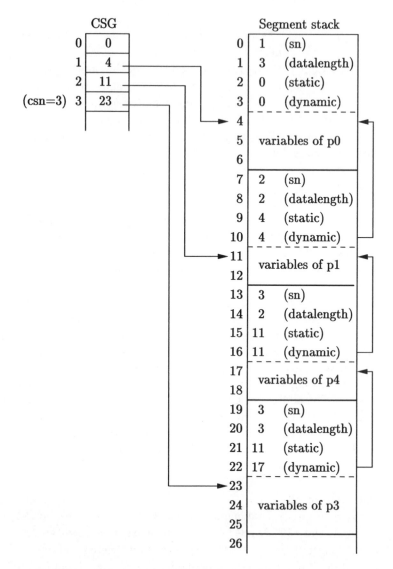

Figure 2.11 Snapshots of CSG and the segment stack.

The configuration of CSG is now as shown in Figure 2.12. The only and current segment group is {S0, S2, S5, S6}. The execution proceeds as follows:

- Termination of p6 at line 13. The segment S6 is removed, csn becomes 3.
- Termination of p5 at line 15. The segment S5 is removed, csn becomes 2.

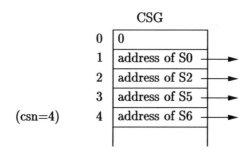

Figure 2.12 Snapshot of CSG.

The current segment group is now {S0, S2}. At the next call of p1 at line 16 a new segment group is created. The same sequence of calls and returns, which we have already seen after the call of p1 at line 18, is again carried out. Note, however, that the segment number of the caller of p1 is 2 instead of 1, because p1 is called from p2 instead of from p0. That gives us (after the call of p3 at line 4) the segment groups {S0, S2}, {S0, S1, S4} and {S0, S1, S3}, where the last group is the current segment group. The previous segment groups are restored by means of the dynamic and static links, both on the return from p3 and from p1. On return from p2, the remaining segment group ({S0, S2}) becomes {S0}. ◇

Having seen how storage management and procedure calls work in VIM, we are now in a position to complete the description of the VIM instruction set (begun in Section 2.2.1).

2.4.2 The instruction set

Addresses in the data memory are 2-tuples (sn,dpl), where sn is the segment number, and dpl is the displacement in the segment. Because the addressing has changed we must redefine the load and store instructions. The instruction ldvar copies the value of a variable from the segment with number sn, and position dpl in the segment, to the top of the stack. The instruction stvar removes the value of a variable from the top of the stack and stores it in the segment with number sn, at position dpl in the segment. To carry out a procedure call we need a jump instruction, which saves the return address (i.e. the address of the next instruction), and transfers control to the first instruction of the procedure block. At the textual end of the procedure block a return instruction is needed to restore the return address in the instruction counter, and thus to transfer control to that instruction. We use the instructions call with an address parameter and return without parameters for this purpose. We also need instructions for storage management (i.e. to create and delete segments, and to create and restore segment

Load and store

instruction	meaning
`ldcon intval`	stores the (integer) value `intval` on the stack
`ldvar sn,dpl`	copies the (integer) value from memory address (`sn,dpl`) to the stack
`stvar sn,dpl`	removes the top (integer) value from the stack and writes it to memory address (`sn,dpl`)

Call and return

instruction	meaning
`call address`	saves the return address, and continues execution at address `address`
`return`	restores the return address, and continues execution at that address

Storage management

instruction	meaning
`crseg sn,length`	creates a segment with number `sn` and data length `length`; if the level of the called procedure is 1 higher than that of the caller, then the new segment is just added to the current group, otherwise a new group is created, and the old group is saved; the new group consists of segments in the old group whose level is less than the level of the called procedure, and the segment of the called procedure; the static and dynamic links of the new segment point to the segment of the surrounding procedure and the caller, respectively
`dlseg`	deletes the segment created last; if the level of the called procedure is 1 higher than that of the caller, then the last created segment is just deleted from the current group, otherwise the old group is restored

Figure 2.13 Instructions of the virtual machine VIM.

groups). These instructions are shown in Figure 2.13.

Earlier we have used the names of the variables and constants in the SLANG program as representatives for the corresponding addresses and values in the VIM program. From now on we will denote the address of variable x by the pair sn_x, dpl_x, and the value of constant y by $intval_y$. Similarly, for a procedure p, we will denote the start address of its block in the program memory by **address**$_p$, and the segment number and the length of its data segment in the data memory by **sn**$_p$ and **length**$_p$, respectively.

Example 2.14
Let us again consider the translation of the assignment statement

    a := b + c

where a and b are variables, and c is a constant. The corresponding VIM instructions that use the new addressing are:

```
ldvar   snb, dplb
ldcon   intvalc
add
stvar   sna, dpla
```

◇

The call-statement

    CALL proc

is translated into the VIM instruction

    call   addressproc

Furthermore, the procedure declaration

```
PROC proc
BEGIN
⋮
END;
```

is translated into the instructions

```
jump      over
crseg     snproc, lengthproc
⋮
dlseg
return
over:
```

Observe that the call is the responsibility of the caller, but the creation and deletion of the segment and the return are the responsibilities of the called procedure. The positions of the call instruction and the return instruction in the VIM code are self-evident. The storage management is delegated to the called procedure, as its level and length are parameters of the create and delete instruction. A jump over the procedure block is needed because the block may only be executed when the procedure is called.

2.4.3   The interpreter

In the light of this new addressing mode we reconsider the execution of a VIM program. The idea of a separate program memory and data memory in VIM is maintained. While no change is made to the organisation of the program memory, the data memory is re-organised.

The data memory is again mapped onto the array *data*, but the latter now behaves as a stack of data segments. The data-stack pointer *dsp* points to the first free position of the array *data*. The administration of segments and segment groups is kept in the segments and in the array CSG. The procedures *create_segment* and *delete_segment* implement the instructions crseg and dlseg, respectively.

The instruction call saves the return address that is restored by the instruction return. Return addresses are saved on a stack, which is represented by an array *return_stack* of type integer. The procedures *push_return* and *pop_return* store an address on, or remove an address from, the return stack, and manipulate the return-stack pointer *rsp*.

Instructions ldvar and stvar have been redefined, and now operate on an address tuple (sn,dpl). The segment number sn is used as an index in CSG to determine the address of the segment, and the displacement dpl is used to indicate the location in the segment.

As the organisation of the data memory and some instructions have changed and some new instructions have been introduced, the interpreter must be changed accordingly. The improved version of the interpreter is shown below.[4]

```
#define  max_prog        1000     /* length of program memory */
#define  max_data        100      /* length of data memory */
#define  max_depth       15       /* maximum nesting depth */
#define  max_stack       100      /* maximum depth of stacks */


typedef enum {
   true = 1, false = 0
} boolean;
```

----

[4]In the interpreter program we use *return_* instead of *return*, because *return* is a reserved word in C.

```
typedef enum {
    neg, abs_, add, sub, mul, dvi, mdl, eq, ne, lt, le, gt, ge, ldcon, ldvar,
    stvar, jump, jift, jiff, call, crseg, dlseg, return_, rdint, wrint, halt
} operation;

typedef struct {
    operation code;
    union {
        /* no operands for:     neg, abs_, add, sub, mul, dvi, mdl, eq, ne, lt,
                                 le, gt, ge, dlseg, return_, rdint, wrint, halt */
        int value;              /* for: ldcon */
        struct {
            int sn1, dpl;       /* for: ldvar, stvar */
        } u1;
        int address;           /* for: jump, jift, jiff, call */
        struct {
            int sn2, length;    /* for: crseg */
        } u2;
    } u;
} instruction;
```

```
int            CSG[max_depth];
instruction    prog[max_prog];
int            data[max_data];
int            stack[max_stack];
int            return_stack[max_stack];
int            sp, dsp, rsp, csn;
```

```
void read_code(void)
{
    /* reads the VIM program from a file and writes it to the array prog */
}
```

```
void push(int x)
{
    stack[sp++] = x;
}
```

```
void pop(int *x)
{
    *x = stack[--sp];
}
```

```
void push_return(int x)
{
    return_stack[rsp++] = x;
}
```

```
void  pop_return(int *x)
{
   *x = return_stack[--rsp];
}


void  read_int(int *x)
{
   /* reads an integer value from the keyboard and assigns it to parameter x */
}


void  write_int(int x)
{
   /* writes the integer value of parameter x to the screen */
}


void  create_segment(int sn, int data_length)
{
   data[dsp++] = sn;
   data[dsp++] = data_length;
   data[dsp++] = CSG[sn - 1];
   data[dsp++] = CSG[csn];
   csn = sn;
   CSG[csn] = dsp;
   dsp += data_length;
}


void  delete_segment(void)
{
   int     current_segment, call_env, sn_caller, i, data_length, static_link, dynamic_link;

   current_segment = CSG[csn];
   data_length = data[current_segment - 3];
   static_link = data[current_segment - 2];
   dynamic_link = data[current_segment - 1];
   if (static_link == dynamic_link) {
     /* caller is in the same segment group */
     csn--;
   } else {   /* caller is in a different segment group */
     call_env = dynamic_link;
     /* restore the segment group of the caller */
     sn_caller = data[dynamic_link - 4];
     for (i = sn_caller; i >= csn; i--) {
       /* restore the caller's environment */
       CSG[i] = call_env;
       call_env = data[call_env - 2];
     }
```

```
      csn  =  sn_caller;
    }
  dsp  -=  data_length + 4;
}


void main(void)
{
  instruction      *instr;
  int              ic, next, left_operand, right_operand, operand, result;
  boolean          truthval, stop;

  read_code();
  ic               = 0;
  sp               = 0;
  dsp              = 0;
  rsp              = 0;
  csn              = 0;
  CSG[csn]         = 0;
  stop             = false;

  while (!stop) {
    next = ic + 1;
    instr = &prog[ic];
    switch (instr->code) {

    case neg:
    case abs_:     /* not shown */
      break;

    case add:
    case sub:
    case mul:
    case dvi:
    case mdl:      /* not shown */
      break;

    case eq:
    case ne:
    case lt:
    case le:
    case gt:
    case ge:       /* not shown */
      break;

    case ldcon:
      push(instr->u.value);
      break;

    case ldvar:
      push(data[CSG[instr->u.u1.sn1] + instr->u.u1.dpl]);
      break;
```

```
      case stvar:
        pop(&data[CSG[instr−>u.u1.sn1] + instr−>u.u1.dpl]);
        break;

      case jump:   /* not shown */
        break;

      case jift:   /* not shown */
        break;

      case jiff:   /* not shown */
        break;

      case call:
        push_return(next);
        next = instr−>u.address;
        break;

      case crseg:
        create_segment(instr−>u.u2.sn2, instr−>u.u2.length);
        break;

      case dlseg:
        delete_segment();
        break;

      case return_:
        pop_return(&next);
        break;

      case rdint:   /* not shown */
        break;

      case wrint:   /* not shown */
        break;

      case halt:
        stop = true;
        break;
      }
      ic = next;
    }
  }
```

The interpreter above does not provide error detection. Note that the only errors that can occur are stack and memory overflow. By adding checks to the routines *push* and *create_segment*, stack and memory overflow can easily be detected.

2.5   Translation from SLANG to VIM

In the previous section we have redefined the storage organisation of the virtual machine VIM in such a way that the data space of procedures can be dynamically created and deleted. We have also introduced special instructions for the creation and deletion of data segments and for the calling of procedures. This means that we are now ready to formally define procedure declarations and procedure calls. The addressing of variables has also changed. Variables are now addressed by means of a segment number and a displacement. This means that we must reconsider the translation of variables.

2.5.1   Procedures

We recall the syntax of the call-statement

> *call_statement*   :   call_token *identifier*.

and the syntax of the procedure declaration

> *procedure_declaration*   :   procedure_token *identifier* *block* separator_token.

The semantics of the call-statement requires that the procedure bound to the identifier be executed, and that the execution be performed in the environment of the declaration of the procedure. The former is taken care of by the instruction `call`, and the latter by the instruction `crseg`. When the execution of the call-statement is finished, the execution must be resumed where it was interrupted, and the old environment must be restored. This is taken care of by the instructions `return` and `dlseg`. For procedure *identifier* we will denote the start address of its block in the program memory by $\text{address}_{identifier}$, and the segment number and the length of its data segment in the data memory by $\text{sn}_{identifier}$ and $\text{length}_{identifier}$.

Given the distribution of the responsibilities over the caller and the callee as discussed in Section 2.4.1, the translations of the call-statement, procedure declaration, block, declaration-part, constant declaration and variable declaration are:

> <*call_statement*>   :   `call` $\text{address}_{identifier}$.
>
> <*procedure_declaration*>   :   <*block*>
> > `return`
> >
> > .
>
> <*block*>   :   <*declaration_part*>
> > `crseg` $\text{sn}_{identifier}$, $\text{length}_{identifier}$
> > <*statement_part*>
> > `dlseg`
> >
> > .

$$<declaration\_part> \quad : \qquad\qquad \{ \quad <constant\_declaration>$$
$$| \quad <variable\_declaration>$$
$$\} \textbf{ clos}$$
$$\{ \quad \texttt{jump} \quad \texttt{over}$$
$$<procedure\_declaration> \textbf{ seq}$$
$$\texttt{over:}$$
$$\} \textbf{ option}$$

.

$$<constant\_declaration> \quad : \quad .$$
$$<variable\_declaration> \quad : \quad .$$

Note that in the translation of the declaration-part we have replaced the construction $<procedure\_declaration>$ **clos** by $<procedure\_declaration>$ **seq option**. This avoids the inclusion of the instruction jump over when the declaration-part does not contain a procedure declaration. Note also that the translations of the constant and variable declaration are empty. In Sections 3.3.1 and 3.4 we will show that the information associated with constants and variables (i.e. segment numbers, values and displacements) is stored in a table, so that this information can be subsequently used for the translation of statements.

2.5.2   Variables

Identifiers that are variables are specified in the following syntax rules:

$$operand \quad : \quad identifier$$
$$| \quad number$$
$$| \quad expression \textbf{ pack}$$

.

$$left\_part \quad : \quad identifier.$$

$$read\_statement \quad : \quad \texttt{read\_token } identifier \textbf{ list pack}.$$

We will again denote the segment number and displacement of variable *identifier* by $\texttt{sn}_{identifier}$ and $\texttt{dpl}_{identifier}$, respectively, the value of constant *identifier* by $\texttt{intval}_{identifier}$, and the value of number *number* by $\texttt{intval}_{number}$. The translation is then:

$$<operand> \quad : \quad \texttt{ldvar} \quad \texttt{sn}_{identifier}, \texttt{dpl}_{identifier}$$
$$| \quad \texttt{ldcon} \quad \texttt{intval}_{identifier}$$
$$| \quad \texttt{ldcon} \quad \texttt{intval}_{number}$$
$$| \quad <expression>$$

.

$$<left\_part> \quad : \quad \texttt{stvar} \quad \texttt{sn}_{identifier}, \texttt{dpl}_{identifier}.$$

$$<read\_statement> \quad : \quad \{ \quad \texttt{rdint}$$
$$\texttt{stvar} \quad \texttt{sn}_{identifier}, \texttt{dpl}_{identifier}$$
$$\} \quad \texttt{seq}$$

Note that we do not check whether an operand has been initialised.

2.6   Forward references in VIM

In Section 2.3.3 we have used jump instructions and labels in the translation of the if-statement and the while-statement. We have tacitly assumed that these labels are unique, and that they will be translated in some way (e.g. by the assembler) into machine addresses. We will now further extend the architecture of VIM so that jump instructions can be easily handled.

2.6.1   The architecture

Until now we have assumed that arguments of jump instructions are addresses of cells in the program memory. Filling in these arguments may, however, cause problems in the case of forward jumps, as the argument of the jump instruction must be left open until the destination address becomes known. Note that the destination address of backward jumps can be immediately filled in during code generation.

This problem can be easily solved if we first generate an assembly program in which each instruction that is the destination of a jump has a label. The assembler then generates machine code in 2 phases. The first phase consists of building a label table in which each label is associated with an address in the program memory. The second phase consists of building the final machine program in which arguments of jump instructions are addresses in the program memory.

If we do not first generate assembly code, but immediately output machine code, then there are 2 methods to solve the problem of forward jumps: the first method is to complete the jump instruction as soon as the destination address is known. This means of course that we need to "backpatch" the correct destination address in an instruction that we generated earlier. This can be done during a second pass over the program. This requires of course that we remember the addresses of jump instructions. Note that this method is similar to the method that the assembler uses.

In the second method we use a table that stores destination addresses of jump instructions. The argument of a jump instruction is then an index in this table. When a destination address is known it is placed in the table. Of course, in this method, we need to remember the index in the table until we have found the destination address. We will refer to this table as the *address table*.

Unconditional jump

instruction	meaning
jump index	continues execution at the address at position index in the address table

Conditional jumps

instruction	meaning
jift index	removes the top (truth) value, truthval (say), from the stack; if the value of truthval is true then execution is continued at the address at position index in the address table, otherwise the next instruction is executed
jiff index	removes the top (truth) value, truthval (say), from the stack; if the value of truthval is false then execution is continued at the address at position index in the address table, otherwise the next instruction is executed

Call

instruction	meaning
call index	saves the return address, and continues execution at the address at position index in the address table

Create segment

instruction	meaning
crseg sn,index	creates a segment with number sn and length length, (say), which is at position index in the length table; the remainder of the definition is unchanged

Figure 2.14 Instructions of the VIM machine VIM.

A forward-referencing problem occurs with the create-segment instruction as well. The length of the data segment is not known until all the declarations of a procedure have been compiled. Again there are 2 methods: we can complete the create-segment instruction as soon as the length is known (by backpatching), or we can store the length in a *length table*.

The advantage of using the second method, i.e. the address table and the length table, is that generated instructions can be output on-the-fly. We therefore choose this method for jump and create-segment instructions.

2.6.2   The instruction set

In Figure 2.14 we redefine the jump, call and create-segment instructions in VIM to use address and length tables. Both tables are implemented as arrays. The arguments of jump, call and create-segment instructions are indices in these tables. Examples that show the use of the address and length table will be given in Section 3.5.

2.6.3   The interpreter

We now modify the interpreter to handle the new scheme. As before the procedure *read_code* reads the VIM program from a file, and writes it to the array *prog*. It also reads the address and length tables from files, and writes them to the arrays *address_table* and *length_table*. Furthermore, jump, call and create-segment instructions are changed to take their addresses and length from these tables.

```
#define  max_prog        1000      /* length of program memory */
#define  max_table       1000      /* length of address and length table */
#define  max_data        100       /* length of data memory */
#define  max_depth       15        /* maximum nesting depth */
#define  max_stack       100       /* maximum depth of stacks */


typedef enum {
  true = 1, false = 0
} boolean;

typedef enum {
  neg, abs_, add, sub, mul, dvi, mdl, eq, ne, lt, le, gt, ge, ldcon, ldvar,
  stvar, jump, jift, jiff, call, crseg, dlseg, return_, rdint, wrint, halt
} operation;

typedef struct {
  operation code;
  union {
    /* no operands for:    neg, abs_, add, sub, mul, dvi, mdl, eq, ne, lt,
                           le, gt, ge, dlseg, return_, rdint, wrint, halt */
    int value;            /* for: ldcon */
    struct {
      int sn1, dpl;       /* for: ldvar, stvar */
    } u1;
    int index1;           /* for: jump, jift, jiff, call */
    struct {
      int sn2, index2;    /* for: crseg */
    } u2;
  } u;
} instruction;
```

```
instruction         prog[max_prog];
int                 CSG[max_depth];
int                 address_table[max_table];
int                 length_table[max_table];
int                 data[max_data];
int                 stack[max_stack];
int                 return_stack[max_stack];
int                 sp, dsp, rsp, csn;
```

```
/*
** Procedures push, pop, push_return, pop_return, read_int, write_int,
** create_segment and delete_segment are not shown.
*/
```

```
void read_code(void)
{
    /* reads the VIM program from a file and writes it to the array prog */
    /* reads the address table from a file and writes it to the array address_table */
    /* reads the length table from a file and writes it to the array length_table */
}
```

```
void main(void)
{
    instruction         *instr;
    int                 ic, next, left_operand, right_operand, operand, result, length;
    boolean             truthval, stop;

    read_code();
    ic          = 0;
    sp          = 0;
    dsp         = 0;
    rsp         = 0;
    csn         = 0;
    CSG[csn]    = 0;
    stop        = false;

    while (!stop) {
        next = ic + 1;
        instr = &prog[ic];
        switch (instr->code) {

        case neg:
        case abs_:    /* not shown */
            break;

        case add:
        case sub:
        case mul:
        case dvi:
        case mdl:     /* not shown */
            break;
```

```
case eq:
case ne:
case lt:
case le:
case gt:
case ge:        /* not shown */
   break;

case ldcon:     /* not shown */
   break;

case ldvar:     /* not shown */
   break;

case stvar:     /* not shown */
   break;

case jump:
   next = address_table[instr->u.index1];
   break;

case jift:
   pop(operand);
   if (operand == 1)
      next = address_table[instr->u.index1];
   break;

case jiff:
   pop(operand);
   if (operand == 0)
      next = address_table[instr->u.index1];
   break;

case crseg:
   length = length_table[instr->u.u2.index2];
   create_segment(instr->u.u2.sn2, length);
   break;

case dlseg:
   delete_segment();
   break;

case call:
   push_return(next);
   next = address_table[instr->u.index1];
   break;

case return_:
   pop_return(next);
   break;
```

```
case rdint:      /* not shown */
   break;

case wrint:      /* not shown */
   break;

case halt:
   stop = true;
   break;
   }
   ic = next;
 }
}
```

2.7   Exercises

1. Extend the language definition of SLANG so that constants and variables of type Boolean can be declared, and add logical operators that can be applied to Boolean operands.

2. Extend SLANG with a repeat-statement that is defined as follows:

   repeat_statement   :   repeat_token *statement_part*
                            until_token *relation*
                            taeper_token

   Semantics: First the statement-part is executed, and then the relation is evaluated. If the value of the relation is false then the repeat-statement is again executed. If the value of the relation is true no action is taken.

   Give the translation of this repeat-statement, i.e. show the right part of the production of <*repeat_statement*>.

3. Extend SLANG with a for-statement of the form

   FOR i FROM e_1 TO e_2 STEP e_3 DO S OD

   where S is a statement-part and e_1 (initial value), e_2 (final value) and e_3 (increment) are integer-valued expressions. The control variable i is implicitly defined to be of type integer, and its scope is the statement-part between DO and OD.

   S is successively executed for the following values of i:

$$e_1$$
$$e_1 + e_3$$
$$e_1 + 2 * e_3$$
$$\vdots$$
$$e_1 + n * e_3$$

where n the largest integer value ≥ 0, such that:

- if $e_1 \leq e_2$ and $e_3 > 0$
  then $e_1 + n * e_3 \leq e_2$
- if $e_1 \geq e_2$ and $e_3 < 0$
  then $e_1 + n * e_3 \geq e_2$

S will not be executed if:

- $e_2 < e_1$ and $e_3 > 0$
- $e_2 > e_1$ and $e_3 < 0$
- $e_3 = 0$

The expressions e_1, e_2 and e_3 are computed only once during the execution of the for-statement, just before the first execution of S. S is considered a block, and this block is the scope of i. An extra restriction is that i may not be assigned in S.

(a) Give a definition of this for-statement in the style of Section 2.1, i.e. with *syntax, context constraints* and *semantics*.

(b) Explain how this type of for-statement can be expressed in VIM instructions. In particular, explain how the scope rule "S is considered a block, and this block is the scope of i" can be realised.

(c) Finally, show the translation in VIM instructions of the program:

```
BEGIN  VAR INT sum;
       sum := 0;
       FOR i FROM 1 TO 10 STEP 1 DO sum := sum + i OD;
       WRITE (sum)
END.
```

4. Extend SLANG with a case-statement of the form:

```
CASE E OF
     n₁: S₁;
     n₂: S₂;
     ⋮
     nₘ: Sₘ
ESAC
```

where E is an expression, n_i $(1 \leq i \leq m)$ is a number, and S_i $(1 \leq i \leq m)$ is a statement.

The execution of the case-statement proceeds as follows. First, the value of E is computed. This value is compared with n_1. If these values are equal, then S_1 is executed, and the case-statement is then finished. If the values are not equal, then the value of E is compared with n_2, and so on. If the value of E is not equal to any n_i, then nothing is done.

(a) Give a definition of this case-statement in the style of Section 2.1, i.e. with *syntax*, *context constraints* and *semantics*.

(b) Explain how this type of case-statement can be expressed in VIM instructions.

(c) Show the translation in VIM instructions of the program:

```
BEGIN   VAR INT number, result;
        READ (number);
        CASE number * 2 OF
            2:   result := 1;
            4:   result := 2;
            6:   result := 3
        ESAC;
        WRITE (result)
END.
```

Hint: As a result of the computation of E its value will remain on the stack. The value of n_i can be loaded on the stack by means of the instruction ldcon. The instruction **eq** cannot be used to compare these values, because it will remove both values from the stack, whereas the value of E must remain on the stack for the next comparison if the values are not equal. A solution is to introduce an instruction **case index**. This instruction removes both values from the stack in the case of equality, after which the next instruction (the first instruction of S_i) is executed. In the case of inequality, only the value of n_i is removed from the stack, after which the execution continues at the address at position **index** in the address table (the next comparison). It will be necessary to introduce an instruction **remove** that removes the value of E from the stack if nothing is done. Note that the interpreter needs to be extended so that these new instructions can be recognised.

5. Consider the following program, which is an extension of the program in Figure 2.10.

```
BEGIN PROC p1                                            1
      BEGIN VAR ...;                                     2
            PROC p3 BEGIN ...; CALL p4; ...END;          3
```

```
            PROC p4 BEGIN ......END;                    4
            ⋮
            CALL p4;                                    5
            CALL p3;                                    6
            ⋮
        END;                                            7
        PROC p2                                         8
        BEGIN VAR ...;                                  9
            PROC p5                                     10
            BEGIN VAR ...;                              11
                PROC p6 BEGIN ...; CALL p1; ...END;     12
                ⋮
                CALL p6;                                13
                ⋮
            END;                                        14
            ⋮
            CALL p5;                                    15
            CALL p1;                                    16
            ⋮
        END;                                            17
        ⋮
        CALL p1;                                        18
        CALL p2;                                        19
        ⋮
    END.                                                20
```

Show the CSG and the segment stack after the following calling sequence:

(a) p2 at line 19

(b) p5 at line 15

(c) p6 at line 13

(d) p1 at line 12

(e) p4 at line 05

(f) p3 at line 06

(g) p4 at line 03

2.8   Bibliographic notes

The language SLANG can be considered a subset of many contemporary programming languages. Several books are available that deal with aspects of programming languages. A general introduction is given by Pratt [116]. For a systematic discussion of different classes of programming languages we refer to Ghezzi and Jazayeri [53]. A more formal treatment can be found in Tennent [136].

The syntax of SLANG is formally described by means of an extended context-free grammar. A less formal *operational* approach is used to describe the semantics. Other methods are *axiomatic* and *denotational* semantics. For the axiomatic approach we refer to Hoare [75]. An axiomatic definition of Pascal is given by Hoare and Wirth [76]. For introductions to the denotational approach we refer to Gordon [59] and Tennent [136, 135].

The machine language of VIM is an example of a stack-oriented intermediate language. Other kinds of intermediate code include 2- and 3-address instructions, and syntax trees or directed acyclic graphs. For an overview of these intermediate languages see Aho *et al.* [3]. Examples of compiler texts that use an abstract machine are:

- Bennett [22] uses VAM (VSL Abstract Machine), which is a low-level register-oriented machine.
- Elder [39] uses a stack-based hypothetical computer, called Target.
- Holub [78] uses C-code, which is a C subset in which all instructions have direct analogues in most assembly languages.
- Pittman and Peters [115] take abstract syntax trees as intermediate format and use a hypothetical stack computer in a project for the compilation of a subset of Modula-2.
- Waite and Carter [141] generate an abstract syntax tree as intermediate representation, and use a general register architecture as target machine.
- Watt [143] uses a stack-based hypothetical computer, called TAM (Triangle Abstract Machine) as a case study.
- Wirth uses in Chapter 5 of [149] a stack-oriented hypothetical computer, called the PL/0 machine.

The source languages described in the above compiler texts can be found in the bibliographic notes in Chapter 3.

Chapter 3

Building a compiler from scratch

Having defined SLANG and VIM in Chapter 2, we are now in a position to discuss the translation of programs written in SLANG into code that will run on VIM. We start with the presentation of a scanner in Section 3.1, and a context-free parser in Section 3.2. The next step is the implementation of context analysis. To enable us to carry out context analysis, we first discuss symbol-table management in Section 3.3. The parser that we developed in Section 3.2 is extended to a context-sensitive parser in Section 3.4. In Section 3.5, code generation is added to the parser, so that lexical analysis, syntax analysis, context analysis and code generation can be performed in a single pass. Finally, in Section 3.6, we consider error handling.

3.1 A scanner

Scanning is a popular name for *lexical analysis*. Lexical analysis is the first phase in a compiler. Its main aim is the translation of the input character string into a series of tokens. This involves scanning the input text and removing unwanted characters (e.g. spaces), recognising the strings that correspond to tokens, and carrying out various house-keeping tasks such as keeping track of line numbers, generating a listfile, and so on.

A *token* is a name that is given to a set of strings. This set of strings can be a singleton set, a small, finite set, or an infinite set (ignoring implementation restrictions). For example, in Figure 2.4 the name *begin_token* is given to the singleton set {BEGIN}. In other words, the name *begin_token* represents the string "BEGIN".

Some compilers collect related operators in one token, e.g. the name *relop_token* is given to the set {= <> < <= > >=}. Alternatively, a different name can be used for each operator, e.g. the name *equal_token* for the singleton set {=}, the name *not_equal_token* for {<>}, the name *less_than_token* for {<}, and so on. As we saw

91

in Figure 2.4, this is the scheme that we use.

Although in Section 2.1.2 we have defined identifiers and numbers as part of the syntax, in the compiler they will be treated as tokens. We represent the set of identifiers with the token *ident_token* and the set of numbers with the token *num_token*. Both sets are infinite in size. When the scanner recognises an identifier, its token and the identifier itself (called the *lexeme*) will be passed to the parser. Similarly, when the scanner recognises a number, its token and its value will be passed to the parser.

In some compilers, the scanner is responsible for storing the lexeme of an identifier in the symbol table. In that case the token *ident_token* together with the associated pointer to the table entry is passed to the parser. It is also possible to let the parser store the identifier in the symbol table. In that case the scanner will pass the lexeme to the parser. As we shall see, we choose the latter approach.

3.1.1   Regular expressions and languages

Returning now to a scanner for SLANG, let us consider the languages represented by the various tokens that are enumerated in Figure 2.4, and the identifiers and numbers. As we have already mentioned, the token *begin_token* corresponds to a language consisting of only the string "BEGIN" (in capital letters). Other examples of tokens with a one-string language are *becomes_token* and *plus_token*, which correspond to the two-character string ":=" and the one-character string "+", respectively. In the scanner for SLANG, the definitions of the above-mentioned tokens are the following:

```
begin_token      :  BEGIN .
becomes_token    :  := .
plus_token       :  + .
```

In contrast, the sets of strings corresponding to *ident_token* and *num_token* are infinite. In Section 2.1.1 we introduced the syntactic operators concatenation, choice ("|"), option ("**option**"), closure ("**clos**") and sequence ("**seq**"). These operators can be used to build regular expressions, and regular expressions can be used to express infinite sets of strings.

Example 3.1
The following definition specifies *ident_token* and *num_token*:

```
ident_token   :   {a|b|c|d|e|f|g|h|i|j|k|l|m|n|o|p|q|r|s|t|u|v|w|x|y|z}
                  {a|b|c|d|e|f|g|h|i|j|k|l|m|n|o|p|q|r|s|t|u|v|w|x|y|z|
                                          0|1|2|3|4|5|6|7|8|9} clos.
num_token     :   {0|1|2|3|4|5|6|7|8|9} seq.
```
⋄

The expressions on the right-hand side of the above rules are *regular expressions*. Regular expressions are constructed from characters and the above operators. In fact, a regular expression is built up out of simpler regular expressions. As a notational convenience we can use a name in a regular expression of a previously defined regular expression, as long as this does not lead to recursive definitions.

Example 3.2
We can rewrite the above regular expression in the following way:

letter	:	a|b|c|d|e|f|g|h|i|j|k|l|m|n|o|p|q|r|s|t|u|v|w|x|y|z .
digit	:	0|1|2|3|4|5|6|7|8|9 .
ident_token	:	letter { letter| digit} **clos**.
num_token	:	digit **seq**.

Note that these definitions are more intuitive and less cumbersome than the definitions in Example 3.1.   ◇

The language specified by a regular expression is called a *regular language*. The rules used to define tokens are reminiscent of extended context-free grammars, but the difference is that recursion is not allowed. The syntactic operators that we use in token definitions are restricted to concatenation, choice, option, closure and sequence. A more thorough discussion of regular expressions and languages will be presented in Chapter 7.

3.1.2   Finite automata

Regular expressions can be represented by *transition diagrams*. A transition diagram is a directed graph with labelled edges. The edges are also called *transitions*, or *moves*, and the edge labels are input symbols. The nodes in the diagram are called *states*, and these are usually numbered. Exactly one state is designated as the *start state*, and there can be any number of *accept states*. It is customary that a state (node) is drawn as a circle, an accept state as a shaded circle, and that a start state be indicated by a lone arrow. An example of a transition diagram that represents the regular expression $\{a\,|\,b\}c$ is depicted in Figure 3.1.

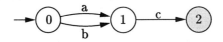

Figure 3.1 Transition diagram for $\{a\,|\,b\}\,c$.

Beginning at the start state, we can traverse a graph by reading the input and making transitions. A transition corresponds to a change of state. In this way, therefore, the transition diagram can be thought of as a machine or, more precisely, an *automaton*. The automaton begins in an initial state 0, and the left-most symbol, a (say), is read from the input. The automaton then goes to some state i if there is an edge from 0 to i with label a in the transition graph. The next symbol can then be read, and the process is repeated. A string is accepted if after all input is read, the final state is an accept state. This means that the input string has been recognised. There are only a finite number of states, hence we call the machine a *finite-state automaton*.

A finite-state automaton can be *deterministic* or *non-deterministic*. In a deterministic finite automaton, there can only be one transition for a given input symbol. In a non-deterministic finite automaton, there may be two or more transitions possible for a given input symbol. In this chapter we will consider finite automata only intuitively, and restrict ourselves to deterministic automata.

Figure 3.2 shows a transition diagram for the pattern ":=". Its start state is state 0, and after reading the characters ":" and "=" the accept state 2 is reached. After the string is recognised, the corresponding token must be given to the parser. We will use the intermediary variable *look_ahead* to pass tokens from the scanner to the parser. In this case, the token *becomes_token* is therefore assigned to *look_ahead*. This finite state automaton is very simple. An even simpler automaton is the one for *plus_token*, which is depicted in Figure 3.3. Similar diagrams can be drawn for other one-character tokens, such as *separator_token*, but not for *less_than_token*, as the character "<" is the first character in the representation of 3 different tokens.

Figure 3.2 Transition diagram for the becomes-token.

Figure 3.3 Transition diagram for the plus-token.

Figure 3.4 shows the combined transition diagram for the relational operators. If we read the input character "<" while in the start state, then the automaton goes to state 2. If the next symbol read is "=", then accept state 3 is reached, and *less_or_equal_token* is produced. If, however, the next symbol read is ">", then the automaton goes to accept state 4, and *not_equal_token* is produced. Otherwise, another token is read, and the automaton moves to accept state 5, in which case *less_than_token* is produced. In the latter case, the last symbol read is not part of *less_than_token*. This means that the pointer in the input string must be retracted so that the next read operation reads the same character again. This is carried out by the action *retract*.

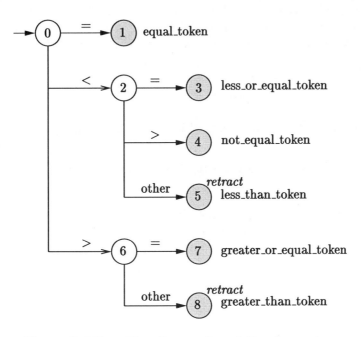

Figure 3.4 Transition diagram for relational operators.

Figure 3.5 shows the automaton that recognises identifiers. When the accept state is reached, the value *ident_token* is produced, i.e. assigned to the variable *look_ahead*. Its lexeme is held in a buffer, which is not shown in this figure. Notice that the input pointer must be retracted, as the last character read does not belong to the identifier.

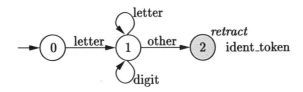

Figure 3.5 Transition diagram for identifiers.

Many languages and compilers treat keywords as reserved identifiers. In that case, after the recognition of an identifier, a pre-defined keyword table must be consulted to see if the string under consideration is a keyword or an identifier. In SLANG, however, we differentiate between keywords and identifiers by representing keywords by upper-case letters, and identifiers by lower-case letters and digits. The automaton for the recognition of keywords is shown in Figure 3.6. The procedure *look_up* compares the upper-case string with the keywords in a keyword table, and returns the keyword token concerned, e.g. *begin_token*, or *end_token*, etc.

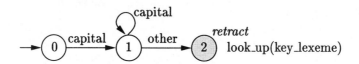

Figure 3.6 Transition diagram for keywords.

We could, of course, use a recogniser for keywords as shown in Figure 3.7, but this would require an automaton with 54 states, which would be more complex to maintain (e.g. delete or change keywords, or extend with new keywords).

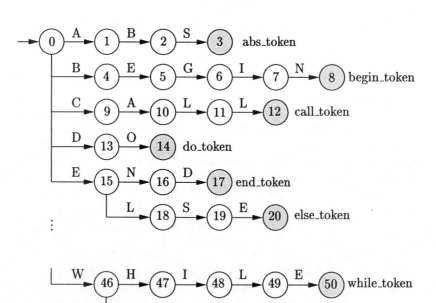

Figure 3.7 Another transition diagram for keywords.

The recogniser for numbers is shown in Figure 3.8. In the accept state, *num_token* with the associated binary value is produced. The binary value is not shown in this figure.

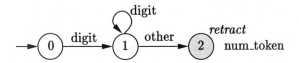

Figure 3.8 Transition diagram for numbers.

Figure 3.9 shows the recognition of comments. Nothing is produced. Representations of tokens may be separated by spaces, tabs and new-lines. Their recognition is depicted in Figure 3.10. The last character read before the accept state is reached, is the first character of the next token. The input pointer is therefore reset. Nothing is produced.

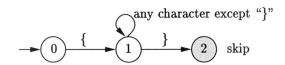

Figure 3.9 Transition diagram for comments.

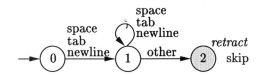

Figure 3.10 Transition diagram for delimiters.

A transition diagram for all the tokens is obtained if we join the transition diagrams of Figure 3.2 through 3.10, excluding Figure 3.7, and renumber the states. The complete transition diagram is shown in Figure 3.11.

3.1.3   Implementation of a scanner

Transition diagrams can be represented, and implemented (although, in general, not efficiently) as tables. In a transition table, each row corresponds to a state,

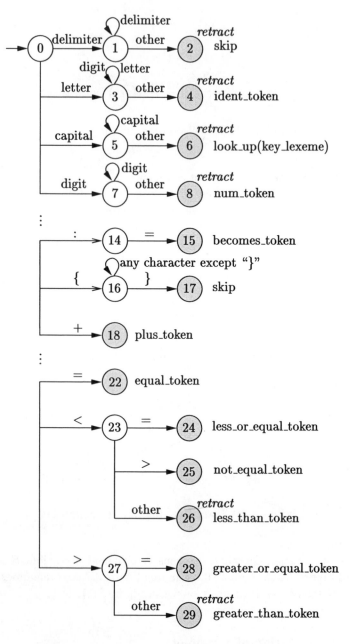

Figure 3.11 Transition diagram for all tokens.

	a	b	c
0	1	1	
1			2
2			

Figure 3.12 Transition table corresponding to the transition diagram shown in Figure 3.1.

and each column to an input symbol. Entries in the table are single states in the case of a deterministic finite automaton, and sets of states in the case of a non-deterministic finite automaton. Empty entries indicate erroneous input. In Figure 3.12, for example, we show the transition table corresponding to the transition diagram that represents the regular expression $\{a\,|\,b\}c$, which is depicted in Figure 3.1.

A transition diagram can also be translated into a program. Typically, such a program reads characters from the input, and uses case or switch-statements to go to new states. Below we show a scanner that is based on this principle. The procedure *next_token*, which returns the recognised token in the variable *look_ahead*, is a translation of the deterministic finite automaton in Figure 3.11. Notice that the recognition of delimiters is not included in the case-statement, but implemented as a while-statement at the beginning of the procedure.

The recognition of identifiers, keywords, numbers and comments is delegated to the procedures *identifier*, *keyword*, *number* and *comment*, respectively. If, at the beginning, we read:

lower-case letter The procedure *identifier* is called, which collects the letters and digits of the identifier in the buffer *ident_lexeme*. Notice that the identifier is terminated by the control character **nul**.

upper-case letter The procedure *keyword* is called, which collects the capital letters of the keyword in the buffer *key_lexeme* and adds a terminating **nul** character. The procedure *look_up* compares the string in the buffer with the keywords (also terminated by the **nul** character) in the keyword table, and returns the keyword concerned.

digit The procedure *number* is called, which reads the digits, computes the associated binary value, and assigns it to the variable *num_value*.

opening brace "{" The procedure *comment* is called, which reads and skips characters until the closing brace "}" is reached.

Details concerning input and table look-up are not shown. Further, error detection and recovery are not implemented. The intermediary variables *look_ahead*, *ident_lexeme* and *num_value* are used to pass tokens and their associated values from the scanner to the parser.

```
#define  max_ident_length          255
#define  max_key_length            5

typedef char                       string[max_ident_length + 1];
typedef char                       capital[max_key_length + 1];

typedef enum {
  true = 1, false = 0
} boolean;

typedef enum {
  ident_token, num_token, begin_token, end_token, int_token, var_token, procedure_token,
  call_token, read_token, write_token, if_token, then_token, else_token, fi_token,
  while_token, do_token, od_token, negate_token, absolute_token, open_token, close_token,
  list_token, period_token, separator_token, becomes_token, open_comment_token,
  close_comment_token, plus_token, minus_token, times_token, over_token, modulo_token,
  equal_token, not_equal_token, less_than_token, less_or_equal_token, greater_than_token,
  greater_or_equal_token
} token;


token                    look_ahead;
string                   ident_lexeme;
int                      num_value;
capital                  key_lexeme;
/* keyword_table         ...; */
char                     ch;
boolean                  retract;


void initialise_scanner(void)
{
  /* enter the keyword tokens and the associated lexemes in the keyword table */
  ch = ' ';    /* initial value */
}

void next_character(void)
{
  /* assign the next character from the input to variable ch */
}

token look_up(capital key_lexeme)
{
  /* assign the keyword token associated with key_lexeme to look_up */
}

void identifier(void)
{
  int index;

  index = 0;
```

```
   do {
     ident_lexeme[index] = ch;
     index++;
     next_character();
   } while (islower(ch) || isdigit(ch));
   ident_lexeme[index] = 0;
   /* terminate the character string by the control character nul */
   look_ahead = ident_token;
   retract = true;
}

void keyword(void)
{
   int index;

   index = 0;
   do {
     key_lexeme[index] = ch;
     index++;
     next_character();
   } while (isupper(ch));
   key_lexeme[index] = 0;
   /* terminate the capital string by the control character nul */
   look_ahead = look_up(key_lexeme);
   /* search the keyword table for the lexeme, and return the associated token */
   retract = true;
}

void number(void)
{
   num_value = 0;
   do {
     num_value = num_value * 10 + ch - '0';
     next_character();
   } while (isdigit(ch));
   look_ahead = num_token;
   retract = true;
}

void comment(void)
{
   do
     next_character();
   while (ch != '}');
}

void next_token(void)
{
   retract = false;
   while (ch <= ' ')
     next_character();
   /* ignore control characters and spaces */
```

```
switch (ch) {

case '(':
  look_ahead = open_token;
  break;

case ')':
  look_ahead = close_token;
  break;

case ',':
  look_ahead = list_token;
  break;

case '.':
  look_ahead = period_token;
  break;

case ';':
  look_ahead = separator_token;
  break;

case ':':
  next_character();
  if (ch == '=') look_ahead = becomes_token;
  break;

case '{':
  comment();
  break;

case '+':
  look_ahead = plus_token;
  break;

case '-':
  look_ahead = minus_token;
  break;

case '*':
  look_ahead = times_token;
  break;

case '/':
  look_ahead = over_token;
  break;

case '|':
  look_ahead = modulo_token;
  break;
```

```
  case '=':
    look_ahead = equal_token;
    break;

  case '<':
    next_character();
    if (ch == '>') look_ahead = not_equal_token;
    else if (ch == '=') look_ahead = less_or_equal_token;
    else {
      look_ahead = less_than_token;
      retract = true;
    }
    break;

  case '>':
    next_character();
    if (ch == '=') look_ahead = greater_or_equal_token;
    else {
      look_ahead = greater_than_token;
      retract = true;
    }
    break;

  default:
    if (islower(ch))
      identifier();
    else if (isupper(ch))
      keyword();
    else if (isdigit(ch))
      number();
  }
  if (!retract) next_character();
}

/* parser routines; see next section */

void main(void)
{
/* main program body; see next section */
}
```

3.2 A context-free parser

In this section we will develop a *predictive recursive-descent parser* for the source language SLANG. In Section 1.5 we have already seen an example of such a recursive-descent parser, in the form of a parser for an expression language.

3.2.1 Predictive recursive-descent parsing

We will first briefly repeat the principles of *recursive-descent parsing*, as given in Section 1.5 and, thereafter, extend this scheme so that a recursive-descent parser for SLANG can be easily written. The basic idea of recursive-descent parsing is that a parsing procedure is associated with each nonterminal of the grammar. Parsing begins by calling the procedure associated with the start symbol. During parsing, each terminal in the right-hand side of a production is matched with the look-ahead symbol, and each nonterminal will result in a call of its associated procedure. The parsing procedures thus descend through the parse tree as they recognise the source program. A parse tree is implicitly defined by the calling sequence of the syntax procedures. In practice, the parse tree may also be generated.

If the right-hand side of a production consists of a number of alternatives (at least 2), then the look-ahead symbol must determine which alternative must be selected. If all alternatives start with a different token, and the look-ahead symbol matches one of these tokens, then the alternative starting with this token will be selected. This is the case in the productions

add_operator	:	plus_token | minus_token.
multiply_operator	:	times_token | over_token | modulo_token.
unary_operator	:	negate_token | absolute_token.

where all alternatives consist of a single token, and also in the production

operand	:	*identifier*
	|	*number*
	|	*expression* **pack**
	.	

where the first and second alternatives consist of a single token (i.e. *ident_token* and *num_token*, respectively), and the last alternative (which is, in fact, *open_token expression close_token*) is also a string that starts with a token.

The selection is not so simple if some or all the alternatives start with a nonterminal, as in

statement	:	*assignment_statement*
	|	*if_statement*
	|	*while_statement*
	|	*call_statement*
	|	*read_statement*
	|	*write_statement*
	.	

In this case we need to know which token strings can be derived from the nonterminals in the right-hand side of the production of *statement*. In Section 1.5 we have therefore introduced FIRST(X) as the set of tokens that can begin a string derivable from X. It is easy to see that the token sets for the various statements are as follows:

$$
\begin{aligned}
\text{FIRST}(\textit{assignment\_statement}) &= \{\text{ident\_token}\} \\
\text{FIRST}(\textit{if\_statement}) &= \{\text{if\_token}\} \\
\text{FIRST}(\textit{while\_statement}) &= \{\text{while\_token}\} \\
\text{FIRST}(\textit{call\_statement}) &= \{\text{call\_token}\} \\
\text{FIRST}(\textit{read\_statement}) &= \{\text{read\_token}\} \\
\text{FIRST}(\textit{write\_statement}) &= \{\text{write\_token}\}
\end{aligned}
$$

These sets are pairwise disjoint, so it is always possible to make a choice between the right-hand sides of *statement*.

Thus far we have compared the look-ahead with the first token(s) of the derivation(s) of each alternative to select the right alternative. This is not possible in the case of an empty alternative. To illustrate this problem, we extend the production of *statement* with a *dummy_statement*, as follows:

```
statement          :   assignment_statement
                   |   if_statement
                   |   while_statement
                   |   call_statement
                   |   read_statement
                   |   write_statement
                   |   dummy_statement
                   .

dummy_statement    :   .
```

The set FIRST(*dummy_statement*) is empty. To select *dummy_statement* during parsing, the tokens that can follow a *dummy_statement* must be known. We therefore define FOLLOW(X) as the set of tokens that can follow a string derivable from X. For example,

$$
\text{FOLLOW}(\textit{dummy\_statement}) = \{\text{end\_token, separator\_token,} \\
\text{else\_token, fi\_token, od\_token}\}
$$

We now introduce the functions EMPTY and DIRSET. EMPTY(X) is a Boolean function that indicates whether X can derive the empty string. DIRSET(X) defines the set of director symbols, and is defined as follows:

$$
\text{DIRSET}(X) = \begin{cases} \text{FIRST}(X), & \text{if } \neg\text{EMPTY}(X) \\ \text{FIRST}(X) \cup \text{FOLLOW}(X), & \text{otherwise} \end{cases}
$$

The director sets for the various statements are as follows:

$$\begin{aligned}
\text{DIRSET}(assignment\_statement) &= \{\text{ident\_token}\} \\
\text{DIRSET}(if\_statement) &= \{\text{if\_token}\} \\
\text{DIRSET}(while\_statement) &= \{\text{while\_token}\} \\
\text{DIRSET}(call\_statement) &= \{\text{call\_token}\} \\
\text{DIRSET}(read\_statement) &= \{\text{read\_token}\} \\
\text{DIRSET}(write\_statement) &= \{\text{write\_token}\} \\
\text{DIRSET}(dummy\_statement) &= \{\text{end\_token, separator\_token,} \\
& \quad \text{else\_token, fi\_token, od\_token}\}
\end{aligned}$$

These sets are pairwise disjoint, and so it is always possible to select the right alternative. Note that alternatives may not only occur as complete right-hand sides, but also as subparts of a right-hand side, as in the production

> *declaration_part* : { *constant_declaration* | *variable_declaration* } **clos**
> *procedure_declaration* **clos**

In this case the director sets

$$\begin{aligned}
\text{DIRSET}(constant\_declaration) &= \{\text{int\_token}\} \\
\text{DIRSET}(variable\_declaration) &= \{\text{var\_token}\}
\end{aligned}$$

are disjoint, as shown above.

In extended context-free grammars (the definition of SLANG is an example) the right-hand sides of the productions are regular expressions. Regular expressions in extended context-free grammars are built up out of terminals, nonterminals, syntactic operators and parentheses.

To choose between different regular expressions we need to re-define the functions FIRST, FOLLOW, EMPTY and DIRSET with regular expressions as arguments. For a regular expressions E, FIRST(E) is the set of tokens that can begin a string derivable from E, FOLLOW(E) is the set of tokens that can follow a string derivable from E, EMPTY(E) indicates whether E can derive the empty string, and DIRSET(E), which defines the set of director symbols, is defined as follows:

$$\text{DIRSET}(E) = \begin{cases} \text{FIRST}(E), & \text{if } \neg\text{EMPTY}(E) \\ \text{FIRST}(E) \cup \text{FOLLOW}(E), & \text{otherwise} \end{cases}$$

In this chapter we restrict ourselves to an informal description of these functions. A formal definition will be given in Chapter 8.

A predictive parser requires that for every regular expression $E_1 \mid E_2 \mid \ldots \mid E_n$, $\forall\, i,j\ (1 \le i < j \le n)$, the sets of symbols that are representative for the choice of E_i and E_j are disjoint, i.e. DIRSET(E_i) $\cap$ DIRSET(E_j) $= \emptyset$.

The syntactic operator **option** indicates a choice between zero or one instance of a phrase. A predictive parser requires that for every expression E **option** the set of symbols that are representative for the choice of E and the set of symbols that may follow E **option** must be disjoint, i.e. $\neg$EMPTY(E) $\wedge$ (FIRST(E) $\cap$ FOLLOW(E **option**) $= \emptyset$).

In the language definition of SLANG, the syntactic operator **option** is applied in the following productions:

$$if\_statement \quad : \quad \text{if\_token } relation \text{ then\_token } statement\_part$$
$$\{\text{else\_token } statement\_part\} \textbf{ option}$$
$$\text{fi\_token}$$

$$factor \qquad \quad : \quad unary\_operator \textbf{ option } operand.$$

Note that the functions EMPTY, FIRST and FOLLOW have, with respect to the application of the syntactic operator **option**, the following values:

EMPTY({else_token *statement_part*})	=	false
FIRST({else_token *statement_part*})	=	{else_token}
FOLLOW({else_token *statement_part*} **option**)	=	{fi_token}
EMPTY(*unary_operator*)	=	false
FIRST(*unary_operator*)	=	{negate_token, absolute_token}
FOLLOW(*unary_operator* **option**)	=	{ident_token, num_token, open_token}

The conditions for the syntactic operators **clos**, **seq** and **chain** are similar to **option**. For each regular expression of the form E **clos**:

$$\neg\text{EMPTY}(E) \wedge (\text{FIRST}(E) \cap \text{FOLLOW}(E \textbf{ clos}) = \emptyset)$$

for each regular expression of the form E **seq**:

$$\neg\text{EMPTY}(E) \wedge (\text{FIRST}(E) \cap \text{FOLLOW}(E \textbf{ seq}) = \emptyset)$$

and for each regular expression of the form E_1 **chain** E_2:

$$\text{DIRSET}(E_2) \cap \text{FOLLOW}(E_1 \textbf{ chain } E_2) = \emptyset$$

The reader is invited to transform the regular expressions "E **list**" and "E **pack**" into the regular expressions "E **chain** list_token" and "open_token E close_token", and to check whether the above conditions hold for the productions of SLANG.

3.2.2 Implementation of a parser

We now explain how a recursive-descent parser for an extended context-free grammar can be generated. Let $\Pi(expr)$ represent the parser text for regular expression *expr*. For each production $A : expr$ the parser contains a procedure

```
void A(void)
{
   Π(expr)
}
```

	Regular expression	Parser module
1	a (terminal)	**if** (look_ahead == a) next_token();
2	A (nonterminal)	A(); (i.e. call of procedure associated with A)

3	$E_1 \mid E_2 \mid \ldots \mid E_n$ $(n > 1)$	**if** (look_ahead $\in$ DIRSET(E_1)) {
		    $\Pi(E_1)$
		} **else if** (look_ahead $\in$ DIRSET(E_2)) {
		    $\Pi(E_2)$
		
		    $\vdots$
		
		} **else if** (look_ahead $\in$ DIRSET(E_n)) {
		    $\Pi(E_n)$
		}

4	$E_1 E_1 \ldots E_n$	$\Pi(E_1)$ $\Pi(E_2)$ $\ldots \Pi(E_n)$
5	E **clos**	**while** (look_ahead $\in$ FIRST(E)) { $\Pi(E)$ }
6	$\{E\}$	$\Pi(E)$
7	E **option**	**if** (look_ahead $\in$ FIRST(E)) { $\Pi(E)$ }
8	E **seq**	$\Pi(E)$ **while** (look_ahead $\in$ FIRST(E)) { $\Pi(E)$ }

9	E_1 **chain** E_2	$\Pi(E_1)$
		while (look_ahead $\in$ DIRSET(E_2)) {
		    $\Pi(E_2)$ $\Pi(E_1)$
		}

Figure 3.13 Rules for constructing a parser.

The procedure body $\Pi(expr)$ is generated by replacing the regular expression *expr* (and recursively every subexpression of *expr*) by its corresponding parser module, using the construction rules shown in Figure 3.13. The first 2 rules (i.e. for terminals and nonterminals) shown in this figure are axiomatic rules, the other rules are composition rules. In the following example we illustrate how the rules can be applied to generate a parser routine.

Example 3.3
We will apply the construction rules shown in Figure 3.13 to construct in a stepwise fashion a parser routine for *declaration_part*. SLANG has the following production for *declaration_part*:

> *declaration_part*   :   { *constant_declaration* | *variable_declaration* } **clos**
>   *procedure_declaration* **clos**

Consequently, the general form of the procedure is:

```
void  declaration_part(void)
{
   Π(  {constant_declaration | variable_declaration} clos
       procedure_declaration clos )
}
```

Applying rule 4 from the table in Figure 3.13 yields:

```
void  declaration_part(void)
{
   Π({constant_declaration | variable_declaration} clos)
   Π(procedure_declaration clos)
}
```

We now apply rule 5,

```
void  declaration_part(void)
{
   while (look_ahead == int_token || look_ahead == var_token) {
      Π(constant_declaration | variable_declaration)
   }
   while (look_ahead == procedure_token) {
      Π(procedure_declaration)
   }
}
```

Note that the set FIRST(*constant_declaration | variable_declaration*) consists of the tokens *int_token* and *var_token*, and that the membership test *look_ahead* ∈ FIRST(*constant_declaration | variable_declaration*) has been written as

```
look_ahead == int_token || look_ahead == var_token
```

We next apply rule 3, which results in:

```
void  declaration_part(void)
{
   while (look_ahead == int_token || look_ahead == var_token) {
      if (look_ahead == int_token) {
         Π(constant_declaration)
      } else if (look_ahead == var_token) {
         Π(variable_declaration)
      }
   }
```

```
   while (look_ahead == procedure_token) {
      Π(procedure_declaration)
   }
}
```

Finally, application of rule 2 results in:

```
void declaration_part(void)
{
   while (look_ahead == int_token || look_ahead == var_token) {
      if (look_ahead == int_token) {
         constant_declaration();
      } else if (look_ahead == var_token) {
         variable_declaration();
      }
   }
   while (look_ahead == procedure_token) {
      procedure_declaration();
   }
}
```

◇

3.2.3   A parser for SLANG

Shown below is a parser for SLANG. Some parts (concerning the scanner) are only shown schematically. This parser does not provide error recovery.

```
/* constant and type declarations are not shown */

token    look_ahead;
string   ident_lexeme;
int      num_value;
/* other variable declarations are not shown */

void initialise_scanner(void)
{
   /* initialises the scanner */
}

void next_token(void)
{
   /* assigns the next token to the variable look_ahead */
}

/* other scanner functions and parser function prototypes are not shown */
```

```
void program_declaration(void)
{
  block();
  if (look_ahead == period_token) next_token();
}

void block(void)
{
  if (look_ahead == begin_token) next_token();
  declaration_part();
  statement_part();
  if (look_ahead == end_token) next_token();
}

void declaration_part(void)
{
  while (look_ahead == int_token || look_ahead == var_token) {
    if (look_ahead == int_token) {
      constant_declaration();
    } else if (look_ahead == var_token) {
      variable_declaration();
    }
  }
  while (look_ahead == procedure_token) {
    procedure_declaration();
  }
}

void constant_declaration(void)
{
  type_declarer();
  if (look_ahead == ident_token) next_token();
  if (look_ahead == equal_token) next_token();
  if (look_ahead == num_token) next_token();
  while (look_ahead == list_token) {
    if (look_ahead == list_token) next_token();
    if (look_ahead == ident_token) next_token();
    if (look_ahead == equal_token) next_token();
    if (look_ahead == num_token) next_token();
  }
  if (look_ahead == separator_token) next_token();
}

void type_declarer(void)
{
  if (look_ahead == int_token) next_token();
}

void variable_declaration(void)
{
  if (look_ahead == var_token) next_token();
```

```
  type_declarer();
  if (look_ahead == ident_token) next_token();
  while (look_ahead == list_token) {
    if (look_ahead == list_token) next_token();
    if (look_ahead == ident_token) next_token();
  }
  if (look_ahead == separator_token) next_token();
}

void procedure_declaration(void)
{
  if (look_ahead == procedure_token) next_token();
  if (look_ahead == ident_token) next_token();
  block();
  if (look_ahead == separator_token) next_token();
}

void statement_part(void)
{
  statement();
  while (look_ahead == separator_token) {
    if (look_ahead == separator_token) next_token();
    statement();
  }
}

void statement(void)
{
  if (look_ahead == ident_token) {
    assignment_statement();
  } else if (look_ahead == if_token) {
    if_statement();
  } else if (look_ahead == while_token) {
    while_statement();
  } else if (look_ahead == call_token) {
    call_statement();
  } else if (look_ahead == read_token) {
    read_statement();
  } else if (look_ahead == write_token) {
    write_statement();
  }
}

void assignment_statement(void)
{
  left_part();
  if (look_ahead == becomes_token) next_token();
  expression();
}

void left_part(void)
{
```

```
    if (look_ahead == ident_token) next_token();
}

void if_statement(void)
{
    if (look_ahead == if_token) next_token();
    relation();
    if (look_ahead == then_token) next_token();
    statement_part();
    if (look_ahead == else_token) {
        if (look_ahead == else_token) next_token();
        statement_part();
    }
    if (look_ahead == fi_token) next_token();
}

void while_statement(void)
{
    if (look_ahead == while_token) next_token();
    relation();
    if (look_ahead == do_token) next_token();
    statement_part();
    if (look_ahead == od_token) next_token();
}

void call_statement(void)
{
    if (look_ahead == call_token) next_token();
    if (look_ahead == ident_token) next_token();
}

void read_statement(void)
{
    if (look_ahead == read_token) next_token();
    if (look_ahead == open_token) next_token();
    if (look_ahead == ident_token) next_token();
    while (look_ahead == list_token) {
        if (look_ahead == list_token) next_token();
        if (look_ahead == ident_token) next_token();
    }
    if (look_ahead == close_token) next_token();
}

void write_statement(void)
{
    if (look_ahead == write_token) next_token();
    if (look_ahead == open_token) next_token();
    expression();
    while (look_ahead == list_token) {
        if (look_ahead == list_token) next_token();
        expression();
    }
```

```
  if (look_ahead == close_token) next_token();
}

void expression(void)
{
  term();
  while (look_ahead == minus_token || look_ahead == plus_token) {
    add_operator();
    term();
  }
}

void term(void)
{
  factor();
  while (look_ahead == modulo_token || look_ahead == over_token
  || look_ahead == times_token) {
    multiply_operator();
    factor();
  }
}

void factor(void)
{
  if (look_ahead == absolute_token || look_ahead == negate_token) {
    unary_operator();
  }
  operand();
}

void operand(void)
{
  if (look_ahead == ident_token) {
    if (look_ahead == ident_token) next_token();
  } else if (look_ahead == num_token) {
    if (look_ahead == num_token) next_token();
  } else if (look_ahead == open_token) {
    if (look_ahead == open_token) next_token();
    expression();
    if (look_ahead == close_token) next_token();
  }
}

void add_operator(void)
{
  if (look_ahead == plus_token) {
    if (look_ahead == plus_token) next_token();
  } else if (look_ahead == minus_token) {
    if (look_ahead == minus_token) next_token();
  }
}
```

```
void multiply_operator(void)
{
  if (look_ahead == times_token) {
    if (look_ahead == times_token) next_token();
  } else if (look_ahead == over_token) {
    if (look_ahead == over_token) next_token();
  } else if (look_ahead == modulo_token) {
    if (look_ahead == modulo_token) next_token();
  }
}

void unary_operator(void)
{
  if (look_ahead == negate_token) {
    if (look_ahead == negate_token) next_token();
  } else if (look_ahead == absolute_token) {
    if (look_ahead == absolute_token) next_token();
  }
}

void relation(void)
{
  expression();
  relational_operator();
  expression();
}

void relational_operator(void)
{
  if (look_ahead == equal_token) {
    if (look_ahead == equal_token) next_token();
  } else if (look_ahead == not_equal_token) {
    if (look_ahead == not_equal_token) next_token();
  } else if (look_ahead == less_than_token) {
    if (look_ahead == less_than_token) next_token();
  } else if (look_ahead == less_or_equal_token) {
    if (look_ahead == less_or_equal_token) next_token();
  } else if (look_ahead == greater_than_token) {
    if (look_ahead == greater_than_token) next_token();
  } else if (look_ahead == greater_or_equal_token) {
    if (look_ahead == greater_or_equal_token) next_token();
  }
}


void main(void)
{
  initialise_scanner();
  program_declaration();
}
```

Note that the syntactic procedures are a straightforward translation of the corresponding grammar productions according to the rules of Figure 3.13. This is the reason that many tests of the look-head are included twice. Consider, for example, the check for a list-token in procedure *constant_declaration*. Optimisation of the parser procedures is of course possible.

3.3   Symbol-table management

The language definition of SLANG requires that every applied occurrence of an identifier be uniquely associated with a defining occurrence. The defining occurrence (i.e. the declaration) determines the scope (the block), the kind (constant, variable or procedure) and the type (integer) of an identifier. The unique association between applied and defining occurrences implies that there may be only one defining occurrence of an identifier in the same block. Every applied occurrence of an identifier must be in the scope of a defining occurrence of the right kind and type.

To associate applied occurrences of identifiers with defining occurrences, a table is maintained that records for each defining occurrence of an identifier the information of its declaration. Such a table is called a *symbol table*. At every applied occurrence of an identifier, the symbol table must provide fast access to the information collected about the associated defining occurrence of this identifier.

3.3.1   Design of a symbol table

Before we present a design of a symbol table, we first recall the rules about scopes and visibility in SLANG. An identifier is bound to an object in a declaration. The scope of a binding is the block of the procedure in which the declaration occurs. A binding that holds in the block of a procedure also holds in the blocks of its subordinate procedures, unless the identifier is redefined in a subordinate block. From this, the following *visibility rules* can be derived:

- At any point in the program text, only identifiers declared in the current block and in surrounding blocks are accessible.
- If an identifier is declared in more than one block, then only the declaration nearest to the point of the applied occurrence is visible.

Example 3.4
Consider the program in Figure 3.14. This program has 3 scope levels:

1. The main program.
2. The body of procedure "d".
3. The body of procedure "z".

```
BEGIN {level 1}                             1
        VAR INT p, w;                       2
        PROC d                              3
        BEGIN {level 2}                     4
                VAR INT a, r, w;            5
                PROC z                      6
                BEGIN {level 3}             7
                        VAR INT e, p, w;    8
                        ⋮                   9
                END;                        10
                ⋮                           11
        END;                                12
        ⋮                                   13
END.                                        14
```

Figure 3.14 Nesting of scopes.

line	accessible declarations
9	a(2), d(1), e(3), p(3), r(2), w(3), z(2)
11	a(2), d(1), p(1), r(2), w(2), z(2)
13	d(1), p(1), w(1)

Figure 3.15 Visibility of declarations.

The visible declarations at different points in the program are shown in Figure 3.15. The number in parentheses indicates the level of a declaration.   ◇

Symbol tables are usually implemented as hash tables or as binary trees. For block-structured languages (like SLANG) there is also a choice between an individual table for each scope or a single global table. We choose to store the identifiers in a single global binary *identifier tree*. A *tree record* consists of fields for:

- The identifier.
- A pointer to a list of records for different defining occurrences of the identifier.
- Pointers to the left and the right subtree.

For each identifier there is a *definition list*, i.e. a list of definition records. Each *definition record* represents a defining occurrence of the identifier. A definition record consists of fields for:

- The segment number.
- The displacement (of a variable), the value (of a constant) or the index of the address (of a procedure) in the address table.
- The type.
- The kind.
- A pointer to the next definition record.

The list of definition records is organised as a push-down list. When parsing the defining occurrence of an identifier, a definition record will be created, and inserted in front of the list of definition records. A definition record will be removed from the list when we leave the block in which the declaration occurs. This scheme guarantees that, at any time, only declarations from the current block and from surrounding blocks are accessible, and that the declaration nearest to the point of use is found first.

When we leave a block, all definition records created during parsing of this block must be removed from the definition lists. This implies a complicated search of the identifier tree and its definition lists. To optimise the searching process, a *push-down scope list* is maintained. When we enter a block, a scope record is created, and inserted in front of the list of scope records. A *scope record* consists of the following fields:

- A pointer to a list of name records.
- A pointer to the scope record of the previous scope.

The identifiers, which are declared in the current scope, are organised in a *name list*, i.e. a list of name records. A *name record* consists of the following fields:

- The identifier.
- A pointer to the next name-record in the list.

When we leave a block, the identifiers in the name list of the current scope record are searched in the identifier tree. For each identifier that was declared in the current scope, the first definition record is removed from the list of definition records. Finally, the scope record is removed from the scope list, which means that the parser has finished the parsing of the current block, and continues parsing in the surrounding block.

The following declarations describe the records of the identifier tree, the definition list, the scope list and the name list. The type *e_type* enumerates the available type values. The meanings of these type values are:

- *no_type*   no type
- *unknown_type*   unknown
- *int_type*   integer

The type *e_kind* enumerates the possible kinds of the identifiers. The meanings of these kind values are:

- *unknown_kind*   unknown
- *const_kind*   constant identifier
- *var_kind*   variable identifier
- *proc_kind*   procedure identifier

The pointer *ident_tree* points to the identifier tree, and the pointer *scope_list* points to the push-down scope list.

```
#define max_ident_length              255

typedef char                          string[max_ident_length + 1];

typedef enum {
  no_type, unknown_type, int_type
} e_type;

typedef enum {
  unknown_kind, const_kind, var_kind, proc_kind
} e_kind;

typedef struct def_rec {
  int                  sn, dpl_or_value_or_index;
  e_type               type;
  e_kind               kind;
  struct def_rec       *next;
} *def_ptr;

typedef struct ident_rec {
  string               ident;
  def_ptr              def_list;
  struct ident_rec     *left, *right;
} *ident_ptr;

typedef struct name_rec {
  string               ident;
  struct name_rec      *next;
} *name_ptr;

typedef struct scope_rec {
  name_ptr             name_list;
  struct scope_rec     *prev_scope;
} *scope_ptr;

ident_ptr                ident_tree;
scope_ptr                scope_list;
```

Example 3.5

Consider again the program in Figure 3.14. In Figure 3.16 we show the identifier tree and the lists of definition records of the identifiers "p", "w" and "z" when the parser is at level 3 (line 9, in the body of procedure "z"). Note that the first field of the name records contains the segment number. The contents of the second field is the displacement in the case of "p" and "w", and the index (in the address table) in the case of "z". We let this index be 1 in this example. The remaining fields contain the type and kind of the identifier, and the pointer to the next definition record. In Figure 3.17 we show the corresponding scope list and lists of name records.   ◇

In subsequent sections, parsing procedures will use the following local variables to hold information from the symbol table:

- The pointer variable *def* will be used to hold the address of the currently investigated definition record.
- Variables *sn* and *dpl* will be used in 2 ways: to hold the current value of the segment number and the displacement, respectively, and to hold values extracted from the fields of the currently investigated definition record in the symbol table.
- In the case of a constant, the variable *value* will be used to hold the extracted value.
- In the case of a procedure the variable *address* will be used to hold the extracted index of the address in the address table.
- In all the above cases, the variable *kind* holds the extracted kind.

The type will not be extracted from the symbol table because, in the case of a variable or constant, there is only 1 type, namely integer.

3.3.2   The symbol-table interface

At the beginning of the parsing process, the symbol table will be initialised with an empty identifier tree (i.e. the variable *ident_tree* will be set to the null pointer), and the push-down scope list will be initialised with an empty list (i.e. the variable *scope_list* will be set to the null pointer). Also the *nesting depth* will be initialised, i.e. the *scope level* will be set to 0. We now introduce a number of procedures that operate on the symbol table.

When we enter a block, we enter a new scope. A new scope record must therefore be created and pushed onto the scope list. This is done by the procedure

> **void** *enter_scope*(**void**);

which also increments the *scope level*.

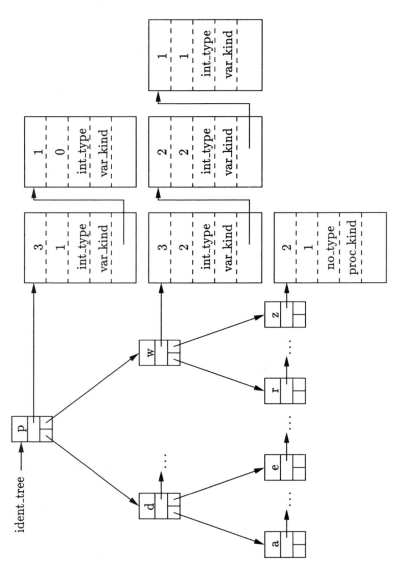

Figure 3.16 Identifier tree and lists of definition records.

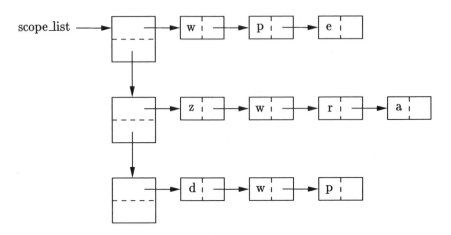

Figure 3.17 Scope list and lists of name records.

When we exit a block, the current scope is exited. All identifiers defined in the current scope become invalid. Their definition records must therefore be removed from the symbol table, and the current scope record must be removed from the top of push-down scope list. These actions are performed by the procedure

> **void** *exit_scope*(**void**);

which also decrements the *scope level.*
   The function

> **int** *current_scope*(**void**);

returns the scope level of the block currently being parsed.
   A definition record must be created for each defining occurrence of an identifier, and both the identifier and its definition record must be added to the symbol table. Moreover, for optimisation reasons, the identifier must be added to the name list on top of the push-down scope list. To handle defining occurrences of identifiers, the following function and procedure are defined:

> *def_ptr create_definition*(**int** *sn*, **int** *dpl_or_value_or_index*,
>   *e_type type, e_kind kind*);
> **void** *insert_definition*(*string ident, def_ptr def*);

Calling the function *create_definition* results in a new definition record being created. The fields of the record are initialised with the arguments that are substituted for the parameters *sn*, *dpl_or_value_or_index*, *type* and *kind*. The function returns a pointer to the created record.

Example 3.6
The assignment

>   *def = create_definition(sn, dpl, int_type, var_kind)*;

creates a definition record for a variable of type integer, with segment number the value of *sn*, and with displacement the value of *dpl*. Similarly, the assignment

>   *def = create_definition(sn, num_value, int_type, const_kind)*;

creates a definition record for a constant of type integer, with segment number the value of *sn*, and with value the current value of *num_value*, as produced by the scanner.   ◇

A call of the procedure *insert_definition* will result in the following actions:

1. The identifier, substituted for the parameter *ident*, is added to the identifier tree, if it is not already there.
2. The definition record pointed to by the argument substituted for parameter *def* is added to the list of definition records for that identifier.
3. The identifier is added to the name list, on top of the push-down scope list. If the name list already has a record for the identifier concerned, then the error message "Double defined identifier" is printed.

Example 3.7
The call

>   *insert_definition(ident_lexeme, def)*;

adds the identifier in the buffer *ident_lexeme* to the identifier tree and to the name list on top of the scope list. Moreover, the record pointed to by *def* is inserted in front of the list of definition records of the identifier concerned.   ◇

To handle applied occurrences of identifiers the following functions are defined:

>   *def_ptr find_definition(string ident)*;
>   **int** *get_sn(def_ptr def)*;
>   **int** *get_dpl(def_ptr def)*;
>   **int** *get_value(def_ptr def)*;
>   **int** *get_address(def_ptr def)*;
>   *e_type get_type(def_ptr def)*;
>   *e_kind get_kind(def_ptr def)*;

The function *find_definition* returns a pointer to the definition record of the identifier, substituted for *ident*. If no definition record for the identifier is found, then the error message "Undefined identifier" is printed. If the identifier does not exist at all in the identifier tree, then the error message "Identifier not found in identifier tree" is printed. In both cases the value *undeclared* is returned, which points to a default definition record. The functions *get_sn*, *get_dpl* (for a variable), *get_value* (for a constant), *get_address* (for a procedure), *get_type* and *get_kind* extract the necessary information from the fields of the definition record. If no definition record exists, then default values (0 for *sn* and *dpl*, *value* and *address*, *unknown_type* for *type*, and *unknown_kind* for *kind*) are returned. Note that the function *get_address* returns the index in the address table at which the address of a procedure is stored and not the address itself.

Example 3.8
The statements

$$def \ = \ find\_definition(ident\_lexeme);$$
$$kind \ = \ get\_kind(def);$$
if (*kind* != *var_kind*) *report_error*("Identifier is not a variable");

return the kind (variable, constant or procedure) of the identifier in the buffer *ident_lexeme*, and check if the identifier is a variable.   ◇

3.4   A context-sensitive parser

In this section we extend the context-free parser of Section 3.2 with actions to check the context constraints.

Every block represents a scope. Therefore, during parsing, when a block is entered, a new scope must be opened, and at the exit of the block, the scope must be terminated. This is done by the procedures *enter_scope* and *exit_scope*, respectively. The procedure *program_declaration* therefore becomes:

```
void program_declaration(void)
{
    enter_scope();
    block();
    exit_scope();
    if (look_ahead == period_token) next_token();
}
```

At the beginning of the declaration-part, the value of the displacement *dpl* is initialised to zero, and the value is incremented for every subsequent variable in the scope—this is the responsibility of the procedure *variable_declaration*. The procedure *variable_declaration* has therefore *dpl* both as input and output parameter. Note that the block of every procedure declaration has its own instantiation of the variable *dpl*. This variable is therefore declared (locally) in the procedure *declaration_part*, which therefore becomes:

```
void declaration_part(void)
{
  int     dpl;

  dpl = 0;
  while (look_ahead == int_token || look_ahead == var_token) {
    if (look_ahead == int_token) {
      constant_declaration();
    } else if (look_ahead == var_token) {
      variable_declaration(&dpl);
    }
  }
  while (look_ahead == procedure_token) {
    procedure_declaration();
  }
}
```

For every defining occurrence of an identifier, its declaration information must be added to the symbol table so that at every applied occurrence, the necessary information can be retrieved from the symbol table. The statements

$$def = create\_definition(sn, \ num\_value, \ int\_type, \ const\_kind);$$
$$insert\_definition(ident\_lexeme, \ def);$$

create a definition record for a constant and add both the identifier and its definition record to the symbol table. For a variable the statements we use are

$$def = create\_definition(sn, \ dpl, \ int\_type, \ var\_kind);$$
$$insert\_definition(ident\_lexeme, \ def);$$

and for a procedure:

$$def = create\_definition(sn, \ proc\_index, \ no\_type, \ proc\_kind);$$
$$insert\_definition(ident\_lexeme, \ def);$$

In the latter the type is *no_type*, as a procedure has no associated type. It is assumed that the variable *proc_index* holds the value of the index in the address table of this procedure. The role of the address table for procedures will be explained in Section 3.5.

Below we show the procedures *constant_declaration*, *variable_declaration* and *procedure_declaration*.

```
void constant_declaration(void)
{
    int          sn;
    def_ptr      def;

    sn= current_scope();
    type_declarer();
    if (look_ahead == ident_token) next_token();
    if (look_ahead == equal_token) next_token();
    if (look_ahead == num_token) next_token();
    def = create_definition(sn, num_value, int_type, const_kind);
    insert_definition(ident_lexeme, def);
    while (look_ahead == list_token) {
        if (look_ahead == list_token) next_token();
        if (look_ahead == ident_token) next_token();
        if (look_ahead == equal_token) next_token();
        if (look_ahead == num_token) next_token();
        def = create_definition(sn, num_value, int_type, const_kind);
        insert_definition(ident_lexeme, def);
    }
    if (look_ahead == separator_token) next_token();
}

void variable_declaration(int *dpl)
{
    int          sn;
    def_ptr      def;

    sn = current_scope();
    if (look_ahead == var_token) next_token();
    type_declarer();
    if (look_ahead == ident_token) next_token();
    def = create_definition(sn, *dpl, int_type, var_kind);
    insert_definition(ident_lexeme, def);
    (*dpl)++;
    while (look_ahead == list_token) {
        if (look_ahead == list_token) next_token();
        if (look_ahead == ident_token) next_token();
        def = create_definition(sn, *dpl, int_type, var_kind);
        insert_definition(ident_lexeme, def);
        (*dpl)++;
    }
    if (look_ahead == separator_token) next_token();
}

void procedure_declaration(void)
{
    int          sn, address;
    def_ptr      def;

    sn = current_scope();
```

```
    if (look_ahead == procedure_token) next_token();
    if (look_ahead == ident_token) next_token();
    address = /* will be explained in the next section */;
    def = create_definition(sn, address, no_type, proc_kind);
    insert_definition(ident_lexeme, def);
    enter_scope();
    block();
    exit_scope();
    if (look_ahead == separator_token) next_token();
}
```

As we remarked at the end of Section 3.2.3, redundant code is generated because of the rules for parser generation shown in Figure 3.13. Consider, for example, the check for a list-token in procedure *constant_declaration*.

In the case of an assignment, the left part must be a variable, otherwise an error message will be printed. The same holds true for the identifiers in the list of a read-statement. The following statements

```
    def = find_definition(ident_lexeme);
    kind = get_kind(def);
    if (kind != var_kind) report_error("Identifier is not a variable");
```

extract the kind of the identifier from the definition record. If the identifier is not declared as a variable, then the error message "Identifier is not a variable" is printed.

Note that type checking between the left part and the right part of an assignment is not needed because SLANG has only one data type.

The procedures *left_part* and *read_statement* become:

```
void left_part(void)
{
    def_ptr       def;
    e_kind        kind;

    if (look_ahead == ident_token) next_token();
    def = find_definition(ident_lexeme);
    kind = get_kind(def);
    if (kind != var_kind) report_error("Identifier is not a variable");
}

void read_statement(void)
{
    def_ptr       def;
    e_kind        kind;

    if (look_ahead == read_token) next_token();
    if (look_ahead == open_token) next_token();
    if (look_ahead == ident_token) next_token();
    def = find_definition(ident_lexeme);
```

```
   kind = get_kind(def);
   if (kind != var_kind) report_error("Identifier is not a variable");
   while (look_ahead == list_token) {
     if (look_ahead == list_token) next_token();
     if (look_ahead == ident_token) next_token();
     def = find_definition(ident_lexeme);
     kind = get_kind(def);
     if (kind != var_kind) report_error("Identifier is not a variable");
   }
   if (look_ahead == close_token) next_token();
}
```

Similarly, the identifier in a call-statement must denote a procedure. The procedure *call_statement* therefore becomes:

```
void  call_statement(void)
{
   def_ptr        def;
   e_kind         kind;

   if (look_ahead == call_token) next_token();
   if (look_ahead == ident_token) next_token();
   def = find_definition(ident_lexeme);
   kind = get_kind(def);
   if (kind != proc_kind) report_error("Identifier is not a procedure");
}
```

Finally, an identifier as operand in an expression must be a variable or a constant. The procedure *operand* therefore becomes:

```
void  operand(void)
{
   def_ptr        def;
   e_kind         kind;

   if (look_ahead == ident_token) {
     if (look_ahead == ident_token) next_token();
     def = find_definition(ident_lexeme);
     kind = get_kind(def);
     if (kind == proc_kind || kind == unknown_kind)
       report_error("Identifier must be a variable or a constant");
   } else if (look_ahead == num_token) {
     if (look_ahead == num_token) next_token();
   } else if (look_ahead == open_token) {
     if (look_ahead == open_token) next_token();
     expression();
     if (look_ahead == close_token) next_token();
   }
}
```

3.5   Code generation

In this section we extend the SLANG parser (as developed in Section 3.2, and extended in Section 3.4) with actions to emit VIM code. For that purpose we introduce procedures that emit code. These procedures differ in the number and the kind of their parameters.

The initialisation and finalisation of code generation is done by the procedures

> **void** *initialise_vimcode*(**void**);
> **void** *finalise_vimcode*(**void**);

The procedure *initialise_vimcode* initialises the generation of VIM instructions. An output file is opened, which will contain the generated instructions. The procedure *finalise_vimcode* first generates the instruction **halt**, then writes the address and length table (remember the explanation of the role of these tables in Section 2.6.1) to other output files, and finally closes the output files. The procedure *program_declaration* now becomes:

```
void program_declaration(void)
{
    initialise_vimcode();
    enter_scope();
    block();
    exit_scope();
    finalise_vimcode();
    if (look_ahead == period_token) next_token();
}
```

When executing a procedure block, a new segment must be available before the start of execution of the first statement of that block. The procedures that emit the instructions **crseg sn,index** and **dlseg** are

> **void** *emit_crseg*(**int** *level,* **int** *index*);
> **void** *emit*(*operation   code*);

The procedure *emit_crseg* is an instruction-specific code-generation action, and the procedure *emit* is used for generating VIM instructions that do not have arguments. The domain of the type *operation* is the instruction set recognised by the machine VIM.

The function *current_scope* produces the current scope level. This is the level that is used in the call to *emit_crseg*. The procedure *emit_crseg* takes its second argument from the length table. A free position in the length table is therefore first claimed by means of the function

> **int** *get_index*(**void**);

which returns this position. The next step is to store the length of the segment at this position. This is done by the procedure

> **void** *enter_length*(**int** *index,* **int** *length*);

The length of the segment is produced by the procedure *declaration_part*, which has therefore an output argument *length*. The procedure *block* becomes:

```
void block(void)
{
    int     level, length_index, length;

    if (look_ahead == begin_token) next_token();
    declaration_part(&length);
    level = current_scope();
    length_index = get_index();
    enter_length(length_index, length);
    emit_crseg(level, length_index);
    statement_part();
    emit(dlseg);
    if (look_ahead == end_token) next_token();
}
```

In the procedure *declaration_part* a jump over the translations of the blocks of the locally declared procedures must be made, as these blocks may only be executed when the procedures are called. We will omit the jump if no local procedures are declared.

VIM instructions, which manipulate the instruction counter (i.e. jump, jift, jiff and call), are emitted by the procedure

> **void** *emit_jump*(*operation code,* **int** *index*);

This procedure takes its second argument from the address table. A free position in the address table is therefore first claimed by means of the function

> **int** *get_label*(**void**);

The assignment

> *over_procs* = *get_label*();

assigns the index of a free position in the address table to *over_procs*. The call

> *emit_jump*(*jump, over_procs*);

uses this position in the address table. The jump address is known at the end of *declaration_part*. At this point the current value of the instruction counter *ic* must be stored in the address table at position *over_procs*. This is done by the procedure

void *emit_label*(**int** *index*);

The procedure *declaration_part* therefore becomes:[1]

```
void  declaration_part(int *length)
{
  int     dpl, over_procs;

  dpl = 0;
  while (look_ahead == int_token || look_ahead == var_token) {
    if (look_ahead == int_token) {
      constant_declaration();
    } else if (look_ahead == var_token) {
      variable_declaration(&dpl);
    }
  }
  *length = dpl;
  if (look_ahead == procedure_token) {
    over_procs = get_label();
    emit_jump(jump, over_procs);
    /* i.e. generation of instruction 'jump over_procs' */
    procedure_declaration();
    while (look_ahead == procedure_token) {
      procedure_declaration();
    }
/* over_procs: */
    emit_label(over_procs);
    /* i.e. definition of label 'over_procs' */
  }
}
```

Note that the final value of *dpl* is returned as the length of the data segment of the procedure.

The procedures *constant_declaration* and *variable_declaration* do not generate any code, but store information in the symbol table. In the case of a constant, we store its value, and in the case of a variable, its segment number and displacement. When we encounter an applied occurrence of a constant or variable, information is retrieved from the symbol table and used to generate code.

The procedure *procedure_declaration* must claim an index in the address table for its address. The value of this index must be stored in the definition record of the procedure in the symbol table, so that the call-statement can find the address

---

[1] See the translation rules in Section 2.5.1.

of the procedure body. A `return` instruction must be emitted after the translation of the procedure *block*. The procedure *procedure_declaration* therefore becomes:

```
void procedure_declaration(void)
{
    int          sn, address;
    def_ptr      def;

    sn = current_scope();
    if (look_ahead == procedure_token) next_token();
    if (look_ahead == ident_token) next_token();
    address = get_label();
    emit_label(address);
    def = create_definition(sn, address, no_type, proc_kind);
    insert_definition(ident_lexeme, def);
    enter_scope();
    block();
    exit_scope();
    emit(return_);
    if (look_ahead == separator_token) next_token();
}
```

No code is generated by the procedures *statement_part* and *statement*. We next consider the specific statements.

For an assignment statement, we must first evaluate the value of the expression, and then assign this value to the variable of the left part. For the assignation we need the instruction `stvar`, which takes as arguments the values of the segment number and the displacement of the variable of the left part. The procedure *left_part* needs to produce these values, and is therefore extended with a parameter list.

The VIM instructions `ldvar sn,dpl` and `stvar sn,dpl` are emitted by the procedures

$$\textbf{void } \textit{emit\_ldvar}(\textbf{int } \textit{sn}, \textbf{int } \textit{dpl});$$
$$\textbf{void } \textit{emit\_stvar}(\textbf{int } \textit{sn}, \textbf{int } \textit{dpl});$$

The procedures *assignment_statement* and *left_part* now become:

```
void assignment_statement(void)
{
    int          sn, dpl;

    left_part(&sn, &dpl);
    if (look_ahead == becomes_token) next_token();
    expression();
    emit_stvar(sn, dpl);
}
```

```
void left_part(int *sn, int *dpl)
{
  def_ptr        def;
  e_kind         kind;

  if (look_ahead == ident_token) next_token();
  def = find_definition(ident_lexeme);
  kind = get_kind(def);
  if (kind != var_kind) report_error("Identifier is not a variable");
  *sn = get_sn(def);
  *dpl = get_dpl(def);
}
```

The translation of the condition and repetition statement must be implemented by means of jump instructions, which use the address table. The procedures *if_statement* and *while_statement* are:

```
void if_statement(void)
{
  int over_then_part, over_else_part;

  if (look_ahead == if_token) next_token();
  relation();
  if (look_ahead == then_token) next_token();
  over_then_part = get_label();
  emit_jump(jiff, over_then_part);
  statement_part();
  if (look_ahead == else_token) {
    over_else_part = get_label();
    emit_jump(jump, over_else_part);
/* over_then_part: */
    emit_label(over_then_part);
    if (look_ahead == else_token) next_token();
    statement_part();
/* over_else_part: */
    emit_label(over_else_part);
  } else /* no else part */
/* over_then_part: */
    emit_label(over_then_part);
  if (look_ahead == fi_token) next_token();
}

void while_statement(void)
{
  int begin_while_stat, end_while_stat;

  if (look_ahead == while_token) next_token();
  begin_while_stat = get_label();
/* begin_while_stat: */
  emit_label(begin_while_stat);
  relation();
  end_while_stat = get_label();
```

```
    emit_jump(jiff, end_while_stat);
    if (look_ahead == do_token) next_token();
    statement_part();
    if (look_ahead == od_token) next_token();
    emit_jump(jump, begin_while_stat);
/* end_while_stat: */
    emit_label(end_while_stat);
}
```

The call-statement needs the index of the address of the procedure body in the address table. The procedure *procedure_declaration* has stored this index in the definition record in the symbol table. The procedure *call_statement* must therefore retrieve this index from this definition record. The procedure *call_statement* becomes:

```
void call_statement(void)
{
    def_ptr      def;
    e_kind       kind;
    int          address;

    if (look_ahead == call_token) next_token();
    if (look_ahead == ident_token) next_token();
    def = find_definition(ident_lexeme);
    kind = get_kind(def);
    if (kind != proc_kind) report_error("Identifier is not a procedure");
    address = get_address(def);
    emit_jump(call, address);
}
```

The read-statement, which reads numbers from the input and assigns them to identifiers in a list, is implemented by means of a sequence of rdint and stvar instructions. The write-statement, which outputs the values of a sequence of expressions, is implemented by means of a sequence of wrint instructions. The value of each expression is left on the stack, and is subsequently moved by the wrint instruction from the stack to the screen.

The procedures *read_statement* and *write_statement* are straightforward:

```
void read_statement(void)
{
    def_ptr      def;
    e_kind       kind;
    int          sn, dpl;

    if (look_ahead == read_token) next_token();
    if (look_ahead == open_token) next_token();
    if (look_ahead == ident_token) next_token();
    def = find_definition(ident_lexeme);
    kind = get_kind(def);
    if (kind != var_kind) report_error("Identifier is not a variable");
```

```
  sn = get_sn(def);
  dpl = get_dpl(def);
  emit(rdint);
  emit_stvar(sn, dpl);
  while (look_ahead == list_token) {
    if (look_ahead == list_token) next_token();
    if (look_ahead == ident_token) next_token();
    def = find_definition(ident_lexeme);
    kind = get_kind(def);
    if (kind != var_kind) report_error("Identifier is not a variable");
    sn = get_sn(def);
    dpl = get_dpl(def);
    emit(rdint);
    emit_stvar(sn, dpl);
  }
  if (look_ahead == close_token) next_token();
}

void write_statement(void)
{
  if (look_ahead == write_token) next_token();
  if (look_ahead == open_token) next_token();
  expression();
  emit(wrint);
  while (look_ahead == list_token) {
    if (look_ahead == list_token) next_token();
    expression();
    emit(wrint);
  }
  if (look_ahead == close_token) next_token();
}
```

The procedures *expression*, *term*, *factor* and *relation* need to know the kind of operator that has to be applied. We therefore extend the procedures *add_operator*, *multiply_operator*, *unary_operator* and *relational_operator* with parameters that indicate the operator concerned. For these parameters the following types are declared:

```
typedef enum { plus, minus                           } add_op;
typedef enum { times, over, modulo                   } mul_op;
typedef enum { absolute, negate                      } unary_op;
typedef enum { equal, not_equal, less_than, less_or_equal,
               greater_than, greater_or_equal        } rel_op;
```

The remaining procedures, except *operand*, are straightforward, and are shown below:

```
void expression(void)
{
  add_op        op;
```

```
  term();
  while (look_ahead == minus_token || look_ahead == plus_token) {
    add_operator(&op);
    term();
    if (op == plus)
      emit(add);
    else if (op == minus)
      emit(sub);
  }
}


void term(void)
{
  mul_op          op;

  factor();
  while (look_ahead == modulo_token || look_ahead == over_token
  || look_ahead == times_token) {
    multiply_operator(&op);
    factor();
    if (op == times)
      emit(mul);
    else if (op == over)
      emit(dvi);
    else if (op == modulo)
      emit(mdl);
  }
}


void factor(void)
{
  unary_op        op;

  if (look_ahead == absolute_token || look_ahead == negate_token) {
    unary_operator(&op);
    operand();
    if (op == negate) emit(neg);
    else if (op == absolute) emit(abs);
  } else /* no unary operator */
    operand();
}


void add_operator(add_op *op)
{
  if (look_ahead == plus_token) {
    if (look_ahead == plus_token) { *op = plus; next_token(); }
  } else if (look_ahead == minus_token) {
    if (look_ahead == minus_token) { *op = minus; next_token(); }
  }
}
```

```
void multiply_operator(mul_op *op)
{
  if (look_ahead == times_token) {
    if (look_ahead == times_token) { *op = times; next_token(); }
  } else if (look_ahead == over_token) {
    if (look_ahead == over_token) { *op = over; next_token(); }
  } else if (look_ahead == modulo_token) {
    if (look_ahead == modulo_token) { *op = modulo; next_token(); }
  }
}


void unary_operator(unary_op *op)
{
  if (look_ahead == negate_token) {
    if (look_ahead == negate_token) { *op = negate; next_token(); }
  } else if (look_ahead == absolute_token) {
    if (look_ahead == absolute_token) { *op = absolute; next_token(); }
  }
}



void relation(void)
{
  rel_op          op;

  expression();
  relational_operator(&op);
  expression();
  if (op == equal) emit(eq);
  else if (op == not_equal) emit(ne);
  else if (op == less_than) emit(lt);
  else if (op == less_or_equal) emit(le);
  else if (op == greater_than) emit(gt);
  else if (op == greater_or_equal) emit(ge);
}

void relational_operator(rel_op *op)
{
  if (look_ahead == equal_token) {
    if (look_ahead == equal_token) { *op = equal; next_token(); }
  } else if (look_ahead == not_equal_token) {
    if (look_ahead == not_equal_token) { *op = not_equal; next_token(); }
  } else if (look_ahead == less_than_token) {
    if (look_ahead == less_than_token) { *op = less_than; next_token(); }
  } else if (look_ahead == less_or_equal_token) {
    if (look_ahead == less_or_equal_token) {
        *op = less_or_equal; next_token();
    }
  } else if (look_ahead == greater_than_token) {
    if (look_ahead == greater_than_token) {
        *op = greater_than; next_token();
    }
```

```
  } else if (look_ahead == greater_or_equal_token) {
    if (look_ahead == greater_or_equal_token) {
      *op = greater_or_equal; next_token();
    }
  }
}
```

An operand can be a variable, a constant, a number or an expression between brackets. For the generation of the instruction `ldcon value` we introduce the instruction-specific code-generation action

> **void** *emit_ldcon*(**int** *value*);

In the case of a constant, the value is retrieved from the definition record in the symbol table, and in the case of a number, the current value of *num_value* is used. The procedure *operand* is:

```
void operand(void)
{
  def_ptr        def;
  e_kind         kind;
  int            sn, dpl, value;

  if (look_ahead == ident_token) {
    if (look_ahead == ident_token) next_token();
    def = find_definition(ident_lexeme);
    kind = get_kind(def);
    if (kind == var_kind) {
      sn = get_sn(def);
      dpl = get_dpl(def);
      emit_ldvar(sn, dpl);
    } else if (kind == const_kind) {
      value = get_value(def);
      emit_ldcon(value);
    } else if (kind == proc_kind || kind == unknown_kind)
      report_error("Identifier must be a variable or a constant");
  } else if (look_ahead == num_token) {
    if (look_ahead == num_token) next_token();
    emit_ldcon(num_value);
  } else if (look_ahead == open_token) {
    if (look_ahead == open_token) next_token();
    expression();
    if (look_ahead == close_token) next_token();
  }
}
```

3.6   Error handling

Thus far we have neglected the detection of, and the recovery from, errors during scanning and context-free parsing, although we have provided error checks for double-defined identifiers, the use of undefined identifiers, and the application of identifiers that do not conform to their definition. We will pay no further attention to the infringement of context constraints, but we will make some remarks on the detection and recovery from lexical and context-free syntactic errors.

3.6.1   Lexical errors

At the level of scanning, error detection is easy, but recovery is hard, as there is not much redundancy. To provide for error handling, we will introduce an extra token, *nonsense_token*, and extend the scanner program for SLANG in 2 places. First, if in the initial state an unexpected character is read, then *nonsense_token* is produced and the next character is read. Second, if we have already read the character ":" (which means that the beginning of *becomes_token* is recognised), and we read any character other than the character "=", then *nonsense_token* is also produced.

The procedure *next_token* of the scanner is therefore extended as follows:

```
void  next_token(void)
{
  retract = false;
  while (ch <= ' ') next_character(); /* ignore control characters and spaces */

  switch (ch) {
  /* single character tokens are not shown */
  case ':':
    next_character();
    if (ch == '=') look_ahead = becomes_token;
    else {
      look_ahead = nonsense_token;
      retract = true;
    }
    break;

  case '<':
    next_character();
    if (ch == '>') look_ahead = not_equal_token;
    else if (ch == '=') look_ahead = less_or_equal_token;
    else {
      look_ahead = less_than_token;
      retract = true;
    }
    break;
```

```
case '>':
  next_character();
  if (ch == '=') look_ahead = greater_or_equal_token;
  else {
    look_ahead = greater_than_token;
    retract = true;
  }
  break;

default:
  if (islower(ch))
    identifier();
  else if (isupper(ch))
    keyword();
  else if (isdigit(ch))
    number();
  else
    look_ahead = nonsense_token;
}
if (!retract) next_character();
}
```

For pragmatic reasons (the size of the buffer *ident_lexeme* and table entry *ident* in record *ident_rec*), there is a restriction on the length of identifiers. Note that a constant *max_ident_length* is defined. The procedure *identifier* must therefore be extended so that at most *max_ident_length* characters are stored. The remaining letters and digits are read but neglected. A warning must be issued if the number of characters in an identifier exceeds *max_ident_length*. Only the first *max_ident_length* characters are considered significant.

There is also a restriction on the size of the buffer *key_lexeme*, for which a constant *max_key_length* is defined. This implies that at most *max_key_length* capital letters can be stored. The remaining capitals are read but neglected. Error messages must be issued if the string is too long or if it is not found in the keyword table. In that case, the token produced is *nonsense_token*.

Finally, there is a restriction on the number of digits in a number. If the digit string is too long, then the calculation of the binary value is stopped. The remaining digits are then read but neglected, and an error message is issued that says the number of digits exceeds a certain maximum.

3.6.2   Syntactic errors

During parsing, each terminal in the right-hand side of a production that is encountered must match the look-ahead. If this condition is violated, then an error is detected. If a choice between a number of alternatives needs to be made, and the look-ahead does not equal a first symbol of any of the alternatives, then no decision can be taken, and again an error is detected. In Figure 3.13 we presented

	Regular expression	Parser module
1	a (terminal)	**if** (look_ahead == a) next_token(); **else** report_error("token a expected");
2	A (nonterminal)	A(); (i.e. call of procedure associated with A)

3	$E_1 \mid E_2 \mid \ldots \mid E_n$ $(n > 1)$	**if** (look_ahead $\in$ DIRSET(E_1)) {
		$\quad$ $\Pi(E_1)$
		} **else if** (look_ahead $\in$ DIRSET(E_2)) {
		$\quad$ $\Pi(E_2)$
		$\quad\vdots$
		} **else if** (look_ahead $\in$ DIRSET(E_n)) {
		$\quad$ $\Pi(E_n)$
		} **else** report_error("incorrect alternative")

4	$E_1 E_2 \ldots E_n$	$\Pi(E_1)\ \Pi(E_2)\ \ldots \Pi(E_n)$
5	E **clos**	**while** (look_ahead $\in$ FIRST(E)) { $\Pi(E)$ }
6	$\{E\}$	$\Pi(E)$
7	E **option**	**if** (look_ahead $\in$ FIRST(E)) { $\Pi(E)$ }
8	E **seq**	$\Pi(E)$ **while** (look_ahead $\in$ FIRST(E)) { $\Pi(E)$ }

9	E_1 **chain** E_2	$\Pi(E_1)$
		while (look_ahead $\in$ DIRSET(E_2)) {
		$\quad$ $\Pi(E_2)\ \Pi(E_1)$
		}

Figure 3.18 Rules for constructing a parser with error detection.

a parser-generation scheme for correct programs. In Figure 3.18 we show a first extension of this scheme that detects errors, but does not provide error recovery. Notice that in the rules 1 and 3 we detect incorrect syntax.

Let us now consider a second extension that does provide error recovery. If an error is detected, then a missing token must be inserted, or an incorrect token must be deleted. But how do we know if a symbol is missing or incorrect?

When parsing the input, the parser advances along the right-hand sides of the productions. At any given moment the parser is busy with one production, and there are some number of unfinished productions (at a higher level). To recover from errors, the parser keeps 3 sets of *markers*:

- **Immediate markers**. The set of tokens that are next expected.
- **Local markers**. The set of tokens that are expected in the rest of the production in which we are working (excluding the immediate markers).
- **Global markers**. The set of tokens that are expected in the rest of all unfinished productions (excluding the local markers, which are the markers in the production in which we are working).

We illustrate the computation of the markers in the following example.

Example 3.9
Consider the following program. From an error-recovery point of view the interesting part of this program is the if-statement, which is embedded in a while-statement, which in turn, is embedded in a program block.

```
BEGIN VAR INT a, b, c;
      a := 1; b := 2;
      WHILE a < b DO
         IF a < b THEN a := b+2 ELSE b := a-2 FI; c := a
      OD
  END.
```

In this example we will explain the computation of the marker sets when parsing this program. In the next example we will show how these marker sets can be used to recover from errors. We will, in particular, discuss the recovery from errors in the if-statement.

Suppose that the parser has advanced to the relation in the if-statement, i.e. the if-token has already been matched and the relation is about to be parsed. The syntactic procedures that up to this point have been called and are not yet finished are therefore: *program_declaration, block, statement_part, statement, while_statement, statement_part* and *statement*, and we are currently working in *if_statement*. In the table below we show the syntactic procedures and computation of the appropriate marker sets. Notice that the procedures are listed in the reverse order of nesting.

immediate markers
    relation: DIRSET(*relation*)
local markers
    if_statement: {then_token}∪ DIRSET(*statement_part*) ∪
                                      DIRSET({else_token *statement_part*} **option**) ∪
                                      {fi_token}
global markers
    statement: ϵ
    statement_part: DIRSET({separator_token *statement*} **clos**)
    while_statement: {od_token}
    statement: ϵ
    statement_part: DIRSET({separator_token *statement*} **clos**)
    block: {end_token}
    program_declaration: {period_token}

Note that we used the construction *statement* {separator_token *statement*} **clos** instead of the construction *statement* **chain** separator_token as the right-hand side of production *statement_part*.

Performing the above computation, we find:

immediate markers: {ident_token, num_token, open_token, absolute_token,
 negate_token}

local markers: {then_token, else_token, fi_token, ident_token, if_token
 while_token, call_token, read_token, write_token}

global markers: {separator_token, od_token, end_token, period_token}

The procedure *if_statement* now calls the procedure *relation*. The immediate and local marker sets are taken from the right-hand side of the production of *relation*, and the global marker set (the new marker set of the environment) is the union of the old local and global marker sets. The tokens in the rest of the right-hand side of *relation* are thus added to the total set of markers. Generally, the total set of markers grows each time we encounter a nonterminal and begin traversing the right-hand side of its production.

When the parsing of the relation is completed, the parser returns to the procedure *if_statement*. The then-token is the next token to be parsed. Immediately before parsing the then-token the 3 marker sets are:

immediate markers: {then_token}

local markers: {else_token, fi_token, ident_token, if_token,
 while_token, call_token, read_token, write_token}

global markers: {separator_token, od_token, end_token, period_token}

After parsing the then-token, the tokens in DIRSET(*statement_part*) become the immediate markers, and these tokens are deleted from the local marker set. The global marker set remains the same. The then-token is thus removed from the total marker set. Every time a part (a grammar symbol, a subexpression between braces or a subexpression followed by one of the operators **option**, **clos** or **seq**) of a production has been parsed, its first set of tokens must be removed from the total marker set. Hence, the total set of markers shrinks each time a part of a right-hand side is parsed.   ◇

The error-recovery strategy is as follows: if the look-ahead symbol is not expected, but is in one of the current marker sets, then the parser assumes that a token is missing, inserts this token and continues parsing. If, however, the not-expected token is not in one of the marker sets, then the parser assumes that the look-ahead symbol is superfluous, deletes it, and continues parsing. We will illustrate this by means of 2 examples.

Example 3.10
Assume that the then-token is missing in the program of Example 3.9. That is, the statement being parsed is:

```
IF a < b     a := b+2 ELSE b := a-2 FI; c := a
```

The look-ahead symbol (i.e. the ident-token corresponding to the left-hand side of the first assignment) is in the local and the global marker sets. The parser, therefore, assumes that the then-token is missing, inserts it, issues the error message "error: then-token inserted", and proceeds.   ◇

Example 3.11
As a second example, assume that the then-token is replaced by a do-token, i.e. the statement being parsed is:

$$\text{IF a < b DO a := b+2 ELSE b := a-2 FI; c := a}$$

The look-ahead symbol, which is the do-token, is this time not in one of the marker sets. The parser, therefore, assumes that the do-token is superfluous, deletes it, and issues the error message "error: do-token deleted". Next, the parser concludes that the then-token is missing and proceeds in the same way as in the previous example.   ◇

For the deletion of superfluous tokens we introduce the procedure *delete_until*, which has a parameter *markers* of type *token_set*, and whose argument is the union of the immediate, local and global marker sets. Tokens are deleted from the input until the look-ahead symbol is in one of these sets.

```
typedef long          *token_set;
/*
** The function in_set() is not listed.
** in_set() returns 1 if a token (1st argument) is a member of
** a token set (2nd argument), else it returns 0.
*/
void delete_until(token_set markers)
{
   while (!in_set((int)look_ahead, markers)) {
     report_error("look_ahead deleted");
     next_token();
   }
}
```

The new rules for parser generation with error recovery are shown in Figure 3.19. Note that in this figure the immediate markers are expressed in terms of first, follow and director sets. For example, the immediate markers in the case of E **clos** are $\text{FIRST}(E) \cup \text{FOLLOW}(E)$.

Error recovery in the case of $\Pi(a)$ involves first deleting superfluous tokens and, second, if the token a is not the look-ahead, inserting this token. In the case of $\Pi(E_1 \mid E_2 \mid \ldots \mid E_n)$, error recovery consists of first deleting superfluous tokens and, second, selecting an alternative. If no alternative can be selected, then the parser acts as if an alternative had been inserted and parsed. Error recovery in the case of subexpressions E **clos**, E **option**, E **seq** and E_1 **chain** E_2 involves deleting superfluous tokens, and investigating whether the subexpression is present.

	Regular expression	Parser module
1	a (terminal)	delete_until($[a]$ ∪ local_markers ∪ global_markers); **if** (look_ahead == a) next_token(); **else** report_error("token a inserted");
2	A (nonterminal)	A(local_markers ∪ global_markers); (i.e. call of procedure associated with A)

3	$E_1 \mid E_2 \mid \ldots \mid E_n$ ($n > 1$)	delete_until(FIRST(E_1) ∪ FIRST(E_2) ∪
		 $\ldots$ ∪ FIRST(E_n) ∪ global_markers);
		 if (look_ahead ∈ DIRSET(E_1)) {
		 $\quad \Pi(E_1)$
		 } **else if** (look_ahead ∈ DIRSET(E_2)) {
		 $\quad \Pi(E_2)$
		 $\quad \vdots$
		 } **else if** (look_ahead ∈ DIRSET(E_n)) {
		 $\quad \Pi(E_n)$
		 } **else** report_error("alternative inserted")

4	$E_1 E_2 \ldots E_n$	$\Pi(E_1)\ \Pi(E_2)\ \ldots \Pi(E_n)$
5	E **clos**	delete_until(FIRST(E) ∪ FOLLOW(E) ∪ local_markers ∪ global_markers); **while** (look_ahead ∈ FIRST(E)) { $\Pi(E)$ }
6	$\{E\}$	$\Pi(E)$
7	E **option**	delete_until(FIRST(E) ∪ FOLLOW(E) ∪ local_markers ∪ global_markers); **if** (look_ahead ∈ FIRST(E)) { $\Pi(E)$ }
8	E **seq**	delete_until(FIRST(E) ∪ FOLLOW(E) ∪ local_markers ∪ global_markers); $\Pi(E)$ **while** (look_ahead ∈ FIRST(E)) { $\Pi(E)$ }

9	E_1 **chain** E_2	$\Pi(E_1)$
		 delete_until(FIRST(E_1) ∪ FIRST(E_2) ∪
		 FOLLOW(E_1) ∪ local_markers ∪
		 global_markers);
		 while (look_ahead ∈ DIRSET(E_2)) {
		 $\quad \Pi(E_2)\ \Pi(E_1)$
		 $\quad$ delete_until(FIRST(E_1) ∪ FIRST(E_2) ∪
		 $\quad\quad$ FOLLOW(E_1) ∪ local_markers ∪
		 $\quad\quad$ global_markers);
		 }

Figure 3.19 Rules for constructing a parser with error detection and recovery.

To illustrate the error-detection and recovery scheme, we extend the (context-free) parsing procedures for *statement, if_statement* and *relation* with the appropriate actions.

```
void statement(token_set global_markers)
{
    token_set        immediate_markers, local_markers, all_markers, local_and_global_markers;

    immediate_markers = create_set(ident_token, if_token, while_token, call_token, read_token,
        write_token, -1);
    local_markers = create_set(-1);
    all_markers = join_sets(immediate_markers, local_markers, global_markers, NULL);
    delete_until(all_markers);
    local_and_global_markers = join_sets(local_markers, global_markers, NULL);
    if (look_ahead == ident_token) {
        assignment_statement(local_and_global_markers);
    } if (look_ahead == if_token) {
        if_statement(local_and_global_markers);
    } if (look_ahead == while_token) {
        while_statement(local_and_global_markers);
    } if (look_ahead == call_token) {
        call_statement(local_and_global_markers);
    } if (look_ahead == read_token) {
        read_statement(local_and_global_markers);
    } if (look_ahead == write_token) {
        write_statement(local_and_global_markers);
    } else report_error("alternative inserted");
}
/*
** The functions create_set() and join_sets() are not listed,
** create_set()    creates a token set of a variable number of tokens terminated by -1,
** join_sets()     joins a variable number of token sets, terminated by the NULL pointer,
**                 into a new token set.
*/
void if_statement(token_set global_markers)
{
    token_set        immediate_markers, local_markers, all_markers, local_and_global_markers;
    int              over_then_part, over_else_part;

    immediate_markers = create_set(if_token, -1);
    local_markers = create_set(ident_token, num_token, open_token, absolute_token,
        negate_token, then_token, else_token, fi_token, if_token, while_token,
        call_token, read_token, write_token, -1);
    all_markers = join_sets(immediate_markers, local_markers, global_markers, NULL);
    delete_until(all_markers);
    if (look_ahead == if_token) next_token();
    else report_error("if_token inserted");
    local_markers = create_set(then_token, else_token, fi_token, ident_token,
        if_token, while_token, call_token, read_token, write_token, -1);
    local_and_global_markers = join_sets(local_markers, global_markers, NULL);
    relation(local_and_global_markers);
    immediate_markers = create_set(then_token, -1);
```

```
    local_markers = create_set(else_token, fi_token, ident_token, if_token,
        while_token, call_token, read_token, write_token, −1);
    all_markers = join_sets(immediate_markers, local_markers, global_markers, NULL);
    delete_until(all_markers);
    if (look_ahead == then_token) next_token();
    else report_error("then_token inserted");
    over_then_part = get_label();
    emit_jump(jiff, over_then_part);
    local_markers = create_set(else_token, fi_token, −1);
    local_and_global_markers = join_sets(local_markers, global_markers, NULL);
    statement_part(local_and_global_markers);
    immediate_markers = create_set(else_token, fi_token, −1);
    local_markers = create_set(fi_token, −1);
    all_markers = join_sets(immediate_markers, local_markers, global_markers, NULL);
    delete_until(all_markers);
    if (look_ahead == else_token) {
        over_else_part = get_label();
        emit_jump(jump, over_else_part);
/* over_then_part: */
        emit_label(over_then_part);
        immediate_markers = create_set(else_token, −1);
        local_markers = create_set(fi_token, ident_token, if_token, while_token, call_token,
            read_token, write_token, −1);
        all_markers = join_sets(immediate_markers, local_markers, global_markers, NULL);
        delete_until(all_markers);
        if (look_ahead == else_token) next_token();
        else report_error("else_token inserted");

        local_markers = create_set(fi_token, −1);
        local_and_global_markers = join_sets(local_markers, global_markers, NULL);
        statement_part(local_and_global_markers);
/* over_else_part: */
        emit_label(over_else_part);
    } else   /* no else part */
/* over_then_part: */
        emit_label(over_then_part);
    immediate_markers = create_set(fi_token, −1);
    local_markers = create_set(−1);
    all_markers = join_sets(immediate_markers, local_markers, global_markers, NULL);
    delete_until(all_markers);
    if (look_ahead == fi_token) next_token();
    else report_error("fi_token inserted");
}

void relation(token_set global_markers)
{
    token_set        local_markers, local_and_global_markers;

    local_markers = create_set(equal_token, not_equal_token, less_than_token,
        less_or_equal_token, greater_than_token, greater_or_equal_token,
        ident_token, num_token, open_token, absolute_token, negate_token, −1);
    local_and_global_markers = join_sets(local_markers, global_markers, NULL);
```

```
    expression(local_and_global_markers);
    local_markers = create_set(ident_token, num_token, open_token, absolute_token,
        negate_token, −1);
    local_and_global_markers = join_sets(local_markers, global_markers, NULL);
    relational_operator(local_and_global_markers);
    local_markers = create_set(−1);
    local_and_global_markers = join_sets(local_markers, global_markers, NULL);
    expression(local_and_global_markers);
}
```

The above syntactic procedures are a straightforward translation of the corresponding grammar productions following the rules of Figure 3.19. This is the reason why some tests are superfluous. An example is the test for the if-token. This token will certainly be present, because otherwise the procedure *if_statement* would not have been called. A second example is the test for the else-token, which will also be found, because the else-token is used to decide that the else-part is present. The deletion of superfluous tests from the parser procedures is straightforward.

This simple method of error recovery works satisfactorily in many cases, but may, as any error-recovery method, in some cases take the wrong action. We will illustrate this in the following example.

Example 3.12
Consider the if-statement:

```
            IF a < b < c THEN a := b+2 ELSE b := a−2 FI; c := a
```

which, as before, is embedded in a while-statement, which in turn is embedded in a program block. As soon as the parser finds the second "<" an error is detected. This token is not in one of the marker sets and is therefore deleted by the parser, with the error message "less-than-token deleted". The next token found, the ident-token (the identifier c), is in the local marker set. This token could be the beginning of the first statement-part in the if-statement, which is, of course, not true, and the parser issues a number of confusing messages. First, the error message "then-token inserted" is issued. The parser assumes that the first statement-part of the if-statement is being parsed. The identifier c is considered the left part of an assignment statement, but then a new error is encountered. The error messages "then-token deleted" and "becomes-token inserted" are issued. The reader is invited to discover that the confusion lasts until the else-token is found as the look-ahead symbol.   ◇

A solution to this problem is to use a *sieve*, which prevents certain tokens from becoming members of marker sets. A candidate to be stopped by the sieve is the ident-token. Notice that our last example works well if the ident-token is not in the marker sets.

3.7   Exercises

1. Consider the program:

```
BEGIN VAR INT i;                    1
       PROC p                       2
       BEGIN VAR INT i;             3
              ⋮                     4
       END;                         5
       PROC q                       6
       BEGIN ...                    7
       END;                         8
          ⋮                         9
END.                                10
```

   Show the symbol table during parsing at the ends of lines 3, 7 and 8.

2. Assume that SLANG is extended with a repeat-statement, as defined in Exercise 2 of Section 2.7. Construct the associated procedure that performs syntax analysis and code generation.

3. Assume that SLANG is extended with a for-statement, as explained in Exercise 3 of Section 2.7. Construct a procedure that performs syntax analysis, context analysis and code generation for this statement. Explain the necessary changes to the symbol table and the actions that operate on the table for the handling of the control variable.

4. Assume that SLANG is extended with a case-statement, as explained in Exercise 4 of Section 2.7. Construct a procedure that performs syntax analysis and code generation for this statement.

3.8   Bibliographic notes

Many books on compiler construction discuss principles, and use as illustration language constructs taken from Ada, C, Modula or Pascal. Typical examples are Aho *et al.* [3], Fischer and LeBlanc [45], Waite and Goos [142] and Wilhelm and Maurer [148]. Other books treat compiler construction by systematically developing a compiler for a full language. Examples are:

- Bennett [22] writes a compiler for VSL (Very Simple Language), which is a simple block-structured procedural language with assignment statements, while-loops, if-then-else branches and simple expressions.

- Elder [39] contains a working compiler for a substantial subset of Modula-2.
- Holub [78] implements an ANSI-compatible subset of C.
- Pittman and Peters [115] use Modula-2 as the programming language for illustrative code.
- Most of the specific examples in Waite and Carter [141] involve subsets of Pascal.
- Watt [143] uses the programming language Δ as a case study.
- Wirth describes in Chapter 5 of [149] a recursive-descent compiler for the language PL/0, which is a subset of Pascal.

The systematic way of generating a parser from context-free grammars can be found in research papers and books, e.g. Heckmann [67] and Lewi *et al.* [96, 97, 98].

In this chapter we presented a single model for a symbol table. More on symbol-table organisation and access techniques can be found in Aho *et al.* [3], McKeeman [102] and Tremblay and Sorenson [138].

The error detection and recovery method described in this chapter was inspired by van de Snepscheut [128], who presented this approach for recursive-descent parsers derived from context-free grammars. We adapted the method for extended context-free grammars. A similar approach can be found in [64, 129]. There is a large amount of research literature on error-recovery methods. An overview is presented in [65]. Other contributions are given in [27, 46, 87, 96, 101, 109, 125, 126, 130, 145]. In the bibliographic notes in Chapter 8 we also address the issue of error handling and repair.

Chapter 4

Generating a compiler

In Section 3.1 we have shown that the tokens of a language can be described by means of regular expressions, that regular expressions can be represented by transition diagrams, and that transition diagrams can be translated into a program. This program is, in fact, a scanner. From now on, we will no longer manually write a scanner, but instead use a scanner generator that automatically generates a scanner. Essentially, the input of a scanner generator is a set of regular expressions that describe the tokens of a language, and the output is a scanner for this language.

In Section 3.2 we have shown how a recursive-descent parser can be derived from an extended context-free grammar. The rules to generate a parser from such a grammar are shown in Figure 3.13. In Section 3.6 this parser generation scheme is extended to rules which also provide for error detection and recovery. Essentially, the input of a parser generator is a context-free grammar that specifies a programming language, and the output is a parser for this language. From now on we will assume that a scanner generator and a parser generator are available. Both will, in fact, be treated as black boxes, which means that as long as the input specification is correct, the generators will do the rest.

In Section 3.4 we have shown how a context-free parser can be extended with actions to check context constraints and to generate code. This is also a systematic process, although we did not present a generation scheme. What we need, in fact, are a context-analyser generator and a code-generator generator. Such generators exist and are usually based on *attribute grammars*. Attribute grammars form an extension of the context-free grammar framework in the sense that information is associated with programming-language constructs by attaching attributes to the grammar symbols representing these constructs. Attribute grammars have shown themselves to be a useful formalism for specifying the context-sensitive syntax and the semantics of programming languages, as well as for implementing editors, compilers and compiler-writing systems.

In Section 4.1 we will give a general introduction to attribute grammars, and in Section 4.2, we will augment extended context-free grammars with attributes and attribute-evaluation rules. This will allow us to use attribute-evaluation rules to specify the context constraints and code to be emitted. A compiler generator that comprises a scanner generator, and a parser generator based on attributed extended context-free grammars, is presented in Section 4.3. Scanner and parser specifications for SLANG will be given as input to this generator.

4.1   Attribute grammars

In this section we will present a number of examples of attribute grammars. In Section 4.1.1 we will enhance a given context-free grammar with attribute-evaluation rules that check the types of operators and operands in arithmetic expressions. We then develop the attribute scheme and illustrate 2 methods of reporting type errors. In Section 4.1.2 we consider top-down parsing and attribute evaluation.

4.1.1   Introduction

Many programming languages are not context-free, but have context-constraints, e.g. scope and type rules. Scope rules determine the scope of each declaration and allow the declaration of each identifier to be located. Type rules make it possible to infer the type of each expression and thus to ensure that each operator is supplied with operands of the correct type.

Example 4.1
Consider the following context-free grammar for arithmetic expressions:

$$
\begin{array}{lll}
expr_0 & : & expr_1 \text{ plus\_token } term. \\
expr & : & term. \\
term_0 & : & term_1 \text{ times\_token } factor. \\
term & : & factor. \\
factor & : & \text{open\_token } expr \text{ close\_token.} \\
factor & : & \text{ident\_token.}
\end{array}
$$

Note that multiple occurrences of the same grammar symbol in a production are distinguished by subscripts. This grammar is assumed to be a part of a larger grammar, which also specifies how declarations are written. We omit, however, for the moment, the productions that specify these declarations, and simply assume that every identifier represents a variable that is in the scope of its declaration, so that its type is known. The 2 possible types are integer and real. The plus and the times operator can be applied to either type. Further, we assume the grammar is strongly typed, i.e. the type of any subexpression should be deducible from its operators and the types of its operands at compile time.   ◇

The grammar in Example 4.1 is a context-free grammar, but not an extended context-free grammar as syntactic operators are not used. Further, instead of using the vertical bar "|" to denote an alternative production, we write each production out explicitly. These simplifications make it easier to enhance the productions with attribute-evaluation rules. Moreover, the grammar is left recursive, which implies that a recursive-descent parser does not exist for this grammar.[1] At the end of this section we will transform this left-recursive grammar into a right-recursive grammar, and in Section 4.2 we will apply extended context-free grammars to eliminate left recursion. We will then also return to the scheme of 1 production for each nonterminal. In this section we will only consider the context-free grammar scheme of Example 4.1.

Given an expression, type computation could proceed in 2 steps:

1. The syntax analyser constructs the parse tree.
2. The constraint analyser applies the type rules in a bottom-up order to compute the types of all subexpressions.

The nodes in the parse tree can be implemented as records, each with some number of fields. One field identifies the grammar symbol that labels the node, and for each child there is a field that contains a pointer to the child. Additional fields may hold context-sensitive and semantic information. The type of a subexpression is, for example, stored in a field of the record. This field has the name *type*, and can hold the type value, which must be either integer or real. In this way a parse tree is decorated with type information.

We can extend the context-free grammar shown in Example 4.1 to a context-sensitive grammar that describes typed expressions by associating an *attribute* with each nonterminal that represents a (sub)expression. This attribute specifies the *type* of the (sub)expression. The type rules, which specify the type of an expression as a function of the types of its subexpressions, are called *attribute-evaluation rules*.

Example 4.2
Consider the following production:

$$expr_0 \quad : \quad expr_1 \text{ plus\_token } term.$$

We would like to specify in this production that the type of $expr_0$ is integer if the types of both $expr_1$ and $term$ are integer, otherwise the type of $expr_0$ is real. This can be done by means of the following attribute-evaluation rule:

if (*type* **of** $expr_1$ == **real**) *type* **of** $expr_0$ = **real**;
else *type* **of** $expr_0$ = *type* **of** *term*;

⋄

In productions that consist of a sole nonterminal on the left and right-hand side we often use what is referred to as a *copy rule*. A copy rule simply copies

---

[1]There are, however, other parsing methods that can handle left recursion. For example, bottom-up methods, which are briefly discussed at the end of Chapter 8.

the value of the attribute of the right-hand side nonterminal to the left-hand side nonterminal.

Example 4.3
The production:

>   *expr* : *term.*

has the copy rule:

>   *type* **of** *expr* = *type* **of** *term;*

◇

   In the above examples we have associated the attribute *type* with the grammar symbols *expr* and *term*, and added attribute-evaluation rules to the productions to compute the value of attribute *type* **of** *expr*. In a similar way, we can associate the attribute *type* with the grammar symbol *factor*, and add attribute-evaluation rules to the other productions.
   As in Chapter 3, we assume that the scanner translates every identifier into the token *ident_token* and its *lexeme*. The lexeme is used to access the associated definition record in the symbol table. The definition record contains, among other things, the type of the identifier. The grammar symbol *ident_token* has an attribute *lexeme*, and the function call

>   extract_type (*lexeme* **of** ident_token)

extracts the type from the symbol table. Note that the function *extract_type* is, in fact, a combination of the functions *find_definition* and *get_type* that are defined in Chapter 3.

Example 4.4
The attribute grammar, consisting of productions and attribute-evaluation rules (enclosed in square brackets) corresponding to the context-free grammar in Example 4.1 is shown below:

> $expr_0$: $expr_1$ plus_token *term.*
>   [**if** (*type* **of** $expr_1$ == **real**) *type* **of** $expr_0$ = **real**;
>   **else** *type* **of** $expr_0$ = *type* **of** *term*;
>   ]
>   *expr*   : *term.*
>   [*type* **of** *expr* = *type* **of** *term*;]
> $term_0$: $term_1$ times_token *factor.*
>   [**if** (*type* **of** $term_1$ == **real**) *type* **of** $term_0$ = **real**;
>   **else** *type* **of** $term_0$ = *type* **of** *factor*;
>   ]
>   *term*   : *factor.*
>   [*type* **of** *term* = *type* **of** *factor*;]

factor : open_token *expr* close_token.
  [*type* **of** *factor* = *type* **of** *expr*;]
factor : ident_token.
  [*type* **of** *factor* = extract_type(*lexeme* **of** ident_token);]

◇

Figure 4.1 shows the attributed parse tree of the expression $(a + b) * c$, where a is of type real, and b and c are of type integer, using the above attribute grammar. In this figure, every identifier is represented by *ident_token* and the value of its attribute *lexeme*. The symbols $+$, $*$ and parentheses are shown as they appear in the input. Notice that in every production the information flows from the right-hand side to the left-hand side. From this it follows that the attributes can be computed during a single bottom-up traversal of the parse tree. The computation starts at the leaves, and the type of the root is computed last. The attributes in this example are called *synthesised* attributes. The value of a synthesised attribute at a node in the parse tree is computed from the values of attributes at the children of that node.

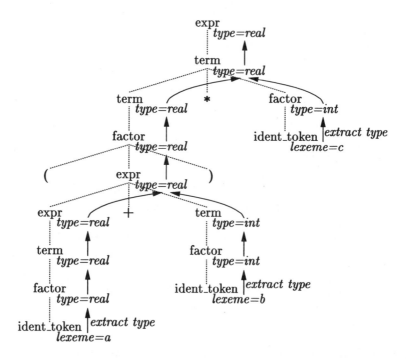

Figure 4.1 Attributed parse tree of an expression.

We now introduce *inherited* attributes. The value of an inherited attribute at a node in the parse tree is computed from the attributes at the parent and the siblings of that node. Generally speaking, a synthesised attribute attached to a tree node contains information concerning the subtree at that node. Inherited attributes are convenient for expressing the dependence of a language construct on the context in which it appears.

Example 4.5
In this example we demonstrate the application of inherited attributes to distribute type information to the various identifiers in declarations.

> *declaration*   :   *type_declarer identifier_list*.
>   [*itype* **of** *identifier_list* = *stype* **of** *type_declarer*;]
> *type_declarer*   :   int_token.
>   [*stype* **of** *type_declarer* = `int`;]
> *type_declarer*   :   real_token.
>   [*stype* **of** *type_declarer* = `real`;]
> *identifier_list*$_0$:   *identifier_list*$_1$ list_token ident_token.
>   [*itype* **of** *identifier_list*$_1$ = *itype* **of** *identifier_list*$_0$;
>   enter_type(*lexeme* **of** ident_token, *itype* **of** *identifier_list*$_0$);
>   ]
> *identifier_list*   :   ident_token.
>   [enter_type(*lexeme* **of** ident_token, *itype* **of** *identifier_list*);]

A declaration consists of the keyword **integer** or **real**, followed by a number of identifiers. The nonterminal *type_declarer* has a synthesised attribute *stype*, whose value is determined by the production in which it is assigned, i.e. by the keyword in the declaration.

The first production and attribute-evaluation rule in the grammar above assigns the value of the synthesised attribute *stype* **of** *type_declarer* to the inherited attribute *itype* **of** *identifier_list*. The productions for *identifier_list* pass the type value down the parse tree by means of the inherited attribute *itype* **of** *identifier_list*. Associated with the productions for *identifier_list* is a function *enter_type* that adds the type of each identifier to its definition record in the symbol table.   ◇

Figure 4.2 shows the attributed parse trees of the declarations **real a** and **integer b, c**, using the above attribute grammar. Notice that the order in which attributes are computed is as follows: the type is determined at the left child of the root, which is then given to the right subtree of the root, whereupon the information flows down to the nodes with label *ident_token*, at which point the type information is entered in the symbol table.

Attribute grammars form an extension of the context-free grammar framework in the sense that attributes are associated with grammar symbols. Each *attribute* has a (possibly infinite) value domain. Attribute values are defined by *attribute-evaluation rules* associated with the productions of the grammar.

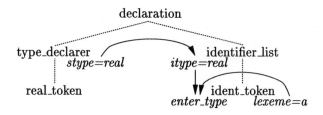

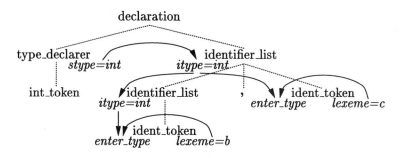

Figure 4.2 Attributed parse trees of declarations.

Attributes can be divided into 2 disjoint classes: the *synthesised* attributes and the *inherited* attributes. The attribute-evaluation rules associated with a production define the synthesised attributes attached to the grammar symbol on the left-hand side and the inherited attributes attached to the grammar symbols on the right-hand side of the production.

A non-ambiguous context-free grammar defines a single parse tree for each sentence. The values of the synthesised attributes at a tree node and the inherited attributes at its immediate descendants are defined by the attribute-evaluation rules associated with the production applied at that node. The value of a synthesised attribute of the parent is computed from the values of the attributes at its children and (possibly) other attributes of the parent itself. The value of an inherited attribute of a child is computed from the values of the attributes at its parent and its siblings and (possibly) other attributes of the child itself.

Generally speaking, a synthesised attribute attached to a tree node contains information concerning the subtree at that node. In other words, it comprises the information from the terminal string derived from the nonterminal symbol labelling that node. Inherited attributes are convenient for expressing the dependence of a programming language construct on the context in which it appears. Attributes can also be used to verify context conditions, e.g. to determine whether operands

operators	operand types		result type
$+,-,*$:	(integer,integer)	$\rightarrow$	integer
:	(integer,real)	$\rightarrow$	real
:	(real,integer)	$\rightarrow$	real
:	(real,real)	$\rightarrow$	real
$/$:	(any,any)	$\rightarrow$	real
$\div,\vert$:	(integer,integer)	$\rightarrow$	integer

Figure 4.3 Arithmetic operators and the types of their operands and result.

of an expression have the correct type. Such a condition can be expressed as a *predicate* on attribute values.

We end this section with 2 more-involved examples that show how an attribute grammar can be used to specify a *type checker* for arithmetic expressions. The purpose of this grammar is to check that operators have correctly-typed operands. When we emit code it is also necessary to know which operator (i.e. integer or real) we are dealing with. Further, in the case of mixed types, an operand of type integer needs to be converted to an operand of type real. In the examples we first list the grammar symbols, then the types and descriptions of the attributes, and we finish with the productions and attribute-evaluation rules of the grammar.

Example 4.6
Let us assume that our arithmetic expressions have operators for addition $(+)$, subtraction $(-)$, multiplication $(*)$, real $(/)$ and integer $(\div)$ division, and modulus $(\vert)$. The priority and the associativity of the operators is expressed by the underlying context-free grammar. The operators $+$, $-$, $*$ and $/$ are overloaded in the sense that they apply to both integers and reals. The operators $\div$ and $\vert$ require both operands to be of type integer. The table shown in Figure 4.3 specifies for each operator the possible operand and result types.

The following grammar makes use of the synthesised attributes *type*, *op* and *lexeme*, to specify the type of an operand, the kind of an operator, and the lexeme of an identifier, respectively. The lexeme is of type *string*, which is a sequence of characters. We use a procedure "report_error" to report detected errors. If there is a type error, then it is reported after the whole right-hand side expression has been seen.

grammar symbols:
    nonterminals: *assignment, left_part, expr, term, factor, add_operator,*
                       multiply_operator.
    terminals: ident_token, becomes_token, open_token, close_token,
                       plus_token, minus_token, times_token, real_division_token,
                       integer_division_token, modulo_token.
    start symbol: *assignment.*

attribute types:
> **type** mode   = (int, real);
>   operation = (add, sub, mul, rdv, idv, mdl).

description of attributes:
> *type*   : mode   **syn of** *left_part, expr, term, factor;*
> *op*   : operation **syn of** *add_operator, multiply_operator;*
> *lexeme* : string   **syn of** ident_token.

productions and attribute-evaluation rules:
> *assignment* : *left_part* becomes_token *expr.*
>   [**if** (*type* **of** *left_part* == int && *type* **of** *expr* == real)
>   report_error("type conflict: int vs. real")
>   ]
> *left_part* : ident_token.
>   [*type* **of** *left_part* = extract_type(*lexeme* **of** ident_token);]
> $expr_0$: $expr_1$ *add_operator term.*
>   [**if** (*type* **of** $expr_1$ == real) *type* **of** $expr_0$ = real;
>   **else** *type* **of** $expr_0$ = *type* **of** *term;*
>   ]
> *expr* : *term.*
>   [*type* **of** *expr* = *type* **of** *term;*]
> $term_0$: $term_1$ *multiply_operator factor.*
>   [**switch** (*op* **of** *multiply_operator*) {
>   **case mul:**   **if** (*type* **of** $term_1$ == real) *type* **of** $term_0$ = real;
>   **else** *type* **of** $term_0$ = *type* **of** *factor;*
>   **break;**
>   **case rdv:**   *type* **of** $term_0$ = real;
>   **break;**
>   **case idv:**
>   **case mdl:**   *type* **of** $term_0$ = int;
>   **if** (*type* **of** $term_1$ == real)
>   report_error("left operand not of type int");
>   **if** (*type* **of** *factor* == real)
>   report_error("right operand not of type int");
>   }
>   ]
> *term* : *factor.*
>   [*type* **of** *term* = *type* **of** *factor;*]
> *factor* : open_token *expr* close_token.
>   [*type* **of** *factor* = *type* **of** *expr;*]
> *factor* : ident_token.
>   [*type* **of** *factor* = extract_type(*lexeme* **of** ident_token);]
> *add_operator* : plus_token.
>   [*op* **of** *add_operator* = add;]

add_operator : minus_token.
    [*op* **of** *add_operator* = **sub**;]
multiply_operator : times_token.
    [*op* **of** *multiply_operator* = **mul**;]
multiply_operator : real_division_token.
    [*op* **of** *multiply_operator* = **rdv**;]
multiply_operator : integer_division_token.
    [*op* **of** *multiply_operator* = **idv**;]
multiply_operator : modulo_token.
    [*op* **of** *multiply_operator* = **mdl**;]

◇

In Figure 4.4 we show the attributed parse tree of the statement a := b + c | d, where a and b are of type real, and c and d are of type integer.

The next example is a more sophisticated type checker. It uses an inherited attribute to detect type errors earlier, in fact, at the moment that an identifier of an incorrect type is read.

Example 4.7
In this example, the inherited attribute *etype* (short for *expected type*) indicates the expected type of an operand within the context of the assignment statement. Its value can be **intexp** or **unspec**. The first is an abbreviation for **integer expected**, the latter for **unspecified**. The attribute *etype* is used to pass the expected type down to the level of the identifiers. The synthesised attribute *atype* (short for *actual type*) plays the same role as the attribute *type* in Example 4.6. If the value of *etype* is **intexp**, then the value of *atype* must be **int**. If the value of *etype* is however **unspec**, then the value of *atype* may be either **int** or **real**.

grammar symbols:
  nonterminals: *assignment, left_part, expr, term, factor, add_operator, multiply_operator.*
  terminals: ident_token, becomes_token, open_token, close_token, plus_token, minus_token, times_token, real_division_token, integer_division_token, modulo_token.
  start symbol: *assignment.*

attribute types:
  type model = (int, real);
          mode2 = (intexp, unspec);
          operation = (add, sub, mul, rdv, idv, mdl).

description of attributes:
  atype : model   **syn of** *left_part, expr, term, factor;*
  etype : mode2   **inh of** *expr, term, factor;*
  op   : operation **syn of** *add_operator, multiply_operator;*
  lexeme : string   **syn of** ident_token.

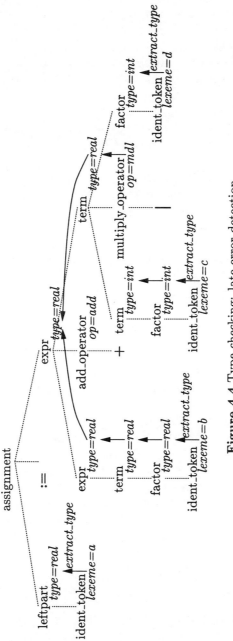

Figure 4.4 Type checking: late error detection.

productions and attribute-evaluation rules:

assignment : *left_part* becomes_token *expr*.
   [**if** (*atype* **of** *left_part* == int) *etype* **of** *expr* = intexp;
     else *etype* **of** *expr* = unspec;
   ]

left_part : ident_token.
   [*atype* **of** *left_part* = extract_type(*lexeme* **of** ident_token);]

$expr_0$: $expr_1$ add_operator *term*.
   [*etype* **of** $expr_1$ = *etype* **of** $expr_0$;
     etype **of** *term* = *etype* **of** $expr_0$;
     if (*atype* **of** $expr_1$ == real) *atype* **of** $expr_0$ = real;
     else *atype* **of** $expr_0$ = *atype* **of** *term*;
   ]

expr : *term*.
   [*etype* **of** *term* = *etype* **of** *expr*;
     atype **of** *expr* = *atype* **of** *term*;
   ]

$term_0$: $term_1$ multiply_operator *factor*.
   [**if** (*etype* **of** $term_0$ == intexp ||
      op **of** *multiply_operator* == idv ||
      op **of** *multiply_operator* == mdl) {
     etype **of** $term_1$ = intexp;
     etype **of** *factor* = intexp;
   }
   else{
     etype **of** $term_1$ = unspec;
     etype **of** *factor* = unspec;
   }
   switch (*op* **of** *multiply_operator*) {
     case mul: **if** (*atype* **of** $term_1$ == real)
             atype **of** $term_0$ = real;
          else *atype* **of** $term_0$ = *atype* **of** *factor*;
         break;
     case rdv: **if** (*etype* **of** $term_0$ == intexp) {
          report_error("real division in integer expression");
          atype **of** $term_0$ = int;
         }
         else *atype* **of** $term_0$ = real;
         break;
     case idv:
     case mdl: *atype* **of** $term_0$ = int;
   }
   ]

term : *factor*.

      [*etype* **of** *factor* = *etype* **of** *term*;
         atype **of** *term* = *atype* **of** *factor*;
      ]
factor :   open_token *expr* close_token.
      [*etype* **of** *expr* = *etype* **of** *factor*;
         atype **of** *factor* = *atype* **of** *expr*;
      ]
factor :   ident_token.
      [**if** (*etype* **of** *factor* == `intexp` &&
           extract_type(*lexeme* **of** ident_token) == `real`) {
         report_error("real operand in integer expression");
         atype **of** *factor* = `int`;
      }
      else *atype* **of** *factor* = extract_type(*lexeme* **of** ident_token);
      ]
add_operator :   plus_token.
      [*op* **of** *add_operator* = `add`;]
add_operator :   minus_token.
      [*op* **of** *add_operator* = `sub`;]
multiply_operator :   times_token.
      [*op* **of** *multiply_operator* = `mul`;]
multiply_operator :   real_division_token.
      [*op* **of** *multiply_operator* = `rdv`;]
multiply_operator :   integer_division_token.
      [*op* **of** *multiply_operator* = `idv`;]
multiply_operator :   modulo_token.
      [*op* **of** *multiply_operator* = `mdl`;]

                                          ◇

Figure 4.5 shows the attributed subtree for the right-hand side of the assignment in Figure 4.4, using the new attribute grammar.

4.1.2   Top-down parsing and attribute evaluation

An *attribute evaluator* computes the values of all instances of attributes attached to a parse tree. In general, the order of evaluation is unimportant, with the only constraint being that an evaluation rule cannot be executed before the values of its arguments are available. Initially the values of all attribute instances attached to the tree are undefined, with the exception of the synthesised attribute instances attached to the leaves. These are determined by the scanner. The evaluator chooses at each step an attribute instance whose value can be computed. The evaluation process continues until all attribute instances are defined or until none of the remaining attribute instances can be evaluated.

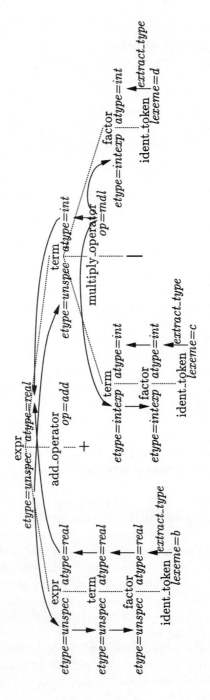

Figure 4.5 Type checking: early error detection.

In this chapter we will not consider attribute evaluation in general, but we will restrict ourselves to the evaluation of attributes during a single pass of the parse tree, where a *pass* is a left-to-right traversal of the tree.

The following example demonstrates the evaluation of attributes from left to right. It describes the scope rules of a language, in which variables must be declared before use. The language has a block structure. A *block* is built from declarations and statements. A *declaration* is a *variable_declaration*, which consists of a single identifier, like **var** *a*. A *statement* is a *simple_statement* (like **use** *a*) or a *block*.

In Chapter 3 we introduced a symbol table that records the information from the declarations in a program. We also used this approach in the type-checking examples in this chapter. In the following example we will store the declaration information in symbol tables that are attribute instances of the parse tree. In this sense, the example is very inefficient as almost identical symbol tables are scattered as attribute instances all over the parse tree, but it clearly demonstrates how declaration information is collected from and distributed over the tree nodes.

The attributes *or*, *up* and *us* (short for *original*, *updated* and *used*, respectively) represent symbol tables. The attributes *or* and *up*, associated with *declaration_part*, are used to collect declaration information to be used in statements. The updated symbol table of *declaration_part* contains the information of the original table plus the declarations that are part of *declaration_part*. The attribute *decl*, associated with *declaration* and *variable_declaration*, represents a single declaration. The attribute *us*, associated with *block*, *statement_part*, *statement* and *simple_statement*, is a symbol table that contains all identifiers that are valid for the grammar symbol concerned.

Example 4.8

An attribute grammar in which the scope rules of the language are implemented using a 1-pass scheme. Variables must be declared before use.

grammar symbols:
    nonterminals: *program_declaration, block, declaration_part, declaration, variable_declaration, statement_part, statement, simple_statement.*
    terminals: begin_token, end_token, var_token, use_token, ident_token.
    start symbol: *program_declaration.*

attribute types:
    { the definition of type symbol_table is not shown. }

description of attributes:

or	:	symbol_table	**inh of** *declaration_part*;
up	:	symbol_table	**syn of** *declaration_part*;
us	:	symbol_table	**inh of** *block, statement_part, statement, simple_statement*;
decl	:	string	**syn of** *declaration, variable_declaration.*
lexeme	:	string	**syn of** ident_token.

functions:
>   symbol_table
>   new_table(**void**)
>   {   /*creates an empty table */
>   }
>
>   symbol_table
>   append(string *decl*, /* **to** */ symbol_table *table*)
>   {   /*adds a new declaration to the table,
>   reporting an error, if a double declaration is found */
>   }
>
>   symbol_table
>   concatenate (symbol_table *local_table*, symbol_table *global_table*)
>   {   /*returns a symbol table by concatenating the local and the global
>   table; in the case of identical names the declaration from the local
>   table will be found first */
>   }
>
>   **void** check_declaration(string *name*, symbol_table *table*)
>   {   /*reports an error if the name is not in the table */
>   }

productions and attribute-evaluation rules:
>   *program_declaration* : *block*.
>   [**us of** *block* = new_table();]
>   *block* : begin_token *declaration_part* *statement_part* end_token.
>   [**or of** *declaration_part* = new_table();
>   **us of** *statement_part* =
>   concatenate (**up of** *declaration_part*, **us of** *block*);
>   ]
>   *declaration_part$_0$* : *declaration_part$_1$* *declaration*.
>   [**or of** *declaration_part$_1$* = **or of** *declaration_part$_0$*;
>   **up of** *declaration_part$_0$* =
>   append (*decl* **of** *declaration*, /*to*/ **up of** *declaration_part$_1$*);
>   ]
>   *declaration_part* : *declaration*.
>   [**up of** *declaration_part* =
>   append (*decl* **of** *declaration*, /*to*/ **or of** *declaration_part*);
>   ]
>   *declaration* : *variable_declaration*.
>   [*decl* **of** *declaration* = *decl* **of** *variable_declaration*;]
>   *variable_declaration* :   var_token ident_token.
>   [*decl* **of** *variable_declaration* = *lexeme* **of** ident_token]

$statement\_part_0$: $statement\_part_1$ *statement.*
    [*us* **of** $statement\_part_1$ = *us* **of** $statement\_part_0$;
       us **of** *statement* = *us* **of** $statement\_part_0$;
    ]
statement_part : *statement.*
    [*us* **of** *statement* = *us* **of** *statement_part*;]
statement : *simple_statement.*
    [*us* **of** *simple_statement* = *us* **of** *statement*;]
statement : *block.*
    [*us* **of** *block* = *us* **of** *statement*;]
simple_statement : use_token ident_token.
    [check_declaration (*lexeme* **of** ident_token, *us* **of** *simple_statement*);]

An attributed parse tree for the program

> **begin**
>   **var** a
>   **use** a
>   **begin**
>   **var** b
>   **use** b
>   **end**
> **end**

is shown in Figure 4.6. Observe that, when we parse declarations, information is added to the symbol table only when the evaluator moves bottom-up. This means that it is possible to delete attribute *or* and to compile declarations only making use of attribute *up*.   ◇

It has already been mentioned that the space management of the above example is inefficient. The attributes *or*, *up* and *us* are symbol tables, and these attributes occur in many places in the parse tree. We will now remove this inefficiency by implementing the attributes *or*, *up* and *us* as pointers to lists of declarations. The function *new_table* creates a scope record that consists of the following fields:

- A pointer to a name list.
- A pointer to the scope record of the surrounding scope.

The initial values of the pointers of the scope record are **nul**.

The identifiers, which are declared in the current scope, are organised in a list of name records. A name record consists of the following fields:

- The identifier.
- A pointer to the next name record in the list.

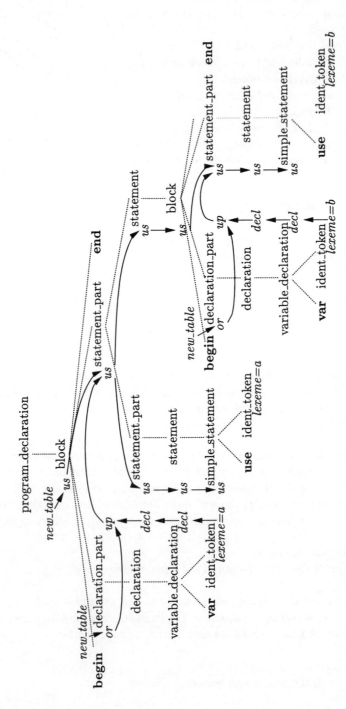

Figure 4.6 Attribute evaluation in 1 pass.

The function *append* creates a new name record, and inserts it in front of the list of name records of the current scope. The call append(*decl* **of** *declaration, or* **of** *declaration_part*) results in the creation of a name record with as identifier the value of attribute *decl* **of** *declaration*. The value of attribute *or* **of** *declaration_part* is a pointer to the scope record of the current scope. The name record is added to the list of name records of this scope record. The value of the function *append* is a pointer value, which is the address of the scope record of the current scope. Note that this address is equal to the value of *or* **of** *declaration_part*.

The function *concatenate* adds the scope record of the current scope to the list of scope records of surrounding scopes. The call concatenate(*up* **of** *declaration_part, us* **of** *block*) has two pointers as arguments. The value of *up* **of** *declaration_part* is a pointer to the scope record of the current scope. The value of *us* **of** *block* is a pointer to the scope record of the surrounding scope. The latter value is now included in the scope record of the current scope. Note that scope records of parallel blocks point to the scope record of the same surrounding block. Contrary to the scheme in Chapter 3, where we used a function *exit_scope*, the scope record and the name records of a block that is exited are not removed. We will return to the old scheme in Section 4.3.3.

The following declarations describe the records of the *scope list* and the *name list*. The type *symbol_table* is a pointer type. An attribute of type *symbol_table* will point to a scope record, which in turn will point to a list of name records.

```
#define  max_ident_length        255

typedef char                     string[max_ident_length + 1];

typedef struct name_rec {
    string              ident;
    struct name_rec     *next;
} *name_ptr;

typedef struct scope_rec {
    name_ptr            name_list;
    struct scope_rec    *prev_scope;
} *scope_ptr;

typedef scope_ptr                symbol_table;
```

Notice that the same organisation was used for the scope list in Section 3.3.1.

We will now combine top-down parsing and attribute evaluation. We first make the following observations:

1. During parse-tree construction, top-down parsers recognise tree nodes and the productions to be applied in pre-order.

2. During an evaluation pass over a parse tree each node is visited twice. Inherited attribute instances of a node are evaluated during the pre-order visit and synthesised attribute instances during the post-order visit.

From these observations it can be concluded that attribute instances can be evaluated during top-down parsing if the attribute instances can be evaluated during a single left-to-right pass over the parse tree.

It is easy to augment a recursive-descent parser in such a way that it can also evaluate attributes during parsing. The inherited attributes of a nonterminal A correspond with input parameters of the procedure for A, and the synthesised attributes correspond with its output parameters. It is self-evident that the input parameters of a procedure (the inherited attributes of the nonterminal) must be computed before the procedure is called. The output parameters (the synthesised attributes of the nonterminal) become available after the execution of the call-statement is finished. This will be expressed by writing the evaluation rules in the productions, as we did earlier in translation schemes in Section 1.5. The position of an evaluation rule within a production determines when it is executed during parsing. Syntactically, an evaluation rule can be viewed as another nonterminal with an empty right-hand side.

Consider, for example, the production for *block* in the attribute grammar shown in Example 4.8.

> *block* : begin_token *declaration_part statement_part* end_token.
> [*or* **of** *declaration_part* = new_table();
>   *us* **of** *statement_part* =
>   concatenate (*up* **of** *declaration_part*, *us* **of** *block*);
>]

This production can be rewritten as:

> *block* : begin_token
>   [*or* **of** *declaration_part* = new_table();]
>   *declaration_part*
>   [*us* **of** *statement_part* :=
>   concatenate (*up* **of** *declaration_part*, *us* **of** *block*);
>   ]
>   *statement_part*
>   end_token

We will now develop the corresponding parsing procedure for *block*. We first apply the rules of Figure 3.13 to construct the syntactic part of the procedure, then copy every attribute-evaluation rule literally into the procedure, and finally replace the inherited and synthesised attributes by corresponding input and output parameters.

```
void block (symbol_table used_of_block)
{
   symbol_table      or_of_declaration_part,
                     up_of_declaration_part,
                     us_of_statement_part;

   if (look_ahead == begin_token) next_token();
   or_of_declaration_part = new_table();
   declaration_part(or_of_declaration_part, &up_of_declaration_part);
   us_of_statement_part = concatenate(up_of_declaration_part, us_of_block);
   statement_part(us_of_statement_part);
   if (look_ahead == end_token) next_token();
}
```

Notice that in the body of this procedure all attributes of nonterminals that occur in the right-hand side of the production for *block* have been declared as local variables. Further, the inherited attribute *us* of *block* is assumed to be available when the procedure is entered.

The execution of the parsing procedure for *block* will proceed as follows: the inherited attribute *or* of *declaration_part* is first computed. The procedure for *declaration_part* then uses this attribute to compute the synthesised attribute *up* of *declaration_part*. This attribute, together with *us* of *block*, will then be used to compute the inherited attribute *us* of *statement_part*. Finally, the procedure *statement_part* is called with *us* of *statement_part* as input parameter.

The attribute grammar of Example 4.8 is not suitable, however, for top-down parsing as its productions for *declaration_part* and *statement_part* are left recursive. In the following example we show a transformed version of the attribute grammar. In this new grammar we have used right recursion, and we have transformed the attribute-evaluation rules accordingly. We have also taken the opportunity to optimise the attribute grammar in the sense that declaration information is collected only during bottom-up moves of the evaluator. The attribute *or* has been removed and the attribute *up* is now called *decls*.

Example 4.9

A transformed version of the attribute grammar of Example 4.8. Note that we have continued to place the attribute-evaluation rules at the end of the productions.

productions and attribute-evaluation rules:

    program_declaration   :   *block*.
         [*us* **of** *block* = new_table();]
    block :   begin_token *declaration_part statement_part* end_token.
         [*us* **of** *statement_part* =
             concatenate (*decls* **of** *declaration_part*, *us* **of** *block*);
         ]

declaration_part : *declaration more_declarations.*
 [*decls* **of** *declaration_part* =
   append (*decl* **of** *declaration*, /*to*/ *decls* **of** *more_declarations*);
 ]
more_declarations$_0$: *declaration more_declarations*$_1$.
 [*decls* **of** *more_declarations*$_0$ =
   append (*decl* **of** *declaration*, /*to*/ *decls* **of** *more_declarations*$_1$);
 ]
more_declarations : ϵ .
 [*decls* **of** *more_declarations* = new_table();]
declaration : *variable_declaration.*
 [*decl* **of** *declaration* = *decl* **of** *variable_declaration*;
 ]
variable_declaration : var_token ident_token.
 [*decl* **of** *variable_declaration* = *lexeme* **of** ident_token]
statement_part : *statement more_statements.*
 [*us* **of** *statement* = *us* **of** *statement_part*;
  us **of** *more_statements* = *us* **of** *statement_part*;
 ]
more_statements$_0$: *statement more_statements*$_1$.
 [*us* **of** *statement* = *us* **of** *more_statements*$_0$;
  us **of** *more_statements*$_1$ = *us* **of** *more_statements*$_0$;
 ]
more_statements$_0$: ϵ .
 []
statement : *simple_statement.*
 [*us* **of** *simple_statement* = *us* **of** *statement*;]
statement : *block.*
 [*us* **of** *block* = *us* **of** *statement*;]
simple_statement : use_token ident_token.
 [check_declaration (*lexeme* **of** ident_token, *us* **of** *simple_statement*);]

◇

We mentioned earlier that right-recursive productions sometimes make it hard to handle left-associative operators, which are normally expressed by left-recursive productions. To avoid both left and right-recursive productions, we can use extended context-free grammars (which we have extensively used in Chapters 2 and 3). We will study these in the next section.

4.2 Attributed extended context-free grammars

The underlying context-free grammar of the attribute grammar shown in Example 4.8 can be rewritten into an extended context-free grammar as follows:

program_declaration	:	*block.*
block	:	begin_token *declaration_part statement_part* end_token.
declaration_part	:	*declaration* **seq**.
declaration	:	*variable_declaration.*
variable_declaration	:	var_token ident_token.
statement_part	:	*statement* **seq**.
statement	:	*simple_statement.*
statement	:	*block.*
simple_statement	:	use_token ident_token.

We now need to augment this extended context-free grammar with attributes and attribute-evaluation rules. From now on we will omit the square brackets around the attribute-evaluation rules. We require every terminal, nonterminal, attribute and evaluation function to be declared, so that they can be easily distinguished.

Let us first have a look at the production

declaration_part   :   *declaration* **seq**.

We assume that, as in Example 4.8, nonterminal *declaration_part* has inherited attribute *or* and synthesised attribute *up*, and that nonterminal *declaration* has synthesised attribute *decl*.

For this sequence of declarations, we want that attribute *up* **of** *declaration_part* initially gets the value of *or* **of** *declaration_part*, and that every time a variable declaration is parsed, the current value of *decl* **of** *declaration* is added to the value of *up* **of** *declaration_part*.

The original definition of attribute grammars, however, requires that every occurrence of an attribute in a production be assigned exactly once, in order to avoid ambiguity. Ambiguity arises, for example, if 2 evaluation rules assign different values to an attribute, so that it is unclear which value the attribute will eventually receive. If we keep this restriction, then it is impossible to ever update an attribute value as is necessary in the above situation. We could, of course, forego this restriction, and allow an attribute value to be updated. However, we will keep the above-mentioned restriction for the inherited and synthesised attributes, and introduce special attributes to hold intermediate values that may change. These special attributes only play a local role in a production; hence they are called *local attributes*.

A local attribute must be declared as local in a production. The scope of such an attribute is the production in which it is defined. We will allow a local attribute to be updated. In the above situation we will first collect the values of the declarations of the sequence in a local attribute *local_table*, and finally assign the value of *local_table* to *up* **of** *declaration_part*. The attributed production for *declaration_part* now becomes:

declaration_part (**local** *local_table*: symbol_table)
    : *local_table* = *or* **of** *declaration_part*;

```
    { declaration
      local_table = append (decl of declaration, /*to*/ local_table);
    } seq
    up of declaration_part = local_table;
```

We can now rewrite the attribute grammar shown in Example 4.8 into an extended context-free form. This is shown below.

Example 4.10
The scope rules in the language (described in Example 4.8) are expressed using an extended context-free grammar.

productions and attribute-evaluation rules

program_declaration
   : *us* **of** *block* = new_table();
   block

block
   : begin_token
   or **of** *declaration_part* = new_table();
   declaration_part
   us **of** *statement_part* = concatenate (*up* **of** *declaration_part*, *us* **of** *block*);
   statement_part
   end_token

declaration_part (**local** *local_table*: symbol_table)
   : *local_table* = *or* **of** *declaration_part*;
    { *declaration*
     local_table = append (*decl* **of** *declaration*, /*to*/ *local_table*);
    } **seq**
    up **of** *declaration_part* = *local_table*;

declaration
   : *variable_declaration*
   decl **of** *declaration* = *decl* **of** *variable_declaration*;

variable_declaration
   : var_token
   ident_token
   decl **of** *variable_declaration* = *lexeme* **of** ident_token;

statement_part
   : { *us* **of** *statement* = *us* **of** *statement_part*;

> *statement*
> } **seq**

.

statement
> : *us* **of** *assignment_statement* = *us* **of** *statement;*
> *assignment_statement*

.

statement
> : *us* **of** *block* = *us* **of** *statement;*
> *block*

.

simple_statement
> : use_token
> ident_token
> check_declaration (*lexeme* **of** ident_token, *us* **of** *simple_statement*);

.

◇

Let us have a closer look at the attributed production for *declaration_part* in Example 4.10. Before we develop the corresponding parsing procedure, we will first rewrite the syntactic construct that uses the **seq** operator into an equivalent construct that uses the **clos** operator, as follows:

declaration_part (**local** *local_table*: symbol_table)
> : *local_table* = *or* **of** *declaration_part;*
> *declaration*
> *local_table* = append (*decl* **of** *declaration*, /*to*/ *local_table*);
> { *declaration*
> *local_table* = append (*decl* **of** *declaration*, /*to*/ *local_table*);
> } **clos**
> *up* **of** *declaration_part* = *local_table;*

.

We will now show the corresponding parsing procedure for *declaration_part*. We apply the rules of Figure 3.13 to construct the syntactic part of the procedure, copy the attribute-evaluation rules into the procedure, and add input and output parameters that correspond to the inherited and synthesised attributes. The corresponding parsing procedure becomes:

---

void *declaration_part* (*symbol_table or_of_declaration_part,*
                            *symbol_table *up_of_declaration_part*)
{
  symbol_table   *local_table;*
  string   *decl_of_declaration;*

```
local_table  =  or_of_declaration_part;
declaration(&decl_of_declaration);
local_table  =  append(decl_of_declaration,  /* to */  local_table);
while (look_ahead  ==  var_token) {
  declaration(&decl_of_declaration);
  local_table  =  append(decl_of_declaration,  /* to */  local_table);
}
*up_of_declaration_part  =  local_table;
}
```

Notice that the body of this procedure contains declarations of 2 local variables, namely the variable *local_table* that corresponds to the local attribute *local_table* and the variable *decl_of_declaration* that corresponds to the attribute *decl* of *declaration*. The nonterminal *declaration* occurs in the right-hand side of the production for *declaration_part*.

The extended context-free grammar, presented at the beginning of this section, does not contain a syntactic construct with a **chain** operator. To illustrate the use of the **chain** operator in combination with local attributes, we will change the grammar so that declarations are separated by separator-tokens. A *declaration_part* can then be defined as:

> *declaration_part* : *declaration* **chain** separator_token .

The corresponding attributed production becomes:

declaration_part (**local** *local_table*: symbol_table)
  : *local_table* = *or* **of** *declaration_part*;
    { *declaration*
      local_table = append (*decl* **of** *declaration*, /*to*/ *local_table*);
    } **chain** separator_token
    up **of** *declaration_part* = *local_table*;

If we rewrite the **chain**-construct

> *declaration* **chain** separator_token

into

> *declaration* {separator_token *declaration*} **clos**

then the associated parsing procedure becomes:

```
void declaration_part (symbol_table or_of_declaration_part,
                         symbol_table *up_of_declaration_part)
{
  symbol_table    local_table;
  string          decl_of_declaration;
```

```
    local_table  =  or_of_declaration_part;
    declaration(& decl_of_declaration);
    local_table  =  append(decl_of_declaration, /* to */ local_table);
    while (look_ahead == separator_token) {
      if (look_ahead == separator_token) next_token();
      declaration(& decl_of_declaration);
      local_table  =  append(decl_of_declaration, /* to */ local_table);
    }
    *up_of_declaration_part  =  local_table;
}
```

The specification in Example 4.6 does not contain a syntactic construct with an **option** operator. To illustrate the use of the **option** operator in combination with local attributes, we will make another change to the grammar, and make the occurrence of a declaration-part in a block optional. The production for *block* is then

> *block* : begin_token *declaration_part* **option** *statement_part* end_token.

If the declaration-part is present, then the attribute-evaluation rules

> *or* **of** *declaration_part* = new_table();
> *us* **of** *statement_part* = concatenate (*up* **of** *declaration_part*, *us* **of** *block*);

must be applied. If, however, the declaration-part is not present, then the evaluation rule

> *us* **of** *statement_part* = *us* **of** *block*;

must be used. These evaluation rules can be put together in the following attributed production:

block (**local** *local_table*: symbol_table)
    : begin_token
    local_table = new_table();
    { *or* **of** *declaration_part* = new_table();
      declaration_part
      local_table = *up* **of** *declaration_part*;
    } **option**
    us **of** *statement_part* = concatenate (*local_table*, *us* **of** *block*);
    statement_part
    end_token

The associated parsing procedure becomes:

```
void block (symbol_table  us_of_block)
{
    symbol_table      or_of_declaration_part,
                      up_of_declaration_part,
                      us_of_statement_part,
                      local_table;

    if (look_ahead == begin_token) next_token();
    local_table = new_table();
    if (look_ahead == var_token) {
        or_of_declaration_part = new_table();
        declaration_part(or_of_declaration_part, &up_of_declaration_part);
        local_table = up_of_declaration_part;
    }
    us_of_statement_part = concatenate(local_table, us_of_block);
    statement_part(us_of_statement_part);
    if (look_ahead == end_token) next_token();
}
```

This concludes the introduction to attributed extended context-free grammars. In the next section we present a compiler generator based on this kind of attribute grammar, and we give scanner and parser specifications for SLANG as input for this generator. The parser specification will contain attributes and actions that check the context constraints, and that emit code. As in Chapter 3, a symbol table will be maintained that can be referenced from any place in the grammar. This means that declaration information is no longer stored as attribute instances in the parse tree, hence attributes *or*, *up* and *us* will no longer be used.

4.3   A compiler generator

In this section we will use a generator to specify a compiler that translates SLANG programs into VIM code.

The scanner generator and combined parser and attribute-evaluator generator together form a *compiler generator*. Figure 4.7 shows the role the compiler generator plays in generating a compiler. The scanner generator produces a scanner module and a set of token definitions from a set of regular expressions. The parser generator produces an attributed-parser program from an attributed extended context-free grammar and the set of token definitions that come from the scanner generator. This parser is a recursive-descent parser in which attributes are implemented as procedure parameters. The scanner, parser and attribute evaluator form a *compiler*. The compiler reads a source program and generates a VIM

program. The interpreter, which implements the machine VIM, reads the VIM
program and executes it.

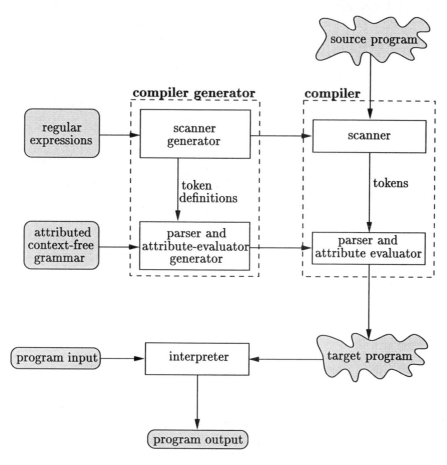

Figure 4.7 The role of the compiler generator.

In this chapter we will treat the compiler generator as a black box, i.e. we do not
explain the way in which a scanner and parser are generated from specifications.
For this we refer to Chapters 7 and 8. We will not formally define the specification
languages of the scanner and the parser and attribute-evaluator generator, but
instead simply demonstrate the languages by way of examples. These examples
will, of course, be taken from the specification of SLANG.

Attribute-evaluation rules are represented by *actions*, which are, in fact, procedures or functions. As a convenience to the user we can pre-define a number of
actions that convert strings from one type or representation to another, operate on

action	meaning
get_repr ( ): string	returns the representation of the scanned token
convert_to_lower ( ): string	returns the lower-case version of the representation
convert_to_upper ( ): string	returns the upper-case version of the representation
int_encode ( ): integer	returns an integer-typed version of the representation

Figure 4.8 Scanner actions.

the symbol table and emit code. The procedures defined in Chapter 3, for example, could be considered a useful set of actions.

4.3.1   The scanner specification

The *scanner generator* constructs a *scanner* from token definitions. The tokens are defined using regular expressions. In Section 3.1 we have seen that regular expressions can be represented by a finite automaton and that a finite automaton can be translated into a program. This program will always recognise the longest possible string matching a regular expression. In this section we will explain the different "sections" that make up the *scanner specification.*

Tokens are defined in 3 sections: the *symbols section, keywords section* and *rules section*. Character sets and strings, which may be used in the rules, can be defined in the *charsets section* and the *strings section*. The symbols, keywords and left-hand sides of rules (excluding the left-hand sides of rules that define a character string that must be skipped) form the set of terminals for the parser.

The scanner generator allows terminals to have synthesised attributes that are typed. The types that are available are integer, real, Boolean, character and (character) string. Attributes can be declared in the *attributes section.*

Actions. When the scanner is in an accept state, and an identifier, a keyword or a number has been recognised, then we need actions that operate on the representation of the token concerned. These actions produce the representation of the token, convert a string from lower to upper-case or vice versa, and convert a digit string to a binary number. A number of actions are defined in Figure 4.8. Notice that an action definition consists of an action name and a result-type. Every action always has 1 formal input parameter of type string. The type of the parameter is therefore not specified.

Attributes. Attributes are declared in the *attributes section*. For each attribute, its type, and the terminals for which the attribute is defined, must be specified.

Example 4.11

We can define the synthesised attributes *ident_lexeme* of terminal *ident_token* and *num_value* of terminal *num_token* in the following way:

attributes

    ident_lexeme   :   string   **syn of** ident_token.
    num_value   :   integer   **syn of** num_token.

                                                                        ◇

The attribute types must be one of the available types. If during the error recovery by the (generated) parser a missing terminal is inserted, its attributes are assigned a default value. Attributes of type integer and real are set to 0; attributes of type Boolean are set to false; attributes of type character are set to the ASCII value **nul**, and attributes of type string are set to the empty string. These values are assigned to the attributes using default actions, which are generated by the scanner generator.

Symbols. The external representations of the symbols to be recognised are declared in the *symbols section*. A specification of an external representation must be surrounded by white space (i.e. space or tab characters). If the syntactic operators **list** and **pack** are used in the parser-generator specification, the accompanying generated scanner must be able to recognise the symbols ",", "(" and ")". Therefore, when using these operators, the tokens *list_token*, *open_token* and *close_token* must be defined in the scanner-generator specification.

Example 4.12

In this example the symbols *open_token*, *close_token*, *list_token* and some other tokens are declared. Notice that their representations are surrounded by white space.

symbols

    open_token   :   (.
    close_token   :   )   .
    list_token   :   ,   .
    period_token   :   .   .
    separator_token :   ;   .
    becomes_token   :   :=   .

                                                                        ◇

Keywords. The external representations of the keywords are defined in the *keywords section*. A specification of an external representation must also be surrounded by white space.

Example 4.13

The keywords *begin_token* and *end_token* can be defined in the following way:

keywords

    begin_token   :   BEGIN .
    end_token   :   END   .

◇

In contrast to symbols, the external representations of keywords are not directly translated into a finite automaton. Instead, a representation rule for the keywords must be specified in the *rules section* of the scanner specification. We show how this is done shortly when we discuss the *rules section*.

Character sets. In the *charsets section*, specific sets of characters are specified that may be used in the *rules section* to denote a particular character set. A definition in the *charsets section* consists of a name and a denotation.

Example 4.14
In this example the character sets *ascii*, *rbrace*, *letter*, *capital* and *digit* are defined. The character set *ascii* represents the set of characters in the range from **nul** to **del**, *rbrace* consists of a single character, *letter* of lower-case letters, *capital* of upper-case letters, and *digit* of decimal digits.

charsets

    ascii   :   [**nul** .. **del**] .
    rbrace :   ["}"] .
    letter   :   ["a" .. "z"] .
    capital :   ["A" .. "Z"] .
    digit   :   ["0" .. "9"] .

◇

Strings. In the *strings section* character strings are defined. The defined string names may be used in the *rules section* to denote the character string. The string representation must be enclosed in either single or double quotes.

Example 4.15
The strings *lbrace* and *quote* can be defined as follows:

strings

    lbrace :   "{".
    quote   :   """.

◇

Rules. In the *rules section* the representation rules are specified that recognise groups of terminal symbols like keywords, identifiers and numbers. If the left-hand side of a representation rule has an attribute, then an action must be specified that assigns a value to the attribute. This action may start with the keyword **reserved**, which is used in the case that a rule matches a keyword and an identifier at the same time. The keyword **reserved** may optionally be followed by a conversion action of the recognised string, followed by the keyword **else**. After the keyword **else**, only attribute assignations are allowed. Using the keyword **reserved**, the generated scanner is directed to first check the keyword table for the converted recognised string. If the string concerned is found, then the associated keyword token is returned, otherwise the else-section is executed.

Example 4.16
The following rule defines keywords as reserved words, and both identifiers and keywords as case-insensitive.

rules
 ident_token : *{letter | capital}* *{letter | capital | digit}* **clos**
        reserved convert_to_upper ( )
        else *ident_lexeme* = get_repr ( ).

Here we have used the definitions of *letter*, *capital* and *digit* from Example 4.14 Notice that the keywords are handled as a subset of the identifiers. After the recognition of an identifier, it is first checked to see if the external representation found matches the representation of a keyword. If this is not the case, then the external representation must be an identifier.   ◇

If a rule is used only to recognise the keywords, then the keyword **verify** must occur in the left-hand side. In this case, the generated scanner checks the keyword table for the recognised string and returns the appropriate token if the keyword is found.

Example 4.17
This example illustrates the case that keywords are represented by capital letters, and identifiers by lower-case letters and digits.

rules
 verify   : *capital* **seq**.
 ident_token : *letter {letter | digit}* **clos**
        ident_lexeme = get_repr ( ) .

A finite automaton will be built that recognises strings of capital letters. Every string found will be compared to the keyword representations in the *keywords section*. If the capital letter string matches a keyword representation, then the associated keyword token is returned.   ◇

If a rule describes a sequence of characters that should be skipped, then the keyword **skip** should be used in the left-hand side.

Example 4.18
Comments defined as text between left and right braces can be skipped by using the following rule:

rules

> **skip**   :   *lbrace* {*ascii* − *rbrace*} **clos** *rbrace* .

Notice that we have used the syntactic operator "−" here. This operator computes the difference between 2 character sets.   ◇

4.3.2   A scanner specification for SLANG

To illustrate the ideas above, we now present a *scanner specification* for SLANG from which the compiler generator can generate a *scanner*. In the *rules section* we define keywords as strings of upper-case letters. Identifiers are strings of lower-case letters and digits, but must begin with a lower-case letter. Numbers are strings of digits. A comment is written between braces and will be skipped by the scanner. Strings of spaces will also be skipped by the scanner. The *charsets section* and the *strings section* contain definitions of character sets and strings that are used in the *rules section*. The symbols and keywords are defined in the *symbols section* and the *keywords section*, respectively. The *attributes section* defines a synthesised attribute *ident_lexeme* for identifiers, and a synthesised attribute *num_value* for numbers.

attributes

ident_lexeme	:	string	**syn of** ident_token.
num_value	:	integer	**syn of** num_token.

symbols

open_token	:	(	.
close_token	:	)	.
list_token	:	,	.
period_token	:	.	.
separator_token	:	;	.
becomes_token	:	:=	.
open_comment_token	:	{	.
close_comment_token	:	}	.
plus_token	:	+	.
minus_token	:	−	.
times_token	:	*	.
over_token	:	/	.
modulo_token	:			.
equal_token	:	=	.
not_equal_token	:	<>	.
less_than_token	:	<	.
less_or_equal_token	:	<=	.
greater_than_token	:	>	.
greater_or_equal_token	:	>=	.

keywords

begin_token	:	BEGIN	.
end_token	:	END	.
int_token	:	INT	.
var_token	:	VAR	.
procedure_token	:	PROC	.
call_token	:	CALL	.
read_token	:	READ	.
write_token	:	WRITE	.
if_token	:	IF	.
then_token	:	THEN	.
else_token	:	ELSE	.
fi_token	:	FI	.
while_token	:	WHILE	.
do_token	:	DO	.
od_token	:	OD	.
negate_token	:	NEG	.
absolute_token	:	ABS	.

charsets

blank	:	[**ht** .. **lf, sp**] .
ascii	:	[**nul** .. **del**] .
rbrace	:	["}"] .
letter	:	["a" .. "z"] .
capital	:	["A" .. "Z"] .
digit	:	["0" .. "9"] .

strings

lbrace	:	"{" .

rules

verify	:	*capital* **seq** .
ident_token	:	*letter* {*letter* | *digit*} **clos**
		$ident_lexeme = $ get_repr ( ) .
num_token	:	*digit* **seq**
		$num_value = $ int_encode ( ) .
skip	:	*blank* **seq** .
skip	:	*lbrace* {*ascii* − *rbrace*} **clos** *rbrace* .

4.3.3   The parser specification

The parser generator is based on the attributed extended context-free grammar formalism. In this section we will explain the different "sections" that may occur in the *parser specification*.

The parser generator allows terminals and nonterminals to have typed attributes. As in the scanner generator, the available types are integer, real, Boolean, character and (character) string. Moreover, there is an enumerated type *operation* that contains the operation codes of the instructions (e.g. **add**, **sub** or **eq**). The attributes, attributed production rules and start symbol are defined in the *attributes section*, *rules section* and *root section*, respectively.

Syntax conditions. The parser generator constructs a predictive top-down parser. A predictive top-down parser that is based on an extended context-free grammar satisfies the following 5 conditions (see also Section 3.2.1):

1. For each regular expression $E_1 \mid E_2 \mid \ldots \mid E_n$,
   $\forall\, i, j \ (1 \leq i < j \leq n)$: $\mathrm{DIRSET}(E_i) \cap \mathrm{DIRSET}(E_j) = \emptyset$.
2. For each regular expression E **option**:
   $\neg \mathrm{EMPTY}(E) \wedge (\mathrm{FIRST}(E) \cap \mathrm{FOLLOW}(E\,\textbf{option}) = \emptyset)$.
3. For each regular expression E **clos**:
   $\neg \mathrm{EMPTY}(E) \wedge (\mathrm{FIRST}(E) \cap \mathrm{FOLLOW}(E\,\textbf{clos}) = \emptyset)$.
4. For each regular expression E **seq**:
   $\neg \mathrm{EMPTY}(E) \wedge (\mathrm{FIRST}(E) \cap \mathrm{FOLLOW}(E\,\textbf{seq}) = \emptyset)$.
5. For each regular expression E_1 **chain** E_2:
   $\mathrm{DIRSET}(E_2) \cap \mathrm{FOLLOW}(E_1\,\textbf{chain}\,E_2) = \emptyset$.

The *parser generator* first computes the functions EMPTY, FIRST, FOLLOW and DIRSET, and then verifies the above syntactic conditions. If the conditions are fulfilled, then a *predictive recursive-descent parser* is generated according to the rules of Figure 3.13.

The generated parser supports *syntactic error recovery* (see Section 3.6.2). At any moment during parsing, the parser maintains a look-ahead set of markers. A marker is simply a token that the parser may expect, sometime in the future. If the next token that is read by the parser is illegal, but is a member of the marker set, then the parser assumes a token is missing, inserts the missing token, and continues. If the illegal token is not in the marker set, then the parser assumes the next token is superfluous, deletes it, and continues. This error-recovery strategy is included in the generated parser (the parser is generated according to the rules of Figure 3.19).

Actions. While parsing, we need *actions* for context-sensitive analysis and code generation. An *action definition* consists of an action name, followed by a list of parameter specifications between parentheses. Action names are followed by parentheses, even if they have no parameters. A parameter specification consists of its kind, its name and its type. The kind is represented by the keyword **in**, **out** or **inout**, indicating that the parameter is of kind input, output, or both input and output. The type must be one of the available types.

An *action call* consists of an action name, followed by an argument list between parentheses. The argument list corresponds to the parameter list of the action definition. The arguments may be attributes, and integer, character or string denotations. Denotations may only be input arguments.

In Figures 4.9 through 4.13 we show a number of action definitions that we will use in the parser specification for SLANG. Actions for storing information in, and retrieving information from, the symbol table are shown in Figure 4.9. Note that the 2 functions *get_sn* and *get_dpl* that are defined in Chapter 3 have been replaced by the single action *get_sn_dpl*, which retrieves both the segment number and the displacement from the symbol table. Also note that the current segment number is an implicit parameter in the action *create_definition*. An action to check if an identifier has the correct kind (constant, variable or procedure) is shown in Figure 4.10. The action call *check_kind*(proc_kind,*def*,true), for example, checks if the identifier, pointed to by def, is declared as a procedure. The action call *check_kind*(proc_kind,*def*,false) on the other hand, checks that the identifier is not declared as a procedure, i.e. if its kind is var_kind or const_kind. Actions for manipulating the address and length tables are given in Figure 4.11. Actions for code generation are presented in Figure 4.12. Special attention should be given to the action *emit_load*, which generates an ldcon instruction for a constant and an ldvar instruction for a variable. The *kind* field of the definition record indicates which instruction must be generated. Finally, some actions to evaluate attributes are shown in Figure 4.13. Note that the action *assign_op* can be used to assign the value of an operation code (e.g. add or eq) to an attribute. The action *clear_op* can be used to assign the default operation code noop to an attribute.

Attributes. It is possible to define 3 types of attributes in the *attributes section*:

- attributes associated with (non)terminals, i.e. inherited and synthesised attributes
- global attributes
- local attributes

Both synthesised and inherited attributes can be defined for nonterminals, but only synthesised attributes are allowed for terminals. The same attribute name can be defined for different (non)terminals. An *inherited attribute* can be assigned in the production in which it occurs in the right-hand side. A *synthesised attribute* can be assigned in the production in which it occurs in the left-hand side.

In some systems, the attribute evaluator aborts as soon as a syntactic error is detected. A parser generated by the compiler generator, however, continues to evaluate attributes after encountering a syntactic error. This means that the generated parser keeps verifying the context constraints, even after program text has been deleted or inserted. Deleting a superfluous token cannot cause an attribute to become unassigned, but inserting a missing token can. The compiler generator, therefore, requires that the declarations of all synthesised attributes include a *default* action. This default action is executed if the nonterminal is not encountered in the input of the generated parser. Default values are not needed for the inherited attributes because the inserted symbols are not parsed.

action	meaning
enter_scope ( )	creates a new scope record, and increments the scope level
exit_scope ( )	deletes the definition records of all identifiers in the current scope; deletes the current scope record, and decrements the scope level
current_scope (**out** *level*: integer)	returns in *level* the scope level of the block currently being parsed
create_definition (**out** *def*: def_ptr; **in** *dpl_or_value_or_index*: integer; **in** *type*: e_type; **in** *kind*: e_kind)	creates a new definition record, and initialises its fields with the values of *dpl_or_value_or_index*, *type* and *kind*; the parameter *sn* is implicit; output parameter *def* points to the created record
insert_definition (**in** *name*: string; **in** *def*: def_ptr)	adds the name *name* to the identifier tree, and the record, pointed to by *def*, to the definition list of the symbol table
find_definition (**out** *def*: def_ptr; **in** *name*: string)	returns in *def* a pointer to the current definition record of identifier *name*
get_sn_dpl (**out** *sn*, *dpl*: integer; **in** *def*: def_ptr)	returns in *sn* the segment number and in *dpl* the displacement of the identifier defined in the definition record, pointed to by *def*
get_address (**out** *address*: integer; **in** *def*: def_ptr)	returns in *address* the index in the address table of the procedure defined in the definition record, pointed to by *def*

Figure 4.9 Actions for symbol-table management.

action	meaning
check_kind (**in** *kind*: e_kind; **in** *def*: def_ptr; **in** *truthval*: Boolean)	checks if the kind of the record, pointed to by *def*, is equal or not equal to *kind*

Figure 4.10 Actions for checking context constraints.

action	meaning
get_label (**out** *index*: integer)	a free position in the address table is returned in *index*
get_index (**out** *index*: integer)	a free position in the length table is returned in *index*
emit_label (**in** *index*: integer)	the current value of *ic* is stored at position *index* in the address table
enter_length (**in** *index*, *length*: integer)	the value of *length* is stored at position *index* in the length table

Figure 4.11 Actions for manipulating the address and length table.

Example 4.19
In this example we show definitions of an inherited attribute and 2 synthesised attributes with default actions.

attributes:

inh_dpl	:	integer	**inh of** *variable_declaration.*
syn_dpl	:	integer	**syn of** *variable_declaration, left_part* **with default** clear_int.
length	:	integer	**syn of** *declaration_part* **with default** clear_int.

◇

Note that the generated scanner assigns values to the attributes of the terminals, and not the generated parser. The scanner generator produces a token file that contains all terminals, their synthesised attributes, and associated default actions. These default actions may be executed by the parser if tokens are missing and inserted in the input.

The same attributes are sometimes used in many productions. This can result in many copy actions of an attribute value (see the examples in Sections 4.1.2 and 4.2). In order to prevent these copy actions and to save space, *global attributes* can be used. Global attributes can be assigned values repeatedly. Moreover, global attributes are shared by all nonterminals, i.e. the global attributes are associated with the total language and form a shared storage that can be referred to from any place in the grammar. Global attributes can also be used as arguments in action calls. However, the use of global attributes has 2 drawbacks:

- Unlike inherited, synthesised and local attributes, the parser generator does not check whether global attributes have a value before they are used.
- It is generally considered poor programming practice to use global attributes (except in the case of the symbol table).

In the compiler generator the symbol table can be used as a global attribute. The definition of the attribute is implicit and need not be done by the user.

action	meaning
`initialise_vimcode ( )`	initialises the generation of VIM code; opens the code file
`finalise_vimcode ( )`	generates a `halt` instruction; writes the address and length table to output files, and closes the files
`emit_crseg (in` *level, index*: `integer)`	generates a `crseg` instruction with the values of *level* and *index* as arguments
`emit (in` *code*: `operation)`	creates a parameter-less instruction
`emit_stvar (in` *sn, dpl*: `integer)`	generates an `stvar` instruction with the values of *sn* and *dpl* as arguments

`emit_jump (`
`in` *code*: `operation;`
`in` *index*: `integer)`
	generates a jump instruction with the value of *index* as index in the address table

`emit_load (in` *def*: `def_ptr)`	determines if *def* points to the record of a constant or a variable, and generates an `ldcon` or `ldvar` instruction; the value, or the segment number and displacement, are taken from the record, pointed to by *def*
`emit_ldcon (in` *value*: `integer)`	generates an `ldcon` instruction with the value of *value* as argument

Figure 4.12 Actions for code generation.

action	meaning

`assign_int (`
`out` *dest*: `integer;`
`in` *source*: `integer)`
	assigns the integer value of *source* to *dest*

`clear_int (out` *dest*: `integer)`	assigns the value 0 to *dest*

`increment_int (`
`inout` *dest*: `integer;`
`in` *value*: `integer)`
	increments the integer value of *dest* by the integer value *value*

`assign_op (`
`out` *dest*: `operation;`
`in` *source*: `operation)`
	assigns the operation value *source* to *dest*

`clear_op (out` *dest*: `operation)`	assigns the operation value `noop` to *dest*

Figure 4.13 Actions for attribute evaluation.

Within a production we can define *local attributes*. The use of local attributes is explained in the *rules section*, which we describe next.

Rules. The productions of the grammar are defined in the *rules section*. A production must be defined for each nonterminal. The right-hand side of a production consists of terminals, nonterminals, action calls and syntactic operators.

An attribute that occurs as an argument of an action call in a production is a combination of a (non)terminal occurrence and its attribute. In order to distinguish different occurrences of the same (non)terminal in a production, the occurrences are assigned unique numbers. The occurrence of an attribute is specified as a **of** $X \# i$, where:

- a is the attribute name;
- X is the (non)terminal name;
- i is the occurrence number of (non)terminal X in the production.

The occurrence number of the left-hand side nonterminal is 0. The occurrence numbers of the (non)terminals on the right-hand side start at 1. If a (non)terminal occurs only once in the production, then no occurrence number has to be specified. In that case, the default occurrence number of the left-hand side is 0, and of the right-hand side (non)terminals is 1.

Local attributes are associated with a specific production, and can be used for intermediate calculations. Like global attributes, local attributes can be assigned values repeatedly. Local attributes may be used as arguments in action calls.

The position of an action call in a production determines when it is executed. Syntactically, an action call can be viewed as a nonterminal whose production has an empty right-hand side—thus, an action call may never be directly followed by a syntactic operator, as this would lead to a parsing conflict (see the syntax conditions at the beginning of this section).

Example 4.20
The attributed production of the nonterminal *declaration_part* of SLANG is the following:[2]

declaration_part (**local** *dpl*, *over_procs*: integer)
  : clear_int (*dpl*)
    { *constant_declaration*
    | assign_int (*inh_dpl* **of** *variable_declaration*, *dpl*)
    variable_declaration
    assign_int (*dpl*, *syn_dpl* **of** *variable_declaration*)
    } **clos**
    assign_int (*length* **of** *declaration_part*, *dpl*)
    { get_label (*over_procs*)

---

[2]See the translation rules in Section 2.5.1.

      emit_jump (**jump**, *over_procs*)
      procedure_declaration **seq**
      emit_label (*over_procs*)
} **option**

.

We assume that the attribute declarations in Example 4.19 hold for this production, i.e. nonterminal *variable_declaration* has inherited attribute *inh_dpl* and synthesised attribute *syn_dpl*, and nonterminal *declaration_part* has synthesised attribute *length*.

We now explain the right-hand side of the above production for *declaration_part*. The reader should compare this production with the procedure *declaration_part* in Section 3.5. The above production is the specification from which the compiler generator can generate the corresponding procedure.

Every variable in a block has a displacement. The displacement must be 0 for the first variable in the scope, and this value must be incremented for every subsequent variable. The latter is the responsibility of *variable_declaration*.

This production has a local attribute *dpl*. At the beginning of *declaration_part*, the action *clear_int* sets the value of *dpl* to 0. Each time a variable declaration is parsed, the action *assign_int* will assign the current value of *dpl* to the inherited attribute *inh_dpl* **of** *variable_declaration*. The variable declaration, in turn, will assign this value to its own local attribute *dpl*, which will be incremented for each variable that is encountered. At the end of the variable declaration, the value of *dpl* is returned in the synthesised attribute *syn_dpl* **of** *variable_declaration*. The action *assign_int* will then assign this value to the local attribute *dpl* of *declaration_part*. This process is repeated for every variable declaration that is parsed. After all variable declarations have been parsed, the current value of *dpl* is the length of the segment. The action *assign_int* assigns, therefore, the value of *dpl* to the synthesised attribute *length* **of** *declaration_part*.

If the declaration part contains 1 or more procedure declarations, then a jump over the translations of the blocks of the locally declared procedures must be made, as these blocks may only be executed when the procedures are called. The action *get_label* claims a free position in the address table, and assigns its index to the local attribute *over_procs*. The action *emit_jump* then emits a jump instruction. Finally, when all procedure declarations have been parsed, the action *emit_label* stores the current value of the instruction counter in the address table at position *over_procs*.   ◇

The parser generator verifies that all input arguments are assigned in each action call. The system has no provisions to verify whether the output arguments will be assigned, because the procedure bodies (associated with the action definitions) are beyond the field of view of the generator system.

The parser generator performs 2 tests on the attributed input grammar: the reachability test and the availability test. In the *reachability test*, the generator system verifies for every occurrence of an attribute a **of** X that acts as a parameter of an action call whether a reference to X is allowed from this position in the production.

Example 4.21
Consider the production

A : {*action*$_1$ X | *action*$_2$ Y} Z.

Clearly, X or Y will occur in a parse tree, but not both X and Y. Thus, neither may *action*$_1$ refer to Y, nor may *action*$_2$ refer to X. Similarly, in the rule

A : X **option** *action* Y.

action may not refer to X because it is not known whether X will occur in the parse tree. ◇

In the *availability test*, the generator system verifies for every production whether all synthesised attributes of its left-hand side, and all inherited attributes of its right-hand side, are defined. Moreover, for every action it verifies whether the input arguments are available on time if the input text is parsed from left to right.

Root. The start symbol of the grammar is defined in the *root section*. Actions that must be performed before and after parsing the root can be specified in this section.

Example 4.22
In this example the nonterminal *program_declaration* is defined.

root
    initialise_vimcode ( )
    program_declaration
    finalise_vimcode ( )
    .

Notice that the actions *initialise_vimcode* and *finalise_vimcode* are performed before and after parsing the root. In Chapter 3 these actions were part of the procedure *program_declaration*. ◇

4.3.4 A parser specification for SLANG

To illustrate the ideas above, we now present a *parser specification* for SLANG from which the compiler generator can generate a context-sensitive parser and code generator. In the specification we first list the attribute definitions in the *attributes section*, then the start symbol in the *root section*, and we finish with the attributed productions in the *rules section*.

Notice that the input and output parameters that were used in the procedures in Chapter 3 are now defined as inherited and synthesised attributes, respectively, and that many local variables in these procedures are now defined as local attributes. The reader is invited to carefully compare the specification in this chapter and the implementation in Chapter 3. It should then become clear that there is a close correspondence between the specification and the implementation.

attributes

syn_sn	:	integer	**syn of** *left_part* **with default** clear_int.
inh_dpl	:	integer	**inh of** *variable_declaration.*
syn_dpl	:	integer	**syn of** *variable_declaration, left_part* **with default** clear_int.
length	:	integer	**syn of** *declaration_part* **with default** clear_int.
op	:	operation	**syn of** *add_operator, multiply_operator,* *unary_operator, relational_operator* **with default** clear_op.

root

> initialise_vimcode ( )
> *program_declaration*
> finalise_vimcode ( )

> .

rules

program_declaration
  : enter_scope ( )
    block
    exit_scope ( )
    period_token

  .

block (**local** *level, length_index*: integer)
  : begin_token
    declaration_part
    current_scope (*level*)
    get_index (*length_index*)
    enter_length (*length_index,* length **of** *declaration_part*)
    emit_crseg (*level, length_index*)
    statement_part
    emit (**dlseg**)
    end_token

  .

declaration_part (**local** *dpl*, *over_procs*: integer)
  : clear_int (*dpl*)
    { *constant_declaration*
    | assign_int (*inh_dpl* **of** *variable_declaration*, *dpl*)
      variable_declaration
      assign_int (*dpl*, *syn_dpl* **of** *variable_declaration*)
    } **clos**
    assign_int (*length* **of** *declaration_part*, *dpl*)
    { get_label (*over_procs*)
      emit_jump (**jump**, *over_procs*)
      procedure_declaration **seq**
      emit_label (*over_procs*)
    } **option**
    .

constant_declaration (**local** *def*: def_ptr)
  : *type_declarer*
    { ident_token
      equal_token
      num_token
      create_definition (*def*, *num_value* **of** num_token, int_type, const_kind)
      insert_definition (*ident_lexeme* **of** ident_token, *def*)
    } **list**
    separator_token
    .

type_declarer
  : int_token
    .

variable_declaration (**local** *dpl*: integer; *def*: def_ptr)
  : var_token
    type_declarer
    assign_int (*dpl*, *inh_dpl* **of** *variable_declaration*)
    { ident_token
      create_definition (*def*, *dpl*, int_type, var_kind)
      insert_definition (*ident_lexeme* **of** ident_token, *def*)
      increment_int (*dpl*, 1)
    } **list**
    assign_int (*syn_dpl* **of** *variable_declaration*, *dpl*)
    separator_token
    .

procedure_declaration (**local** *address*: integer; *def*: def_ptr)
  : procedure_token
    ident_token
    get_label (*address*)
    emit_label (*address*)
    create_definition (*def*, *address*, **no_type**, **proc_kind**)
    insert_definition (*ident_lexeme* **of** ident_token, *def*)
    enter_scope ( )
    block
    exit_scope ( )
    emit (**return**)
    separator_token
  .

statement_part
  : *statement* **chain** separator_token
  .

statement
  : *assignment_statement*
  | *if_statement*
  | *while_statement*
  | *call_statement*
  | *read_statement*
  | *write_statement*
  .

assignment_statement
  : *left_part*
    becomes_token
    expression
    emit_stvar (*syn_sn* **of** *left_part*, *syn_dpl* **of** *left_part*)
  .

left_part (**local** *def*: def_ptr)
  : ident_token
    find_definition (*def*, *ident_lexeme* **of** ident_token)
    check_kind (**var_kind**, *def*, true)
    get_sn_dpl (*syn_sn* **of** *left_part*, *syn_dpl* **of** *left_part*, *def*)
  .

if_statement (**local** *over_then_part, over_else_part*: integer)
  : if_token
     relation
     then_token
     get_label (*over_then_part*)
     emit_jump (jiff, *over_then_part*)
     statement_part
     { get_label (*over_else_part*)
       emit_jump (jump, *over_else_part*)
       emit_label (*over_then_part*)
       else_token
       statement_part
       emit_label (*over_else_part*)
     | (* no else_part *)
       emit_label (*over_then_part*)
     }
     fi_token
     .

while_statement (**local** *begin_while_stat, end_while_stat*: integer)
  : while_token
     get_label (*begin_while_stat*)
     emit_label (*begin_while_stat*)
     relation
     get_label (*end_while_stat*)
     emit_jump (jiff, *end_while_stat*)
     do_token
     statement_part
     od_token
     emit_jump (jump, *begin_while_stat*)
     emit_label (*end_while_stat*)
     .

call_statement (**local** *address*: integer; *def*: def_ptr)
  : call_token
     ident_token
     find_definition (*def, ident_lexeme* of ident_token)
     check_proc (proc_kind, *def*, true)
     get_address (*address, def*)
     emit_jump (call, *address*)
     .

read_statement (**local** *sn*, *dpl*: integer; *def*: def_ptr)
  : read_token
    { ident_token
     find_definition (*def*, *ident_lexeme* **of** ident_token)
     check_kind (**var_kind**, *def*, true)
     get_sn_dpl (*sn*, *dpl*, *def*)
     emit (**rdint**)
     emit_stvar (*sn*, *dpl*)
    } **list pack**
  .

write_statement
  : write_token
    { *expression*
     emit (**wrint**)
    } **list pack**
  .

expression
  : *term*
    { *add_operator*
     term
     emit (*op* **of** *add_operator*)
    } **clos**
  .

term
  : *factor*
    { *multiply_operator*
     factor
     emit (*op* **of** *multiply_operator*)
    } **clos**
  .

factor
  : *unary_operator*
    operand
    emit (*op* **of** *unary_operator*)
  | *operand*
  .

operand (**local** *def:* def_ptr)
  : ident_token
    find_definition (*def, ident_lexeme* **of** ident_token)
    check_proc (**proc_kind**, *def*, false)
    emit_load (*def*)
  | num_token
    emit_ldcon (*num_value* **of** num_token)
  | *expression* **pack**
  .

add_operator
  : plus_token
    assign_op (*op* **of** *add_operator*, add)
  | minus_token
    assign_op (*op* **of** *add_operator*, sub)
  .

multiply_operator
  : times_token
    assign_op (*op* **of** *multiply_operator*, mul)
  | over_token
    assign_op (*op* **of** *multiply_operator*, dvi)
  | modulo_token
    assign_op (*op* **of** *multiply_operator*, mdl)
  .

unary_operator
  : negate_token
    assign_op (*op* **of** *unary_operator*, neg)
  | absolute_token
    assign_op (*op* **of** *unary_operator*, abs)
  .

relation
  : *expression*
    relational_operator
    expression
    emit (*op* **of** *relational_operator*)
  .

relational_operator
  : equal_token
    assign_op (*op* **of** *relational_operator*, eq)

| not_equal_token
     assign_op (*op* **of** *relational_operator*, **ne**)
| less_than_token
     assign_op (*op* **of** *relational_operator*, **lt**)
| less_or_equal_token
     assign_op (*op* **of** *relational_operator*, **le**)
| greater_than_token
     assign_op (*op* **of** *relational_operator*, **gt**)
| greater_or_equal_token
     assign_op (*op* **of** *relational_operator*, **ge**)

.

4.4   Exercises

1. Figure 4.6 shows for the sentence

   begin
       variable_declaration
       assignment_statement
         begin
           variable_declaration
           assignment_statement
         end
     end

   the attributed parse tree according to the attribute grammar of Example 4.8. Give for this sentence also the attributed parse trees according to the attribute grammars of Examples 4.9 and 4.6. Show the attribute dependencies with arrows as in Figure 4.6.

2. Rewrite the attribute grammars of Examples 4.8 and 4.6 so that the attribute *or* has been removed. Declarations are thus collected purely bottom-up, i.e. by means of the attribute *up* only. You may give *up* a different name, if you wish. Show the information flow of both attribute grammars by means of an example of an attributed parse tree.

3. Consider the specification of the if-statement in Section 4.3.4. Give the corresponding procedure that performs parsing and attribute evaluation. Follow exactly the method of the compiler generator, i.e. generate a parser according to the rules of Figure 3.13, and insert actions as described in Section 4.2. Compare your result with the procedure for if-statement in Section 3.5. What is the difference and how do you explain this?

4. Assume that SLANG is extended with a repeat-statement, as defined in Exercise 2 of Section 2.7. Construct the attributed parser specification for this repeat-statement.

5. Assume that SLANG is extended with a for-statement, as explained in Exercise 3 of Section 2.7. Construct the attributed parser specification for this for-statement. Explain the necessary changes to the symbol table and the actions that operate on the table for the handling of the control variable.

6. Assume that SLANG is extended with a case-statement, as explained in Exercise 4 of Section 2.7. Construct the attributed parser specification for this case-statement.

4.5   Laboratory

The language we describe is intended as a laboratory assignment in a computer-science course. The language differs from SLANG in that it is based on the concept of expressions. Normally, we differentiate between statements and expressions: the former are used to carry out actions, and the latter to compute values. In the language that is proposed here, statements not only carry out actions, they also compute values.

There are some other differences with SLANG. Declarations and statements may occur in any order. The only restriction is that the declaration of a variable or constant must precede its use. The language has more types and operators than SLANG, and the language allows a multiple assignment.

The student is invited to develop a lexical syntax (i.e. a specification of the tokens) and context-sensitive syntax (i.e. an attribute grammar) that implements this language. The underlying (extended) context-free grammar must be predictive. While the student will find suggestions for the syntax of this language in this chapter, the student is encouraged to choose his or her own syntax.

It is suggested that a lexical specification be developed first, followed by an extended context-free grammar. The major problem with the context-free grammar will be making it predictive. Context-sensitive features (e.g. attributes) can then be added to the grammar. In the more difficult extensions to the language, which involve more complex data structures, this may also involve extending the symbol table. Finally, actions that generate code can be added to the grammar. This will probably require the student to create his or her own actions that do type checking, emit interpreter instructions and manipulate the symbol table. It may also require the student to add new instructions to the interpreter. A possible extension of the instruction set of VIM is presented in Figure 4.14. In order to understand how these and other instructions of VIM can be used, it is important to know how data are represented. We will use 3 types of data: integer, Boolean and character.

These data have an external representation on the keyboard and the screen, and an internal representation in memory. Boolean and character values are internally represented by integer values. The logical value **true** is internally represented by 1, and the value **false** by 0. Characters are internally represented by their ordinal value in the ASCII set.

We begin by describing the basic expression language in Section 4.5.1. We then describe 2 extensions to this language:

- a conditional statement, in Section 4.5.2, and
- a while statement, in Section 4.5.3.

These extensions involve scope rules that are more complicated than those in SLANG. In Chapter 5 we extend the expression language still further by adding procedures, functions, arrays, records and pointers.

4.5.1   Basic expression language

In the basic expression language we have declarations and expressions. An expression can be an arithmetic expression, an assignment statement, a read statement or a print statement. Every variable and constant must be declared, and the declaration of a variable or constant (called the defining occurrence) must precede its use (applied occurrence) in the text.

An *arithmetic expression* consists of a number of operands separated by operators. An operator can have the type integer, Boolean and character. An operand can be a variable, constant and denotation, and also have the type integer, Boolean and character. Examples of integer, Boolean and character denotations are 12, **true** and "a" (respectively). Not all types of operands, however, can be used in combination with all operators. The operators, their relative priorities (from highest to lowest), and the permitted combination of types is shown in the table in Figure 4.15. Note that the operators $=$ and $<>$ are overloaded.

An *assignment statement* generates a result. This result is the value of the variable on the left-hand side of the assignment symbol. The type of an assignment statement is the type of its left-hand side variable. Further, the type of the left-hand side variable must be equal to the type of the right-hand side. Because an assignment statement has a value, it can be used as a "sub-expression" in another statement or expression. Consider the following example:

$$x := y := x + y$$

The value of the assignment statement $y := x + y$ is the value of $x + y$. This value is assigned to x, and is, therefore, also the value of the total statement. Notice that the operator $:=$ is implicitly right-associative.

An assignment statement cannot be used everywhere in an expression, however. The following expression, for example, is not allowed:

$$x + y := 1 + y$$

Removal and copy

instruction	meaning
pop	removes the value on top of the stack
copy	duplicates the value on top of the stack

Unary logical operation

This instruction first removes the top (logical) value, boolval (say), from the stack, and performs the following action:

instruction	meaning
not	stores the logical value ¬boolval on the stack

Binary logical operations

These instructions first remove the 2 top (logical) values, boolval2 and boolval1 (say), in this order from the stack, and perform for each instruction the following actions:

instruction	meaning
and	stores the logical value boolval1 $\land$ boolval2 on the stack
or	stores the logical value boolval1 $\lor$ boolval2 on the stack

Input and output

instruction	meaning
rdint	reads an integer value from the keyboard and stores its internal representation on the stack
rdbool	reads a logical value from the keyboard and stores its internal representation on the stack
rdchar	reads a character value from the keyboard and stores its internal representation on the stack
wrint	removes the top value from the stack and writes its external integer representation to the screen
wrbool	removes the top value from the stack and writes its external logical representation to the screen
wrchar	removes the top value from the stack and writes its external character representation to the screen

Figure 4.14 Instructions of the virtual machine VIM.

priority	operators	valid operand types	result type
1	(unary) $-$, $+$	integer	integer
	(unary) **not**	Boolean	Boolean
2	$*$, $/$, **mod**	integer	integer
3	$+$, $-$	integer	integer
4	$<$, $<=$, $>=$, $>$	integer	Boolean
	$=$, $<>$	integer, Boolean, character	Boolean
5	**and**	Boolean	Boolean
6	**or**	Boolean	Boolean

Figure 4.15   Arithmetic operators, their relative priorities, and the types of their operands and result.

Depending on their relative priorities, we could evaluate this expression as $x + (y := 1) + y$, which is $x + 2$, or as $(x + y) := (1 + y)$. Neither is desirable. We avoid this kind of construction by stipulating that there may only be a single variable on the left-hand side of an assignment operator.

A *read statement* has the general form **read** (*varlist*), where *varlist* is a list of variables (at least 1). A read statement also generates a result. The type of a read statement depends on what is read:

- If only 1 variable is read, then the type of the read statement is equal to the type of this variable, and the result is its value.
- If more than 1 variable is read, then the read statement has type *void*.

A result that has type void corresponds to a value that cannot be used. More precisely, it corresponds to the empty value. The following expression, for example, is not allowed because the read statement has type void:

   $x + $ **read** (y, z)

A *print statement* has the general form **print** (*exprlist*), where *exprlist* is a list of expressions (at least 1). A print statement is analogous to a read statement, with the exception that not only can variables be printed, but also expressions.

- Each expression in a print statement must have a type that is not void.
- If only 1 expression is printed, then the type of the print statement is equal to the type of this expression, and the result is its value.
- If more than 1 expression is printed, then the print statement itself has type void.

For example, the following statement prints the value of x, and then increments x:

   $x := $ **print** $(x) + 1$

In contrast to a statement or expression, a declaration does not generate a result. A declaration is said to have type *no_type*.

The basic expression language also has a *compound expression*, which is a sequence of expressions and declarations, separated by semicolons. However, because a compound expression must also generate a result, we stipulate that a compound expression must end in an expression (and must not end in a declaration). The result and type, then, of the compound expression is the result and type of this (final) expression. The scope of any declaration in the compound expression is the compound expression itself, but declaration must precede use. Consider, for example, the compound expression that reads 2 Boolean variables and evaluates a Boolean expression:

> **var boolean:** a; **read** (a);
> **var boolean:** b; **read** (b);
> $(a$ **and not** $b)$ **or** $($**not** a **and** $b)$

This compound expression has type Boolean, and generates the *exclusive-or* of the 2 variables. Note that the syntax that we have used here for the declaration is only a suggestion. We could also have written the declarations using the form **var boolean** a, for example, or even **var** a: **boolean**.

A compound expression that is enclosed in parentheses, or the keywords **begin** and **end**, is called a *closed compound expression*. The result and type of a closed compound expression is the same as the result and type of the enclosed compound expression. Because a closed compound expression generates a result, it can also be an operand. For example, we can assign the result of the above compound expression to some Boolean variable c as follows:

> $c :=$ (**var boolean:** a; **read**(a);
>   **var boolean:** b; **read**(b);
> $(a$ **and not** $b)$ **or** $($**not** a **and** $b)$
>   )

Note that the Boolean variables a and b are only defined inside the closed compound expression.

To understand the consequences of treating statements as expressions, particularly from an implementation point of view, let us look at some program constructs. Consider the following program fragment:

> $x := y := 1$;
> $z := 2$

The result of the assignment statement $y := 1$ is the value 1. This value is then assigned to x. In a sense, this value is being re-used. The assignment to x also generates a value 1. This value, however, is redundant and must be discarded. The following assignment statement $(z := 2)$ is then executed, and generates the value 2. Depending on the context of this fragment, this value may also have to be discarded. In practice, when an expression is executed, it leaves a value on the arithmetic stack, ready to be used by another expression. If this value is not used, then it must be popped off the stack. This situation arises when we have 2 expressions separated by a semicolon.

We will see that there are other situations where values need to be discarded. The value generated by the last expression in the main program, for example, must also be discarded (the program does not generate a result). Consider, for example, the following program:

> **begin**
> $\quad x := 1;$
> $\quad$ **print** (x)
> **end**.

When the print statement is executed, it generates the value of x, namely 1. This value must be discarded.

Care should be taken in building the compiler to ensure that values that are generated by expressions are either re-used or explicitly discarded.

4.5.2   The conditional statement

We can extend and improve the basic expression language by adding a conditional statement. A conditional statement adds more expressive power to the language. Like assignment, read and print statements, a conditional statement generates a result. We can use it in the following way, for example:

> $x :=$ **if** b **then** 0 **else** 1 **fi**

Depending on the value of b, x will be set to 0 or 1. Because a conditional statement generates a result, it can be used as an operand. Possible operands, then, in the extended expression language are conditional statements, closed compound expressions, and variables, constants and denotations of type integer, Boolean and character.

The general form of a conditional statement is as follows:

> **if** comp_expr$_0$ **then** comp_expr$_1$ **else** comp_expr$_2$ **fi**

where comp_expr is a compound expression. Note that this is only a suggested syntax. The else part (i.e. **else** comp_expr$_2$) in a conditional statement is optional. The following conditions on the types apply:

- The type of comp_expr$_0$ must be Boolean.
- If there is no else part, then the statement has type void.
- If there is an else part, then:
  - If comp_expr$_1$ and comp_expr$_2$ have the same type, then this is the type of the conditional statement.
  - If comp_expr$_1$ and comp_expr$_2$ have different types, then the conditional statement has type void.

Further, the following special scope rules apply.

- The scope of declarations in comp_expr$_0$ is all 3 compound expressions.

- The scope of declarations in comp_expr$_1$ is only itself.
- The scope of declarations in comp_expr$_2$ is only itself.

4.5.3 The while statement

An iterative construct is added to the expression language in the form of a while statement. A while statement has the general form

while comp_expr$_0$ **do** comp_expr$_1$ **od**

The following conditions on the type and scope apply:

- The while statement has type void.
- The type of comp_expr$_0$ is Boolean.
- The scope of declarations in comp_expr$_0$ is both compound expressions.
- The scope of declarations in comp_expr$_1$ is only itself.

Because a while statement has type void, it cannot be used as an operand. In fact, a while statement is an expression, along with assignment statements, read statements and print statements. Consider the following example of a while statement:

while b **do**
    $x := x + 1;$
    print (x)
od

The print statement within the while statement generates a result. This result must be discarded because the while statement has type void.

4.6 Bibliographic notes

Context-free grammars and attribute grammars have proved to be the two fundamental formalisms for compiler construction.

In 1968 Knuth [90], and later [91], introduced the basic concepts of attribute grammars (i.e. inherited and synthesised attributes and evaluation rules). The idea of synthesised attributes is, however, older and dates back to 1961 when Irons [83] used them to specify the translation of ALGOL 60. Since Knuth's papers a wealth of literature has appeared on attribute grammars, in particular evaluation methods. See the references contained in Chapter 9. Examples 4.6 and 4.7 in this chapter have been adapted from Wilhelm [146], and Example 4.8 was inspired by Bochmann [24].

Many compiler generators are based on attribute grammars. Most of them generate multi-phase compilers in which the first phase is restricted to scanning and parsing, and subsequent phases (context analysis, optimisation and code generation) are based on attribute grammars. Examples of systems that combine parsing and attribute evaluation are CWS2 by Bochmann and Ward [25]; the Language Implementation LAboratory LILA (distributed under the name MIRA), developed by a group under Lewi [97, 98]; the compiler generator Coco [118], a microprocessor-based system, developed by Rechenberg and Mössenböck; and TCGS (Twente Compiler-Generator System) due to Alblas, Groen, Schaap-Kruseman and Schepers [16, 17, 61]. For each of these systems, however, facilities are available to produce multi-phase compilers.

Chapter 5

Extensions to the source language and virtual machine

In this chapter we add *arrays* and *procedure parameters* to SLANG. The arrays are *dynamic* in the sense that the bounds are expressions that may contain variables and procedure parameters. The bounds are computed when the array declaration is executed, i.e. after entering the procedure in which the array is declared. The procedure parameters are *value* and *reference parameters*. The extended source language will be discussed in Section 5.1. The new language features require some modifications to the memory organisation, instruction set and interpreter of the virtual machine VIM. The extended version of VIM will be discussed in Section 5.2 and 5.4. The translation from SLANG to VIM is discussed in Section 5.3 and 5.5. Finally, in Section 5.6 we discuss the compilation of programs written in SLANG into code that will run on VIM.

5.1 Extensions to SLANG

This section defines extensions to the language definition of SLANG, as presented earlier in Section 2.1.2. The language constructs that refer to arrays and procedure parameters need to be redefined. Procedure parameters can be specified with the tokens that are already available. For the specification of arrays, however, we need 3 new special symbols, namely the left and right-bracket token and the up-to token. These are defined in the table in Figure 5.1.

Special symbols

left_bracket_token	:	[.	right_bracket_token	:	] .
up_to_token	:	...			

Figure 5.1 The representation of new special symbols in SLANG.

We will now consider the language constructs that deal with arrays and procedure parameters. These are specified by the following productions in the context-free grammar. For each construct, we will also describe the context constraints, and the semantics. Note that, in this section, we do not consider language constructs that have not changed.

Variable declarations

variable_declaration	:	var_token *type_declarer*
		{*identifier bound_part* **option**} **list** separator_token
		.

type_declarer	:	int_token.
bound_part	:	left_bracket_token *bound_pair* **list** right_bracket_token.
bound_pair	:	*lower_bound* up_to_token *upper_bound*.
lower_bound	:	*expression*.
upper_bound	:	*expression*.

Context constraints: Every identifier in the variable declaration denotes a variable. It is a simple variable if the bound-part (which is optional) is empty, and an array variable if the bound-part is not empty. The scope of a variable is the block in which the declaration occurs. An identifier may not be declared twice in the same block.

Unlike a normal expression, a bound expression (i.e. an expression that is used as a lower or upper bound in a variable declaration) has the extra restriction that every identifier in the expression that denotes a variable or a constant must be declared in a surrounding block. Note that there is no restriction on the identifiers in a bound expression that denote parameters. These may be taken from the parameter list of the procedure in which the array variable is declared or from a surrounding procedure.

Semantics: For each identifier in the variable declaration that denotes a simple variable, a new location, *loc* (say), is obtained in the store, and *loc* is bound to the identifier.

For each identifier in the variable declaration that denotes an array variable, 3 steps are performed:

1. Let n be the number of bound pairs in the bound-part. For every bound pair, the lower-bound expression and the upper-bound expression are computed. Let the values of the pairs be $(lo_1, up_1), (lo_2, up_2), \ldots, (lo_n, up_n)$.
2. The relation $lo_i \leq up_i$ is checked for every pair (lo_i, up_i) ($1 \leq i \leq n$).
3. A number $m = (up_1 - lo_1 + 1) * (up_2 - lo_2 + 1) * \ldots * (up_n - lo_n + 1)$ of consecutive locations, starting at *loc* (say), is obtained in the store, and *loc* and m are bound to the identifier.

For each bound pair, the value of the lower bound must be smaller than or equal to the value of the upper bound.

Procedure declarations

procedure_declaration	:	procedure_token *identifier*
		{*parameter_part* **chain** separator_token} **pack option**
		block separator_token
		.
parameter_part	:	*val_parameter_part*
	|	*ref_parameter_part*
		.
val_parameter_part	:	*type_declarer identifier* **list**.
ref_parameter_part	:	var_token *type_declarer identifier* **list**.

Context constraints: The identifier (further referred to as *procedure identifier*) in the procedure declaration denotes a procedure. The scope of a procedure is the block in which the declaration occurs. An identifier may not be declared twice in this block.

Every identifier in a val-parameter-part denotes a value parameter. Every identifier in a ref-parameter-part denotes a reference parameter. The scope of a parameter is the block of the procedure declaration. A value parameter represents a value (like a constant), which means that the parameter may be used, but not assigned. A reference parameter represents a simple variable or an indexed variable, which means that the parameter may be both used and assigned.

An identifier may not be declared twice in a parameter-part and in the block of the same procedure.

Semantics: The block is bound to the procedure identifier.

Assignment statements

assignment_statement	:	*left_part* becomes_token *expression*.
left_part	:	*identifier index_part* **option**.
index_part	:	left_bracket_token *index* **list** right_bracket_token.
index	:	*expression*.

Context constraints: The assignment statement must occur in the scope of the identifier in the left part, and the identifier must denote a variable.

If the index-part of the identifier is not empty, then the identifier must denote an array variable, otherwise the identifier must denote a simple variable or a reference parameter. The number of indices in the index-part of an indexed variable must be equal to the number of bound pairs in the declaration of the associated array variable.

Semantics: 2 steps are performed:

1. The destination of the assignment is determined. In the case of an identifier that denotes a simple variable, the destination is the location bound to the identifier. For an identifier that denotes an array variable, the expressions in the index-part are computed. Their values, together with the identifier,

determine the location of the indexed variable. For an identifier that denotes a reference parameter, the destination is the location of the argument that is substituted for the parameter.

2. The expression is evaluated, and its value is written to the location determined in step 1.

Call-statements

call_statement	:	call_token *identifier argument* **list pack option**.
argument	:	*identifier index_part* **option**
		| *expression*

Context constraints: The call-statement must occur in the scope of the identifier, and the identifier must denote a procedure. The call-statement must also occur after the identifier of the declaration of the procedure.

The call-statement may contain a list of arguments that may be empty. The corresponding procedure declaration must contain an equal number of parameters. The correspondence between arguments and parameters is established by the position of the arguments and parameters in the call-statement and procedure declaration, respectively. In the case of a value parameter, the argument must be an expression (a denotation of a number, a constant, simple variable, indexed variable or parameter is a simple case). In the case of a reference parameter, the argument must be a simple variable, an indexed variable, or a reference parameter from a surrounding procedure.

The call-statement must occur in the scope of every identifier in the parameter list. If the index-part of an identifier is not empty, then the identifier must denote an array variable, otherwise the identifier must denote a simple variable, constant or parameter. The number of indices in the index-part of an indexed variable must be equal to the number of bound pairs in the declaration of the associated array variable.

Semantics: Every value parameter represents a value. The value of the argument expression is bound to the parameter. This value is determined when the procedure is called.

Every reference parameter represents a simple variable or an indexed variable. The location bound to the argument is bound to this parameter. The location is determined when the procedure is called. If the argument is an indexed variable, its expressions in the index-part are computed when the procedure is called. The same location remains bound to the variable during the execution of the block of the procedure.

The block bound to the identifier is executed in the environment in which the identifier was declared. When the execution of the call-statement is finished, the execution of the statement-part (of which the call-statement forms a part) is resumed at the point it was interrupted.

Read-statements

> *read_statement* : read_token {*identifier index_part* **option**} **list pack**.

Context constraints: The read-statement must occur in the scope of every identifier in the list, and every identifier must denote a variable.

If the index-part of an identifier is not empty, then the identifier must denote an array variable, otherwise the identifier must denote a simple variable or a reference parameter. The number of indices in the index-part of an indexed variable must be equal to the number of bound pairs in the declaration of the associated array variable.

Semantics: For each identifier in the list, and in the order of occurrence, 2 steps are performed:

1. The location of the destination is determined. For an identifier that denotes a simple variable, the destination is the location bound to the identifier. For an identifier that denotes an array variable, the expressions in the index-part are computed. Their values, together with the identifier, determine the location of the indexed variable. For an identifier that denotes a reference parameter, the destination is the location of the argument that is substituted for the parameter.
2. The first number of the input is written to the location, determined in step 1, and then removed from the input.

Expressions

> | *expression* | : | *term* **chain** *add_operator*. |
> | *term* | : | *factor* **chain** *multiply_operator*. |
> | *factor* | : | *unary_operator* **option** *operand*. |
> | *operand* | : | *identifier index_part* **option** |
> | | \| | *number* |
> | | \| | *expression* **pack** |
>
> | | . | |
> | *add_operator* | : | plus_token \| minus_token. |
> | *multiply_operator* | : | times_token \| over_token \| modulo_token. |
> | *unary_operator* | : | negate_token \| absolute_token. |

Context constraints: The expression must occur in the scope of every identifier that occurs as an operand in the expression. If the index-part of an identifier is not empty, then the identifier must denote an array variable, otherwise the identifier must denote a simple variable, constant or parameter. The number of indices in the index-part of an indexed variable must be equal to the number of bound pairs in the declaration of the associated array variable.

Semantics: An expression is a rule for computing a numerical value of type integer. The value is obtained by applying the arithmetic operators on the actual values of the operands of the expression. The actual value of an operand is obvious in the case of a denotation of a number, or an identifier that denotes a constant. For an identifier that denotes a simple variable, it is the current value at its location. For an identifier that denotes an array variable, the expressions in the index-part are computed. Their values, together with the identifier, determine the location of the indexed variable. The current value at this location is the actual value of the operand. For an identifier that denotes a parameter, it is the current value of the argument that is substituted for the parameter.

The arithmetic operators plus, minus, times, over (division with truncation), modulo, negate and absolute have the conventional meanings. The syntax specifies the following precedence rules:

> **highest priority:** negate, absolute
> **second highest priority:** times, over, modulo
> **lowest priority:** plus, minus

An expression enclosed between left and right parentheses is first evaluated and this value is used in subsequent calculations. Consequently, the order of application of operators within an expression can always be arranged by appropriate positioning of parentheses.

5.2 Extensions to VIM: arrays

We now reconsider the architecture, instruction set and interpreter of the virtual machine VIM. We extend the machine model so that the declaration and use of *arrays* can be easily handled. Parameter passing is not yet considered. This will be done in Section 5.4.

5.2.1 The architecture

In this section, we will explain how indexed variables can be addressed, and how dynamic arrays can be mapped onto the data segments of the memory.

Addressing of indexed variables. Let us consider an n-dimensional array of the form $A[lo_1..up_1, lo_2..up_2, \ldots, lo_n..up_n]$. The data segments of VIM (and computer memories in general) have a linear structure. We will therefore linearise the n-dimensional array A and map it onto a 1-dimensional array $M[offset .. offset + (up_1 - lo_1 + 1) * (up_2 - lo_2 + 1) * \ldots * (up_n - lo_n + 1) - 1]$. Linearisation is possible in several ways, e.g. as a sequence of rows or as a sequence of columns. We will map the arrays of SLANG row-wise on the linear memory of VIM, i.e. we will apply the method where the last index changes the fastest. For a 3-dimensional array this means:

```
p = offset;
  for (i = lo₁; i <= up₁; i++)
    for (j = lo₂; j <= up₂; j++)
      for (k = lo₃; k <= up₃; k++)
        { M[p] = A[i][j][k]; p++; }
```

Index i indicates the planes, index j the rows, and index k the elements in a row.
The index in M that corresponds to the indexed variable

$$A[i, j, k] \quad (lo_1 \leq i \leq up_1, lo_2 \leq j \leq up_2, lo_3 \leq k \leq up_3)$$

is

$$
\begin{aligned}
p = offset \quad &+ \quad (i - lo_1) \quad * \quad (up_2 - lo_2 + 1) * (up_3 - lo_3 + 1) \\
&+ \quad (j - lo_2) \quad * \quad (up_3 - lo_3 + 1) \\
&+ \quad (k - lo_3)
\end{aligned}
$$

In other words, we begin by going through $(i - lo_1)$ planes, then through $(j - lo_2)$
rows, and finally through $(k - lo_3)$ elements before we find the indexed variable
$A[i, j, k]$.

In every index calculation we need the values of $(up_2 - lo_2 + 1) * (up_3 - lo_3 + 1)$
and $(up_3 - lo_3 + 1)$. We will therefore rewrite the formula as

$$
\begin{aligned}
p = offset \quad &+ \quad (i - lo_1) \quad * \quad d_2 * d_3 \\
&+ \quad (j - lo_2) \quad * \quad d_3 \\
&+ \quad (k - lo_3)
\end{aligned}
$$

where $d_2 = (up_2 - lo_2 + 1)$ and $d_3 = (up_3 - lo_3 + 1)$. Alternatively we could write

$$
\begin{aligned}
p = offset \quad &+ \quad (i - lo_1) \quad * \quad s_1 \\
&+ \quad (j - lo_2) \quad * \quad s_2 \\
&+ \quad (k - lo_3) \quad * \quad s_3
\end{aligned}
$$

where $s_1 = d_2 * d_3$, $s_2 = d_3$ and $s_3 = 1$.

Returning to the n-dimensional array $A[lo_1..up_1, lo_2..up_2, \ldots, lo_n..up_n]$, the index
in M of the indexed variable $A[ix_1, ix_2, \ldots, ix_n]$ is

$$
\begin{aligned}
p = offset \quad &+ \quad (ix_1 - lo_1) \quad * \quad s_1 \\
&+ \quad (ix_2 - lo_2) \quad * \quad s_2 \\
&\quad \vdots \\
&+ \quad (ix_n - lo_n) \quad * \quad s_n
\end{aligned}
$$

where $d_k = (up_k - lo_k + 1)$ $(1 \leq k \leq n)$, and $s_{k-1} = d_k * \ldots * d_n$ $(1 \leq k \leq n)$, $s_n = 1$.

The computation of the s_k proceeds as follows:

$$
\begin{aligned}
s_n \quad &= \quad 1 \\
s_{k-1} \quad &= \quad d_k * s_k \quad (1 \leq k \leq n)
\end{aligned}
$$

n
offset
s_0
lo_1
s_1
lo_2
s_2
$\vdots$
s_{n-1}
lo_n

Figure 5.2 Descriptor of an array.

The value of s_0 does not play a role in the computation of the index in M; s_0 is, however, the size of the total array, and is, therefore, important for space reservation purposes.

The values of the lo_i and s_i provide sufficient information for *bound checking*, as is shown below. For each k $(1 \leq k \leq n)$ the restriction

$$lo_k \leq ix_k \leq up_k$$

can be rewritten into

$$0 \leq (ix_k - lo_k) * s_k \leq (up_k - lo_k) * s_k$$

Since

$$(up_k - lo_k) * s_k = (up_k - lo_k + 1) * s_k - s_k = d_k * s_k - s_k = s_{k-1} - s_k$$

we can write

$$0 \leq (ix_k - lo_k) * s_k \leq s_{k-1} - s_k$$

Above we have seen that the necessary information for space reservation, address calculation and bound checking are the values of n (the dimension), the *offset*, and the values of s_i $(0 \leq i \leq n-1)$ and lo_i $(1 \leq i \leq n)$. This information is therefore put together in an array *descriptor* (also called *dope vector*), as shown in Figure 5.2. The descriptor will be stored in the data segment of the block in which the array is declared.

Memory management of arrays. As every simple variable has a fixed size, the space needed for simple variables in a block is known at compile time. The size of an array variable, however, is generally not known at compile time as the bounds are expressions that may contain variables whose values are only known at execution time. In the definition of array bounds it is stated that the operands of the bound expressions can be simple and indexed variables as well as constants that need to be defined in a surrounding block, and parameters. This means that the operands have a value at the moment the block is activated. As the sizes of arrays are not known at compile time, their offsets can also not be determined at compile time. The size of the descriptor is, however, known at compile time. The length of the descriptor of an array of dimension n is $2 * n + 2$, i.e. 1 position for n, 1 position for the *offset*, n positions for the *lower bounds* and n positions for the *s*-values.

We assume, therefore, that a data segment has a static and a dynamic part. The static part contains cells for simple variables and cells to store the descriptors of array variables. Simple variables and descriptors of arrays are assigned a *displacement* in the order in which they occur in the declaration-part. The dynamic part contains cells for the arrays themselves.

The computation of the offsets and the lengths of the arrays, and the extension of the data segment with the dynamic part, proceeds as follows. Initially, the current length of the data segment is equal to the length of the static part of the segment. The *offset* of an array is equal to the current length of the data segment. The size of the array is computed and added to the current length of the segment. The new current length will be the *offset* of the next array in the declaration-part.

5.2.2   The instruction set

In this section, we add new instructions for manipulating indexed variables and for handling declarations of dynamic arrays.

The instruction `ldvar` copies the value of a simple variable from the segment with number `sn`, and position `dpl` in the segment, to the top of the stack. The instruction `stvar` removes the value of a simple variable from the top of the stack and stores it in the segment with number `sn`, at position `dpl` in the segment. For indexed variables we need different load and store instructions. These will be called `ldxvar` and `stxvar`. Both instructions operate on the address tuple (`sn,dpl`) that indicates the address of the descriptor in the data segment. The indices of the indexed variable are assumed to be on the stack. Both instructions check that each index lies within its lower and upper bound. If this is not the case an error will be reported and the execution halts.

For the computation of the fields of descriptors, and the recomputation of the segment length, we introduce the instruction `descr sn,dpl,n`, where (`sn,dpl`) is the address of the descriptor and `n` the dimension of the array. The length of the data segment is kept in the administration part of the segment (see Figure 2.11). The initial value (the length of the static part) is put in the data segment by means of the instruction `crseg sn,index`, where `sn` is the segment number and `index` the position of the length in the address table. The instruction `descr sn,dpl,n` fills the descriptor, recomputes the segment length and puts the new value in the data segment. The load and store instructions and the instruction for

Load and store

instruction	meaning
`ldcon intval`	stores the (integer) value `intval` on the stack
`ldvar sn,dpl`	copies the (integer) value from memory address `(sn,dpl)` to the stack
`stvar sn,dpl`	removes the top (integer) value from the stack and writes it to memory address `(sn,dpl)`
`ldxvar sn,dpl`	computes the address of an indexed variable; the descriptor of the array variable has memory address `(sn,dpl)`, and the indices are taken (and removed) from the stack; copies the (integer) value from the memory address of the indexed variable to the stack
`stxvar sn,dpl`	computes the address of an indexed variable; the descriptor of the array variable has memory address `(sn,dpl)`, and the indices are taken (and removed) from the stack; removes the top (integer) value from the stack and writes it to the memory address of the indexed variable

Descriptor handling

instruction	meaning
`descr sn,dpl,n`	computes the fields of the descriptor of an array variable, and recomputes the segment length; the descriptor of the array has memory address `(sn,dpl)`, the dimension is `n`, and the array bounds are taken (and removed) from the stack

Figure 5.3 Instructions of the virtual machine VIM.

handling descriptors (i.e. the computation of the fields and the recomputation of the segment length) are shown in Figure 5.3.

In the following examples we show how indexed variables are addressed, and array declarations are handled.

Example 5.1
Consider the assignment statement

$$a[2*p,q] := b[p+3,7]$$

where p and q are simple variables. The address of a simple variable x is denoted by the pair sn_x, dpl_x, and the address of the descriptor of an array m by sn_m, dpl_m. The VIM instructions corresponding to this assignment statement are:

```
ldvar   sn_p,dpl_p
ldcon   3
add
ldcon   7
ldxvar  sn_b,dpl_b
ldcon   2
ldvar   sn_p,dpl_p
mul
ldvar   sn_q,dpl_q
stxvar  sn_a,dpl_a
```

◇

Example 5.2
Consider the following procedure

```
PROC proc
BEGIN VAR INT a, b[1..10], c, d[1..q,2*p..q+4];
      ⋮
END;
```

The simple variables p and q are declared (and assigned a value before proc is called) in a surrounding block. The translation into VIM instructions is shown below. Note that sn_{proc}, sn_b and sn_d represent the same segment number.

```
crseg   sn_proc,length_index_proc
ldcon   1
ldcon   10
descr   sn_b,dpl_b,1
ldcon   1
ldvar   sn_q,dpl_q
ldcon   2
ldvar   sn_p,dpl_p
mul
ldvar   sn_q,dpl_q
ldcon   4
add
descr   sn_d,dpl_d,2
⋮
dlseg
return
```

◇

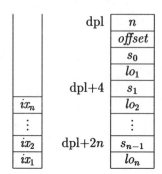

Figure 5.4 Stack (left) and descriptor (right) just before the address calculation of an indexed variable.

5.2.3   The interpreter

An indexed variable $A[ix_1, ix_2, \ldots, ix_n]$ is translated into code for n index expressions and the instruction **ldxvar sn,dpl**, where (**sn,dpl**) is the address of the descriptor. The values of the index expressions are (as usual) on the stack. The instruction **ldxvar sn,dpl** is implemented by means of the procedure *index_dpl* and a push operation. The procedure *index_dpl* computes the displacement **xdpl** of the indexed variable, and the push operation stores its value on the stack. The instruction **ldxvar sn,dpl** operates on the descriptor and on the top positions of the stack. The stack contents (just before the instruction **ldxvar** is executed) and the descriptor are depicted in Figure 5.4. If an indexed variable $A[ix_1, ix_2, \ldots, ix_n]$ must be assigned, then the instruction **stxvar sn,dpl** must be applied. This instruction is implemented by means of the procedure *index_dpl* and a pop operation.

The declaration of an array $A[lo_1..up_1, lo_2..up_2, \ldots, lo_n..up_n]$ is translated into code for n pairs of bound expressions and the instruction **descr sn,dpl,n**, where (**sn,dpl**) is the address of the descriptor and **n** is the dimension. The values of the bound expressions are on the stack. The procedure *descriptor* implements the instruction **descr sn,dpl,n** and operates on the descriptor and on the top positions of the stack. The stack contents (just before the instruction **descr** is executed) and the descriptor (after its fields have been computed) are depicted in Figure 5.5.

As some new instructions have been introduced, the interpreter must be extended. The new version of the interpreter is shown below.

#define *max_prog*	1000	/* length of program memory */
#define *max_table*	1000	/* length of address and length table */
#define *max_data*	100	/* length of data memory */
#define *max_depth*	15	/* maximum nesting depth */
#define *max_stack*	100	/* maximum depth of stacks */

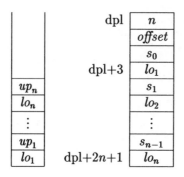

Figure 5.5   Stack (left) just before, and descriptor (right) just after, the processing of an array declaration.

```
typedef enum {
    true = 1, false = 0
} boolean;

typedef enum {
    neg, abs_, add, sub, mul, dvi, mdl, eq, ne, lt, le, gt, ge, ldcon, ldvar,
    stvar, ldxvar, stxvar, jump, jift, jiff, call, descr, crseg, dlseg, return_,
    rdint, wrint, halt
} operation;

typedef struct {
    operation code;
    union {
        /* no operands for:    neg, abs_, add, sub, mul, dvi, mdl, eq, ne, lt,
                               le, gt, ge, dlseg, return_, rdint, wrint, halt */
        int value;            /* for: ldcon */
        struct {
            int sn1, dpl;     /* for: ldvar, stvar, ldxvar, stxvar */
        } u1;
        int index1;           /* for: jump, jift, jiff, call */
        struct {
            int sn2, dpl2, n; /* for: descr */
        } u2;
        struct {
            int sn3, index3;  /* for: crseg */
        } u3;
    } u;
} instruction;


int             CSG[max_depth];
instruction     prog[max_prog];
int             address_table[max_table];
int             length_table[max_table];
```

```
int                data[max_data];
int                stack[max_stack];
int                return_stack[max_stack];
int                dsp;

void descriptor(int sn, int dpl, int n)
{
  int length, s, k, up, lo;

  s = 1;                              /* s_n */
  data[CSG[sn]+dpl] = n;
  for (k = dpl+n*2+1; k >= dpl+3; k -= 2) {
    pop(&up);                         /* up_k */
    pop(&lo);                         /* lo_k */
    if (up < lo) report_error("upper bound smaller than lower bound");
    data[CSG[sn]+k] = lo;             /* lo_k */
    s *= up-lo+1;                     /* s_{k-1} = (up_k-lo_k+1)*s_k */
    data[CSG[sn]+k-1] = s;            /* s_{k-1} */
  }
  length = data[CSG[sn]-3];          /* current segment length */
  data[CSG[sn]+dpl+1] = length;      /* offset */
  length += s;                       /* s_0 */
  data[CSG[sn]-3] = length;          /* new segment length */
  dsp += s;
}


int index_dpl(int sn, int dpl)
{
  int ix, k, lo, n, s, s1, offset, xdpl;

  n = data[CSG[sn]+dpl];
  offset = data[CSG[sn]+dpl+1];
  k = dpl+n*2;
  pop(&ix);                          /* ix_n */
  lo = data[CSG[sn]+k+1];            /* lo_n */
  xdpl = ix-lo;                      /* ix_n-lo_n */
  s1 = data[CSG[sn]+k];              /* s_{n-1} */
  if (ix-lo < 0 || ix-lo > s1-1) report_error("index of array out of bounds");
  while (k >= dpl+4) {
    pop(&ix);                        /* ix_k */
    lo = data[CSG[sn]+k-1];          /* lo_k */
    s = data[CSG[sn]+k];             /* s_k */
    xdpl += (ix-lo)*s;               /* (ix_k-lo_k)*s_k */
    s1 = data[CSG[sn]+k-2];          /* s_{k-1} */
    if ((ix-lo)*s < 0 || (ix-lo)*s > s1-s)
      report_error("index of array out of bounds");
    k -= 2;
  }
  xdpl += offset;
  return xdpl;
}
```

```
/*
    procedures read_code, push, pop, push_return, pop_return, read_int,
    write_int, create_segment and delete_segment are not shown
*/

void main(void)
{
    instruction      *instr;
    int              ic, next, sp, rsp, csn, xdpl, left_operand,
                     right_operand, operand, result, length;
    boolean          truthval, stop;

    read_code();
    ic               = 0;
    sp               = 0;
    dsp              = 0;
    rsp              = 0;
    csn              = 0;
    CSG[csn]         = 0;
    stop             = false;

    while (!stop) {
        next = ic+1;
        instr = &prog[ic];
        switch (instr->code) {

        case neg:
        case abs_:
            /* not shown */
            break;

        case add:
        case sub:
        case mul:
        case dvi:
        case mdl:
            /* not shown */
            break;

        case eq:
        case ne:
        case lt:
        case le:
        case gt:
        case ge:
            /* not shown */
            break;

        case ldcon:
            push(instr->u.value);
            break;
```

```
        case ldvar:
          push(data[CSG[instr->u.u1.sn1]+instr->u.u1.dpl1]);
          break;

        case stvar:
          pop(&(data[CSG[instr->u.u1.sn1]+instr->u.u1.dpl1]));
          break;

        case ldxvar:
          xdpl = index_dpl(instr->u.u1.sn1, instr->u.u1.dpl1);
          push(data[CSG[instr->u.u1.sn1]+xdpl]);
          break;

        case stxvar:
          xdpl = index_dpl(instr->u.u1.sn1, instr->u.u1.dpl1);
          pop(&(data[CSG[instr->u.u1.sn1]+xdpl]));
          break;

        case jump:
        case jift:
        case jiff:
        case call:
          /* not shown */
          break;

        case descr:
          descriptor(instr->u.u2.sn2, instr->u.u2.dpl2, instr->u.u2.n);
          break;

        case crseg:
        case dlseg:
        case return_:
          /* not shown */
          break;

        case rdint:
        case wrint:
          /* not shown */
          break;

        case halt:
          stop = true;
          break;
      }
      ic = next;
    }
}
```

5.3   Translation of arrays

In the previous section we have redefined the storage organisation of VIM so that dynamic arrays can be handled. We have introduced special instructions to process array declarations and to load and store indexed variables. This means that we must reconsider the translation of variables.

5.3.1   Declarations

Before we discuss the translation of variable declarations, we first reconsider the translation of procedure declarations, blocks and declaration-parts. Their productions are:

procedure_declaration : procedure_token *identifier*
                            {*parameter_part* **chain** separator_token} **pack option**
                            block separator_token

.

block : begin_token *declaration_part statement_part* end_token.

declaration_part : {*constant_declaration* | *variable_declaration*} **clos**
                       procedure_declaration **seq option**

.

For a procedure *identifier* we will denote its segment number by $sn_{identifier}$, and the index of its segment length in the length table by $length\_index_{identifier}$. If we neglect for the moment the parameters, then the translations are:

<procedure_declaration> : *<block>*
                              `return`

.

<block> : `crseg` $sn_{identifier}$, $length\_index_{identifier}$
              <declaration_part>
              <statement_part>
              `dlseg`

.

<declaration_part> :   { *<constant_declaration>*
                         | *<variable_declaration>*
                         } **clos**
                         { `jump`   `over`
                             <procedure_declaration> **seq**
              `over:`
                         } **option**

.

Note that, in contrast to the translation in Section 2.5.1, the instruction **crseg** is now the first instruction of the translation of block. The reason is that the data segment must be available when the declaration-part is executed, in particular the array variables, as their descriptors must be filled.

During compilation, it is no problem to emit the instruction **crseg** before the declarations are parsed, and while the static length of the data segment is not yet known. The length can be stored later in the address table, namely when the declarations have been parsed.

We next consider the translation of a variable declaration. The productions are:

variable_declaration	:	var_token *type_declarer*
		{*identifier bound_part* **option**} **list** separator_token
		.
type_declarer	:	int_token.
bound_part	:	left_bracket_token *bound_pair* **list** right_bracket_token.
bound_pair	:	*lower_bound* up_to_token *upper_bound*.
lower_bound	:	*expression*.
upper_bound	:	*expression*.

We will denote the segment number and the displacement of a variable *identifier* by $\mathrm{sn}_{identifier}$ and $\mathrm{dpl}_{identifier}$, respectively. The translations are then:

$<variable\_declaration>$

    :   {simple variable}

   | $<bound\_part>$ {indexed variable}

        descr $\mathrm{sn}_{identifier}, \mathrm{dpl}_{identifier}, \mathrm{n}$

    .

$<bound\_part>$	:	$<bound\_pair>$ **seq**.
$<bound\_pair>$	:	$<lower\_bound>$
		$<upper\_bound>$
		.
$<lower\_bound>$	:	$<expression>$.
$<upper\_bound>$	:	$<expression>$.

Note that the translation of the declaration of a simple variable is empty, i.e. no VIM code is generated for a simple variable. The same holds for the declaration of a constant. In Sections 3.3.1, 3.4 and 3.5 it was shown that the necessary information is stored in the symbol table, and is subsequently used for the translation of statements.

5.3.2 Variables

Identifiers that are variables are specified in the following productions:

operand : *identifier index_part* **option**
        | *number*
        | *expression* **pack**
        .

left_part : *identifier index_part* **option**.

read_statement : read_token {*identifier index_part* **option**} **list pack**.

The index-part of indexed variables is defined in the productions:

index_part : left_bracket_token *index* **list** right_bracket_token.
index   : *expression*.

We will denote the segment number and displacement (of the descriptor) of variable *identifier* by $\mathrm{sn}_{identifier}$ and $\mathrm{dpl}_{identifier}$, respectively, the value of constant *identifier* by $\mathrm{intval}_{identifier}$, and the value of number *number* by intval_{number}. The translations are then:

\<operand> :	ldvar $\mathrm{sn}_{identifier},\mathrm{dpl}_{identifier}$	{simple variable}
|	*\<index_part>*	{indexed variable}
	ldxvar $\mathrm{sn}_{identifier},\mathrm{dpl}_{identifier}$	
|	ldcon $\mathrm{intval}_{identifier}$	{constant}
|	ldcon intval_{number}	{number}
|	*\<expression>*	{(expression)}
	.	

\<left_part> :	stvar $\mathrm{sn}_{identifier},\mathrm{dpl}_{identifier}$	{simple variable}
|	*\<index_part>*	{indexed variable}
	stxvar $\mathrm{sn}_{identifier},\mathrm{dpl}_{identifier}$	
	.	

\<read_statement>
     : { rdint
           { stvar $\mathrm{sn}_{identifier},\mathrm{dpl}_{identifier}$ {simple variable}
           | *\<index_part>*   {indexed variable}
             stxvar $\mathrm{sn}_{identifier},\mathrm{dpl}_{identifier}$
           }
        } **seq**
        .

\<index_part> : *\<index>* **seq**.
\<index>   : *\<expression>*.

5.4   Extensions to VIM: parameters

In this section we reconsider the architecture, instruction set and interpreter of VIM and extend the machine model so that *parameters* can be handled.

5.4.1   The architecture

In Section 5.1, value and reference parameters were defined. The argument that corresponds to a *value parameter* must be an expression. Its operands can be simple and indexed variables, numbers and parameters. The argument that corresponds to a *reference parameter* must be a simple or an indexed variable, or a reference parameter from a surrounding procedure. Note that the caller and the callee can be in different segment groups, so that it may be impossible for the callee to compute the arguments. The computation of the arguments is therefore the responsibility of the caller. It is, however, the responsibility of the callee to store the arguments in its data segment, after it has created the segment.

In VIM, the evaluation of an expression is organised so that the result remains on the stack. This means that the caller stores the argument value on the stack, so that the callee can find it. We will do the same with arguments that correspond to reference parameters. The caller stores the arguments on the stack, where the callee can find them. The stack is therefore used as an intermediary store to pass arguments from the caller to the callee. In the case of a value parameter, the caller simply leaves the value of the computation on the stack. The callee pops this value from the stack and stores it in its data segment. In the case of a reference parameter, the location of a simple or indexed variable must be bound to the parameter. The address of this variable is determined by the caller and pushed onto the stack. This address is popped from the stack by the callee and stored in its data segment. The callee can then read from, and write to, the location of this variable by means of *indirect addressing*.

Thus far we have used pairs (sn,dpl) as addresses. However, the caller and callee can be in different segment groups, so that the same segment number sn may represent different segments in both groups. It is, therefore, necessary to compute the *index* in the data memory *data* that corresponds to the pair (sn,dpl), and to pass this *absolute address* instead of the pair (sn,dpl) from the caller to the callee. The argument for a reference parameter will thus be the address value CSG[sn]+dpl.

We assume that parameters and variables are stored in the data segment in the following order:

1. Parameters, in the order in which they occur in the parameter list.
2. Simple variables and descriptors of array variables, in the order in which the variables occur in the declaration-part.
3. Arrays, in the order in which they occur in the declaration-part.

To conclude, parameter passing proceeds as follows. The caller computes the arguments in the order in which they occur in the argument list.

- In the case of a value parameter, the value is computed and pushed onto the stack.
- In the case of a reference parameter, the absolute address CSG[sn]+dpl is computed and pushed onto the stack

The callee must remove these arguments from the stack and store them in its data segment. The first argument has the lowest dpl, and the last argument has the highest dpl. However, the arguments are popped from the stack in reverse order, which means that the parameter section of the data segment must be filled from the highest to the lowest displacement. We will not burden the compiler writer with this complicated transfer of arguments from the stack to the data segment, and instead introduce a special action that takes care of the generation (in the right order) of the necessary stvar instructions.

5.4.2   The instruction set

We need new instructions to manipulate addresses of reference parameters. The instruction varaddr sn,dpl computes the address CSG[sn]+dpl, and pushes this onto the stack. The instruction xvaraddr sn,dpl reads the indices of an indexed variable from the stack, takes the address (sn,dpl) of the descriptor, computes the displacement xdpl of the indexed variable, and then the absolute address CSG[sn]+xdpl, and pushes the latter onto the stack. For the access to reference parameters we need *indirect addressing*. The instruction ldind expects an absolute address on top of the stack. This address is removed from the stack, and the value at this address is pushed onto the stack. The instruction stind expects an absolute address and a value on top of the stack. The address and the value (in this order) are removed from the stack, and the value is stored at the address.

The instructions to build absolute addresses and to load and store values are shown in Figure 5.6.

Example 5.3
Consider the procedure declaration

```
PROC proc (INT a, b; VAR INT c, d, e)
BEGIN
        ⋮
    c := a;
    d := b + c * e;
        ⋮
END;
```

Building absolute addresses

instruction	meaning
varaddr sn,dpl	pushes the address CSG[sn]+dpl onto the stack
xvaraddr sn,dpl	pushes the address CSG[sn]+xdpl onto the stack, where xdpl is the displacement of an indexed variable; the descriptor of the array has memory address (sn,dpl), and the indices are taken (and removed) from the stack

Load and store

instruction	meaning
ldcon intval	stores the (integer) value intval on the stack
ldvar sn,dpl	copies the (integer) value from memory address (sn,dpl) to the stack
stvar sn,dpl	removes the top (integer) value from the stack and writes it to memory address (sn,dpl)
ldxvar sn,dpl	computes the address of an indexed variable; the descriptor of the array variable has memory address (sn,dpl), and the indices are taken (and removed) from the stack; copies the (integer) value from the memory address of the indexed variable to the stack
stxvar sn,dpl	computes the address of an indexed variable; the descriptor of the array variable has memory address (sn,dpl), and the indices are taken (and removed) from the stack; removes the top (integer) value from the stack and writes it to the memory address of the indexed variable
ldind	removes the absolute address from the top of the stack and copies the (integer) value at this address to the stack
stind	removes the absolute address and the (integer) value (in this order) from the top of the stack and writes the value to the address

Figure 5.6 Instructions of the virtual machine VIM.

and the call-statement

```
CALL proc (3, p+q, x[i], y, z)
```

where i, p, q and y are simple variables, x[i] is an indexed variable, and z is a reference parameter from a surrounding procedure.

The VIM instructions corresponding to the procedure declaration are:

```
crseg      snproc, length_indexproc
stvar      sne, dple
stvar      snd, dpld
stvar      snc, dplc
stvar      snb, dplb
stvar      sna, dpla
  ⋮
ldvar      sna, dpla
ldvar      snc, dplc
stind
ldvar      snb, dplb
ldvar      snc, dplc
ldind
ldvar      sne, dple
ldind
mul
add
ldvar      snd, dpld
stind
  ⋮
dlseg
return
```

Note that sn_{proc}, sn_a, sn_b, sn_c, sn_d and sn_e represent the same segment number.

The instructions corresponding to the procedure call are:

```
ldcon      3
ldvar      snp, dplp
ldvar      snq, dplq
add
ldvar      sni, dpli
xvaraddr   snx, dplx
varaddr    sny, dply
ldvar      snz, dplz
call       address_indexproc
```

Note that the instruction `ldvar` sn_z, dpl_z loads the absolute address of the argument associated with reference parameter z, and not its value.   ◇

5.4.3   The interpreter

As some new instructions have been introduced, the interpreter must again be
extended. The improved version of the interpreter is shown below.

```
#define  max_prog      1000    /* length of program memory */
#define  max_table     1000    /* length of address and length table */
#define  max_data      100     /* length of data memory */
#define  max_depth     15      /* maximum nesting depth */
#define  max_stack     100     /* maximum depth of stacks */

typedef enum {
  true = 1, false = 0
} boolean;

typedef enum {
  neg, abs_, add, sub, mul, dvi, mdl, eq, ne, lt, le, gt, ge, ldcon, ldvar,
  stvar, ldxvar, stxvar, varaddr, xvaraddr, ldind, stind, jump, jift, jiff,
  call, descr, crseg, dlseg, return_, rdint, wrint, halt
} operation;

typedef struct instruction {
  operation  code;
  union {
    /* no operands for:    neg, abs_, add, sub, mul, dvi, mdl, eq, ne, lt, le, gt,
                           ge, ldind, stind, dlseg, return_, rdint, wrint, halt */
    int value;             /* for: ldcon */
    struct {
      int sn1, dpl;        /* for: ldvar, stvar, ldxvar, stxvar, varaddr, xvaraddr */
    } u1;
    int index1;            /* for: jump, jift, jiff, call */
    struct {
      int sn2, dpl2, n;    /* for: descr */
    } u2;
    struct {
      int sn3, index3;     /* for: crseg */
    } u3;
  } u;
} instruction;

int          CSG[max_depth];
instruction  prog[max_prog];
int          address_table[max_table];
int          length_table[max_table];
int          data[max_data];
int          stack[max_stack];
int          return_stack[max_stack];

/*
  procedures read_code, push, pop, push_return, pop_return, read_int, write_int,
  create_segment, delete_segment, descriptor and index_dpl are not shown
*/
```

```
void main(void)
{
    instruction     *instr;
    int             ic, next, sp, dsp, rsp, csn, xdpl, i, left_operand,
                    right_operand, operand, result, length, address;
    boolean         truthval, stop;

    read_code();
    ic          = 0;
    sp          = 0;
    dsp         = 0;
    rsp         = 0;
    csn         = 0;
    CSG[csn]    = 0;
    stop        = false;

    while (!stop) {
        next = ic + 1;
        instr = &prog[ic];
        switch (instr->code) {

        case neg:
        case abs_:
            /* not shown */
            break;

        case add:
        case sub:
        case mul:
        case dvi:
        case mdl:
            /* not shown */
            break;

        case eq:
        case ne:
        case lt:
        case le:
        case gt:
        case ge:
            /* not shown */
            break;

        case ldcon:
            push(instr->u.value);
            break;

        case ldvar:
            push(data[CSG[instr->u.u1.sn1] + instr->u.u1.dpl1]);
            break;
```

```
case stvar:
    pop(&(data[CSG[instr->u.u1.sn1] + instr->u.u1.dpl1]));
    break;

case ldxvar:
    xdpl = index_dpl(instr->u.u1.sn1, instr->u.u1.dpl1);
    push(data[CSG[instr->u.u1.sn1] + xdpl]);
    break;

case stxvar:
    xdpl = index_dpl(instr->u.u1.sn1, instr->u.u1.dpl1);
    pop(&(data[CSG[instr->u.u1.sn1] + xdpl]));
    break;

case varaddr:
    push(CSG[instr->u.u1.sn1] + instr->u.u1.dpl1);
    break;

case xvaraddr:
    xdpl = index_dpl(instr->u.u1.sn1, instr->u.u1.dpl1);
    push(CSG[instr->u.u1.sn1] + xdpl);
    break;

case ldind:
    pop(&address);
    push(data[address]);
    break;

case stind:
    pop(&address);
    pop(&(data[address]));
    break;

case jump:
case jift:
case jiff:
case call:
    /* not shown */
    break;

case descr:
    descriptor(instr->u.u2.sn2, instr->u.u2.dpl2, instr->u.u2.n);
    break;

case crseg:
case dlseg:
case return_:
    /* not shown */
    break;

case rdint:
case wrint:
```

```
      /* not shown */
      break;

   case halt:
      stop = true;
      break;
   }
   ic = next;
 }
}
```

5.5 Translation of parameters

In the previous section we have redefined the storage organisation of VIM so that parameters can be stored. We have introduced special instructions to handle value and reference parameters. This means that we must reconsider the translation of procedures and variables.

5.5.1 Procedures

We consider again the syntax of a procedure declaration and block

> *procedure_declaration* : procedure_token *identifier*
> {*parameter_part* **chain** separator_token} **pack option**
> *block* separator_token
>
> .

> *block* : begin_token *declaration_part* *statement_part* end_token.

and the syntax of a call-statement

> *call_statement* : call_token *identifier* *argument* **list pack option**.
> *argument* : *identifier* *index_part* **option**
> | *expression*
>
> .

Note that the first alternative of *argument* denotes a reference argument, and the second a value argument.

We will denote the segment number and the displacement (of the descriptor) of variable *identifier* by $\text{sn}_{identifier}$ and $\text{dpl}_{identifier}$, respectively. The index of procedure *identifier* in the address table is denoted by $\text{address\_index}_{identifier}$, the index of its segment length in the length table by $\text{length\_index}_{identifier}$, and the number of its parameters by $\text{nr\_of\_pars}_{identifier}$. The translations are then:

$<procedure\_declaration>$: crseg   sn$_{identifier}$,length_index$_{identifier}$
{ stvar   sn$_{identifier}$,nr_of_pars$_{identifier}-1$
stvar   sn$_{identifier}$,nr_of_pars$_{identifier}-2$
$\vdots$
stvar   sn$_{identifier}$,1
stvar   sn$_{identifier}$,0
} **option**
$<block>$
dlseg
return

$\cdot$

$<block>$: $<declaration\_part>$
$<statement\_part>$

$\cdot$

Note that, in contrast to the translation in Sections 2.5.1 and 5.3.1, the instruction crseg is now the first instruction of the translation of procedure declaration. The reason is that the data segment must be available before the arguments are transferred from the stack to the data segment. For reasons of symmetry, we have also included the instruction dlseg in the translation of procedure declaration.

$<call\_statement>$: $<argument>$ **seq option**
call   address_index$_{identifier}$

$\cdot$

$<argument>$
: varaddr   sn$_{identifier}$,dpl$_{identifier}$ {simple variable,
reference argument}
| ldvar   sn$_{identifier}$,dpl$_{identifier}$ {reference parameter,
reference argument}
| $<index\_part>$ {indexed variable,
xvaraddr   sn$_{identifier}$,dpl$_{identifier}$ reference argument}
| $<expression>$ {expression,
value argument}

$\cdot$

We see here that the instruction ldvar is used to load an absolute address from a memory location in the case where a reference parameter from a surrounding procedure is used as a reference argument.

5.5.2   Variables

We consider again the translation of variables. Variables can be simple and indexed variables, and value and reference parameters. Identifiers that are variables are specified in the following syntax rules.

operand : *identifier index_part* **option**
　　　| *number*
　　　| *expression* **pack**

　　　.

left_part : *identifier index_part* **option**.

read_statement : read_token {*identifier index_part* **option**} **list pack**.

index_part : left_bracket_token *index* **list** right_bracket_token.
index　　　: *expression*.

We will denote the segment number and the displacement (of the descriptor) of variable *identifier* by $\text{sn}_{identifier}$ and $\text{dpl}_{identifier}$, respectively, the value of constant *identifier* by $\text{intval}_{identifier}$, and the value of number *number* by intval_{number}. The translations are then:

<*operand*>
　　　: ldvar $\text{sn}_{identifier}, \text{dpl}_{identifier}$　　{simple variable}
　　　| ldvar $\text{sn}_{identifier}, \text{dpl}_{identifier}$　　{value parameter}
　　　| ldvar $\text{sn}_{identifier}, \text{dpl}_{identifier}$　　{reference parameter}
　　　　ldind
　　　| <*index_part*>　　　　　　　　{indexed variable}
　　　　ldxvar $\text{sn}_{identifier}, \text{dpl}_{identifier}$
　　　| ldcon $\text{intval}_{identifier}$　　　　{constant}
　　　| ldcon intval_{number}　　　　{number}
　　　| <*expression*>　　　　　　　　{(expression)}

　　　.

<*left_part*>
　　　: stvar $\text{sn}_{identifier}, \text{dpl}_{identifier}$　　{simple variable}
　　　| ldvar $\text{sn}_{identifier}, \text{dpl}_{identifier}$　　{reference parameter}
　　　　stind
　　　| <*index_part*>　　　　　　　　{indexed variable}
　　　　stxvar $\text{sn}_{identifier}, \text{dpl}_{identifier}$

　　　.

<read_statement>
```
    :  {  rdint
          {  stvar  sn_identifier, dpl_identifier      {simple variable}
          |  ldvar  sn_identifier, dpl_identifier      {reference parameter}
             stind
          |  <index_part>                              {indexed variable}
             stxvar  sn_identifier, dpl_identifier
          }
       }  seq
```

<index_part> : *<index>* seq.
<index>   : *<expression>*.

5.6   Generating a compiler from SLANG to VIM

In this section we discuss the specification of a compiler that translates programs written in SLANG into code that will run on VIM. We first discuss in Section 5.6.1 the necessary extensions to the symbol-table organisation. In Section 5.6.2 we present a set of useful actions for context-sensitive parsing and code generation. In Sections 5.6.3 and 5.6.4 we specify the scanner and the context-sensitive parser and code generator of SLANG.

5.6.1   Extensions to the symbol table

The organisation of the *identifier tree* and the *push-down scope list* remains the same. All identifiers (this includes not only the names of constants and simple variables, but also the names of arrays and parameters) are stored in the identifier tree and the name lists of the push-down scope list. However, more declaration information needs to be stored, as we have introduced array variables and parameters. For the declaration of an array variable, we must store its dimension, and for the declaration of a procedure, we must store the number of its parameters, and for each parameter whether it is a value or a reference parameter. For each identifier there is again a list of definition records. Each *definition record* represents a defining occurrence of the identifier. A definition record contains the following fields:

- The segment number.
- The displacement (of a simple variable or the descriptor of an array variable), the value (of a constant), or the index of the address (of a procedure) in the address table.
- The type.

- The kind.
- The dimension (of an array variable), or the number of parameters (of a procedure).
- A pointer to a list of records for the parameters of the procedure.
- A pointer to the next definition record.

For each parameter there is a *parameter record*. Such a parameter record contains the following fields:

- The access method, i.e. value or reference.
- A pointer to the next parameter record.

The following declarations describe the records of the identifier tree, the definition list and the parameter list. As in Section 3.3.1, the type *e_type* enumerates the type values *no_type*, *unknown_type* and *int_type*. The type *e_kind* enumerates the possible kinds of the identifiers. The meanings of these kind values are:

- *unknown_kind*   unknown
- *const_kind*   constant identifier
- *svar_kind*   simple variable identifier
- *avar_kind*   array variable identifier
- *proc_kind*   procedure identifier
- *vpar_kind*   value parameter identifier
- *rpar_kind*   reference parameter identifier

The type *e_access* defines the possible access methods of the parameters. These access-method values and their meanings are as follows:

- *val_access*   value parameter
- *ref_access*   reference parameter

The new declarations are:

```
#define max_ident_length        255

typedef char                    string[max_ident_length + 1];

typedef enum {
  no_type, unknown_type, int_type
} e_type;

typedef enum {
  unknown_kind, const_kind, svar_kind, avar_kind, proc_kind, vpar_kind, rpar_kind
} e_kind;
```

```
typedef enum {
    val_access, ref_access
} e_access;

typedef struct par_rec {
    e_access                access;
    struct par_rec          *next;
} par_rec;

typedef struct def_rec {
    int                     sn, dpl_or_value_or_index;
    e_type                  type;
    e_kind                  kind;
    int                     dim_or_nr_of_pars;
    par_rec                 *par_list;
    struct def_rec          *next;
} def_rec;

typedef struct ident_rec {
    string                  ident;
    def_rec                 *def_list;
    struct ident_rec        *left, *right;
} ident_rec;
```

5.6.2   Actions

Having added arrays and parameters to SLANG, we must reconsider the actions
that we need for context-sensitive analysis and code generation. In Figures 5.7
through 5.11 we show the action definitions that we will use in the parser specification for SLANG. Comparing Figures 5.7 through 5.11 to Figures 4.9 through
4.13, we see some actions have been redefined, new actions have been included,
and some actions that are no longer needed have been deleted.

Compared to Figure 4.9, the following changes have taken place in Figure 5.7.
The action *create_definition* has an extra parameter *dim_or_nr_of_pars*, which represents the dimension of an array or the number of parameters of a procedure. The
action *find_definition* has an extra parameter *is_bound*, which has the value true if
the operand is part of a bound expression. If this is the case, we must search for
a constant or variable in the surrounding block. The symbol-table management
provides new actions for arrays and parameters. The action *get_dimension* returns
the dimension of an array, and the action *get_nr_of_parameters* the number of parameters of a procedure. There are actions that add parameter records to, and find
parameter records in, the symbol table, and actions that retrieve the *access_kind* of
a parameter record, which indicates whether the parameter is a value or reference
parameter.

action	meaning
enter_scope ( )	creates a new scope record, and increments the scope level
exit_scope ( )	deletes the definition records of all identifiers in the current scope; deletes the current scope record, and decrements the scope level
current_scope (**out** *level*: integer)	returns in *level* the scope level of the block currently being parsed
create_definition (**out** *def*: def_ptr; **in** *dpl_or_value_or_index*: integer; **in** *type*: e_type; **in** *kind*: e_kind; **in** *dim_or_nr_of_pars*: integer)	creates a new definition record, and initialises its fields with the values of *dpl_or_value_or_index*, *type*, *kind* and *dim_or_nr_of_pars*; the parameter *sn* is implicit; output parameter *def* points to the created record
insert_definition (**in** *name*: string; **in** *def*: def_ptr)	adds the name *name* to the identifier tree, and the record, pointed to by *def*, to the definition list of the symbol table
find_definition (**out** *def*: def_ptr; **in** *name*: string; **in** *is_bound*: Boolean)	returns in *def* a pointer to a definition record of identifier *name*; if *is_bound* is false, then the current definition is taken; if *is_bound* is true, then a parameter is taken from the current block, and a constant or variable from a surrounding block

Figure 5.7 Actions for symbol-table management.

The actions for checking context constraints in Figure 5.8 are more complicated than the actions in Figure 4.10 as more cases have to be distinguished. The action *check_if_false* is included so that the value of a Boolean attribute can be checked. The actions *check_if_too_many* and *check_if_too_few* can be used to check whether the number of arguments of a procedure call is equal to the number of parameters of the corresponding procedure declaration. These actions can also be used to check whether the number of indices of an indexed variable is equal to the dimension (i.e. the number of bound pairs) of the corresponding array declaration. Checking the number of arguments of a procedure call proceeds as follows. The actions *check_if_too_many* and *check_if_too_few* have an argument *nr*. The initial value of *nr* is the number of parameters of the procedure declaration. This value is decremented by 1 each time an argument of the procedure call is parsed. The action *check_if_too_many* is used to check if there are more arguments than parameters. This is the case when the value of *nr* has become 0 and there are still arguments to

action	meaning
get_sn_dpl (out *sn*, *dpl*: integer; in *def*: def_ptr)	returns in *sn* the data segment number and in *dpl* the displacement of the identifier defined in the definition record, pointed to by *def*
get_address (out *address*: integer; in *def*: def_ptr)	returns in *address* the index in the address table of the procedure defined in the definition record, pointed to by *def*
get_nr_of_parameters (out *n*: integer; in *def*: def_ptr)	returns in *n* the number of parameters of the procedure defined in the definition record, pointed to by *def*
get_dimension (out *n*: integer; in *def*: def_ptr)	returns in *n* the dimension of the array variable defined in the definition record, pointed to by *def*
add_parameter (in *def*: def_ptr; in *access*: e_access)	creates a new parameter record, initialises its field with the value of *access*, adds the record to the list of parameter records of the procedure record, pointed to by *def*, and increments the number of parameters
find_first_parameter (out *def_par*: par_ptr; in *def_proc*: def_ptr)	returns in *def_par* a pointer to the parameter record of the first parameter of the procedure record, pointed to by *def_proc*
find_next_parameter (inout *def_par*: par_ptr)	returns in *def_par* a pointer to the parameter record of the next parameter following the parameter record, pointed to by *def_par*
get_kind_of_parameter (out *is_ref_arg*: Boolean; in *def*: par_ptr)	returns in *is_ref_arg* whether the access_kind of the parameter record, pointed to by *def_par*, is *rpar_kind* or not

Figure 5.7 (continued) Actions for symbol-table management.

be parsed. The action *check_if_too_few* is used to check if there are less arguments than parameters, which is the case when no more arguments are left and *nr* is still not 0. In a similar way it is checked whether the number of indices of an indexed variable equals the number of bound pairs in the corresponding array variable.

Note that no changes have been made in the set of actions for manipulating the address table, i.e. Figure 5.9 is equal to Figure 4.11. Figure 5.10 contains the new actions *emit_descr* and *emit_stargs*. The first generates the **descr** instruction,

action	meaning
check_kind (in *kind*: e_kind; in *def*: def_ptr; in *truthval*: Boolean)	checks if the kind of the record, pointed to by *def*, is equal or not equal to *kind*
check_if_false (in *truthval*: Boolean)	checks if the value of *truthval* is false
check_if_too_many (in *nr*: integer)	checks if there are more arguments than parameters, or more indices than bound pairs; *nr* denotes the number of indices or arguments that is still expected
check_if_too_few (in *nr*: integer)	checks if there are more parameters than arguments, or more bound pairs than indices; *nr* denotes the number of indices or arguments that is still expected

Figure 5.8 Actions for checking context constraints.

action	meaning
get_label (out *index*: integer)	a free position in the address table is returned in *index*
get_index (out *index*: integer)	a free position in the length table is returned in *index*
emit_label (in *index*: integer)	the current value of *ic* is stored at position *index* in the address table
enter_length (in *index*, *length*: integer)	the value of *length* is stored at position *index* in the length table

Figure 5.9 Actions for manipulating the address and length table.

the latter the stvar instructions, which pop arguments from the stack and store them in the data segment in reverse order. Note that the action *emit_load* has become more complicated, as not only simple variables and constants must be distinguished, but also indexed variables and value and reference parameters. A similar action *emit_store* has been included. The action *emit_stvar* is no longer needed.

In Figure 5.11 we have defined new actions for attribute evaluation. Examples are actions to increment and decrement integer values, assign Boolean values, and the action *length_of_descriptor*, which computes the length of the descriptor of an array from its dimension.

All the actions defined above will be used in the specification for SLANG, which we present in the next section.

action	meaning
initialise_vimcode ( )	initialises the generation of VIM code; opens the code file
finalise_vimcode ( )	generates a halt instruction; writes the address and length table to output files, and closes the files
emit_crseg (**in** *level*, *index*: integer)	generates a crseg instruction with the values of *level* and *index* as arguments
emit_descr (**in** *sn*, *dpl*, *n*: integer)	generates a descr instruction with the values of *sn*, *dpl* and *n* as arguments
emit_stargs (**in** *n*: integer)	generates *n* stvar instructions; these instructions pop the arguments from the stack and store them in the data segment in reverse order
emit (**in** *code*: operation)	creates a parameter-less instruction
emit_jump (**in** *code*: operation; **in** *index*: integer)	generates a jump instruction with the value of *index* as index in the address table
emit_load (**in** *def*: def_ptr; **in** *is_ref_arg*: Boolean)	determines if *def* points to the record of a constant, a simple or indexed variable, or a value or reference parameter, takes into account the value of *is_ref_arg*, and generates one of the instructions ldcon, ldvar, ldxvar, varaddr or xvaraddr, or the combination of an ldvar and an ldind instruction; the value, or the segment number and displacement are taken from the record, pointed to by *def*
emit_store (**in** *def*: def_ptr)	determines if *def* points to the record of a simple or indexed variable, or a reference parameter, and generates one of the instructions stvar or stxvar, or the combination of an ldvar and an stind instruction; the segment number and displacement are taken from the record, pointed to by *def*
emit_ldcon (**in** *value*: integer)	generates an ldcon instruction with the value of *value* as argument

Figure 5.10 Actions for code generation.

action	meaning

assign_int (
  out *dest*: integer;
  in *source*: integer)
	assigns the integer value of *source* to *dest*

clear_int (**out** *dest*: integer)	assigns the value 0 to *dest*

increment_int (
  inout *dest*: integer;
  in *value*: integer)
	increments the integer value of *dest* by the integer value *value*

decrement_int (
  inout *dest*: integer;
  in *value*: integer)
	decrements the integer value of *dest* by the integer value *value*

assign_true (**out** *dest*: Boolean)	assigns the value true to *dest*
assign_false (**out** *dest*: Boolean)	assigns the value false to *dest*
assign_bool (**out** *dest*: Boolean; **in** *source*: Boolean)	assigns the Boolean value of *source* to *dest*
assign_op (**out** *dest*: operation; **in** *source*: operation)	assigns the operation value *source* to *dest*
clear_op (**out** *dest*: operation)	assigns the operation value noop to *dest*

length_of_descriptor (
  out *size*: integer;
  in *n*: integer)
	assigns the value $2 * n + 2$ to *size*

Figure 5.11 Actions for attribute evaluation.

5.6.3   A scanner specification for SLANG

We now present a *scanner specification* for SLANG from which the compiler generator can generate a scanner. Actually, the scanner specification is the same as shown in Section 4.3.2, except that extra token definitions are needed. We only show these extra definitions. Only 3 new tokens are defined and need to be declared in the *symbols* section of the scanner-generator input, as follows.

symbols
```
    left_bracket_token    :   [    .
    right_bracket_token   :   ]    .
    up_to_token           :   ..   .
```

5.6.4   A parser specification for SLANG

Below we show a *parser specification* for SLANG from which the compiler generator can generate a context-sensitive parser and code generator.

attributes

inh_dim	:	integer	**inh of** *index_part.*
syn_dim	:	integer	**syn of** *bound_part*
			with default clear_int.
inh_dpl	:	integer	**inh of** *block, declaration_part, variable_declaration.*
syn_dpl	:	integer	**syn of** *variable_declaration*
			with default clear_int.
length	:	integer	**syn of** *block, declaration_part*
			with default clear_int.
op	:	operator	**syn of** *add_operator, multiply_operator,*
			unary_operator, relational_operator
			with default clear_op.
is_bound	:	boolean	**inh of** *expression, term, factor, operand.*
is_ref_arg	:	boolean	**inh of** *expression, term, factor, operand.*

root

    initialise_vimcode ( )
    program_declaration
    finalise_vimcode ( )

    .

rules

  program_declaration (**local** *level, length_index:* integer)
   : enter_scope ( )
     current_scope (*level*)
     get_index (*length_index*)
     emit_crseg (*level, length_index*)
     clear_int (*inh_dpl* **of** *block*)
     block
     enter_length (*length_index, length* **of** *block*)
     emit (**dlseg**)
     exit_scope ( )
     period_token

    .

  block
   : begin_token
     assign_int (*inh_dpl* **of** *declaration_part, inh_dpl* **of** *block*)
     declaration_part
     assign_int (*length* **of** *block, length* **of** *declaration_part*)
     statement_part
     end_token

    .

declaration_part (**local** *dpl*, *over_procs*: integer)
:   assign_int (*dpl*, *inh_dpl* **of** *declaration_part*)
    { *constant_declaration*
    | assign_int (*inh_dpl* **of** *variable_declaration*, *dpl*)
      variable_declaration
      assign_int (*dpl*, *syn_dpl* **of** *variable_declaration*)
    } **clos**
    assign_int (*length* **of** *declaration_part*, *dpl*)
    { get_label (*over_procs*)
      emit_jump (**jump**, *over_procs*)
      procedure_declaration **seq**
      emit_label (*over_procs*)
    } **option**

.

constant_declaration (**local** *def*: def_ptr)
:   *type_declarer*
    { ident_token
      equal_token
      num_token
      create_definition (*def*, *num_value* **of** num_token, **int_type**, **const_kind**, 0)
      insert_definition (*ident_lexeme* **of** ident_token, *def*)
    } **list**
    separator_token

.

type_declarer
:   int_token

.

variable_declaration (**local** *sn*, *dpl*, *size*: integer; *def*: def_ptr)
:   var_token
    type_declarer
    assign_int (*dpl*, *inh_dpl* **of** *variable_declaration*)
    { ident_token
      { create_definition (*def*, *dpl*, **int_type**, **svar_kind**, 0)
        increment_int (*dpl*, 1)
      | *bound_part*
        create_definition (*def*, *dpl*, **int_type**, **avar_kind**, *syn_dim* **of** *bound_part*)
        current_scope (*sn*)
        emit_descr (*sn*, *dpl*, *syn_dim* **of** *bound_part*)
        length_of_descriptor (*size*, *syn_dim* **of** *bound_part*)

```
        increment_int (dpl, size)
    }
    insert_definition (ident_lexeme of ident_token, def)
} list
assign_int (syn_dpl of variable_declaration, dpl)
separator_token
```
.

```
bound_part (local nr_of_bound_pairs: integer)
  : left_bracket_token
    clear_int (nr_of_bound_pairs)
    {  bound_pair
       increment_int (nr_of_bound_pairs, 1)
    } list
    assign_int (syn_dim of bound_part, nr_of_bound_pairs)
    right_bracket_token
```
.

```
bound_pair
  : bound
    up_to_token
    bound
```
.

```
bound
  : assign_true (is_bound of expression)
    assign_false (is_ref_arg of expression)
    expression
```
.

```
procedure_declaration (local level, length_index, dpl, address: integer;
                              def_proc, def_par: def_ptr)
  : procedure_token
    ident_token
    get_label (address)
    emit_label (address)
    create_definition (def_proc, address, no_type, proc_kind, 0)
    insert_definition (ident_lexeme of ident_token#1, def_proc)
    enter_scope ( )
    current_scope (level)
    get_index (length_index)
    emit_crseg (level, length_index)
    clear_int (dpl)
```

```
{ {  type_declarer
      {  ident_token
         create_definition (def_par, dpl, int_type, vpar_kind, 0)
         insert_definition (ident_lexeme of ident_token#2, def_par)
         add_parameter (def_proc, val_access)
         increment_int (dpl, 1)
      }  list
   |  var_token
      type_declarer
      {  ident_token
         create_definition (def_par, dpl, int_type, rpar_kind, 0)
         insert_definition (ident_lexeme of ident_token#3, def_par)
         add_parameter (def_proc, ref_access)
         increment_int (dpl, 1)
      }  list
   }  chain separator_token
   emit_stargs (dpl)
}  pack option
assign_int (inh_dpl of block, dpl)
block
enter_length (length_index, length of block)
emit (dlseg)
emit (return)
exit_scope ( )
separator_token
```

.

Note that the actions to enter a new scope and to create a new segment have been moved from the production for *block* to the productions for *program_declaration* and *procedure_declaration*. The reason for this is that the parameters of a procedure belong to the new scope and, therefore, need to be stored in the new segment. The actions *enter_scope* and *emit_crseg* must therefore take place just before the open-token of the parameter list is passed. At this point the displacement must also be initialised to 0, as the parameters occupy the first positions in the segment.

Note that many productions contribute to the computation of the length of the data segment. The length will be finally stored in the length table by the actions of the productions *program_declaration* and *procedure_declaration*.

We have merged the nonterminals *lower_bound* and *upper_bound* into *bound*, as both have *expression* on the right-hand side. Note that *expression* has 2 inherited attributes, namely, *is_bound* and *is_ref_arg*. The value of attribute *is_bound* is set to true if a variable or constant must be taken from a surrounding block, otherwise it is set to false. Attribute *is_bound* is therefore an argument of action *find_definition*. The role of *is_ref_arg* will be explained when we discuss the production for *call_statement*, which we do below.

If we compare the parser specification above to that in Section 4.3.3, we see that the production for *procedure_declaration* has been extended with a parameter list. Further, in the parser specification above, we have merged all the productions associated with *procedure_declaration* into 1 production.

The action *add_parameter* creates a *parameter record*. The first field of this record indicates whether it is a *value* or a *reference* parameter. The second field contains a pointer to the next parameter record. The parameter records are listed in the order in which their corresponding parameters occur in the procedure declaration, i.e. every parameter record is added to the end of the already existing list.

The syntax for *call_statement* is:

> *call_statement* : call_token *identifier argument* **list pack option**.
> *argument* : *identifier index_part* **option**
> | *expression*
> .

The production for *argument* above is not predictive, as the first alternative, *identifier index_part* **option**, is a special case of the second alternative, *expression*. We therefore change the production into

> *argument* : *expression* .

and introduce an inherited attribute *is_ref_arg* that indicates whether an expression (or subexpression) is a reference argument or not. In the case of a reference argument, the expression must be a simple or indexed variable, or a reference parameter from a surrounding procedure. In the case of a value argument, the expression may have a general form.

For each argument we apply the function *get_kind_of_parameter* that extracts the access_method (*ref_access* or *val_access*) of the corresponding parameter from its parameter record, and assigns the value true or false to the attribute *is_ref_arg*. The actions *find_first_parameter* and *find_next_parameter* are applied to find the parameter records. In order to check if the number of arguments equals the number of parameters, we apply the actions *get_nr_of_parameters*, *decrement_int*, *check_if_too_many* and *check_if_too_few*.

The complete specification of the call-statement is as follows:

> *call_statement* (**local** *nr_of_pars*, *address*: integer;
> *def_proc*: def_ptr; *def_par*: par_ptr)
> : call_token
> ident_token
> find_definition (*def_proc*, *ident_lexeme* **of** ident_token, false)
> check_kind (**proc_kind**, *def*, true)
> get_nr_of_parameters (*nr_of_pars*, *def_proc*)
> { find_first_parameter (*def_par*, *def_proc*)

```
    {  check_if_too_many (nr_of_pars)
       assign_false (is_bound of expression)
       get_kind_of_parameter (is_ref_arg of expression, def_par)
       expression
       decrement_int (nr_of_pars, 1)
       find_next_parameter (def_par)
    } list pack
  } option
  check_if_too_few (nr_of_pars)
  get_address (address, def_proc)
  emit_jump (call, address)
```

Nothing has been added to the productions for *statement_part* and *statement*, and for the control statements *if_statement* and *while_statement*. Their specifications, therefore, are not included.

The *assignment_statement* has an ordering problem, as the right part must first be evaluated, and next this value must be assigned to the variable of the left part. In Section 4.3.4, where only simple variables were applied, we solved this problem by temporarily storing the values of the segment number and the displacement in attributes until we were ready to use these values in the *emit_stvar* action. In the extended version of SLANG this solution is no longer possible, as there is no restriction on the number of indices in indexed variables. The VIM code of an indexed variable can thus be arbitrarily long. We solve the ordering problem by means of jumps.

Note that the left part can be a simple or indexed variable, or a reference parameter. The action *emit_store* determines the kind of the identifier concerned (from its definition record) and emits an `stvar` or `stxvar` instruction, or the combination of an `ldvar` and an `stind` instruction. The segment number and displacement are taken from the definition record.

In the production for *index_part* we check if the number of indices of an indexed variable equals the number of bound pairs in the corresponding variable declaration. This is done in a similar way to the counting of the arguments of a call statement. In the specification below we will merge the productions for *index_part* and *index*.

```
assignment_statement (local left, right, after: integer)
  :  get_label (right)
     emit_jump (jump, right)
     get_label (left)
     emit_label (left)
     left_part
     get_label (after)
```

    emit_jump (jump, *after*)
    becomes_token
    emit_label (*right*)
    assign_false (*is_bound* **of** *expression*)
    assign_false (*is_ref_arg* **of** *expression*)
    expression
    emit_jump (jump, *left*)
    emit_label (*after*)

    .

left_part (**local** *def*: def_ptr)
  :   ident_token
    find_definition (*def, ident_lexeme* **of** ident_token, false)
    {   check_kind (**const_kind**, *def*, false)
      check_kind (**avar_kind**, *def*, false)
      check_kind (**proc_kind**, *def*, false)
      check_kind (**vpar_kind**, *def*, false)
      emit_store (*def*)
    | check_kind (**avar_kind**, *def*, true)
      get_dimension (*inh_dim* **of** *index_part, def*)
      index_part
      emit_store (*def*)
    }

    .

index_part (**local** *nr_of_indices*: integer)
  :   left_bracket_token
    assign_int (*nr_of_indices, inh_dim* **of** *index_part*)
    {   check_if_too_many (*nr_of_indices*)
      assign_false (*is_bound* **of** *expression*)
      assign_false (*is_ref_arg* **of** *expression*)
      expression
      decrement_int (*nr_of_indices*, 1)
    } **list**
    check_if_too_few (*nr_of_indices*)
    right_bracket_token

    .

Note that the use of 3 jumps in the translation of an assignment statement is not very efficient. A better solution is to let the production for *left_part* emit an instruction that loads an absolute address on the stack, i.e. a **varaddr** instruction for a simple variable, an **xvaraddr** instruction for an indexed variable, and an **ldvar** instruction for a reference parameter. The production for *assignment_statement* must then emit a `swap` and an `stind` instruction after the code for the right part has been generated. The `swap` instruction exchanges 2 operands on top of the arithmetic stack, so that the destination address and the value to be stored are in the right order. The `stind` instruction removes both the address and the value from the stack and stores the value at the address.

The production for *read_statement* has the same characteristics as the production for *left_part*. In the production for *write_statement* we must set the inherited attributes *is_bound* and *is_ref_arg* of *expression* to false, to indicate that the expression is neither a bound expression nor a reference argument.

read_statement (**local** *sn, dpl*: integer; *def*: def_ptr)
  : read_token
    { ident_token
      find_definition (*def, ident_lexeme* **of** ident_token, false)
      emit (`rdint`)
      { check_kind (`const_kind`, *def*, false)
        check_kind (`avar_kind`, *def*, false)
        check_kind (`proc_kind`, *def*, false)
        check_kind (`vpar_kind`, *def*, false)
      | check_kind (`avar_kind`, *def*, true)
        get_dimension (*inh_dim* **of** *index_part, def*)
        index_part
      }
      emit_store (*def*)
    } **list pack**

    .

write_statement
  : write_token
    { assign_false (*is_bound* **of** *expression*)
      assign_false (*is_ref_arg* **of** *expression*)
      expression
      emit (`wrint`)
    } **list pack**

    .

Below we present the productions for *expression, term, factor* and *operand*. The values of attributes *is_bound* and *is_ref_arg* are inherited. The value of *is_bound* is true if a variable or constant must be taken from a surrounding block, otherwise it is false. Attribute *is_bound* is used as an argument in action *find_definition* in production *operand*. The value of *is_ref_arg* is true if the expression represents a reference argument, otherwise it is false. If the expression is a reference argument, then it must not contain an operator. This is checked.

An operand has several alternatives. If the operand is a constant, a simple or indexed variable, or a value or reference parameter, then the action *emit_load* determines whether the operand is a reference argument or not; it also determines the kind of the identifier concerned, and generates one of the instructions ldcon, ldvar, ldxvar, varaddr or xvaraddr, or the combination of an ldvar and an ldind instruction. The segment number and displacement are taken from the definition record. If the operand is a number, then an ldcon instruction is emitted. Finally, if the operand is an expression in parentheses, then the code generation is delegated to this expression.

expression
   : assign_bool (*is_bound* **of** *term*#1, *is_bound* **of** *expression*)
     assign_bool (*is_ref_arg* **of** *term*#1, *is_ref_arg* **of** *expression*)
     term
     { *add_operator*
       assign_bool (*is_bound* **of** *term*#2, *is_bound* **of** *expression*)
       check_if_false (*is_ref_arg* **of** *expression*)
       assign_false (*is_ref_arg* **of** *term*#2)
       term
       emit (*op* **of** *add_operator*)
     } **clos**
     .

term
   : assign_bool (*is_bound* **of** *factor*#1, *is_bound* **of** *term*)
     assign_bool (*is_ref_arg* **of** *factor*#1, *is_ref_arg* **of** *term*)
     factor
     { *multiply_operator*
       assign_bool (*is_bound* **of** *factor*#2, *is_bound* **of** *term*)
       check_if_false (*is_ref_arg* **of** *term*)
       assign_false (*is_ref_arg* **of** *factor*#2)
       factor
       emit (*op* **of** *multiply_operator*)
     } **clos**
     .

factor
   : *unary_operator*
     assign_bool (*is_bound* **of** *operand*#1, *is_bound* **of** *factor*)
     check_if_false (*is_ref_arg* **of** *factor*)
     assign_false (*is_ref_arg* **of** *operand*#1)
     operand
     emit (*op* **of** *unary_operator*)
  | assign_bool (*is_bound* **of** *operand*#2, *is_bound* **of** *factor*)

assign_bool (*is_ref_arg* **of** *operand*#2, *is_ref_arg* **of** *factor*)
operand

.

operand (**local** *sn*, *dpl*: integer; *def*: def_ptr)
  : ident_token
    find_definition (*def*, *ident_lexeme* **of** ident_token, *is_bound* **of** *operand*)
    { check_kind (**avar_kind**, *def*, false)
      check_kind (**proc_kind**, *def*, false)
    | check_kind (**avar_kind**, *def*, true)
      get_dimension (*inh_dim* **of** *index_part*, *def*)
      index_part
    }
    emit_load (*def*, *is_ref_arg* **of** *operand*)
  | num_token
    check_if_false (*is_ref_arg* **of** *operand*)
    emit_ldcon (*num_value* **of** num_token)
  | assign_bool (*is_bound* **of** *expression*, *is_bound* **of** *operand*)
    check_if_false (*is_ref_arg* **of** *operand*)
    assign_false (*is_ref_arg* **of** *expression*)
    expression **pack**

.

Nothing has changed in the productions for operators. Their specifications, therefore, are not included. We end with the specification for *relation*.

relation
  : assign_false (*is_bound* **of** *expression*#1)
    assign_false (*is_ref_arg* **of** *expression*#1)
    expression
    relational_operator
    assign_false (*is_bound* **of** *expression*#2)
    assign_false (*is_ref_arg* **of** *expression*#2)
    expression
    emit (*op* **of** *relational_operator*)

.

5.7 Exercises

1. Consider the following SLANG program:

```
BEGIN VAR INT i,j,k[1..2];
      PROC proc (INT i; VAR INT a,b)
      BEGIN VAR INT j;
            j := b; a := i; b := j-1
      END;
      i := 1; j := 2; k[1] := 1; k[2*i] := 2;
      CALL proc (k[k[j-1]],k[k[2]],k[k[2]])
END .
```

Give the translation of this program in VIM instructions.

2. Consider the following SLANG program:

```
BEGIN VAR INT a;
      PROC proc1 (VAR INT b)
      BEGIN PROC proc2 (VAR INT c)
            BEGIN c := 2*c END;
            CALL proc2 (b);
            b := b+1
      END;
      READ (a);
      CALL proc1 (a);
      WRITE (a)
END .
```

Give the translation of this program in VIM instructions.

3. Consider the following SLANG program:

```
BEGIN VAR INT n;
      PROC exchange (VAR INT a,b)
      BEGIN VAR INT c;
            c := a; a := b; b := c
      END;
      PROC sort (INT n)
      BEGIN VAR INT i,j,a[1..n];
            i := 1;
            WHILE i <= n DO READ (a[i]); i := i+1 OD;
            i := 2;
            WHILE i <= n DO
                IF a[i] < a[i-1] THEN
                    CALL exchange (a[i],a[i-1]);
                    j := i-1;
```

```
                    WHILE j >= 2 DO
                        IF a[j] < a[j-1] THEN
                            CALL exchange (a[j],a[j-1])
                        FI;
                        j := j-1
                    OD
                  FI;
                  i := i+1
              OD;
              i := 1;
              WHILE i <= n DO WRITE (a[i]); i := i+1 OD
          END;
          READ (n);
          CALL sort (n)
      END .
```

Give the translation of this program in VIM instructions.

4. Consider the specification of the procedure declaration in Section 5.6.4. Give the corresponding procedure that performs parsing and attribute evaluation. Follow exactly the method of the compiler generator, i.e. generate a parser according to the rules of Figure 3.13, and insert actions as described in Section 4.2. Your result should be an extension of the procedure for procedure declaration in Section 3.5.

5. Rewrite the productions for *assignment_statement* and *left_part* in the parser specification so that jumps are avoided in the VIM-code. Let the production for *left_part* emit an instruction that loads an absolute address on the stack, and let the production for *assignment_statement* emit a **swap** and an **stind** instruction. The **swap** instruction exchanges 2 operands on top of the stack. This will require you to define a new instruction **swap** and new actions for code generation.

5.8 Laboratory

In Chapter 4 we described a basic expression language as a laboratory assignment, and we extended that language by adding a conditional statement and a while statement. We now wish to extend the basic expression language even further by adding procedures, functions, pointers, arrays and records.

In Section 5.8.1 and 5.8.2 we propose adding procedures and functions. Their implementation is straightforward.

In Section 5.4 we introduced absolute addresses, and used these addresses to implement reference parameters. Absolute addresses can also be used to implement pointers. An extension to our language with pointers is proposed in Section 5.8.3.

In Section 5.1 we introduced dynamic arrays, which require a descriptor in the static part of the data segment, while the array itself is placed in the dynamic part. The arrays that we propose in Section 5.8.4 are different. They have integer denotations as bounds, so that their values are known at compile time and a descriptor is not needed, and the array itself can be placed in the static part of the data segment. Moreover, not only operations on indexed variables, but also on complete arrays are defined. This will require the student to add new instructions to the interpreter, e.g. an instruction stnvar sn,dpl which removes an array from the stack, and writes it at position (sn,dpl) in memory, an instruction eqn n, which compares 2 arrays of length n on the stack, and an instruction popn n, which pops n elements from the stack.

The exercise we propose on records in Section 5.8.5 is the most complicated as we have not as yet discussed records. The records considered, however, are a generalisation of the static arrays in Section 5.8.4. The only difference is that their fields can have different types. The implementation is similar to arrays.

The extensions are described below.

5.8.1   Procedures

The body of a procedure is a closed compound expression that has type void. This means that a procedure cannot be an operand.

A procedure may have value parameters and reference parameters. Both kinds of parameters are, of course, operands, and can be of type integer, Boolean and character.

A procedure must be declared before it is called. However, a procedure can call itself recursively. Further, 2 procedures that call each other must be nested.

5.8.2   Functions

A function is similar to a procedure. The differences are:

- Functions have value parameters only.
- A function call is an operand.
- The closed compound expression that is the body of the function generates a value. This is the value returned by the function. The type of this value (either integer, Boolean and character) is also the type of the function.

Like a variable, constant and procedure, a function must be declared in the text before it is used (called). This means that a function can recursively call itself. It also means that 2 functions that call each other must be nested.

5.8.3 Pointers

We now add pointers to our expression language. A pointer has a value, which is the address of a variable, or **nil**. When a pointer is declared, we must specify the type of the variable to which it points. For example:

var pointer to integer: p, q

Pointers are assigned by using an address function, *address*(*var*), where *var* is a variable. For example:

$p :=$ address(i)

The inverse of this function, *value*(p), yields the value pointed to by pointer p. For example:

$i :=$ value(p)

where, in this case, the variable i would have to be declared as an integer. The value **nil** can also be assigned to a pointer, as in

$q :=$ **nil**

Note that **nil** has no single type—**nil** can be assigned to a pointer of any type.

Like arrays and records, pointers are operators that can be assigned (e.g. $p := q$) and compared (e.g. $p = q$ and $p <> q$).

Note that a pointer to a variable is only valid as long as the variable is within its scope. A pointer to a variable that has "ceased to exist" is called a *dangling* pointer. The compiler must check that pointers do not dangle. Consider, for example, the statement

$p :=$ (**var integer**: i; $i :=$17; address(i))

The value of the closed compound expression is the address of i. The pointer dangles because i is not defined outside the closed compound expression. In general, globally-declared pointers that point to local variables must not be used outside the scope of these variables.

5.8.4 Arrays

Arrays allow data to be conveniently structured. For simplicity, we only consider 1 and 2-dimensional arrays. To declare and use arrays, we add the following language constructs. Note that the syntax used in the examples shown below is for illustrative purposes only.

type declaration: Array types allow a new array data type to be defined. In the type definition, bounds are placed on the indices. These bounds must be integer denotations. For example:

type *barray* = **array** [1..4] **of boolean**,
        iarray = **array** [1..2,1..2] **of integer**

Note that, because the bounds are integers, the bounds can always be statically determined.

variable declaration: Array variables can be declared by using the array type. For example:

var *barray*: *b*, *iarray*: *x*, *y*

variable: Array variables and constants can be used in the program text. Arrays can be assigned (using the assignment operator :=), and they can be compared (the operators = and <>). For example:

if $x <> y$ **then** $x := y$ **fi**

where x and y have been declared above as having an array type.

indexed variable: Indexed array variables can be used to access elements in an array. An index is an integer expression, and is traditionally enclosed in square brackets. For example:

$i := 1$;
$x[i] := y[i]$

denotation: Array denotations are also possible. For example:

$b := [\textbf{true},\textbf{false},\textbf{true},\textbf{false}]$;
$x := [[7,1],[7,31]]$

will initialise the 2 arrays declared above.

Like variables, constants and denotations, therefore, array variables and indexed array variables are operands. In the case of array variables, however, only the operators = and <> can be used. Indexed array variables have the type integer, Boolean and character, and therefore satisfy the table in Figure 4.15.

Constant array declarations. Just as "variables" can be declared as constant, it should also be possible to declare array variables as constant. Consider, for example, the following declaration:

con *barray*: $a = [\textbf{true}, \textbf{true}, \textbf{true}, \textbf{true}]$

The implementation of this construct, however, is more difficult than other array constructs, and for this reason, it is included as an optional extra.

5.8.5   Records

Records can be seen as a generalisation of arrays. The specification of records, therefore, follows the same lines as arrays. It involves adding a record type declaration, record variable declaration, record variables, record field variables (which are analogous to indexed arrays) and record denotations.

A record consists of fields, and these fields can be of type integer, Boolean and character. Below we describe how records are declared and used. As with arrays, the syntax used in the examples is for illustrative purposes only.

type declaration: Record type declarations define the structure of a record. A record consists of a number of field variables. Each field variable has a certain type. For example:

> **type** *mix* = **record** [**integer:** *a*; **boolean:** *b*; **char:** *c*]

In this record type declaration, 3 field variables have been declared.

variable declaration: Record variables can be declared by using the previously declared record type. For example:

> **var** *mix:* *r, s*

variable: Record variables and constants can be used in the program text. Records can be assigned (:=) and they can be compared (= and <>). For example:

> **if** *r* <> *s* **then** *r* := *s* **fi**

field variables: The record field variables are identified by a record and field name, separated by a dot. For example:

> *r.a* := 1;
> *r.b* := **false**;
> *r.c* := 'a'

denotation: Record denotations can be used to initialise a record. A record denotation consists of the record type, followed by the contents of the fields, and surrounded by square brackets. For example:

> *r* := [1, **true**, 'a']

Like variables, constants and denotations, therefore, record variables and field variables are operands. However, only the operators = and <> can be used with record variables. Because field variables can only have the types integer Boolean and character, field variables satisfy the table in Figure 4.15.

Constant record declarations. As an optional extra, we could also consider constant record declarations. Take, for example, the following declaration.

> **con** *mix:* *r* = **record** [1; **true**; 'a']

However, analogous to arrays, the implementation of this construct is more difficult than other record constructs.

5.9   Bibliographic notes

This chapter discusses two extensions to SLANG: arrays and parameters. Other extensions are considered in laboratory assignments. For further information the reader is referred to Fischer and LeBlanc [45], and to a lesser extent to Aho *et al.* [3].

Chapter 6

Code generation

In the course of Chapters 2 and 5 (Sections 2.2.3, 2.4.3, 2.6.3, 5.2.3 and 5.4.3) we have developed in step-wise fashion an interpreter for VIM. This interpreter executes code that has been generated by the compiler. Although an interpreter is simple and convenient to use, it is also inefficient. For example, if we write a program in SLANG that computes the 2000th prime number, and translate this program into VIM code, then the interpreter takes approximately 40 seconds to execute the code. If we rewrite our program in C, then the executable generated by the C-compiler takes approximately $\frac{1}{2}$ of a second to execute![1] Interpreting VIM code is therefore 80 times slower than executing compiled code.

To improve the performance of the system, we need to generate directly executable code from SLANG. We can do this by treating the VIM code as an intermediate code, and using a *code generator* to translate this code into executable target code. Note that by adding a code generator to our system, the compiler that we have been referring to in previous chapters (see Figure 4.7 for example) becomes just the *front-end* of the compiler. The *back-end* of the compiler is then the code generator. We depicted the front and back-ends in Chapter 1, Figures 1.8 and 1.10. So we now differentiate between intermediate-code generation, carried out in the front-end, and "proper" code generation, carried out in the back-end. The main difference is that the code generated by the back-end can be directly "executed" on the target machine. As well as the code generator, the back-end often also consists of an optimiser. The role of the optimiser is to improve the "quality" of the code. The optimiser may be placed before the code generator, in which case it optimises the intermediate code, or after the code generator, in which case it optimises the target code. We may, of course, use both optimisers. Obviously, any optimisations of the intermediate code that we carry out must lead to more efficient target code.

In the following section we will consider code-generation strategies. We will discuss the role that the target code plays, and outline the technique that we will

---

[1] Note that both tests were carried out on an Intel 80486 machine.

use to build a code generator. In Section 6.2 we will describe a code generator that translates VIM code into C-code. We will modify this technique in Section 6.3 to build another translator, this time from VIM code to assembly code. Finally, in Section 6.4 we will consider the performance of the code generated by the 2 translators.

6.1   Code-generation strategies

Code generation is a combination of storage allocation, instruction selection and, because we want to choose the most efficient instructions, optimisation.[2] These *phases*, however, are mutually dependent. This mutual dependency is the classic problem in code generation, and is referred to as the *phase-ordering problem*. Optimisation and storage allocation strongly influence each other, and influence instruction selection, and vice versa. Storage allocation, for example, involves the allocation of stack and memory locations on the one hand, and register allocation on the other hand. The former usually precedes instruction selection, the latter follows it. A complex situation often occurs in ordering the phases, where parts of different phases need to be entwined. Specifying a code-generation algorithm that solves the phase-ordering problem remains an unsolved problem. The search for such a code-generation algorithm is part of a field of research called *automatic code generation*, which we discuss in the bibliographic notes at the end of this chapter.

Unlike scanning, parsing and attribute evaluation, there is little or no formal theory of code generation. In practice, the 3 phases mentioned above are often implemented separately. Usually, the order of the phases is to optimise the intermediate code, select the instructions, allocate registers and, finally, optimise the generated target code. Maybe not surprisingly, the best code generators are hand written. By the term "best" we mean that they generate the fastest code. However, a hand-written code generator can be difficult, if not impossible, to port, and it can be a nightmare to debug. We can minimise porting and debugging problems by automating as much of the process as possible.

A hand-written code generator may be completely written in some programming language, or it may use the help of some formalism. For example, a context-free or attribute grammar can be used to specify the structure of the intermediate language, and semantic actions can be used to generate target code, and even to allocate registers. More generally, we can use some tree-traversal strategy over the parse-tree-like representation of the source program as a basis for a code generator. The advantage of this last approach is that we can "wander" a number of times over the tree, carrying out data-flow and control-flow analyses, and various opti-

---

[2]Actually, a code generator is not a well-defined object. Some people refer to the instruction-selection phase (only) as the code generator, others consider all phases to be equally responsible for the code that is generated, and hence refer to the whole back-end, including separate optimisation phases, as the code generator.

misations, before a final "code-generation" pass is carried out. Better code can be emitted because the analyses and optimisations have a *global* (i.e. complete) view of the intermediate code.

An alternative, far simpler technique of generating code is to directly translate each intermediate instruction into its corresponding target instruction(s). Because this technique uses only local information (i.e. the given intermediate instruction) its ability to optimise is limited. Correspondingly, this technique is sometimes referred to as *blind* or *interpretive*. We refer to the technique as *on-the-fly* because the hallmark of this technique is that each incoming intermediate instruction can be immediately translated into target code. The main advantage of this technique is that it is easy to explain and quick to implement. An on-the-fly code generator actually offers good value for money because, in spite of its simplicity, good quality code can be generated. More complex strategies will generate higher quality code, but there is an exponentially diminishing rate of return here—increasing the complexity will result in increasingly smaller improvements in the quality. There is of course no algorithm that will always generate (truly) *optimal* target code for any given source program.

In this chapter we will use an on-the-fly technique to translate VIM code into target code. Before we discuss this technique, however, we digress slightly and consider the nature of the target code that we wish to generate.

6.1.1 Target code

What, then, is the range of options that are available to us for the choice of target code? Our aim is to generate code that can be directly executed on a given target machine.

- One option is to choose the machine code (i.e. bitstrings) for the particular target machine. The code sequences will then be very complex indeed, difficult to read, write and debug, and difficult to change if we want to generate code for a different target machine. Clearly this is not a sensible option.
- A second option would be to choose assembly instructions, and to use the assembler on the target machine to generate our target program. While assembly code is readable and writeable (at least to some), and is very efficient, it is not portable—to generate code for a different target machine we need to replace all the assembly instructions.
- A third option is to generate high-level instructions. The advantages of high-level code are that it is simple to read, write and debug, and it is very portable. If we generate C-code, for example, then the C-compiler on any target machine can be used to generate executable code. The disadvantage of this option, however, is that we sacrifice efficiency. For example, in a high-level language we cannot usually use hardware registers and addressing modes.

The choice between the second and third options is therefore a trade-off between the efficiency of the assembly code on the one hand, and the ease and portability of high-level code on the other. We depict the second and third options in Figures 6.1 and 6.2. In the first figure we translate VIM code directly into assembly code, but note that we must do this for each individual target machine. In the second figure, the code generator generates high-level code, and a compiler for the high-level code (assuming there is one) on each target machine is used to generate executable code.

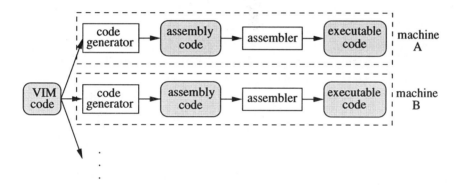

Figure 6.1 Code generators and assemblers on each machine translate VIM code into executable code.

We will first implement the third option. The method that we use can also be used to implement the second option, so once we have shown how to generate high-level code, we will replace the high-level code sequences by assembly instructions. This will result in improved performance.

The obvious important difference between the second and third options is the use of a high-level compiler. It is, of course, possible that there is no suitable high-level compiler available on the target machine (for example, the target machine may be new or experimental). In that case we are forced to use the second option. Actually, if this situation were to arise in practice, we would develop the compiler in stages: initially a bare-bones compiler would be developed that generated assembly code, and once that was running on the target machine, we could write new parts of the compiler in the language that we are compiling, and use the bare-bones compiler to generate assembly code. This is commonly referred to as *bootstrapping*.

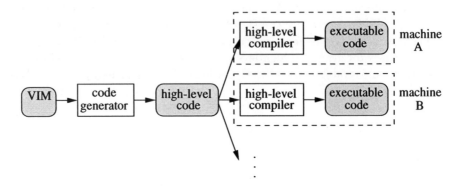

Figure 6.2   A single code generator, and high-level compilers on each machine translate VIM code into executable code.

6.1.2   On-the-fly code generation

We now consider an on-the-fly scheme that translates each VIM instruction into one or more target instructions. There are, of course, only a finite number of kinds of VIM instructions. The machine VIM, for example, has 34 kinds of instructions. We list these instructions in Figure 6.3.

To implement an on-the-fly strategy, we could use the following scheme:

```
while (read(instr)) {
  if (instr == stack_instr₁)
      emit(target_code₁)
  else if (instr == stack_instr₂)
      emit(target_code₂)
  ⋮
  else if (instr == stack_instrₙ)
      emit(target_codeₙ)
  else
      emit("invalid stack instruction")
}
```

where we have used, for the sake of convenience, a C-style notation. In this scheme, *instr* is the VIM instruction, and $n = 34$. Note that the emitted code *target_code* may be a quite long sequence of target instructions.

The on-the-fly scheme above can be implemented in some programming language. A language used for this purpose is referred to as the *implementation language*, and is not necessarily the same language as the code that we are generating.

1	abs			18	ldxvar	sn, dpl
2	add			19	le	
3	call	index		20	lt	
4	crseg	sn, index		21	mdl	
5	descr	sn, dpl, n		22	mul	
6	dlseg			23	ne	
7	dvi			24	neg	
8	eq			25	noop	
9	ge			26	rdint	
10	gt			27	return	
11	halt			28	stind	
12	jiff	index		29	stvar	sn, dpl
13	jift	index		30	stxvar	sn, dpl
14	jump	index		31	sub	
15	ldcon	value		32	varaddr	sn, dpl
16	ldind			33	wrint	
17	ldvar	sn, dpl		34	xvaraddr	sn, dpl

Figure 6.3 The instruction set of VIM.

(In fact, when we generate assembly code, it certainly will not be the same.) There are quite different issues involved in choosing an implementation language. At first glance, C and Pascal may seem suitable candidates. We should realise, however, that the on-the-fly scheme that we illustrate above is more concerned with string manipulation (the strings being the incoming VIM instructions and outgoing target instructions) and involves very few computations. Languages like SNOBOL and AWK would therefore be more suitable as implementation languages.

However, there is yet another way of implementing the on-the-fly scheme, and that is to specify it. In fact, we can use the same specification language(s) that we used for the front-end, namely regular expressions and an attributed context-free grammar, and we can use the same tools (i.e. scanner, parser and attribute-evaluator generators). Instead of generating a front-end, these tools now generate a code generator (i.e. back-end). The advantage of this approach is consistency (the front and back-ends are specified and built in the same way), reliability and ease (the specifications are easier to write and maintain). The disadvantage is that the generated code generator will probably be slower than a programmed code generator, which is not an issue. Note that the quality of the code generated by the code generator should not be less.

In Chapter 4, Figure 4.7, we depicted the compiler and compiler generator, as they were then called. We can now add a back-end to the compiler. The result is shown in Figure 6.4. Note the symmetry in this figure: from the source-language and VIM-language specifications we generate a front-end and a back-end, both consisting of a scanner, parser and attribute evaluator. The output of the front-end (the intermediate program) is the source program of the back-end, and this ties the system together. The target program may be a high-level language or assembly code. To run this program, therefore, a compiler or assembler will be necessary.

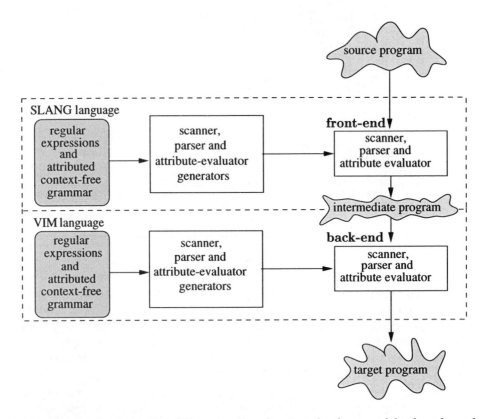

Figure 6.4 A schematic of the compiler showing the front and back-ends and their generators.

Technically, we could refer to the scanner, parser and attribute-evaluator generators for the back-end collectively as a code-generator generator (or a back-end generator), but we should not lose sight of the fact that the generators are the same for the front and back-ends; the difference lies in the specifications and the input language. Note that because the code generated by the front-end is an intermediate code, which is not executed, and the code generated by the back-end is (ultimately) executable, we no longer need the services of an interpreter.

Not shown in Figure 6.4 is a library of routines, called the *run-time system*, that is loaded in with the generated code to produce the target program. These routines declare and provide access to the run-time storage of the program. For example, the allocation and deallocation of, and access to, data structures like stacks and heaps is provided by the run-time system, as well as segmentation, scope and parameter-passing.

6.2   VIM to C-code

The high-level language that we choose to generate is ANSI-C.[3] We choose C because of its power, flexibility, compactness, performance and popularity. It is also possible to program in a low-level way in C (for example, we can use registers and manipulate bit strings), which is useful for optimisation purposes, and narrows the gap with assembly code.

We begin our description of the code generator by presenting in Section 6.2.1 scanner and parser specifications of the input language, VIM. In Section 6.2.2 we describe the associated parser actions and code table. Together, the specifications, actions and code table will allow us to generate a VIM-to-C code generator. Actually, the code generator that we produce is not complete. A run-time system also needs to be provided. We discuss the run-time system in Section 6.2.3.

6.2.1   Specifications

We begin by creating a scanner specification for the VIM instruction set. We assume that the front-end generates a file containing VIM code and an associated segment-length table. We will refer to these together as the intermediate program.

Note that we do not need or see the address table (see Section 3.5). The routine *get_label* in the front-end generates indices that are emitted by *emit_jump* and *emit_label*. In the code these indices act as labels.

Example 6.1
Consider the following SLANG source program:

```
BEGIN VAR INT i, j;
      PROC square(INT a; VAR INT b)
      BEGIN b := a*a END;
      READ(i);
      CALL square(i, j);
      WRITE(j)
END.
```

This program could be translated into the following intermediate program:

---

[3]From now on we will refer to ANSI-C as simply C.

```
        crseg    1   1
        jump     1
2:      crseg    2   2
        stvar    2   1
        stvar    2   0
        ldvar    2   0
        ldvar    2   0
        mul
        ldvar    2   1
        stind
        dlseg
        return_
1:      rdint
        stvar    1   0
        ldvar    1   0
        varaddr  1   1
        call     2
        ldvar    1   1
        wrint
        dlseg
        halt
1:  2
2:  2
```

Observe that a "table" of segment lengths follows the statement **halt**. The second argument of the **crseg** instruction (1 in the first line, and 2 in the third line) is an index of this table. The value at both indices in the program above is 2 because both segments contain 2 variables (i and j in the first segment, a and b in the second).

Note further that on the second line there is a jump-instruction whose destination is the start of the main program, and in the main program there is a call-statement that jumps to the procedure.   ◇

Lexicographically, VIM code consists of keywords (i.e. instruction opcodes), strings of digits (i.e. labels and arguments), and the colon symbol. There are no identifiers. White-space is, of course, ignored. The accompanying segment-length table consists of strings of digits (i.e. indices and segment lengths) and a colon symbol.

A scanner specification that recognises keywords, strings of digits and the colon symbol is shown below. Underscores are appended to the opcodes **return** and **abs**. This is to avoid name clashes later on with reserved words in C and the C-library. Note that the only token that is generated is *lex_token*. We define 1 synthesised attribute, *lexeme*, which points to the lexeme associated with *lex_token*. The routine *get_repr* returns a pointer to a copy of the string represented by *lex_token*.

attributes
    lexeme : string **syn of** lex_token.

symbols
    colon_token : : .

keywords

abs_token	: **abs_** .	ldxvar_token	: **ldxvar** .
add_token	: **add** .	le_token	: **le** .
call_token	: **call** .	lt_token	: **lt** .
crseg_token	: **crseg** .	mdl_token	: **mdl** .
descr_token	: **descr** .	mul_token	: **mul** .
dlseg_token	: **dlseg** .	ne_token	: **ne** .
dvi_token	: **dvi** .	neg_token	: **neg** .
eq_token	: **eq** .	noop_token	: **noop** .
ge_token	: **ge** .	rdint_token	: **rdint** .
gt_token	: **gt** .	return_token	: **return_** .
halt_token	: **halt** .	stind_token	: **stind** .
jiff_token	: **jiff** .	stvar_token	: **stvar** .
jift_token	: **jift** .	stxvar_token	: **stxvar** .
jump_token	: **jump** .	sub_token	: **sub** .
ldcon_token	: **ldcon** .	varaddr_token	: **varaddr** .
ldind_token	: **ldind** .	wrint_token	: **wrint** .
ldvar_token	: **ldvar** .	xvaraddr_token	: **xvaraddr** .

charsets

blank	:	[**sp, lf, cr, ht, ff**] .
digit	:	["0" .. "9"] .
letter	:	["a" .. "z", "_"] .
sign	:	["+","-"] .

rules

skip	:	*blank* **seq** .
verify	:	*letter* **seq** .
lex_token	:	*sign* **option** *digit* **seq**
		lexeme = get_repr ( ) .

We next consider the associated parser specification. The parser specification contains specifications for the VIM code and segment-length table. The VIM code (corresponding to the nonterminal *code*) consists of zero or more instructions and is terminated by a halt instruction (nonterminal *haltinstr*). Each instruction (nonterminal *labinstr*) has an optional label. The segment-length table (nonterminal *table*) consists of colon-separated pairs of numbers. The index and value (which are attributes of *lex_token*) on each line in the table are passed to the action *emit_table*.

There are 34 VIM instructions. These instructions can have up to 3 numerical arguments. These arguments (attributes of *lex_token*) are passed to the action *emit_code*. Note that we are specifying the VIM instructions syntactically in this approach. This high-level specification of the VIM instruction set contrasts with the low-level definition that we used in the interpreter. There we used C-language union-definitions (see Section 5.4.3 for example). The specification is shown below.

root
    code.

constants
    NULL: string.
    LABEL: operation.

rules
code
  : start_code ( )
    labinstr **clos** *haltinstr*
    finish_code ( )
    table **option**

  .

labinstr
  : *label* **option** *instr*

  .

haltinstr
  : halt_token
    emit_code (**halt**, NULL, NULL, NULL)

  .

table
  : start_table ( )
    { lex_token colon_token lex_token
      emit_table (*lexeme* **of** lex_token#1, *lexeme* **of** lex_token#2)
    } **seq**
    finish_table ( )

  .

label
  : lex_token colon_token
    emit_code (LABEL, *lexeme* **of** lex_token, NULL, NULL)

  .

instr

  : abs_token
   emit_code (**abs_** , NULL, NULL, NULL)
  | add_token
   emit_code (**add**, NULL, NULL, NULL)
  | call_token lex_token
   emit_code (**call**, *lexeme* **of** lex_token#1, NULL, NULL)
  | crseg_token lex_token lex_token
   emit_code (**crseg**, *lexeme* **of** lex_token#2, *lexeme* **of** lex_token#3, NULL)
  | descr_token lex_token lex_token lex_token
   emit_code (**descr**, *lexeme* **of** lex_token#4, *lexeme* **of** lex_token#5,
         lexeme **of** lex_token#6)
  | dlseg_token
   emit_code (**dlseg**, NULL, NULL, NULL)
  | dvi_token
   emit_code (**dvi**, NULL, NULL, NULL)
  | eq_token
   emit_code (**eq**, NULL, NULL, NULL)
  | ge_token
   emit_code (**ge**, NULL, NULL, NULL)
  | gt_token
   emit_code (**gt**, NULL, NULL, NULL)
  | jiff_token lex_token
   emit_code (**jiff**, *lexeme* **of** lex_token#7, NULL, NULL)
  | jift_token lex_token
   emit_code (**jift**, *lexeme* **of** lex_token#8, NULL, NULL)
  | jump_token lex_token
   emit_code (**jump**, *lexeme* **of** lex_token#9, NULL, NULL)
  | ldcon_token lex_token
   emit_code (**ldcon**, *lexeme* **of** lex_token#10, NULL, NULL)
  | ldind_token
   emit_code (**ldind**, NULL, NULL, NULL)
  | ldvar_token lex_token lex_token
   emit_code (**ldvar**, *lexeme* **of** lex_token#11, *lexeme* **of** lex_token#12, NULL)
  | ldxvar_token lex_token lex_token
   emit_code (**ldxvar**, *lexeme* **of** lex_token#13, *lexeme* **of** lex_token#14,
         lexeme **of** lex_token#13)
  | le_token
   emit_code (**le**, NULL, NULL, NULL)
  | lt_token
   emit_code (**lt**, NULL, NULL, NULL)
  | mdl_token
   emit_code (**mdl**, NULL, NULL, NULL)

| mul_token
  emit_code (**mul**, NULL, NULL, NULL)
| ne_token
  emit_code (**ne**, NULL, NULL, NULL)
| neg_token
  emit_code (**neg**, NULL, NULL, NULL)
| noop_token
  emit_code (**noop**, NULL, NULL, NULL)
| rdint_token
  emit_code (**rdint**, NULL, NULL, NULL)
| return_token
  emit_code (**return_**, NULL, NULL, NULL)
| stind_token
  emit_code (**stind**, NULL, NULL, NULL)
| stvar_token lex_token lex_token
  emit_code (**stvar**, *lexeme* **of** lex_token#15, *lexeme* **of** lex_token#16, NULL)
| stxvar_token lex_token lex_token
  emit_code (**stxvar**, *lexeme* **of** lex_token#17, *lexeme* **of** lex_token#18,
                      lexeme **of** lex_token#17)
| sub_token
  emit_code (**sub**, NULL, NULL, NULL)
| varaddr_token lex_token lex_token
  emit_code (**varaddr**, *lexeme* **of** lex_token#19, *lexeme* **of** lex_token#20, NULL)
| wrint_token
  emit_code (**wrint**, NULL, NULL, NULL)
| xvaraddr_token lex_token lex_token
  emit_code (**xvaraddr**, *lexeme* **of** lex_token#21, *lexeme* **of** lex_token#22,
                      lexeme **of** lex_token#21)

Note that an argument of *emit_code* is repeated in the case of instructions **ldxvar**, **stxvar** and **xvaraddr**. This repeated argument is not used to generate C-code, but will be used later on to generate assembly code.

The first argument of *emit_code* is an enumerator of the enumerated data type *operation*. The enumeration of *operation* is shown below:

```
typedef enum {
    abs_, add, call, crseg, descr, dlseg, dvi, eq, ge, gt, halt, jiff, jift, jump,
    ldcon, ldind, ldvar, ldxvar, le, lt, mdl, mul, ne, neg, noop, rdint, return_,
    stind, stvar, stxvar, sub, varaddr, wrint, xvaraddr
} operation;
```

The enumerators are used to determine the code (fragment) that corresponds to a given VIM instruction, with the exception of a label, where a constant LABEL of type *operation* is used. We describe the code fragments in the next section.

6.2.2   Parser actions

The actual text of the code generator is generated (emitted) by the 6 routines that are used as actions. Instruction opcodes and any numerical arguments are passed to the routine *emit_code*, and the numerical entries in the segment-length table are passed to the routine *emit_table*. These 2 emit routines write to different files. The file initialisation and termination for these routines is carried out in the routines *start_code* and *finish_code*, and *start_table* and *finish_table*, respectively.

The routine that does most of the work is *emit_code*. This routine is shown below.

```
void
emit_code(operation op, string arg1, string arg2, string arg3)
{
        printf(codetable[op+1], arg1, arg2, arg3);
}
```

It has 4 parameters: the first parameter (i.e. *op*) is an enumerated data type that identifies the instruction that has been matched. The type of this parameter is *operation*. The other 3 parameters are its arguments (if any), and have type *string*. At the heart of the code generator is a table called *codetable*. This table contains C-code fragments that implement the VIM instructions, and these code fragments are emitted. The code table is shown below.

```
char *codetable[] = {
        "l_%s: ",                               /* label */
        "push(abs(pop()));\n",                  /* abs_ */
        "push(pop() + pop());\n",               /* add */
        "{ jmp_buf jmpbuf;\n"                   /* call */
        "  if (setjmp(jmpbuf) == 0) {\n"
        "    call(&jmpbuf);\n"
        "    goto l_%s;\n"
        "  }\n"
        "}\n",
        "crseg(%s, SEGLEN%s);\n",               /* crseg */
        "descr(%s, %s, %s);\n",                 /* descr */
        "dlseg();\n",                           /* dlseg */
        "{ int pop1 = pop();\n"                 /* dvi */
        "  push(pop() / pop1);\n"
        "}\n",
        "push(pop() == pop());\n",              /* eq */
        "push(pop() <= pop());\n",              /* ge */
        "push(pop() < pop());\n",               /* gt */
        "return 0;\n",                          /* halt */
        "if (!pop())\n"                         /* jiff */
        "  goto l_%s;\n",
        "if (pop())\n"                          /* jift */
        "  goto l_%s;\n",
        "goto l_%s;\n",                         /* jump */
```

```
"push(%s);\n",                                    /* ldcon */
"push(getmema(pop()));\n",                        /* ldind */
"push(getmemr(%s, %s));\n",                       /* ldvar */
"{ int sn = %s;\n"                                /* ldxvar */
"  push(getmemr(sn, ixdpl(sn, %s)));\n"
"}\n",
"push(pop() >= pop());\n",                        /* le */
"push(pop() > pop());\n",                         /* lt */
"{ int pop1 = pop();\n"                           /* mdl */
"  push(pop() %% pop1);\n"
"}\n",
"push(pop() * pop());\n",                         /* mul */
"push(pop() != pop());\n",                        /* ne */
"push(-pop());\n",                                /* neg */
"\n",                                             /* noop */
"push(rdint());\n",                               /* rdint */
"{ jmp_buf jmpbuf;\n"                             /* return_ */
"  return_(&jmpbuf);\n"
"  longjmp(jmpbuf, 1);\n"
"}\n",
"{ int pop1 = pop();\n"                           /* stind */
"  putmema(pop1, pop());\n"
"}\n",
"putmemr(%s, %s, pop());\n",                      /* stvar */
"{ int sn = %s, dpl = ixdpl(sn, %s);\n"           /* stxvar */
"  putmemr(sn, dpl, pop());\n"
"}\n",
"push(-pop() + pop());\n",                        /* sub */
"push(varaddr(%s, %s));\n",                       /* varaddr */
"wrint(pop());\n",                                /* wrint */
"{ int sn = %s;\n"                                /* xvaraddr */
"  push(varaddr(sn, ixdpl(sn, %s)));\n"
"}\n",
};
```

The first line in *codetable* is a label string that corresponds to the operation LABEL. This label string is emitted when a label is parsed. The rest of *codetable* consists of the code fragments for the 34 instructions that can be recognised. As each instruction in a given VIM program is parsed, its corresponding code fragment will be generated. When all the VIM instructions have been parsed, a complete C-program will have been emitted. This C-program, called *code.c*, is the C-code. Note that in the code fragment corresponding to the instruction **stxvar**, a temporary variable is used to ensure that the parameters of the call *putmemr* are carried out in the correct order.

There is one problem with the parsing scheme presented above, and that concerns the segment-length table and **crseg** instruction. The second argument of the **crseg** instruction is an index into the segment-length table, but the segment-length table is parsed only after the instructions! So how do we determine the length of a segment when we generate the code for **crseg**? We do this by taking advantage of the fact that we do not actually need to know the segment lengths when we generate C-code; only when C-code is compiled. During parsing, the segment-length argument of the **crseg** instruction is converted into a unique string. This string consists of the letters **SEGLEN** concatenated with the index. When we parse the corresponding index in the segment-length table, we assign to this same unique string the value of the segment length. This is done by converting each line in the segment-length table into a #define-statement. This task is carried out by the routine *emit_table*, shown below.

```
void
emit_table(string index, string value)
{
        printf(seglenfile, "#define SEGLEN%s %s\n", index, value);
}
```

At compilation time, the C-compiler (actually the C-preprocessor) will substitute each (unique) string by its value (as specified by the #define-statement).

Example 6.2
The 2 **crseg** instructions in the VIM code shown in Example 6.1 are translated by *emit_code* into the C-statements crseg(1, SEGLEN1) and crseg(2, SEGLEN2) respectively. The associated segment-length table is converted by *emit_table* into the statements #define SEGLEN1 2 and #define SEGLEN2 2.   ◇

The emitted #define-statements are placed in a file called *seglen.h* (identified by *seglenfile* in the code above), and this file is included into the C-code, *code.c*, by using a #include-statement. When we compile *code.c*, the correct values of the segment lengths will be substituted into the **crseg** instructions.

We have now seen the complete scanner and parser specifications, and the associated actions and code table. Together they form the specification of the code generator. What we have not yet described are the routines, for example, *push* and *pop*, that are called by the code fragments. These routines constitute the run-time system of the code generator, and are loaded in with the C-code when it is compiled. The file that contains these routines is called *rts.h*. We show below the part of *start_code* that generates the first few lines of *code.c*.

```
puts("#include \"rts.h\"");
puts("#include \"seglen.h\"");
puts("int");
puts("main(void)");
puts("{");
```

Note the inclusion of the segment-length file and run-time system.

6.2.3   Run-time system

In Figure 6.5 we show all the components that make up the code generator and its generator(s). In this figure we show the code table that is used by the VIM parser specification, and the generators that, together, generate a code generator. Next to the code generator is the run-time system. Not shown in this figure is the linking of the code generator and run-time system to produce the executable code generator. The code generator is generated, and linked with the run-time system, at compiler-construction time. At compile time the code generator translates the incoming intermediate program (and segment-length table) to a target program. We abbreviate the segment-length table in this figure to *slt*.

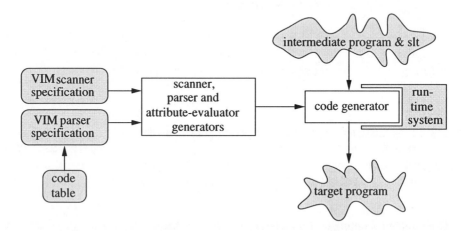

Figure 6.5 The various components that are used to build the code generator.

The C-code fragments in the code table contain calls to routines in the run-time system. These routines simulate the VIM instructions. We can categorise the instructions along architectural lines. The categories, and the run-time system routines that implement instructions in each of the categories, are shown below:

- stack: *push* and *pop*
- segments: *crseg* and *dlseg*
- memory: *getmemr*, *putmemr*, *getmema*, *putmema* and *varaddr*
- dynamic arrays: *descr*, *getseglen*, *incrseglen* and *ixdpl*
- procedure-call mechanism: *call* and *return_*
- reading and writing of integers: *rdint* and *wrint*

We discuss the run-time system routines in each of these categories below.

Stack. An array is used as a stack. The routine *push* pushes an integer onto the stack, and *pop* pops an element off the stack. These routines also ensure that there is no stack underflow or overflow. Actually, because we assume that the VIM code is correct, there can be no stack underflow, only overflow. However, for testing purposes it is safer to include a check for underflow as well. The declarations of the stack, stack pointer and push and pop routines are shown below.

```
static int stack[max_stack], sp = 0;

int
pop(void) /* pop and return a value from the stack */
{
        if (sp > 0)
                return stack[--sp];
        report_error("pop: stack underflow");
        return 0;
}

int
push(int value) /* push a value onto the stack, value is returned */
{
        if (sp < max_stack)
                stack[sp++] = value;
        else
                report_error("push: stack overflow");
        return value;
}
```

Example 6.3
The VIM instruction **add** replaces the top 2 elements on the stack by their sum. This can be implemented in C by popping the stack twice, and pushing the sum of the 2 values that have been popped back onto the stack. This can be expressed concisely by the following code:

```
push(pop() + pop());
```

This code fragment is emitted by *emit_code* when the instruction **add** is parsed. ◇

Example 6.4
The instruction *jift 2* can be implemented by the following code fragment:

```
if (pop())
    goto L_2;
```

Note that the label "2" is an attribute of the instruction, and is an argument of *emit_code*. ◇

Examining the code table, we see that many of the VIM instructions can be implemented simply using standard C and the routines *push* and *pop*. This includes the instructions abs_, add, **dvi**, **eq**, **ge**, **gt**, **halt**, **jiff**, **jift**, **jump**, ldcon, **le**, lt, mdl, **mul**, **ne**, **neg**, **noop** and **sub**. In some of the code fragments, a local variable (*pop1*) is used. In the case of **dvi** and **mdl**, we do this because we need to use the second element on the stack first. In the case of **stind**, it is to ensure that the arguments in the call are evaluated left-to-right.

Segments. As in the interpreter, we use an array *data* to store the segment number, segment length, static and dynamic links, and the segment data. We use *dsp* as an index. The current segment group *CSG* is also an array, and there is a current segment number *csn*. Unlike the interpreter, however, the array *data* that houses the segments is dynamic. Initially this array is completely empty. The declarations are shown below.

```
static int *CSG[max_depth], csn = 0;
static int *data = NULL, dsp = 0;
```

The instructions **crseg** and **dlseg** result in routines of the same names being called. In the previous section we saw how #define-statements can be used to convert an index into a segment length. The segment number and length are arguments of the routine *crseg*, which is called when the instruction **crseg** is parsed. This routine creates a segment, sets the static and dynamic links (using the current segment group) and the level and segment length. The total length of the segment is the segment length plus 4. The current segment group and number are updated, and *dsp* is moved to the end of *data*.

```
void
crseg(int sn, int len)
{
        if (dsp == 0)
                data = (int *)malloc((len+4)*sizeof(int));
        else
                data = (int *)realloc(data, (dsp+len+4)*sizeof(int));
        if (data == NULL) {
                report_error("crseg: not enough memory");
                return;
        }
        data[dsp++] = sn;
        data[dsp++] = len;
        data[dsp++] = CSG[sn − 1]; /* static */
        data[dsp++] = CSG[csn]; /* dynamic */

        csn = sn;
        CSG[csn] = dsp;
        dsp += len;
}
```

Note that the first time *crseg* is called, a number of memory locations are allocated. Every other call to *crseg* results in the array *data* being extended ("reallocated").

The routine *dlseg*, shown below, deletes the current segment given by $CSG[csn]$. If the static and dynamic links are not the same, then the segment group of the caller must be restored. Otherwise the current segment number can be simply decremented. Deleting a segment results in the array *data* shrinking.

```
void
dlseg(void)
{
        int curseg, callenv, i, callsn, len, dynamic_link, static_link;

        if ((curseg = CSG[csn]) < 4) {
                report_error("dlseg: no current segment");
                return;
        }
        len = data[curseg − 3];
        static_link = data[curseg − 2];
        dynamic_link = data[curseg − 1];
        if (static_link != dynamic_link) { /* caller in different group */
                callenv = dynamic_link;
                callsn = data[dynamic_link − 4]; /* restore group */
                for (i = callsn; i >= csn; i−−) {
                        CSG[i] = callenv; /* restore environment */
                        callenv = data[callenv − 2];
                }
                csn = callsn;
        } else {
                if (csn == 0) {
                        report_error("dlseg: no more segments");
                        return;
                }
                CSG[csn−−] = 0; /* same segment group */
        }
        dsp −= len + 4;
        data = (int *)realloc(data, dsp*sizeof(int));
}
```

Memory. There are 5 load and store instructions that require run-time assistance. The instruction `ldvar` places the value at a given segment number and displacement onto the stack. The instruction `stvar` does the reverse. These instructions are implemented using the routines *getmemr* and *putmemr*, which have arguments *sn* and *dpl*. These routines simply read from, and write to, the location $CSG[csn]+dpl$ in the array *data*. Unlike the interpreter, we check that the values of *sn* and *dpl* are consistent. These routines are shown below.

```
int
getmemr(int sn, int dpl)
{
        if (sn >= 0 && sn < max_depth && CSG[sn] > 3 && CSG[sn] < dsp) {
                if (dpl >= 0 && dpl < data[CSG[sn]−3])
```

```
                        return data[CSG[sn]+dpl];
                  report_error("getmemr: wrong displacement");
       } else
                  report_error("getmemr: wrong segment number");
       return 0;
}


void
putmemr(int sn, int dpl, int value)
{
       if (sn >= 0 && sn < max_depth && CSG[sn] > 3 && CSG[sn] < dsp) {
             if (dpl >= 0 && dpl < data[CSG[sn]-3]) {
                    data[CSG[sn]+dpl] = value;
                    return;
             }
             report_error("putmemr: wrong displacement");
       } else
             report_error("putmemr: wrong segment number");
}
```

The above instructions implement relative addressing—only variables that are declared in segments that are "visible" to the current segment can be accessed. Reference parameters for procedures, however, require absolute addressing. An absolute address is simply an index of the array *data*. Absolute addresses are specified by using the instruction **varaddr**. The run-time system routine *varaddr* is in fact almost identical to *getmemr*. The only difference between these routines is that *getmemr* returns with a value from the array *data*, whereas *varaddr* returns with an index (address). We can refer to the value located at the index at any time, from any place in the code, as long as the segment exists. The routine *varaddr* is shown below.

```
int
varaddr(int sn, int dpl)
{
       if (sn >= 0 && sn < max_depth && CSG[sn] > 3
                                      && CSG[sn] < dsp) {
             if (dpl >= 0 && dpl < data[CSG[sn]-3])
                    return CSG[sn] + dpl;
             report_error("varaddr: wrong displacement");
       } else
             report_error("varaddr: wrong segment number");
       return 0;
}
```

To access variables whose indices (absolute addresses) are on the stack, we use the instructions **ldind** and **stind**. These instructions are implemented by the routines *getmema* and *putmema*, respectively. Given an index as parameter, these routines, shown below, simply read from, or write to, the location specified by the index in the array *data*.

```
int
getmema(int idx)
{
        if (idx >= 0 && idx < dsp)
                return data[idx];
        report_error("getmema: illegal absolute address");
        return 0;
}

void
putmema(int idx, int value)
{
        if (idx >= 0 && idx < dsp)
                data[idx] = value;
        else
                report_error("getmema: illegal absolute address");
}
```

Dynamic arrays. Dynamic arrays can be specified by using the instructions descr, ldxvar, stxvar and xvaraddr. These instructions are implemented by the run-time routines *descr* and *ixdpl*.

The instruction descr fills in the descriptor of the particular array. We discussed the role and contents of the descriptor in Section 5.2. The arguments of the descr instruction are passed to the routine *descr*. If the dimension of the array is n, then the n pairs of upper and lower bounds (up_k, lo_k) are popped off the stack (from the highest dimension to the lowest). For each pair (up_k, lo_k), we compute $s_{k-1} = (up_k - lo_k + 1) * \cdots * (up_n - lo_n + 1)$, $1 \le k \le n$. If $k = n$ then $s_n = 1$. The pairs of values (s_{k-1}, lo_k), starting at $k = n$ and descending to $k = 1$, are written to the descriptor (array) at positions $dpl + 2 * n + 1$ down to $dpl + 2$. At position $dpl + 1$ we write the length (*offset*) of the data segment, and at the location dpl itself, the dimension n of the array. The descriptor has now been filled. The total amount of room that we need to store the array is given by s_0. The original memory allocation (*offset* memory locations) must now be expanded (reallocated) to accommodate the s_0 extra locations. This is carried out by the routine *incrseglen*. The routine *getseglen* returns with the length of the data part of the current segment. The routines *descr*, *incrseglen* and *getseglen* are shown below.

```
void
descr(int sn, int dpl, int n)
{
        int offset, s, k, up, lo;

        s = 1;
        for (k = dpl+2*n+1; k >= dpl+3; k -= 2) {
                up = pop();
                lo = pop();
```

```
                    if (up < lo) {
                            report_error("descr: upper bound < lower");
                            return;
                    }

                    s *= (up−lo+1);
                    putmemr(sn, k, lo);
                    putmemr(sn, k−1, s);
            }

            offset = getseglen(sn);
            putmemr(sn, dpl+1, offset);
            incrseglen(sn, s);
            putmemr(sn, dpl, n);
    }


void
incrseglen(int sn, int lenincr)
{
        data[CSG[sn]−3] += lenincr;
        dsp += lenincr;
        if ((data = (int *)realloc(data, dsp*sizeof(int))) == NULL)
                report_error("descr: not enough memory");
}


int
getseglen(int sn)
{
        return data[CSG[sn]−3];
}
```

The instructions ldxvar, stxvar and xvaraddr use the run-time routine *ixdpl*.
When an array variable is used, its indices are stored on the stack. These indices are
popped off the stack by the routine *ixdpl*. The indices, together with the descriptor
of the array, are used to compute the displacement of the indexed variable.

In the case of the instruction ldxvar, the routine *ixdpl* computes the displacement of the indexed variable, *getmemr* determines the value at this displacement,
and *push* places this value on the stack. In the case of stxvar, *ixdpl* again computes the displacement of the indexed variable, and *pop* and *putmemr* move the
value from the top of the stack to this displacement. The routine *ixdpl* is also
used to compute the displacement of an indexed variable that is a reference parameter. Remembering that reference parameters are implemented using absolute
addresses, we can implement the instruction xvaraddr analogously to the instruction varaddr.

```
int
ixdpl(int sn, int dpl)
{
        int ix, k, lo, n, s, s1, offset, xdpl;
```

```
n = getmemr(sn, dpl);
offset = getmemr(sn, dpl+1);
k = dpl + 2*n;
lo = getmemr(sn, k+1);
ix = pop();
xdpl = offset + ix - lo;
s1 = getmemr(sn, k);
if (ix-lo < 0 || ix-lo > s1-1) {
        report_error("ixdpl: index out of bounds");
        return -1;
}
while (k >= dpl+4) {
        ix = pop();
        lo = getmemr(sn, k-1);
        s = getmemr(sn, k);
        xdpl += (ix-lo)*s;
        s1 = getmemr(sn, k-2);
        if ((ix-lo)*s < 0 || (ix-lo)*s > s1-s) {
                report_error("ixdpl: index out of bounds");
                return -1;
        }
        k -= 2;
}
return xdpl;
}
```

Procedure-call mechanism. The code fragments for the instructions `call` and `return_` use the C-library functions *setjmp* and *longjmp* to implement procedure calls. When a label is called, the system-stack environment is saved by a call to *setjmp*. This call to *setjmp* will return with value 0, which is used to make a (conditional) jump to the procedure (label). When we wish to return from a procedure, the environment is restored, and *longjmp* is called with the environment and the value 1 as arguments. The effect of this is that there will be a second call to *setjmp*, but this time it will return with value 1, which causes execution to continue at the statement after the *setjmp* conditional-jump statement.

Because calls to procedures can be nested, we must be able to save a number of different system-stack environments. We do this by using a stack, called *return_stack*, and stack pointer, *rsp*. The routine *call* pushes an environment onto the stack, and *return_* pops an environment off the stack. The declarations of the return stack, its stack pointer, and the routines *call* and *return_* are shown below.

```
static jmp_buf return_stack[max_depth];
static int rsp = 0;

void
call(jmp_buf *jb) /* pushes context jb onto return stack */
{
        if (rsp < max_depth)
```

```
                    memcpy(&return_stack[rsp++], jb, sizeof(jmp_buf));
        else
                    report_error("call: return stack overflow");
}


void
return_(jmp_buf *jb) /* pops the top context from the return stack */
{                    /* and stores it in *jb */
        if (rsp > 0)
                    memcpy(jb, &return_stack[--rsp], sizeof(jmp_buf));
        else
                    report_error("return_: empty return stack");
}
```

Reading and writing. The only VIM instructions that have not yet been mentioned are rdint and wrint. The code fragments for these instructions call routines with the same names, i.e. *rdint* and *wrint*. The routine *rdint* reads a string of digits, and returns the corresponding integer. The routine *wrint* simply emits an integer. The routines are shown below.

```
void
wrint(int value)
{
        printf("%d\n", value);
}


int
rdint(void)
{
        char inputbuf[8];

        fgets(inputbuf, 7, stdin);
        return atoi(inputbuf);
}
```

6.3   VIM to assembly code

In this section we will describe the changes that we need to make to the code generator VIM-to-C so that it will generate assembly code instead of C-code. The C-code that was generated was localised to the parser actions, and mostly in the code table, so most of the changes will be made in the table. Because the source language (VIM) remains the same, the scanner and parser specifications do not have to be changed. In Section 6.3.2 we present the new assembly-code table, and we outline the few minor alterations that are necessary to the actions. The run-time system also needs to be modified. This is described in Section 6.3.3.

However, before describing these changes, we will take time to acquaint ourselves in Section 6.3.1 with the target machine and assembly language.

6.3.1   Target assembler and machine

The target machine is an Intel 80486DX microprocessor. This is a full 32-bit machine with a memory space of 4 gigabytes. It has a pipeline architecture, which means that there are specialised units in the microprocessor that fetch, decode and execute instructions, and generate addresses. The assembler that we use is Borland's Turbo Assembler (version 2.0) that runs on the IBM PC family of computers. This assembler generates instructions for the 8086 and 80x86 processors. In this section we will describe the data representation, instructions and directives in the assembler. Note that we use the convention that assembly instructions are written using upper-case to distinguish them from (lower-case) VIM instructions.

Data. Data is either 8 bits (a byte), 16 bits (word) or 32 bits (double-word), and either signed or unsigned.[4] The data-addressing modes include register, immediate, direct, register indirect, base-plus-index, register relative, base-relative-plus-index and scaled-index. However, the only modes that we use are register and immediate. The registers can be divided into the categories: general purpose, pointer, index, flag and segment registers. We describe each of these categories below:

general purpose The 16-bit general-purpose registers AX (the accumulator), BX (base), CX (count) and DX (data) often appear as operands. Actually, these registers form the lower-half of 32-bit registers that are addressed by EAX, EBX, ECX and EDX. The lowest-quarter (byte) of these registers can also be address by AL, BL, CL and DL.

pointer The 32-bit (only) pointer registers SP and BP are often used to point to the memory location of operands. The stack pointer SP is used with certain instructions (mainly PUSH, POP, CALL and RET) to address stack memory, and the base pointer BP, to address an array of data in memory.

index The source-index register SI is used to address source data indirectly in string instructions. The destination-index register DI is similar, but is used for destination data.

flag The bits of the 32-bit flag register indicate the condition of the machine, and are used to control its operation. The conditional jump instructions use the flag register.

segment These registers are used to access the code, data and additional memory segments.

Numeric constants can be specified by adding a radix suffix to the numerical string. For example, 123D is 123 decimal, and 0fH is 0f hexadecimal. The suffixes are B (binary), O (octal), Q (octal), D (decimal) and H (hexadecimal).

---

[4]We do not consider floating-point numbers.

If we wish to address a symbol at an offset that is relative to the current position, then we can use the OFFSET operator. For example, the operand OFFSET RETADDR will address the position in the segment of the symbol RETADDR. Data types can also be used as operators. For example, instead of the indirect address [BP], which does not make clear whether a byte, word or double-word is being addressed, we would use WORD PTR [BP], which says that BP points to a 16-bit quantity. The data type required to store the label-argument in a (conditional) jump instruction can also be specified. The operand SHORT LABEL in a conditional jump instruction says that the relative address (offset or displacement) of the label can be stored in 1 byte. A 1-byte offset has a value between +127 and −128. Note that this jump instruction may be overridden if the JUMP directive is used.

Instructions. The 80486 is a CISC (complex instruction-set computer) microprocessor with approximately 140 instructions. The instructions that we emit can be divided into the following categories:

data transfer The instructions MOV, PUSH and POP are used to move data between (stack) memory and registers.

arithmetic The instructions ADD, SUB, IMUL and IDIV carry out addition, subtraction, signed multiplication and signed division, respectively. We can also compare (CMP), increment (INC), decrement (DEC), negate (NEG), and change format from word to double-word (CWD).

bit manipulation The logical instructions AND and XOR are used, and a logical shift left SHL is handy when we need to multiply by a factor of 2.

program transfer To change the value of the instruction counter, there is an unconditional jump instruction JMP, and conditional jump instructions JG, JGE, JL, JLE, JE, JNE, JZ and JNZ. These conditional instructions test the zero-flag bit in the flag register. Procedures can also be called (CALL) and there is a return instruction (RET).

Finally there is a "no-op" instruction NOP. In total, we can generate 27 different instructions (leaving approximately 113 instructions that are never used).

Borland's Turbo Assembler also supports an extended call instruction that lets you directly call procedures that are written in high-level languages. Arguments to high-level procedures are passed on the stack. The assembler handles the order of the arguments and the clean-up of the stack. The statement CALL FRED, C, AX, BX, for example, calls the procedure FRED with arguments AX and BX. If FRED returns a value, it can be found in register AX.

Directives. As well as instructions, an assembly source program consists of *directives*. Directives are used to carry out various tasks like defining macros, defining and allocating data, controlling the listing, and selecting memory model and language features. We list a number of useful directives below.

- The .MODEL directive allows you to specify a memory model and language support. The memory model determines how the code segment, various data segments, constants and the stack are referenced with (segment) registers, and how they can be combined. The directive .MODEL SMALL, C specifies that a small memory model should be used, and that the procedure-call conventions come from the language C.

- Turbo Assembler also has an include facility. The directive INCLUDE macros will include a file called *macros.asm*.
- The directive JUMPS means that a "complementary" unconditional jump instruction will be generated if the assembler finds that the actual distance of a forward jump is further than a given jump instruction permits.
- The directive .LIST will cause printing of a source listing to commence.
- The directive PUBLIC can be used to "export" a symbol to its environment.
- A string can be assigned to a symbol by using the EQU directive. For example, SEGLEN1 EQU 3 assigns the string 3 to SEGLEN1.
- Macros can be defined by using the MACRO directive. The macro is terminated by a ENDM directive. Within a macro definition, a LOCAL defines temporary symbol names that are replaced by unique symbol names each time the macro is expanded.
- An IRP repeat-directive repeats a block of statements with string substitution. Statements enclosed by the directive IRP PARAM, <ARG1, ... > and its terminator ENDM are repeated, once for each argument in the list < ... >. Instances of the string PARAM in the statements are substituted for by the corresponding argument.

6.3.2 Parser actions

The file initialisation and termination routines perform the same functions as before. The routines *start_code* and *finish_code* open and close the file that will contain the (assembly) program, and emit the head and tail of the assembly program. The head of the code generator is emitted by the following code:

```
puts(".MODEL SMALL, C    ; SMALL model, C calling convention\n");
puts("INCLUDE extmac.asm ; include externals and jump macros\n");
puts("JUMPS              ; for conditional jumps out of range\n");
puts(".LIST              ; begin listing\n");
puts("PUBLIC main        ; export main routine\n");
puts(".DATA              ; start data segment\n");
puts("INCLUDE seglen.asm; include segment length macros\n");
puts(".CODE              ; start code segment\n");
puts("main PROC          ; 8086 assembler of VIM code\n");
```

The routine *emit_code* remains the same.

The routines *start_table* and *finish_table* open and close the file that will contain the segment-length table. The routine *emit_table* that emits the body of the table needs to be changed. In the new version of *emit_table*, the segment length is assigned to a unique string using the EQU directive.

```
void
emit_table(string index, string value)
{
        fprintf(seglenfile, "SEGLEN%s EQU %s\n", index, value);
}
```

Replacing the C-code fragments in the VIM-to-C code table by assembly-code sequences is quite straightforward. One important difference is that we can use the stack memory of the machine instead of our own stack. This means that instead of calling push and pop routines (which form part of the run-time system), we can simply use the assembly instructions PUSH and POP. We illustrate this in the next example.

Example 6.5
In Example 6.3 we saw the C-code that was emitted for the VIM instruction add. Now let us look at the equivalent assembly code. The following assembly code will replace the top 2 elements on the stack by their sum.

```
POP  BX
POP  AX
ADD  AX, BX
PUSH AX
```

This code will be emitted when the VIM instruction add is parsed.   ◇

We show the complete assembly-code table in Figure 6.6. Like the C-code table shown in Section 6.2.2, the assembly-code table consists of code fragments for the 34 different VIM instructions. Further, the code fragments in the C-code table that call functions in the run-time system, also call functions in the run-time system in the assembly-code table, using the so-called extended call instruction. Note that the result that is returned by an extended call instruction is always placed in the register AX.

A number of VIM instructions can be translated directly into assembly code as there are "equivalent" VIM and assembly instructions. For example, dvi, halt, jump, ldcon, mdl, mul, neg, noop and sub. The VIM instructions jiff and jift are also straightforward to implement. We pop the value off the stack into the register AX (say), compare this value with (hexadecimal) 1 using the assembly instruction AND, and use JZ (in the case of jiff) and JNZ (jift) to conditionally jump to the label.

The VIM instructions eq, ge, gt, le, lt and ne are implemented by using macros. Actually, we can be more concise and use a repeat macro (IRP). In the following IRP, we define 6 macros: CMPE, CMPGE, CMPG, CMPLE, CMPL and CMPNE, corresponding to the VIM instructions above. A macro call CMP*str* AX, BX, for

```
static char *codetable[]= {
 "L_%s:\n",
 "POP     AX              ; abs_\n"
 "CALL    _ABS C, AX\n"
 "PUSH    AX\n",
 "POP     BX              ; add\n"
 "POP     AX\n"
 "ADD     AX, BX\n"
 "PUSH    AX\n",
 "XCALL   L_%s            ; call\n",
 "MOV     AX, %s          ; crseg\n"
 "MOV     BX, SEGLEN%s\n"
 "CALL    CRSEG C, AX, BX\n",
 "DESCR   %s, %s, %s      ; descr\n",
 "CALL    DLSEG C         ; dlseg\n",
 "POP     BX              ; dvi\n"
 "POP     AX\n"
 "CWD     \n"
 "IDIV    BX\n"
 "PUSH    AX\n",
 "POP     BX              ; eq\n"
 "POP     AX\n"
 "CMPE    AX, BX\n"
 "PUSH    AX\n",
 "POP     BX              ; ge\n"
 "POP     AX\n"
 "CMPGE   AX, BX\n"
 "PUSH    AX\n",
 "POP     BX              ; gt\n"
 "POP     AX\n"
 "CMPG    AX, BX\n"
 "PUSH    AX\n",
 "RET                     ; halt\n",
 "POP     AX              ; jiff\n"
 "AND     AX, 0001H\n"
 "JZ      L_%s\n",
 "POP     AX              ; jift\n"
 "AND     AX, 0001H\n"
 "JNZ     L_%s\n",
 "JMP     L_%s            ; jump\n",
 "PUSH    %s              ; ldcon\n",
 "POP     BX              ; ldind\n"
 "CALL    GETMEMA C, BX\n"
 "PUSH    AX\n",
 "MOV     BX, %s          ; ldvar\n"
 "MOV     CX, %s\n"
 "CALL    GETMEMR C, BX, CX\n"
 "PUSH    AX\n",
 "IXDPL   %s, %s          ; ldxvar\n"
 "CALL    GETMEMR C, %s, CX\n"
 "PUSH    AX\n",
 "POP     BX              ; le\n"
 "POP     AX\n"
 "CMPLE   AX, BX\n"
 "PUSH    AX\n",
 "POP     BX              ; lt\n"
 "POP     AX\n"
 "CMPL    AX, BX\n"
 "PUSH    AX\n",
 "POP     BX              ; mdl\n"
 "POP     AX\n"
 "CWD     \n"
 "IDIV    BX\n"
 "PUSH    DX\n",
 "POP     BX              ; mul\n"
 "POP     AX\n"
 "IMUL    BX\n"
 "PUSH    AX\n",
 "POP     BX              ; ne\n"
 "POP     AX\n"
 "CMPNE   AX, BX\n"
 "PUSH    AX\n",
 "MOV     BP, SP          ; neg\n"
 "NEG     WORD PTR[BP]\n",
 "NOP                     ; noop\n",
 "CALL    RDINT C         ; rdint\n"
 "PUSH    AX\n",
 "CALL    POPRETADDR C    ; return_\n"
 "PUSH    AX\n"
 "RET     \n",
 "POP     BX              ; stind\n"
 "POP     AX\n"
 "CALL    PUTMEMA C, BX, AX\n",
 "MOV     BX, %s          ; stvar\n"
 "MOV     CX, %s\n"
 "POP     AX\n"
 "CALL    PUTMEMR C, BX, CX, AX\n",
 "IXDPL   %s, %s          ; stxvar\n"
 "POP     AX\n"
 "CALL    PUTMEMR C, %s, CX, AX\n",
 "POP     BX              ; sub\n"
 "POP     AX\n"
 "SUB     AX, BX\n"
 "PUSH    AX\n",
 "MOV     BX, %s          ; varaddr\n"
 "MOV     CX, %s\n"
 "CALL    VARADDR C, BX, CX\n"
 "PUSH    AX\n",
 "POP     AX              ; wrint\n"
 "CALL    WRINT C, AX\n",
 "IXDPL   %s, %s          ; xvaraddr\n"
 "CALL    VARADDR C, %s, CX\n"
 "PUSH    AX\n",
};
```

example, compares the contents of **AX** and **BX** for the condition *str*, and stores the Boolean result in **AX**. Here *str* is one of **E**, **GE**, **G**, **LE**, **L** and **NE**.

```
IRP        COND,    <E, GE, G, LE, L, NE>
CMP&COND   MACRO    DEST, SRC
           LOCAL    LTRUE, LEXIT
           CMP      DEST, SRC       ;; does dest<=>src?
           J&COND   SHORT LTRUE     ;; yes, go to Ltrue
           XOR      DEST, DEST      ;; no, let dest=0
           JMP      SHORT LEXIT     ;; and go to exit
LTRUE:     MOV      DEST, 1         ;; and let dest=1
LEXIT:
           ENDM                     ;; end of macro
           ENDM                     ;; end of IRP
```

In this macro, the contents of the destination and source (registers) are compared, and depending on the value of COND, one of the 6 conditional jump instructions JE, JGE, JG, JLE, JL and JNE (respectively) will be carried out. This results in the contents of the destination being set to 0 or 1.

6.3.3   Run-time system

We have already mentioned that the routines *push* and *pop* are not used by the assembly-code fragments. These routines can therefore be removed from the run-time system. Only the routines that are concerned with procedure calls and dynamic arrays need to be changed. We describe these changes below.

Procedure calls. The routines *call* and *return_* need to be modified as these routines use the C-library routines *setjmp* and *longjmp* to implement the procedure-call mechanism. We again use a stack (also called *return_stack*) to store the return addresses. Instead of a stack of elements of type *jmp_buf*, however, this time we only need a stack of integers. A C-routine *pushretaddr* that pushes an address (integer) onto the stack, and a routine *popretaddr* that pops an address off the stack are used. The declarations of the return stack, its pointer, and the push and pop routines are shown below.

```
static int returnstack[max_depth], rsp = 0;

void
pushretaddr(int retaddr)
{
        if (rsp < max_depth)
                returnstack[rsp++] = retaddr;
        else
                report_error("pushretaddr: return stack overflow");
}
```

```
int
popretaddr(void)
{
        if (rsp > 0)
                return returnstack[−−rsp];
        else
                report_error("popretaddr: empty return stack");
        return 0;
}
```

We use the return-stack push routine in the macro XCALL. This macro, shown below, implements the instruction `call` by first determining the return address, calling *pushretaddr* to save this address, and then jumping to the given label.

```
XCALL     MACRO   LABEL                     ;; call subroutine
          LOCAL   RETADDR
          MOV     AX, OFFSET RETADDR        ;; get return address in ax
          CALL    PUSHRETADDR C, AX         ;; save ax on the return stack
          JMP     LABEL                     ;; go to the subroutine
RETADDR:
          ENDM
```

The return address is popped off the return stack by a direct call to *popretaddr* from the assembly-code fragment for the instruction `return_`. The result of this call is that the return address is placed in the register AX. The value in this register is pushed onto the stack, where it is used by the instruction RET to jump to the correct address.

Dynamic arrays. We saw in the VIM-to-C code generator how the run-time routines *descr* and *ixdpl* implement dynamic arrays. Because these routines pop elements off the stack, these routines must be translated into assembly code. The 2 macros DESCR and IXDPL are shown below. Note that, for the sake of simplicity, we have left out bounds checking.

```
DESCR     MACRO SN, DPL, N                  ;; descr(sn, dpl, n)
          LOCAL LDLOOP, LDTEST

          MOV     AX, N                     ;; n
          SHL     AX, 1                     ;; 2*n
          MOV     BX, DPL                   ;; dpl
          ADD     BX, AX                    ;; dpl + 2*n
          INC     BX                        ;; dpl + 2*n + 1
          MOV     DI, BX                    ;; k= dpl + 2*n + 1
          MOV     SI, 1                     ;; s= 1
          JMP     SHORT LDTEST
LDLOOP:
          POP     AX                        ;; up= pop()
          POP     BX                        ;; lo= pop()
          SUB     AX, BX                    ;; up - lo
          INC     AX                        ;; up - lo + 1
```

```
            IMUL  SI
            MOV   SI, AX            ;; s *= up - lo + 1
            CALL  PUTMEMR C, SN, DI, BX ;; putmemr(sn, k, lo)
            MOV   AX, DI            ;; k
            DEC   AX               ;; k - 1
            CALL  PUTMEMR C, SN, AX, SI ;; putmemr(sn, k-1, s)
            SUB   DI, 2            ;; k -= 2
LDTEST:
            MOV   AX, DPL           ;; dpl
            INC   AX               ;; dpl + 1
            CMP   AX, DI            ;; dpl + 1 < k
            JL    SHORT LDLOOP
            CALL  GETSEGLEN C, SN      ;; offset= getseglen(sn)
            CALL  PUTMEMR C, SN, DI, AX ;; putmemr(sn, k, offset)
            CALL  INCRSEGLEN C, SN, SI  ;; incrseglen(sn, s)
            CALL  PUTMEMR C, SN, DPL, N ;; putmemr(sn, dpl, n)
            ENDM

ixdpl       MACRO SN, DPL            ;; int ixdpl(sn, dpl)
            LOCAL LXLOOP, LXTEST

            CALL  GETMEMR C, SN, DPL   ;; getmemr(sn, dpl)
            SHL   AX, 1
            MOV   BX, DPL
            ADD   BX, AX
            MOV   DI, BX             ;; k= dpl + 2*getmemr(sn, dpl)
            MOV   AX, DPL            ;; dpl
            INC   AX               ;; dpl+1
            CALL  GETMEMR C, SN, AX
            MOV   SI, AX             ;; xdpl= getmemr(sn, dpl+1)
            MOV   AX, DI            ;; k
            INC   AX               ;; k+1
            CALL  GETMEMR C, SN, AX
            SUB   SI, AX             ;; xdpl -= getmemr(sn, k+1)
            POP   BX
            ADD   SI, BX             ;; xdpl += pop()
            JMP   SHORT LXTEST
LXLOOP:
            MOV   BP, SP             ;; pop() but leave sp
            MOV   AX, DI            ;; k
            DEC   AX               ;; k-1
            CALL  GETMEMR C, SN, AX
            SUB   WORD PTR[BP], AX     ;; pop() - getmemr(sn, k-1)
            CALL  GETMEMR C, SN, DI     ;; getmemr(sn, k)
            IMUL  WORD PTR[BP]         ;; (pop()-getmemr(sn,k-1))*prev
            ADD   SI, AX             ;; xdpl += prev
            SUB   DI, 2            ;; k -= 2
            ADD   SP, 2            ;; pop() only update sp
LXTEST:
            MOV   AX, DPL           ;; dpl
            ADD   AX, 2            ;; dpl+2
            CMP   AX, DI            ;; dpl+2 < k
```

```
JL      SHORT LXLOOP
MOV     CX, SI                  ;; result in register cx
ENDM
```

This is the extent of the changes to the run-time system.

6.4   Performance

We call the code generators that we have presented in the previous 2 sections *v2c* (VIM to C-code) and *v2a* (VIM to assembly code). In the next section we compare the speed of the code generated by *v2c* and *v2a*, and the interpreter. In Section 6.4.2 we analyse and improve the efficiency of the code generated by *v2c*.

6.4.1   Comparison

At the beginning of this chapter we mentioned programs in SLANG and C that compute the 2000th prime number. We noted that the interpreter was 80 times slower than the C-executable. In this section we will use the prime benchmark to see how fast the code generated by *v2c* and *v2a* is.

Before doing so, however, we briefly review the procedure for compiling and executing SLANG programs. Given a program written in SLANG, the front-end is used to generate a VIM (intermediate) program. To "run" this program, we can do 3 things:

1. We can execute it directly with the interpreter.
2. We can use *v2c* to translate it into C-code,[5] compile the C-code, and then run the executable.
3. We can use *v2a* to translate it into assembly code, assemble this code, and then run the executable.

In the table in Figure 6.7, we show the time taken by the interpreter, and code generated by *v2c* and *v2a* for the prime benchmark. Notice that the C-code generated by *v2c* is more than 5 times faster than the interpreter, and that the assembly code generated by *v2a* is more than 10 times faster. These results typify all the testing that was done.

6.4.2   Efficiency

Now let us look more closely at the quality of the code generated by *v2c* and *v2a*, and analyse its behaviour.

---

[5]The Borland C Compiler was used, and no optimisation switches.

	time (seconds)
interpreter	40
v2c	7.1
v2a	3.7

Figure 6.7   The time taken to compute the 2000th prime number by the interpreter, and the code generated by *v2c* and *v2a*.

The code generator *v2c* generates "naive" code. It is naive in the sense that, because VIM instructions are translated individually, there is no account taken of the context. It is possible, for example, that a pop of a particular variable is directly followed by a push of the same variable. Further, heavy use is made of function calls, particularly *push* and *pop*.

Example 6.6
Consider the intermediate code that was generated in Example 6.1. The corresponding C-code is shown below. On the right in the code we have added comments that explain the effect of each line of C-code. We denote the value of a variable a (say) by $val(a)$, and an indirect reference to a variable b by $ind(b)$.

```
#include "rts.h"
#include "seglen.h"
int
main(void)
{
crseg(1, SEGLEN1);              /* 1. create seg. 1 of length SEGLEN1 */
goto L1;                        /* 2. go to start of "main" at label L_1 */
L2: crseg(2, SEGLEN2);          /* 3. create seg. 2 of length SEGLEN2 */
putmemr(2, 1, pop());           /* 4. move val(b) from stack to seg. 2 */
putmemr(2, 0, pop());           /* 5. move val(a) from stack to seg. 2 */
push(getmemr(2, 0));            /* 6. copy val(a) from seg. 2 to stack */
push(getmemr(2, 0));            /* 7. copy val(a) from seg. 2 to stack */
push(pop() * pop());            /* 8. replace top 2 elements by val(a*a) */
push(getmemr(2, 1));            /* 9. copy val(b) from seg. 2 to stack */
{ int pop1= pop();
  putmema(pop1, pop());         /* 10. move val(a*a) to the address val(b) */
}
dlseg();                        /* 11. delete seg. 2 */
{ jmp_buf jmpbuf;
  return_(&jmpbuf);             /* 12. restore env. from call stack */
  longjmp(jmpbuf, 1);           /* 13. return to setjmp() == 1 */
}
L1: push(rdint());              /* 14. read val(i), copy val(i) to stack */
putmemr(1, 0, pop());           /* 15. move val(i) to seg. 1 */
push(getmemr(1, 0));            /* 16. copy val(i) from seg. 1 to stack */
push(varaddr(1, 1));            /* 17. copy ind(j) from seg. 1 to stack */
{ jmp_buf jmpbuf;
```

routine	time %	count
main	29	1
pop	26	74176
push	25	74176
getmemr	11	29816
putmemr	2	6948
"others"	≤ 1	

Figure 6.8 A profile of the prime benchmark for *v2c*.

```
   if (setjmp(jmpbuf) == 0) {  /* 18. save env. in jmpbuf, setjmp() == 0 */
      call(&jmpbuf);           /* 19. move env. to call stack */
      goto L2;                 /* 20. go to proc. "square" at label l_2 */
   }
}
push(getmemr(1, 1));           /* 21. copy val(j) from seg. 1 to stack */
wrint(pop());                  /* 22. move val(j) from stack to output */
dlseg();                       /* 23. delete seg. 1 */
return 0;                      /* 24. end */
}
```

Examining this code, we can see when the segments are created and deleted, how variable parameters are implemented, and how procedures are called using *setjmp*. Notice that we *move* a value from the stack to a segment (i.e. we leave nothing behind), but that we *copy* a value from a segment onto the stack. With regard to the efficiency, we note the following:

- In lines 5 and 6, and 15 and 16, the value of "a" is moved from the stack to the segment and back again. These instructions are therefore redundant.
- In line 8, the C-code fragment *push(pop()∗pop())* means that 3 function calls (each involving a stack-bounds check) are necessary to replace the top 2 elements on the stack by their product.

$\diamond$

While a single-pass on-the-fly code-generation scheme cannot, in general, carry out optimisations that involve knowledge of the (global) structure of the program, it is possible to locally optimise the code. We can do this by making the scheme more "intelligent". For example, we can add a *stack descriptor* that keeps track of variables that are on the stack. We can determine when push operations are redundant by checking the stack descriptor. We do not consider optimisations of this sort here because we wish to keep the code generator as simple as possible.

We can, however, do something about the (zealous) use of functions in the implementation of *v2c*. The data flow in a VIM program is mainly to and from the stack. One would expect, therefore, that the push and pop routines from the run-time system to be heavily used. In the table in Figure 6.8, we show the

routine	time %	count
getmemr	39	29816
main	35	1
putmemr	10	6948
putmema	6	4545
"others"	≤ 1	

Figure 6.9 A profile of the prime benchmark for the in-lined version of *v2c*.

percentage of the total run time that is spent in each routine, and the number of times each routine is called for the prime benchmark. (For the purposes of this analysis, only the 200th prime is computed.) Note that the push and pop routines are called 148,352 times in total, and account for more than half the time. Each of the routines listed as "others" uses less than 1% of the total time.

Instead of using the functions *push* and *pop*, we could in-line the code belonging to these functions in the code fragments.

Example 6.7
Let us again consider the C-code fragment *push(pop()∗pop())* that corresponds to the VIM instruction mul. We can replace this code fragment by the following:

```
if (−−sp>0)
    stack[sp−1] = stack[sp−1] * stack[sp]
else
    report_error("stack underflow");
```

This code has the same effect as the original code fragment, but it involves no function calls, and there is only 1 bounds check.   ◇

We can replace all the references to *push* and *pop* in the code table by code that explicitly references the stack. The new version of *v2c* that uses the new code table will generate a C-program in which part of the run-time system has been "in-lined". The profile of the generated code for the prime benchmark (again, only the 200th prime is computed) using this new in-lined version of *v2c* is shown in Figure 6.9. Note that the push and pop routines are no longer present, and that more than half the time in the benchmark is now spent accessing "memory" (i.e. calling *getmemr, putmemr* and *getmema*). Again, each of the routines in "others" uses less than 1% of the total time.

Applying the in-lined version of *v2c* to our 2000th prime benchmark results in an execution time of 4.9 seconds. The execution time was 7.1 seconds (see Figure 6.7)—this is an improvement of approximately $\frac{1}{3}$.

We could continue this process, of course, and in-line more of the run-time system. However, while the gains are worthwhile, we choose not to present an in-lined version of the code table because it is less readable and less intuitive. The table consists mainly of low-level stack operations. The straightforward approach has the added advantage that it is easier to add new VIM instructions to the code table and specifications. This property is called *extendibility*.

We could speed up the code generated by *v2a* by rewriting heavily used routines into assembly code. For the purposes of this text, however, we have tried to minimise and localise the differences between *v2c* and *v2a*. A run-time system written in assembly code would be a nuisance to port, of course.

A big advantage of the on-the-fly technique is its simplicity and directness, and in the case of *v2c*, its portability. We can compile a source program on any computer that has a C-compiler by using *v2c*. The potential of this technique can be seen in *v2a*, which, despite its simplicity, generates surprisingly fast code when compared to a commercial C-compiler.

Note that we have not considered modifying the front-end to generate "better" intermediate code. The front-end can make optimisations to the code that the back-end cannot make because the front-end has full knowledge of the structure of the program. For example, identifying and removing common subexpressions is typically carried out in the front-end. The front-end can identify loops, and can pass information about the use of variables to the back-end. We must avoid, however, "optimising" the front-end in such a way that it becomes target-machine dependent. If the front-end has knowledge of the target machine, and uses this knowledge to generate "more efficient" intermediate code, then the front-end will be biased and less portable. Nearly all optimisations involve weighing up the pros and cons: is a particular optimisation worth the effort, and what is the price that we pay?

The code-generator generator that generates *v2c* and *v2a* is a welcome addition to the compiler generator. By "replacing" the interpreter with a code generator, we have improved the performance by an order of magnitude. The code generator *v2c* is particularly useful. It is a take-anywhere code generator that also generates reasonably fast code.

6.5 Exercises

1. Modify *v2c* to generate code for the new instructions listed below.

   (a) `pop` This instruction removes the value on top of the stack.

   (b) `copy` This instruction duplicates the value on top of the stack.

   (c) `swap` This instruction reverses the order of the top 2 values on the stack.

   (d) `not` This instruction carries out a logical *not* operation on the top (logical) value on the stack. The top value is replaced by the result.

   (e) `and, or` These instructions carry out logical *and* and *or* operations on the top 2 (logical) values on the stack. The top 2 values are replaced by the result.

(f) `rdbool, wrbool`   The instruction `rdbool` reads a (logical) value from the keyboard and stores its internal representation on the stack. The instruction `wrbool` removes the top value from the stack and writes its external logical representation to the screen.

(g) `rdchar, wrchar`   The instruction `rdchar` reads a (character) value from the keyboard and stores its internal representation on the stack. The instruction `wrchar` removes the top value from the stack and writes its external character representation to the screen.

Do this by:

- adding the instruction to the VIM scanner and parser specifications,

- adding appropriate code fragments to the code table, and

- adding any necessary routines to the run-time system.

The instructions above were listed in Section 4.5 (Figure 4.14) as part of the laboratory, except for the instruction **swap**, which was mentioned in Section 5.6.4.

2. Having modified *v2c* in Exercise 1, now modify *v2a* to generate 80486 code for these instructions.

3. In Example 6.7 we showed how the code fragment for the instruction **mul** can be in-lined. In-line the code fragments in the rest of the code table.

4. In Section 6.4.2 we mentioned that a stack descriptor can be used to keep track of variables on the stack. This stack descriptor enables us to avoid generating some redundant code.

   (a) By analysing the code table, determine in which situations the descriptor could be used.

   (b) Implement a stack-descriptor scheme.

5. What other optimisations are possible to *v2c*?

6.6   Bibliographic notes

For more information on the 80486 microprocessor and assembly language, the reader is referred to Brey [26].

Since the 1970s, research in code generation has been mainly concerned with so-called *automatic code generation*. In automatic code generation, a code generator is generated from a (high-level) description of the target machine by a code-generator generator. Various methods have been used to build a code-generator generator. In these notes we will briefly survey these methods.

The Production-Quality Compiler Compiler (PQCC) project. This was an ambitious project [29, 150] in the late 1970s and early 1980s. Its aim was to automatically generate a high-quality code generator, and to solve the phase-ordering problem. It used, for example, 2 instruction-selection phases that sandwich a register allocator. Although this system was partially successful in achieving its aims, this research faded from view in the early 1980s. See [138] for a description of this technique.

A code generator based on a peephole-optimiser. This unusual "code generator" was developed by Davidson and Fraser [21, 33, 34, 49]. It was unusual because a very simple code generator was first used to translate the intermediate code into *register transfer instructions*. In effect, these instructions acted as a second intermediate code. The accompanying *peephole optimiser* is then used to translate the register-transfer instructions into (efficient) target code. A peephole optimiser replaces a "window" of instructions (usually 2 or 3) by a single instruction, if possible. The David and Fraser optimiser worked symbolically and was derived from a machine description. This technique was extensively studied throughout the 1980s, albeit by only a small group of researchers.

A template-matching dynamic-programming code generator. This scheme was originally formulated by Aho and Johnson in 1976 [2], and was further developed and implemented by various researchers (e.g. [1, 82, 84]). It has had a chequered history. Notable successes have been the portable C-compiler [85] that runs on countless different machines, and the *twig* system [1]. The basic philosophy of this scheme is to first estimate the resources (registers) that are needed to evaluate subtrees in a bottom-up pass of the expression (syntax) tree. These estimates are used to allocate registers, and to evaluate the order of evaluation.

The Graham–Glanville scheme. This scheme was formulated in 1977/78 by Glanville and Graham [57, 58], and was extensively developed by Ganapathi and Fischer [50, 51]. It attracted a great deal of attention throughout the 1980s. In Graham and Glanville's original work, a bottom-up (shift/reduce) parser generator was modified to act as a code-generator generator. In [57], Glanville "proved" that the code generator generated correct code, and could not block. The elegance, simplicity and effectiveness of this technique, and its "formal" basis, astounded the research world when it was introduced. Ganapathi and Fischer's contribution was to extend the technique to use a more sophisticated attribute scheme and parser.

By the end of the 1980s, however, it was realised that the technique could not adequately handle real (i.e. non-uniform) instruction sets, and that other phases (such as register allocation and optimisation) could also not be adequately handled. A description and bibliographic survey of this technique can be found in [105] and [138].

Bottom-up pattern matching (BUPM). Techniques based on bottom-up pattern matching, and using either *regular tree grammars* or *term rewrite systems* have been studied for 20 years now, and are still popular. Kron [93], Hoffmann and O'Donnell [77] and Chase [30] have laid the foundations of this technique.

Chase [30] implemented a BUPM by specifying patterns using a regular tree grammar. A regular tree grammar is a context-free grammar with prefix notation on the right-hand sides of the productions. This prefix notation represents trees. Chase found that the tables generated by the pattern matcher were enormous, requiring extensive use of compression techniques. A formalisation of Chase's table-compression technique can be found in Hemerik and Katoen [70]. An asymptotic improvement in both space and time to Chase's algorithm is given by Cai *et al.* [28].

Hatcher and Christopher [66] extended the work of Chase, and they built a complete system. Their work was a milestone in that they carried out *static* cost analysis, which is a cost analysis carried out at code-generator generation time. In a *dynamic* cost analysis, the code generator itself performs the cost analysis. This is a space–time trade-off. Static cost-analysis makes the code-generator generator more complex and requires a lot of space for tables. In effect, pattern selection is encoded into the tables. The resulting code generator, however, is simple and fast. In both the static and dynamic BUPMs, the cost analysis is usually carried out using dynamic programming [144]. For a comparison of the performance of static and dynamic BUPMs, see Henry and Damron [73, 74] and Henry [71, 72]. Two notable attempts to improve the efficiency of the dynamic (BUPM) code generator have been Emmelmann *et al.* [41], who developed the BEG system, and Fraser *et al.* [47], who developed the IBURG system.

In 1990, Balachandran *et al.* [19] used a regular tree grammar and techniques based on the work of Chase, Hatcher and Christopher to build a static BUPM. Ferdinand *et al.* [44] reformulated the (static) BUPM algorithm (based on regular tree grammars) in terms of finite tree automata, using a subset-construction algorithm to carry out the static cost analysis.

Pelegrí-Llopart and Graham [113, 114] combined the static cost analysis concept from Hatcher and Christopher, the pattern-matching and table-compression techniques from Chase, and, most importantly, term rewrite systems (rather than regular tree grammars) to develop a system called BURS, which stands for *bottom-up rewrite system*. A BURS is, in fact, a generalisation of a BUPM, and is more powerful. The term rewrite system in a BURS consists of rewrite rules that define transformations between *terms*. A term, which is represented by a tree, consists of operators and operands (which are analogous to nonterminals and terminals in context-free grammars). However, *variables* that can match any tree are also allowed. The advantage of using a term rewrite system is that, as well as the usual rewrite rules that reduce the expression tree, we can use rules that transform the expression tree. Algebraic properties of terms can therefore be incorporated into the code-generation process. The "BURS theory" that Pelegrí-Llopart and Graham developed is quite complex, however. In 1996, Nymeyer *et al.* [107] reworked and formalised BURS theory. Instead of a static cost analysis, however, they used a dynamic (heuristic) search algorithm (called the A* algorithm).

Mainly theoretical research into the role of term rewrite systems in code generation has been carried out by Emmelmann [40] and Giegerich and Schmal [55, 56].

In 1992, Fraser *et al.* [48] presented a new implementation of a BURS. However, their system, called BURG, was based on a tree grammar, and not a term rewrite system. The table-generation algorithm that they used is described in [117].

Summing up. Advances in the theory of grammars during the 1960s and 1970s resulted in general-purpose parser generators that made hand-written parsers obsolete. Looking back on 20 years of research into automatic code generation, one could be forgiven for concluding that researchers are really no closer to finding a theory of code generation, or general-purpose code-generator generators, that will make hand-written code generators obsolete.

Part II

Principles

Chapter 7

Scanning

In this chapter we show how a lexical analyser (scanner) can be generated from a specification. In other words, we show how a scanner generator works. To do this, we must first describe the theory of finite automata. This theory forms the basis of a number of construction algorithms that together can be used to translate a specification (in the form of a regular expression) into a scanner. These construction algorithms therefore make up a scanner generator.

As we saw in Section 3.1, the main responsibility of the lexical analyser is to recognise tokens in the stream of input characters. These tokens are then passed to the parser, which uses them to verify the syntax. Why do we have a separate lexical analyser and syntax analyser? There are 2 main reasons for this:

- **Efficiency**. Character processing is time-consuming. It can be more effectively optimised if localised. Furthermore, the lexical analyser can identify and remove language constructs like comments, blanks, tabs and new-lines that play no further active part in compilation.
- **Design**. The lexical and syntax analysers work on different levels of language abstraction—the lexical analyser processes characters and words, and the syntax analyser processes words and sentences. Separating the specification of the syntax and the sentence structure results in a more readable, portable and maintainable compiler specification.

Before discussing the construction and structure of the lexical analyser, it is worthwhile to consider the different terminology used in scanning and parsing, both here and in the literature, and the roles that the scanner and parser play in compilation.

As stated above, a lexical analyser is responsible for recognising strings of symbols, or words, in a programming language. The symbols are, of course, simply characters. A word, then, is a string of characters. A set of words is represented by a token. A set of words is also a language, hence a token represents a language. In lexical analysis, a language (or token) is specified by a regular expression. Such a language is therefore called a regular language. Note that there is no concept of sentence in lexical analysis—the words in the language can occur in any order.

The symbols used by the syntax analyser (parser) correspond to the tokens generated by the lexical analyser. These symbols are referred to as terminals. A string of symbols in a syntax analyser is referred to as a sentence (remember in a lexical analyser we referred to a string of symbols as a word) and a language is a set of sentences. Typically the syntax analyser is responsible for recognising the sentence structure in a programming language, where a sentence corresponds to a complete input program. We specify a language by a context-free grammar. Such a language is referred to as a context-free language.

In summary then, while the symbols in a lexical and a syntax analyser differ, in abstract terms, both lexical and syntax analysis handle strings of symbols and languages that are sets of strings.

7.1   Regular expressions

We begin by defining an *alphabet* as a finite, non-empty set of *symbols*, and a *string* as a finite row of symbols. A special string is the empty string—this string consists of no symbols, and is denoted by ϵ. A language over an alphabet T is a set of strings, and is a subset of T^*.

There is a special class of languages called regular languages. These languages can be specified by *regular expressions*. A regular expression is an expression that is constructed from the elements of an alphabet T, ϵ and the operators *choice*, *concatenation* and *closure*. A regular expression E is built up out of simpler regular expressions. Correspondingly, the language specified by a regular expression *L(E)* is built up out of the languages specified by its constituent simpler regular expressions. The following rules are used to construct regular expressions over an input alphabet T.

1. ϵ is a regular expression that specifies the language consisting only of the empty string $L(\epsilon) = \{\epsilon\}$.
2. If $a \in T$ then a is a regular expression that specifies the language $L(a) = \{a\}$.
3. If E and E' are regular expressions, then so are the following:

   choice: $E \mid E'$ specifying the language $L(E) \cup L(E')$
   concatenation: $E E'$ specifying the language $L(E)\, L(E')$
   closure: E^* specifying the language $\bigcup_{i=0}^{\infty} L(E)^i$
   bracketing: $\{E\}$ specifying the language $L(E)$

Actually, certain notational conveniences have been used here. In rule 1, we use the same name "ϵ" for the empty regular expression and the empty string, and in rule 2, we use the same name "a" to refer to the regular expression, the string and the symbol. To be technically correct, regular expressions, strings and symbols are different entities, hence their names should be distinct.

Notice in rule 3 that the choice and closure operators are explicitly represented by "|" and "*", but that the concatenation operator is implicit. The closure operator is sometimes called the *Kleene closure*. It can also be represented as **clos**. The use of braces to affect priorities is also defined in rule 3. In the literature, parentheses are often used instead of braces. Note that we also use braces to denote sets in this book.

We can reduce the number of braces in a regular expression by adopting the convention that all operators are left-associative, and by assigning the following relative priorities to the operators. From highest to lowest, the priorities are:

1. closure
2. concatenation
3. choice

Regular expressions have algebraic properties. For example, concatenation and choice are associative, hence we can write $\{E_1E_2\}E_3 = E_1\{E_2E_3\} = E_1E_2E_3$, and, $\{E_1 \,|\, E_2\} \,|\, E_3 = E_1 \,|\, \{E_2 \,|\, E_3\} = E_1 \,|\, E_2 \,|\, E_3$. Also, concatenation is distributive over choice, so $E_1\{E_2 \,|\, E_3\} = E_1E_2 \,|\, E_1E_3$.

Let's have a look at some examples. The regular expression a specifies a language $L(a) = \{a\}$, which is a set containing one string, namely a. The regular expression $a \,|\, b$ specifies $L(a) \cup L(b) = \{a\} \cup \{b\} = \{a, b\}$. More interestingly, the regular expression a^* specifies an infinite set of strings, namely $\bigcup_{i=0}^{\infty} L(a)^i = \{\epsilon\} \cup \{a\} \cup \{aa\} \cup \ldots = \{\epsilon, a, aa, \ldots\}$. Mixing the closure and choice operators, the regular expression $\{a \,|\, b\}^*$ specifies an infinite set of strings made up of zero or more instances of an a or b, namely $\bigcup_{i=0}^{\infty}(L(a) \cup L(b))^i = \{\epsilon, a, b, aa, ab, ba, bb, \ldots\}$. Finally, we have that $a\{a \,|\, b\}^*b$ specifies any string consisting of a's and b's that begins with a and ends with b.

7.2 Finite automata

In Section 3.1.2 we introduced the concept of a transition diagram and a finite automaton. It was briefly stated that a finite automaton may be *deterministic* or *non-deterministic*. In this section we examine finite automata more closely, and we show how to implement a deterministic finite automaton. We abbreviate deterministic and non-deterministic finite automata to DFA and NFA, respectively.

A finite automaton A is defined by the quintuple (Q, T, M, Z, F) where

Q is a finite, non-empty set of states,

T is a finite input alphabet,

$Z \in Q$ is the start state,

$F \subseteq Q$ is a set of accept states,

and in the case of a DFA

M is a mapping from $Q \times T \to Q$

and in an NFA

M is a mapping from $Q \times (T \cup \{\epsilon\}) \to Q^*$

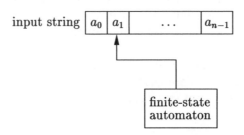

Figure 7.1 A schematic of a finite-state automaton.

In Figure 7.1 we show a schematic of a finite-state automaton. At any given moment, the automaton is in a particular state. At the start, it is in state Z. After reading an input symbol, the automaton changes state. When all the input has been read (and is correct), it is in one of the states in the set F. In the case of a DFA, if the input is the string of n symbols $a_0 \ldots a_{n-1}$, $a_i \in T$, $i = 0, \ldots, n-1$, then, after reading symbol a_i, the automaton is in state

$$Q_{i+1} = M(Q_i, a_i)$$

where $Q_0 = Z$. The string is accepted if $Q_n \in F$.

Notice in the definition of the mapping M above that the input alphabet in an NFA is extended by $\{\epsilon\}$. This means that transitions in an NFA can also be labelled with the symbol ϵ. These transitions are called ϵ-transitions. An ϵ-transition can occur without input being read. Notice also that we do not have the restriction in an NFA that the mapping must generate a single state. This means that, given a state and an input symbol, it is possible to change to more than 1 state.

In the case of an NFA, after reading symbol a_i, the automaton will be in a set of states

$$\Xi_{i+1} = \epsilon\text{-closure}\,(M(\Xi_i, a_i))$$

The mapping $M(\Xi_i, a_i)$ generates a set of states—in fact, it generates those states that are reachable from a state in Ξ_i given input symbol a_i. In other words, if $\Xi_i = \{Q_1, \ldots, Q_k\}$, then $M(\Xi_i, a_i) = \bigcup_{j=1}^{k} M(\{Q_j\}, a_i)$. If the generated set of states $\Xi_p = \{Q_1, \ldots, Q_l\}$, then $\epsilon\text{-closure}(\Xi_p) = \Xi_p \cup \bigcup_{j=1}^{l} M(\{Q_j\}, \epsilon)$. In other words, we add to Ξ_p all those states that can be reached by one or more ϵ-transitions. The input string is accepted if there exists $Q_i \in \Xi_n \cap F$. Note that a DFA is a special case of an NFA.

Transition diagrams can be represented and implemented (although, in general, not efficiently) as tables. In a transition table, each row corresponds to a state, and each column to an input symbol, or to ϵ in the case of an NFA. Entries in the table are single states in the case of a DFA, and sets of states in an NFA. Empty entries indicate erroneous input.

In Figure 7.2 we show an example of a DFA and 2 NFAs, corresponding to the regular expression ab^*b. In Figure 7.3, we give corresponding transition tables for the same regular expression.

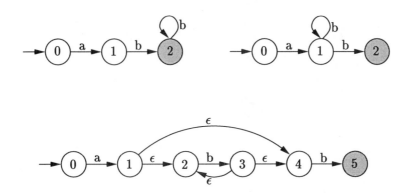

Figure 7.2   A DFA (top left) and 2 NFAs corresponding to the regular expression ab^*b.

We have now considered regular expressions and the languages that they specify, and finite automata. In fact, it can be proved that for every regular expression E, there exists a finite automaton A such that $L(E) = L(A)$. This proof is done by induction on each of the 3 operators: concatenation, choice and closure. What this says is that regular expressions and finite automata are equivalent.

Why is it, then, that we are interested in finite automata? As the name suggests, a finite automaton is a program, a program that will recognise (or match) strings in a language specified by a corresponding regular expression. This program, in fact, forms the basis of our lexical analyser.

Example 7.1
Consider the DFA shown on the left in Figure 7.4. This DFA recognises identifiers

	a	b
0	{1}	
1		{2}
2		{2}

	a	b
0	{1}	
1		{1,2}
2		

	a	b	ϵ
0	{1}		
1			{2,4}
2		{3}	
3			{2,4}
4		{5}	
5			

Figure 7.3 Transition tables corresponding to the finite automata in Figure 7.2.

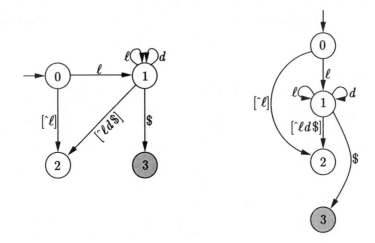

Figure 7.4 A DFA for the regular expression $\ell\{\ell\,|\,d\}^*\$$, drawn 2 ways.

of the form $\ell\{\ell\,|\,d\}^*\$$. The edges in this DFA are labelled ℓ and d, which stand for letter and digit; $\$$, which is the end-of-text symbol; $[\hat{}\,\ell]$, which is any symbol but a letter; and $[\hat{}\,\ell d\$]$, which is any symbol but a letter, digit or end-of-text symbol. The rationale behind this DFA should be obvious—the DFA will accept a letter followed by any number (including zero) of letters and digits, and terminated by an end-of-text symbol. Incorrect input causes a transition to a "reject" state (2), and correct input to an accept state (3).

In Figure 7.5 we show a program that is a direct translation of this DFA. For convenience we have let $\$$ be a new-line symbol. This program will "accept" identifiers that are terminated by a new-line, and "reject" all else.   ◇

Notice in the program in Figure 7.5 that states are indicated by labels (i.e. the program counter), and that edges are given by if-goto statements. We have used an "unstructured", "goto" style of programming in this example to highlight the equivalence between the DFA and the program. This program (lexical analyser) truly mimics the control flow in the DFA. This is easy to see if the program is compared with the redrawn DFA, shown on the right in Figure 7.4. More usually, however, if-statements or case-statements are used to implement a DFA. (See Chapter 3.)

Normally, of course, an identifier is only one of the many syntactic constructs that we wish to recognise in a programming language. If we assume that each construct has its own transition diagram, then we can consider the start states of all the transition diagrams to be linked. In a given transition diagram, if we encounter a symbol that does not match any transition, then we must assume that this symbol belongs to some other token. This symbol must therefore be returned

```
main()
{
  char c;

L0:
  c = getchar();
  if (islower(c)) goto L1;
  /* otherwise */ goto L2;
L1:
  c = getchar();
  if (islower(c)) goto L1;
  if (isdigit(c)) goto L1;
  if (c == '\n') goto L3;
  /* otherwise */ goto L2;
L2:
  printf("Rejected\n");
  return;
L3:
  printf("Accepted\n");
  exit(0);
}
```

Figure 7.5 A lexical analyser for the regular expression $\ell\{\ell\,|\,d\}^*\$$.

to the input queue (to allow it to be re-read), and we must go to the start state of the next transition diagram. Only after all start states have been exhausted can we flag an error.

7.3   Constructing a finite automaton

In this section we construct non-deterministic and deterministic finite automata from a given regular expression. As noted earlier, the essential difference between an NFA and a DFA is the number of transitions that are possible in a state; in an NFA there can be more than 1, in a DFA there can be at most 1. Because more than 1 state is possible in an NFA, some kind of backtracking (or parallel) algorithm is needed to undo "incorrect" decisions. However, backtracking has a number of disadvantages: it makes error handling difficult, it is hard to undo other actions that are associated with state transitions, and the time required to parse a string may increase exponentially with the length of the string. It is for these reasons that an NFA can be difficult to implement. This is in contrast to a DFA, which, as we saw in the previous section (see Figure 7.5), was very straightforward to implement.

Unfortunately, we cannot easily construct a DFA directly from a regular expression. We must first construct an NFA, and then convert the NFA into a DFA.

We describe 2 techniques to construct an NFA from a regular expression. The first technique, described in the next section, is called *Thompson's construction*. In this technique, an NFA is constructed that often contains many ϵ-transitions. This can cause a serious space problem, however, when used on non-toy languages. This technique is therefore often considered impractical, although it may still be used because of its conceptual simplicity. A second more efficient technique, which we call *element construction*, is described in Section 7.3.2. In this technique, we construct an NFA that contains no ϵ-transitions, hence there is no intrinsic space problem. Both techniques work on the abstract-syntax-tree representation of the regular expression.

In Section 7.3.3 we describe a *subset-construction* algorithm that converts an NFA, generated by either of the above techniques, into a DFA. Finally, in Section 7.3.4, we give a *state-minimisation* algorithm that minimises the number of states in a DFA.

7.3.1   Thompson's construction

To build an NFA, we need to construct an abstract syntax tree of the given regular expression. In the abstract syntax tree, the concatenation, choice and closure operators are internal nodes, and the input symbols are leaf nodes.

Example 7.2
The abstract syntax tree of $\ell\{\ell\,|\,d\}^*$ is

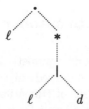

Notice that we represent the concatenation operator by a dot, and that, as it happens, all 3 operators occur in this tree.   ◇

In fact, it is possible to draw a syntax tree for each of the operators, namely $E\,E'$, $E\,|\,E'$ and E^*, where E and E' are regular expressions. These syntax trees have the following appearance:

We can indicate the control flow in these subtrees, and thereby produce *control-flow graphs*. In the case of $E\ E'$, for example, we must traverse both regular expressions E and E', starting at the root of the syntax tree. That is, we go from the root to E, traverse the tree represented by E, then we go to E', traverse the tree represented by E', and finally go back to the root again. Pictorially, this looks like:

In this graph, the syntax tree is shown dotted. Following the arrows, then, we traverse $0 \rightarrow 1$, the tree E, $2 \rightarrow 3$, the tree E', and finally $4 \rightarrow 5$. In the case of $E\,|\,E'$, we need to do either E or E'. That is, starting at the root, we go to E and back, or to E' and back. This results in the following graph:

Traversing the graph, we find that control flows along $0 \rightarrow 1$ and $2 \rightarrow 5$, and $0 \rightarrow 3$ and $4 \rightarrow 5$. Finally, we consider E^*. In closure, we can skip E altogether, or we can do E one or more times. This results in:

To skip E, we traverse $0 \rightarrow 3$. To do E once, we traverse $0 \rightarrow 1$, the tree E and $2 \rightarrow 3$. To repeat E, we need to go back to the beginning of E again, i.e. we traverse $2 \rightarrow 1$.

We have now handled all the operators. We can also construct control-flow graphs for the leaf nodes. A leaf is either an input symbol a (say), or an ϵ. These

```
state = 0;

traverse(node)
{
        traverse(left);
        traverse(right);
        node.i = state;
        state = state+1;
        node.s = state;
        state = state+1;
        if (node.n∈T || node.n == ε)
                ℑ[node.i][node.n] = {node.s};
        else if (node.n == concatenate) {
                ℑ[node.i][ε] = {left.i};
                ℑ[left.s][ε] = {right.i};
                ℑ[right.s][ε] = {node.s};
        }
        else if (node.n == choice) {
                ℑ[node.i][ε] = {left.i, right.i};
                ℑ[left.s][ε] = {node.s};
                ℑ[right.s][ε] = {node.s};
        }
        else if (node.n == close) {
                ℑ[node.i][ε] = {left.i, node.s};
                ℑ[left.s][ε] = {left.i, node.s};
        }
}
```

Figure 7.6 Thompson's construction algorithm.

can be represented by the following graphs.

$$0 \xrightarrow{\text{a}} 1 \qquad\qquad 0 \longrightarrow 1$$

The control-flow graphs for the 3 types of operator nodes and 2 types of leaf nodes can be used to construct a control-flow graph for any given regular expression. As we shall see, a control-flow graph corresponds to an NFA.

Thompson's construction algorithm can be used to construct a control-flow graph for a given syntax tree. This algorithm is shown in Figure 7.6. In this algorithm, the control-flow graph is represented by a transition table $\mathfrak{S}$. The syntax tree is traversed bottom-up and left-to-right, by recursively calling the procedure *traverse* with the parameter *node*, where *node* is an input symbol, ϵ, or an operator. Nodes with no children (i.e. input symbols and ϵ) are first processed by the procedure, followed by the operator nodes. Choice nodes and concatenation nodes have 2 children, referred to by *left* and *right* in the procedure, and closure has 1 child, referred to by *left*.

Each node has an associated attribute *node.n* that designates its name. A name is either *concatenate, choice, close*, the empty string ϵ, or the actual input symbol. Nodes also have 2 other attributes, *node.i* and *node.s*, which designate the states that the automaton is in before and after traversing the tree rooted at that node (respectively). As we ascend the syntax tree, we compute the attributes *node.i* and *node.s*, first for the leaves, and then for each of the operators, until finally the root of the tree is reached. For each node *node*, the attributes *node.i* and *node.s* are computed using the global variable *state*, and transitions are added to the transition table $\Im$. These transitions correspond to the control-flow graphs described above.

Consider the case of a choice node, for example. In the algorithm, *node.n* is equal to *choice*, and the transitions we add to the transition table are from *node.i* to *left.i* and to *right.i*, from *left.s* to *node.s*, and from *right.s* to *node.s*. These transitions correspond to the following control-flow graph:

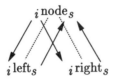

There are some things to notice about Thompson's construction algorithm. First of all, the transitions added by the operator nodes are all ϵ-transitions. Secondly, every state, except the accept state, must have either 1 or 2 successors. Nodes with 2 successors, of course, are non-deterministic. There are only 3 places in the algorithm where we can we add non-determinism to $\Im$; once in choice, and twice in closure. Thirdly, the initial state is given by the ".i" attribute of the root node, and the accept state, by the ".s" attribute. The accept state is unique and has no successors. Because the initial and accept states are attributes of the root node, these are the last 2 states to be enumerated. The input nodes, in order of occurrence, are the first to be enumerated. Finally, if there are N input and operator nodes in the syntax tree, then the resulting graph will contain $2*N$ states. (Every node, or symbol, is allocated 2 states.)

Example 7.3
Consider again the syntax tree corresponding to $\ell\{\ell\,|\,d\}^*$ shown in Example 7.2. Applying Thompson's construction algorithm to this tree, we construct the transition table shown on the left in Figure 7.7. There are 6 symbols in the expression $\ell\{\ell\,|\,d\}^*$. (Do not forget that there is an implicit concatenation operator.) We see in the table that there are 12 transitions. From the table it is simple to construct the control-flow graph. This is shown on the right in Figure 7.7.   ◇

	ℓ	d	ϵ
0	{1}		
1			{8}
2	{3}		
3			{7}
4		{5}	
5			{7}
6			{2,4}
7			{6,9}
8			{6,9}
9			{11}
10			{0}
11			

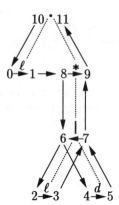

Figure 7.7 A transition table and control-flow graph corresponding to $\ell\{\ell\,|\,d\}^*$.

Redrawing the control-flow graph, it assumes its more conventional appearance as an NFA.

Example 7.4
We can redraw the control-flow graph in Figure 7.7 and produce the automaton in Figure 7.8. ◇

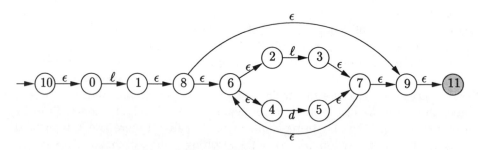

Figure 7.8 The NFA corresponding to $\ell\{\ell\,|\,d\}^*$.

7.3.2 Element construction

In element construction, we distinguish between the occurrences of a symbol in a regular expression. An occurrence of a symbol is called an *element*. A regular expression, therefore, is made up of operators and elements, and each element is unique. Each symbol in a given input string will be matched by at least 1 element in the corresponding regular expression.

Subscripts are usually used to distinguish between the symbols in a regular expression. For example, if we have the regular expression a^*ab, then we can write $a_1^*a_2b$, where a_1, a_2 and b are elements. Notice that since there is only 1 b, it needs no subscript. If we have an input string $aaab$, then the first 2 a symbols are matched by the element a_1, the third a symbol is matched by the element a_2, and the symbol b is matched by the element b.

First and last sets. Element construction involves computing the set of elements $\text{FIRST}(E)$ that can match the first symbol in a string matched by the regular expression E, and the set of elements $\text{LAST}(E)$ that can match the last symbol in a string matched by E. To compute these sets, we first need to compute the Boolean function $\text{EMPTY}(E)$ that says whether E can match the empty string ϵ or not.

Basic rules to compute EMPTY, FIRST and LAST for ϵ, an element a (say), and expressions of the form E^*, $E \mid E'$ and $E\,E'$ are used to compute EMPTY, FIRST and LAST for more complicated regular expressions. These basic rules are given in Figure 7.9. Consider the following cases:

ϵ The element ϵ will always match ϵ, so $\text{EMPTY}(\epsilon)$ is true, but as we have no symbols, $\text{FIRST}(\epsilon)$ and $\text{LAST}(\epsilon)$ are empty.

a If we have a regular expression consisting only of the element a, $\text{EMPTY}(a)$ is false since a must match the input symbol a. Further, $\text{FIRST}(a)$ and $\text{LAST}(a)$ are both $\{a\}$ as a is the only symbol that we have.

E^* By definition, E^* can match the empty string, hence $\text{EMPTY}(E^*)$ is true. Furthermore, since E^* denotes any number of repeats of E, the first elements in E and E^* will be the same, and the last elements in E and E^* will also be the same. Hence $\text{FIRST}(E^*)$ is $\text{FIRST}(E)$, and $\text{LAST}(E^*)$ is $\text{LAST}(E)$.

$E \mid E'$ The regular expression $E \mid E'$ can match either E or E', so we can write $\text{EMPTY}(E \mid E')$ as $\text{EMPTY}(E) \vee \text{EMPTY}(E')$. The first and last elements of $E \mid E'$ can include elements from both sides, so both E and E' will contribute to the first and last sets. In other words, $\text{FIRST}(E \mid E')$ must be $\text{FIRST}(E) \cup \text{FIRST}(E')$, and $\text{LAST}(E \mid E')$ must be $\text{LAST}(E) \cup \text{LAST}(E')$.

$E\,E'$ This regular expression will match ϵ if both E and E' match ϵ. Hence $\text{EMPTY}(E\,E')$ can be written as $\text{EMPTY}(E) \wedge \text{EMPTY}(E')$. The computation of the first and last sets is slightly more complicated. If E can never be empty (i.e. $\text{EMPTY}(E)$ is false), then E will always precede E', and $\text{FIRST}(E\,E')$ will be $\text{FIRST}(E)$. If E can match ϵ, then either E or E' can come first, and hence $\text{FIRST}(E\,E')$ is $\text{FIRST}(E) \cup \text{FIRST}(E')$.

The computation for $\text{LAST}(E\,E')$ is similar. If E' cannot match ϵ, then E' will always succeed E, and $\text{LAST}(E\,E')$ will be $\text{LAST}(E')$, otherwise $\text{LAST}(E\,E')$ will be $\text{LAST}(E) \cup \text{LAST}(E')$.

RE	EMPTY
ϵ	true
a	false
E^*	true
$E\,\vert\,E'$	$\mathrm{EMPTY}(E) \vee \mathrm{EMPTY}(E')$
$E\,E'$	$\mathrm{EMPTY}(E) \wedge \mathrm{EMPTY}(E')$

RE	FIRST
ϵ	$\{\}$
a	$\{a\}$
E^*	$\mathrm{FIRST}(E)$
$E\,\vert\,E'$	$\mathrm{FIRST}(E) \cup \mathrm{FIRST}(E')$
$E\,E'$	$\begin{cases} \mathrm{FIRST}(E), & \text{if } \neg\mathrm{EMPTY}(E) \\ \mathrm{FIRST}(E) \cup \mathrm{FIRST}(E'), & \text{otherwise} \end{cases}$

RE	LAST
ϵ	$\{\}$
a	$\{a\}$
E^*	$\mathrm{LAST}(E)$
$E\,\vert\,E'$	$\mathrm{LAST}(E) \cup \mathrm{LAST}(E')$
$E\,E'$	$\begin{cases} \mathrm{LAST}(E'), & \text{if } \neg\mathrm{EMPTY}(E') \\ \mathrm{LAST}(E) \cup \mathrm{LAST}(E'), & \text{otherwise} \end{cases}$

Figure 7.9 Rules to compute the function EMPTY and sets FIRST and LAST for regular expressions.

Given a syntax tree of a regular expression, we can compute the function EMPTY, and the sets FIRST and LAST bottom-up using the rules in Figure 7.9.

Example 7.5
Below we see the values of EMPTY, FIRST and LAST for the regular expression $\ell_1\{\ell_2\,\vert\,d\}^*$. Each node is annotated with the value at that node.

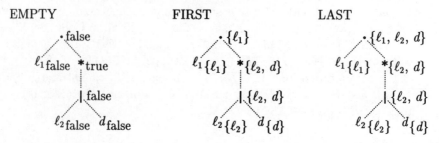

For example, consider the syntax tree corresponding to FIRST. Starting at the leaf nodes, and using the rules given in Figure 7.9, we can write $\text{FIRST}(\ell_1)=\{\ell_1\}$, $\text{FIRST}(\ell_2)=\{\ell_2\}$ and $\text{FIRST}(d)=\{d\}$. Working up the tree, at the choice node we compute,

$$
\begin{aligned}
\text{FIRST}(\ell_2\,|\,d) &= \{\ell_2\}\cup\{d\} \\
&= \{\ell_2,\,d\}
\end{aligned}
$$

and at the closure node,

$$
\begin{aligned}
\text{FIRST}(\{\ell_2\,|\,d\}^{\star}) &= \text{FIRST}(\ell_2\,|\,d) \\
&= \{\ell_2,\,d\}
\end{aligned}
$$

Finally, at the root, because $\text{EMPTY}(\ell_1)$ is false, we compute

$$
\begin{aligned}
\text{FIRST}(\ell_1\{\ell_2\,|\,d\}^{\star}) &= \text{FIRST}(\ell_1) \\
&= \{\ell_1\}
\end{aligned}
$$

where we have used $\text{EMPTY}(\ell_1)=\text{false}$. ◇

Follow sets. The first and last sets can be used to compute the set of elements $\text{FOLLOW}(e)$, which is the set of elements that match the next symbol in the input string after the symbol that e matches. Notice that FOLLOW is a function of an element, unlike FIRST and LAST, which are functions of regular expressions.

Example 7.6
Consider again the regular expression $\ell_1\{\ell_2\,|\,d\}^{\star}$. This regular expression will match strings like ℓ, $\ell\ell$, ℓd, $\ell\ell\ell$, $\ell\ell d$, $\ell d\ell$, ℓdd and so on. The elements in $\text{FOLLOW}(\ell_1)$ match all the input symbols that can appear after the symbol that ℓ_1 matches. Now, the element ℓ_1 matches the first ℓ in each of the above strings, and we can see that the next symbol is either another ℓ (in strings $\ell\ell$, $\ell\ell\ell$ and $\ell\ell d$) or a d (strings ℓd, $\ell d\ell$ and ℓdd). These symbols are matched by elements ℓ_2 and d, respectively, hence $\text{FOLLOW}(\ell_1)$ is $\{\ell_2,d\}$. What is $\text{FOLLOW}(\ell_2)$? In strings $\ell\ell\ell$ and $\ell\ell d$, we see that the symbol that ℓ_2 matches (the second ℓ) is followed by another ℓ, or a d. These are matched by the elements ℓ_2 and d, respectively, and hence $\text{FOLLOW}(\ell_2)$ is also $\{\ell_2,d\}$. Analogous reasoning will show that $\text{FOLLOW}(d)$ is also $\{\ell_2,d\}$. ◇

In general, of course, we cannot compute the follow sets by inspecting the regular expression and possible inputs, as we did above. The information needed to compute the follow sets for each element can be found in the first and last sets in the syntax tree. There are only 2 ways that regular expressions can follow each other, namely through either a concatenation or a closure operation.

When 2 regular expressions E and E' are concatenated, it should be obvious that the last elements of E will be followed by the first elements of E'. The follow set of <u>each element</u> in $\text{LAST}(E)$, then, must include elements in the set $\text{FIRST}(E')$.

When we take the closure of a regular expression E, we simply concatenate E with itself, some number of times. The last elements of E, therefore, can be followed by its own first elements. Hence, the follow set of <u>each element</u> in $\text{LAST}(E)$ must include the elements in the set FIRST(E). We can express these 2 rules in the following way:

RE	FOLLOW
$E\,E'$	$\forall e \in$ LAST(E): FOLLOW(e) = FOLLOW$(e) \cup$ FIRST(E')
E^*	$\forall e \in$ LAST(E): FOLLOW(e) = FOLLOW$(e) \cup$ FIRST(E)

Using these rules, we can compute FOLLOW for each element in a regular expression. Note that each concatenation and closure operation in the regular expression can contribute to the follow set of an element in the regular expression. As in Thompson's construction, we use the syntax tree to apply the rules, but this time we can traverse the syntax tree in any order.

Example 7.7

We again consider the regular expression $\ell_1\{\ell_2 \mid d\}^*$ and use the previous computation of first and last sets, and the above rules, in a top-down traversal of the syntax tree. The root node is a concatenate node, with left branch representing ℓ_1, and right branch $\{\ell_2 \mid d\}^*$. Given LAST$(\ell_1)=\{\ell_1\}$, when we apply the first rule we find that FOLLOW$(\ell_1)=\emptyset\cup$FIRST$(\{\ell_2 \mid d\}^*)=\{\ell_2,d\}$. The next contributing node is the closure node. Given LAST$(\ell_2 \mid d)=\{\ell_2,\ d\}$, we find FOLLOW$(\ell_2)=$FOLLOW$(d)=\emptyset\cup$FIRST$(\ell_2 \mid d)=\{\ell_2,d\}$. There are no more concatenation or closure nodes, hence we have computed all the follow sets. In tabular form, the follow sets are:

element	follow
ℓ_1	$\{\ell_2, d\}$
ℓ_2	$\{\ell_2, d\}$
d	$\{\ell_2, d\}$

Consider the first row in this table. This says that after the input symbol ℓ is matched by element ℓ_1, the next input symbol will be matched by either the element ℓ_2 or d. Similarly for the second and third rows. ◇

Algorithm to construct an NFA. Given FOLLOW$(e_i)=\{e_{f_1},\ldots,e_{f_n}\}$ for each element e_i in a regular expression R, and FIRST(R) and LAST(R), we can construct an NFA using the following steps:

1. Assign to each element e_i in R a unique number, starting with 1. These are the states of the NFA. For the purposes of this construction algorithm, we consider states and elements as synonymous.

2. Create a start state (0), and construct transitions from the start state to each of the states in FIRST$(R)=\{e_{g_1},\ldots,e_{g_m}\}$. A transition from 0 to state e_{g_j} is labelled by the symbol corresponding to e_{g_j}.

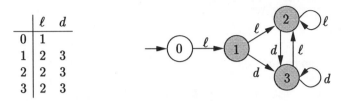

	ℓ	d
0	1	
1	2	3
2	2	3
3	2	3

Figure 7.10 A transition table and NFAcorresponding to $\ell\{\ell\,|\,d\}^*$.

3. Construct transitions from the state e_i to each of the states in FOLLOW(e_i). A transition from e_i to state e_{f_j} is labelled by the symbol corresponding to e_{f_j}.
4. Indicate as accept states those states in LAST(R)=$\{e_{l_1}, \ldots, e_{l_p}\}$.

Example 7.8
We will apply the above steps to the regular expression $\ell\{\ell\,|\,d\}^*$.

1. We begin by numbering the elements in $\ell_1\{\ell_2\,|\,d\}^*$. We let ℓ_1 be 1, ℓ_2 be 2, and d be 3.
2. We now draw a transition from the start state (i.e. state 0) to each of the states in the first set of the root node. The first set of the root node is $\{\ell_1\}$, so we draw a transition from state 0 to state 1. We label this transition by ℓ.
3. Using FOLLOW(ℓ_1)=$\{\ell_2, d\}$, we draw a transition from state 1 (which is ℓ_1) to state 2 (which is ℓ_2), and from state 1 to state 3 (which is d). Similarly, using FOLLOW(ℓ_2)=$\{\ell_2, d\}$, we draw a transition from state 2 to itself and from state 2 to state 3, and using FOLLOW(d)=$\{\ell_2, d\}$, we draw a transition from state 3 to state 2 and from state 3 to itself. In each case the transition to state 2 is labelled by ℓ, and the transition to state 3 by d. Summing up all these transitions, we produce the transition table shown on the left in Figure 7.10.
4. In the last step we identify the accept states, which are those states given by the last set of the root node, namely $\{\ell_1, \ell_2, d\} = \{1, 2, 3\}$. In this automaton, then, every state except the start state is an accept state.

The resulting transition diagram is shown on the right in Figure 7.10.   ◇

Notice that there are no ϵ-transitions in the finite automaton in Figure 7.10. The observant reader should also notice that this finite automaton is deterministic. In general, the automaton that is constructed by the element method will in fact be non-deterministic. (Remember that a DFA is a special case of an NFA.) It is easy to see why the constructed automaton will be non-deterministic if we consider the elements in the first and follow sets. While transitions to elements in these sets will be unique, 2 (or more) elements in a set may, of course, correspond to the same input symbol, in which case, the labels on transitions from the same state will not be unique.

$S_0 = \epsilon-closure(\{0\});$
$\Xi = \{S_0\};$
unmark $S_0;$
for (*each unmarked state* $S \in \Xi$) {
      mark $S;$
      for (*each input symbol* $a \in T$) {
            $S_a = \epsilon-closure(move(S,a));$
            $\Im[S][a] = S_a;$
            if ($S_a \notin \Xi$) {
                  unmark $S_a;$
                  $\Xi = \Xi \cup \{S_a\};$
            }
      }
}

Figure 7.11 A subset-construction algorithm to convert an NFA into a DFA.

7.3.3 Subset construction

To convert an NFA into a DFA we use a subset-construction algorithm. This algorithm is given in Figure 7.11. In this algorithm, Ξ is the set of (new) states that make up the DFA, and each state in Ξ is itself a set of NFA states. T is the set of input symbols. In essence, we compute in this algorithm new groups of NFA states by examining the transitions of each state for each input symbol.

The algorithm uses 2 functions, namely *move* and ϵ-*closure*. The *move* of a set of NFA states $Q = \{s_1, \ldots, s_m\}$ given an input symbol a, is defined by

$$move(Q, a) = \{q \mid \exists \text{ a transition from } s_i \in Q \text{ to } q \text{ given symbol } a\}$$

and the ϵ-*closure* by

$$\epsilon\text{-}closure(Q) = Q \cup \{q \mid q \text{ is reachable from } s_i \in Q \text{ with } \epsilon\text{-transitions}\}$$

Note that we add NFA states to the set Q when we compute the ϵ-*closure*. Furthermore, if all states in Q have no ϵ-transitions, then obviously ϵ-*closure*$(Q) = Q$.

This algorithm generates a DFA transition table $\Im[Q, a]$. There is a transition in the DFA $\Xi = \{Q_0, \ldots, Q_n\}$ from Q_i to Q_j given input symbol a if ϵ-*closure*$(move(Q_i, a)) = Q_j$. In the algorithm, this is written as $\Im[Q_i, a] = Q_j$. The accept states in the DFA Ξ are those states that contain at least 1 NFA accept state.

Example 7.9
Consider the NFA for $\ell\{\ell \mid d\}^*$ that was constructed by Thompson's construction. This is shown in Figure 7.8. The input alphabet T of $\ell\{\ell \mid d\}^*$ is $\{\ell, d\}$. Following the algorithm in Figure 7.11, we initialise by letting

$A = \epsilon\text{-}closure(\{10\})$
$\quad = \{10, 0\}$

At this point, then, our DFA consists of $\Xi = \{A\}$. The state A is unmarked, so we mark it, and compute $Q_a = \epsilon\text{-}closure(move(A,a))$ for all $a \in T$. The first input symbol is ℓ, so we need to compute $move(A,\ell)$. This is equal to $\{1\}$, since there is a transition from state 0 to state 1 on ℓ. We can now compute:

$$\epsilon\text{-closure}(move(A, \ell)) = \epsilon\text{-closure}(\{1\})$$
$$= \{1, 2, 4, 6, 8, 9, 11\}$$

We have not seen this state before, so we call it B, we unmark B, and we let $\Im[A, l] = B$. The second input symbol is d, so we now compute $move(A,d)=\{\}$. The ϵ-closure of the empty set is the empty set, so this does not generate any new states. We are now finished with state A, and our DFA consists of $\Xi = \{A, B\}$, of which only A is marked. We continue the above calculation using B. The full calculation is shown in Figure 7.12. State A is a start state, and all the rest (i.e. B, C and D) are accept states, since they all contain the NFA state 11. The resulting DFA transition diagram, produced from the transition table $\Im$, is

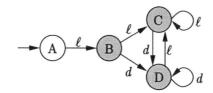

$\diamond$

7.3.4   State minimisation

The DFA constructed using the subset-construction algorithm will often be sub-optimal, in the sense that there will be more states than necessary. Every DFA can be reduced to a unique (up to the state names) minimal DFA. Of course, the language accepted remains the same.

A refinement algorithm can be used to minimise the number of states in a DFA. In this algorithm, we begin with a partition of the states, and continually refine this partition, based on the observed behaviour of the automaton. The obvious initial partition is to place all non-accept states in 1 group, and accept states in another. We now try to distinguish between states in a group by examining their behaviour given each of the input symbols. If we have a partition consisting of the states $(Q_1, \ldots, Q_n)$, then we distinguish states Q_i and Q_j if there are transitions to a state in a <u>different</u> group on some input symbol a, or one has a transition, and the other does not. This process is repeated until no new partitions can be constructed. All the states in a group in the final partition have the same behaviour, and can be considered equivalent (a representative from the group is usually chosen).

$$\epsilon\text{-closure}(\{10\}) \qquad = \{10,0\} \qquad\qquad \equiv A$$
$$\text{move}(A,\ell) \qquad\quad = \{1\}$$
$$\epsilon\text{-closure}(\text{move}(A,\ell)) \quad = \{1,2,4,6,8,9,11\} \quad \equiv B \qquad \ldots \mathfrak{I}[A,\ell] = B$$
$$\text{move}(A,d) \qquad\quad = \{\}$$
$$\epsilon\text{-closure}(\text{move}(A,d)) \quad = \{\}$$
$$\text{move}(B,\ell) \qquad\quad = \{3\}$$
$$\epsilon\text{-closure}(\text{move}(B,\ell)) \quad = \{2,3,4,6,7,9,11\} \quad \equiv C \qquad \ldots \mathfrak{I}[B,\ell] = C$$
$$\text{move}(B,d) \qquad\quad = \{5\}$$
$$\epsilon\text{-closure}(\text{move}(B,d)) \quad = \{2,4,5,6,7,9,11\} \quad \equiv D \qquad \ldots \mathfrak{I}[B,d] = D$$
$$\text{move}(C,\ell) \qquad\quad = \{3\}$$
$$\epsilon\text{-closure}(\text{move}(C,\ell)) \quad = C \qquad\qquad\qquad\qquad \ldots \mathfrak{I}[C,\ell] = C$$
$$\text{move}(C,d) \qquad\quad = \{5\}$$
$$\epsilon\text{-closure}(\text{move}(C,d)) \quad = D \qquad\qquad\qquad\qquad \ldots \mathfrak{I}[C,d] = D$$
$$\text{move}(D,\ell) \qquad\quad = \{3\}$$
$$\epsilon\text{-closure}(\text{move}(D,\ell)) \quad = C \qquad\qquad\qquad\qquad \ldots \mathfrak{I}[D,\ell] = C$$
$$\text{move}(D,d) \qquad\quad = \{5\}$$
$$\epsilon\text{-closure}(\text{move}(D,d)) \quad = D \qquad\qquad\qquad\qquad \ldots \mathfrak{I}[D,d] = D$$

Figure 7.12   The computation of DFA states from NFA states using the subset-construction algorithm.

Example 7.10
The DFA corresponding to $\ell\{\ell|d\}^*$ constructed in Example 7.9 contains more states than is necessary. To minimise the number of states, we first partition the states into those that are accept states (BCD), and those that are not (A). We cannot partition group (A), so we consider group (BCD). With input ℓ, each of the states in the group undergoes a transition to state C. Furthermore, given input d, each of these states goes to state D. There is no way, therefore, of distinguishing between the states in this group, so all states in this group are considered equivalent. We coalesce states B, C and D, and call the new state B. The minimum DFA can be redrawn in the following way:

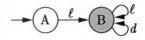

Example 7.11
Consider the regular expression $\ell\{\ell \mid d\}^*\ell d$. This specifies identifiers that begin with a letter, and end with a letter and a digit. A DFA for this regular expression is shown below:

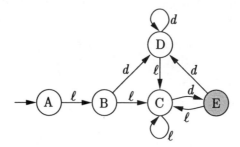

Applying state minimisation, we begin by partitioning the states into the groups $(ABCD)$ and (E). With input ℓ and d, we find that states in the first group have the following transitions:

ℓ : A→B, B→C, C→C, D→C

d : B→D, C→E, D→D

Input symbol d reveals that A, which has no transition, and C, which has a transition to a state in a different group, should be separated from the group. The resulting partition is $(A)(BD)(C)(E)$. Checking the transitions again, we find that:

ℓ : B→C, D→C

d : B→D, D→D

We cannot distinguish between the behaviour of B and D, so we coalesce B and D, and call the new state B. The resulting minimal-state DFA is shown below:

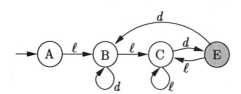

◇

7.4 Exercises

1. Consider the language defined by $\{\alpha aaa\beta \mid \alpha, \beta \in (a|b)^*\}$, and with alphabet $\{a,b\}$. Each string in this language contains at least one instance of the sub-string aaa. Construct a finite automaton that accepts this language.

2. Construct an NFA and a DFA for the language defined by $(a|b)^*a(a|b)(a|b)$, and with alphabet $\{a,b\}$.

3. Consider the (finite) language defined by {I,II,III,IV,V,VI,VII,VIII,IX}, with alphabet {I,V,X}.

   (a) By assigning an accept state to each string in the language, construct a finite automaton that accepts this language.

   (b) Minimise the number of states.

4. An NFA over {0,1} is

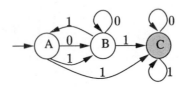

   (a) What is the language accepted by this NFA?

   (b) Construct a DFA that accepts the same language.

5. A language of real numbers can be specified by the regular expression

$$(+|-|\epsilon)\, d\, d^*(.d^*\,|\,\epsilon)(E(+|-|\epsilon)\, d^*\,|\,\epsilon)$$

   where the alphabet is {+,−,.,d,E}. Construct the corresponding DFA.

6. Consider the regular expression $(d^*.d\,|\,d.d^*)$, with alphabet {d,.}.

   (a) Construct an NFA from the regular expression.

   (b) Construct a DFA from the NFA.

   (c) Minimise the total number of states in the DFA.

   In each case show the intermediate steps in the algorithm used.

7. Consider the regular expression $(a|b)^*abb$, with alphabet {a,b}.

   (a) Use Thompson's construction to construct an NFA from the regular expression.

   (b) Now use element construction to construct an NFA from the regular expression. Show in your solution the null, first and last sets. Also show the follow-set table.

   (c) Convert the NFA generated using element construction into a DFA.

   (d) Minimise the number of states in the DFA.

8. Consider the regular expression $a^*ba\,|\,aba^*$, with alphabet {a,b}, where the usual priority and associativity rules apply.

   (a) Construct a NFA for this expression by using element construction.

   (b) Construct a DFA from the NFA.

   (c) Minimise the number of states in the DFA.

7.5   Bibliographic notes

The theory of regular expressions is dealt with by Hopcroft and Ullman [81]. While almost all compiler texts treat scanning, surprisingly few treat finite automaton and scanner generation. This is probably due to the fact that, even today, many compiler builders choose to write a scanner by hand. The best coverage of the theory of lexical analysis can be found in Aho *et al.* [3], Fischer and LeBlanc [45], Holub [78], Parsons [110] and Gough [60]. Parson's book is introductory, but nevertheless it is very informative. Holub's book is a must for anyone who is considering building a scanner generator. In spite of the many newer offerings, one of the most useful and practical works on lexical analysis remains Aho *et al.*'s book.

Research into lexical analysis in recent years has been mainly concerned with performance improvements of the scanner and of the scanner generator. In [140], for example, a higher-performance scanner is described that is hard-coded (instead of the traditional table-driven). In [62] a high-performance scanner generator (called *rex*) is described. This generator can build a scanner in linear time for practical cases. Other scanner generators are *flex* [111] and *alex* [103]. Incremental and lazy scanner generators have also been investigated. The incremental scanner generator built by [133], called *LexAGen*, maintains a deterministic finite-state automaton incrementally on the basis of a regular grammar. In [68, 69], a lazy incremental scanner generator called ISG is described. It constructs an automaton by need. Notwithstanding these developments, the classical UNIX lexical-analyser generator *lex* [95], now 2 decades old, still enjoys popularity in the computer-science community. (See [63] for a comparison of *lex*, *flex* and *rex*.)

The seminal paper describing Thompson's construction was written by Ken Thompson (of UNIX fame) in 1968 [137]. Thompson described in detail a compiler that generated a pattern matcher. The input to the compiler was a regular expression, and the input to the generated program was some text. The generated program searched for strings in the text that matched the regular expression. Because the compiler and generated program had to work in a text editor, they had to be fast. The compiler was written in ALGOL 60, and the compiler generated IBM 7094 assembler. Actually, what we now call Thompson's construction refers to the compiler that Thompson developed. The program that the compiler generated (the pattern matcher), simulated an NFA. This is tantamount to building a DFA, and is commonly referred to as the subset-partitioning algorithm.

Thompson's construction can be found in most references on compiler building. Invariably, however, the construction algorithm is presented using "bubble" diagrams. The presentation used here (syntax transition trees) is more useful, intuitive and relates better to the implementation.

In an interactive system like an editor, both the build and execution time must be relatively short. In that case, because the input strings are not too long, Thompson's implementation performs well. In a compiler, one is usually more interested in minimising the execution time. If the regular expression and input string have lengths n and m, then to build the NFA requires $O(n)$ in space and time, and simulating the NFA requires $O(n \times m)$. A DFA, on the other hand, can occupy $O(2^n)$ in space, but is, of course, very fast, taking $O(m)$ in time. These are all worst-case scenarios.

Element construction is an NFA construction algorithm that is also referred to as the "followpos" algorithm in the literature ([3, 23]).

An NFA has certain advantages over a DFA. In applications where choice is inherent, an NFA provides a more natural and concise means of specification. NFAs can also be easily composed, which means that NFAs can be trivially modularised. The composition (modularisation) of DFAs, on the other hand, is a complex task. The composed DFA corresponding to 2 regular expressions must be generated from the combined regular expression.

Nymeyer [106] used an attribute grammar to specify a backtracking scheme and Thompson's construction. Nymeyer also considered *pathological* regular expressions, which are regular expressions that contain an ϵ-loop. An ϵ-loop is generated when we take the closure of a regular expression that can be ϵ.

Chapter 8

Parsing

In the previous chapter we showed how a lexical analyser can be generated from a specification. The lexical analyser recognises words (strings) in the program text, and translates them into a sequence of tokens. In this chapter we show how these tokens can then be used by the syntax analyser (or parser, we use the terms interchangeably) to determine whether the input program is syntactically correct. We also show how the syntax analyser can be generated from a specification (of the language of the input program). This specification is a context-free grammar.

While it is convenient for reasons of efficiency and design to separate the lexical and syntax analysers, it is also true, in general, that the syntax analyser can assume the task of the lexical analyser, but not vice versa. For example, programming constructs that can be nested to an arbitrary depth like blocks, statements, expressions and even parentheses can be specified by a context-free grammar but cannot be specified by regular expressions. As we shall see, a syntax analyser that is based on a context-free grammar has a "memory" (in the form of a stack) that enables it to match far more complicated programming constructs than a lexical analyser. In contrast to a lexical analyser, which we saw in the previous chapter was based on a finite-state automaton, a syntax analyser is based on a *stack automaton*.

The syntax analyser should not only determine whether an input program is syntactically correct—it should also generate a representation of the structure of the program. This representation is usually required by subsequent phases in the compiler to generate a target program. Sometimes the generation of the target code is interwoven with the parser. It is, however, conceptually easier to present the parser module as an algorithm that only checks whether the program is syntactically correct and generates a parse tree of the program. This parse tree, usually augmented with some semantically-relevant information (e.g. attributes associated with nodes of the parse tree), is the input of the next phase of the compiler (either an optimiser or a code generator).

Actually, syntax analysers do not only arise in the context of building compilers for programming languages. In principle, any program that reads structured data consists of a parser. If the data can be described by a context-free grammar, then the parser can be generated. Of course, this is also true of the program that translates a context-free grammar into a parser, which is called a parser generator. The input of a parser generator is a context-free grammar; the output is a parser. The input grammar of a parser generator (or anything else) can also be specified by a context-free grammar. A grammar that specifies a grammar is called a meta-grammar.

There are many kinds of parsers, or to be more precise, there are many kinds of *parsing strategies*. A distinction is usually made between top-down strategies and bottom-up strategies, although there are strategies that are a mixture of the two. In this chapter we will concentrate on *top-down parsing*, and for the purposes of comparison, we will also briefly explain *bottom-up parsing*.

The aim of this chapter is to build a type of top-down parser, called an LL(1) parser, and an extended version called ELL(1). We do this in stages. First we need to fix our notation and nomenclature, and lay a basis for the theoretical treatment that will follow. We do this in Section 8.1. In Section 8.2 we relate a recursive-descent parser, as was developed in Chapters 1 and 3, to a table-driven top-down parser. Particularly important here is the role that the table plays in a table-driven parser. Section 8.3 presents LL(1) grammars, which form a restricted class of context-free grammars for which efficient top-down parsers can easily be constructed. We also consider transformations of context-free grammars into LL(1) form. In Section 8.4 we revisit the regular-expression formalisms, and introduce extended context-free grammars, and we examine the class of extended LL(1), or ELL(1), grammars. A recursive-descent parser and a table-driven ELL(1) parser are described in Section 8.4.4. Finally, in Section 8.5, we briefly discuss bottom-up parsing.

8.1   Context-free grammars

The study of context-free grammars has its origins in the study of natural languages. In 1956, Noam Chomsky first used a context-free grammar as a grammatical model for English. The first use of context-free grammars to model programming languages was in 1963 by John Backus and Peter Naur, who used a context-free grammar to describe the syntax of ALGOL 60. As a recognition of their contribution, their context-free-grammar notation is sometimes referred to as Backus–Naur Form (or BNF for short).

Context-free grammars have generally been unsuccessful in modelling natural languages because natural languages are firstly, highly ambiguous, and secondly, context-sensitive. Consider, for example, the sentence "He walked to the woman with a limp." This sentence is syntactically ambiguous because we cannot tell from the sentence who has a limp. As example of context-sensitivity is the word "saw": Are we referring to a tool or an action? There are parsing methods that can handle ambiguous grammars, but they fall outside the traditional field of compiler-building. Here we are only concerned with parsing methods for unambiguous context-free grammars. These grammars can more than adequately describe most programming languages.

A context-free grammar G is denoted by a 4-tuple (N, T, P, S), where N is a finite, nonempty set of nonterminal symbols, T is a finite, nonempty set of terminal symbols and $S \in N$ is the start symbol of the grammar. The set $N \cup T$ is denoted by V, the alphabet of G. P is a finite set of productions or rules of the form $A \rightarrow \alpha$, where $A \in N$ and $\alpha \in V^*$. If a production has the form $A \rightarrow \epsilon$, then the production is called an ϵ-production. The nonterminal A is sometimes referred to as the nonterminal on the left-hand side (of the production), and α as the right-hand side of the production.

A context-free grammar is a specification of a rewrite system. When we apply a production to an input string, we rewrite an instance of the left-hand side nonterminal in the string, independent of its context. Hence the term *context-free*. Note that a *context-sensitive grammar* consists of productions of the form $\beta A\gamma \rightarrow \beta\alpha\gamma$, where α is not empty.

At this point it is useful to consider the notation that we will use to refer to a terminal, nonterminal, string of terminals and string of nonterminals. Conventionally, upper-case letters A, B, C and so on, are used to denote nonterminals, and lower-case letters a, b, c and so on, to denote terminals. However, an exception to this general rule is that we sometimes use X, Y and Z to denote a "symbol" in the grammar (i.e. a nonterminal <u>or</u> terminal), and S to denote the start symbol (nonterminal).

Strings of terminals are also denoted with lower-case letters, but taken from the other end of the alphabet; namely u, v, w and so on. Strings of nonterminals cannot be denoted by letters from the other end of the upper-case alphabet, as these are already in use. Instead, the Greek letters η, μ and ν are used. Finally, we denote random strings of terminals and nonterminals by the Greek letters α, β, γ and δ. The symbol ϵ is special and denotes the empty string. In the table below we summarise the major points of the notation:

	symbol	string of symbols
terminals	a, b, c, ... $\in$ T	u, v, w, ... $\in$ T*
nonterminals	A, B, C, ... $\in$ N	η, μ, $\nu \in$ N*
terminals and nonterminals	X, Y, Z $\in$ V	α, β, γ, $\delta \in$ V*

However, sometimes more meaningful names and symbols are used to refer to terminals and nonterminals. For example, names like *expr*, *term* and *factor* may be used as nonterminals, and symbols like $+$, $*$ and $-$, and digits, as terminals.

Example 8.1

In Section 1.5 we defined a context-free grammar for constant arithmetic expressions. We consider the grammar again, omitting the nonterminal *const_expr*. This grammar, which we refer to by G_1, is defined by the 4-tuple (N, T, P, S) with $N = \{expr, term, factor, digit\}$, $T = \{+, *, (,), 0, 1, 2, 3, 4, 5, 6, 7, 8, 9\}$, start symbol *expr*, and P the following productions.

$$
\begin{aligned}
expr &\to expr + term & expr &\to term & term &\to term * factor \\
term &\to factor & factor &\to (\ expr\ ) & factor &\to digit \\
digit &\to 0 & digit &\to 1 & digit &\to 2 \\
digit &\to 3 & digit &\to 4 & digit &\to 5 \\
digit &\to 6 & digit &\to 7 & digit &\to 8 \\
digit &\to 9
\end{aligned}
$$

This grammar describes arithmetic expressions consisting of the operators multiplication and addition, parenthesised expressions, and the digits 0 until 9.   ◇

Two notational conveniences are often used. The first is that a context-free grammar can be given only by its rules, in which case it is understood that the symbols on the left-hand sides of the productions are the nonterminals (the first one of which is the start symbol), and the rest of the symbols are terminals. The second notational convenience is that productions that have the same left-hand side nonterminal can be written in an abbreviated form. For example, the productions $expr \to expr + term$ and $expr \to term$ can be rewritten as $expr \to expr + term\ |\ term$.

Example 8.2
The context-free grammar G_1 can also be expressed in the following way:

$$
\begin{aligned}
expr &\to expr + term\ |\ term \\
term &\to term * factor\ |\ factor \\
factor &\to (\ expr\ )\ |\ digit \\
digit &\to 0\ |\ 1\ |\ 2\ |\ 3\ |\ 4\ |\ 5\ |\ 6\ |\ 7\ |\ 8\ |\ 9
\end{aligned}
$$

◇

The productions of a context-free grammar $G = (N, T, P, S)$ are used to rewrite strings. If $A \in N$, $\alpha, \beta, \gamma \in V^*$ and $A \to \beta \in P$, then the string $\alpha A \gamma$ can be rewritten as $\alpha \beta \gamma$. This is called a one-*step*, or *direct*, *derivation*, and is written as $\alpha A \gamma \Rightarrow \alpha \beta \gamma$. Note that β may be the empty string ϵ.

In the direct derivation $wA\gamma \underset{l}{\Rightarrow} w\beta\gamma$, $w \in T^*$, the nonterminal A is the left-most nonterminal. This is called a *direct left-derivation*. Analogously, if A is the right-most nonterminal, and $\alpha A u \underset{r}{\Rightarrow} \alpha \beta u$, $u \in T^*$, then we have a *direct right-derivation*.

More generally, a *derivation* of a string $\delta \in V^*$ from a string $\alpha \in V^*$, written as $\alpha \Rightarrow^* \delta$, means that some number $n \geq 0$ of direct derivations are applied in succession. If $n = 0$, then $\delta = \alpha$, otherwise we have $\alpha \Rightarrow \alpha_0 \Rightarrow \ldots \Rightarrow \alpha_{n-1} \Rightarrow \delta$. If each direct derivation in $\alpha \Rightarrow^* \delta$ is a direct left-derivation, then we have a *left-derivation*. This is written as $\alpha \underset{l}{\Rightarrow}^* \delta$. Similarly, if each direct derivation in $\alpha \Rightarrow^* \delta$ is a direct right-derivation, then we have a *right-derivation*, and this is written as $\alpha \underset{r}{\Rightarrow}^* \delta$. If we wish to exclude the possibility that $n = 0$, then we can write $\alpha \Rightarrow^+ \delta$.

A *sentential form* of G is a string $\alpha \in V^*$ derivable from the start symbol S. That is, $S \Rightarrow^* \alpha$. The *language* generated or defined by G is the set $L(G) = \{w\ |\ S \Rightarrow^* w; w \in T^*\}$. Such an element w in G is called a *sentence* in $L(G)$.

Example 8.3

The string $(3 + 0) * 2$ is a sentence in the language described by the context-free grammar shown in Examples 8.1 and 8.2. This sentence can be derived in the following way:

$$expr \Rightarrow term \Rightarrow term * factor \Rightarrow factor * factor \Rightarrow (expr) * factor \Rightarrow$$
$$(expr + term) * factor \Rightarrow (term + term) * factor \Rightarrow (factor + term) * factor \Rightarrow$$
$$(digit + term) * factor \Rightarrow (3 + term) * factor \Rightarrow (3 + factor) * factor \Rightarrow$$
$$(3 + digit) * factor \Rightarrow (3 + 0) * factor \Rightarrow (3 + 0) * digit \Rightarrow (3 + 0) * 2$$

This is a left-derivation: $expr \underset{1}{\Rightarrow} (3 + 0) * 2$. Each of the strings in the derivation, including the start symbol *expr* and the resulting sentence $(3+0)*2$, is a sentential form.

$\diamond$

A derivation can be pictorially represented as a *parse tree*. Each derivation step corresponds to adding branches to a nonterminal leaf in the parse tree. The leaves of these branches are the symbols on the right-hand side of the production corresponding to the nonterminal. The leaves of a parse tree consist only of the terminals in the context-free grammar, and the internal nodes, of the nonterminals in the grammar. We saw examples of parse trees in Chapter 1 (Section 1.2).

Two context-free grammars G_1 and G_2 are called (weakly) equivalent if $L(G_1) = L(G_2)$, i.e. they generate the same language.

Example 8.4

Consider the context-free grammar G_2 defined by the following productions:

$$expr \rightarrow expr + expr \mid expr * expr \mid (expr) \mid 0 \mid 1 \mid 2 \mid 3 \mid 4 \mid 5 \mid 6 \mid 7 \mid 8 \mid 9$$

This grammar generates the same language as G_1. Notice that this grammar contains only 1 nonterminal (the start symbol), but that the set of terminals in G_1 and G_2 is the same. (In general, if 2 grammars describe the same language, then they must, of course, have the same set of terminals.)

A derivation of the string $(3 + 0) * 2$ using G_2 is the following:

$$expr \Rightarrow expr * expr \Rightarrow (expr) * expr \Rightarrow (expr + expr) * expr \Rightarrow$$
$$(3 + expr) * expr \Rightarrow (3 + 0) * expr \Rightarrow (3 + 0) * 2$$

Notice that this left-derivation $expr \underset{1}{\Rightarrow} (3+0)*2$ takes 6 steps, whereas the derivation of the same sentence using G_1 took 14 steps.

$\diamond$

While grammar G_2 is much more concise than G_1, it is also less precise. In fact, G_2 is really an under-specification of the required language. This is because the grammar is *ambiguous*. We introduced the concept of ambiguity in Section 1.2. If a context-free grammar is ambiguous, then there exists at least 1 sentence that has at least 2 parse trees. In other words, $S \Rightarrow w$ is not unique for some $w \in T^*$, $S \in N$. Note that every parse tree corresponds to a left and right derivation. If a sentence has 2 parse trees, then it has 2 left derivations, and 2 right derivations. This sentence is said to be ambiguous in the grammar.

Example 8.5
Consider the sentence $1 + 2 * 3$ and the context-free grammar G_2. This sentence is ambiguous in grammar G_2 because it has 2 left-derivations:

$expr \Rightarrow expr * expr \Rightarrow expr + expr * expr \Rightarrow 1 + expr * expr \Rightarrow$
  $1 + 2 * expr \Rightarrow 1 + 2 * 3$

and

$expr \Rightarrow expr + expr \Rightarrow 1 + expr \Rightarrow 1 + expr * expr \Rightarrow$
  $1 + 2 * expr \Rightarrow 1 + 2 * 3$

⋄

A context-free grammar is called *cyclic* if there is a derivation $A \Rightarrow^+ A$ for some nonterminal A. A context-free grammar that is cyclic has at least one sentence with an unbounded number of left-derivations. Such a grammar is therefore ambiguous.

Example 8.6
Any context-free grammar that contains a production $A \Rightarrow A$, where A is a nonterminal, obviously is cyclic, and is therefore ambiguous. Consider, for example, the grammar $S \Rightarrow S \mid a$. There is an unbounded number of parse trees corresponding to the only possible sentence a in the language.   ⋄

It is possible to define a context-free language that can only be described by ambiguous context-free grammars. Such a language is called *inherently ambiguous*.

Example 8.7
In 1966, R.J. Parikh devised an inherently ambiguous language consisting of strings of a's, b's and c's, where the number (greater than or equal to 0) of either a's and b's, or b's and c's, is the same. Examples of sentences in this language are *aabc*, *aabb* and *abbcc*. The sentence *abbc* is not in the language.   ⋄

A context-free grammar is said to be *left recursive* if $A \Rightarrow^+ A\alpha$ for some $A \in N$ and $\alpha \in V^*$. Every context-free grammar that is left recursive can be transformed into an equivalent context-free grammar that is not left recursive. Analogously for right recursive.

A context-free grammar is called *reduced* if, for all $X \in V$, there is at least one derivation $S \Rightarrow^* \alpha X \beta \Rightarrow^* w$, for some $\alpha, \beta \in V^*$ and $w \in T^*$. In other words, a reduced context-free grammar does not contain any nonterminals that can never appear in the derivation of some sentence. Obviously, if there is such a nonterminal, it is redundant. Every context-free grammar that is not reduced can be transformed into an equivalent context-free grammar that is reduced.

As we stated in the introduction to this chapter, context-free grammars can describe many important programming-language constructs. They cannot, however, describe everything. For example, in some programming languages, variables must be declared before they are used. This requirement cannot be described by context-free productions. In a real compiler, this requirement is checked as part of the context analysis (usually with the help of a symbol table).

8.2 Top-down parsing

In Chapter 1 (Section 1.3.2), we showed how a parse tree can be used to visualise the process of parsing an input string. Let us refresh our memories. We begin top-down parsing by selecting a production in the context-free grammar with the start symbol on the left-hand side. This production forms the top of the parse tree. We then check whether the leading terminal symbols of the yield of this tree match the leading symbols of the input. If the leading terminal symbols match, we take the left-most nonterminal symbol in the tree and we apply a production with this nonterminal as left-hand side. We continue this process until we have no nonterminals left at the leaves. If we select the correct production at each step, then we will always succeed in constructing a parse tree for the input string (assuming that the string is generated by the grammar).

8.2.1 Recursive-descent

The above parsing scheme was implemented in Chapters 1 and 3 using the principle of recursive-descent. In Section 1.5 we constructed a simple one-pass translator that was based on a recursive-descent parser. In a recursive-descent parser, a procedure is associated with each nonterminal N in the grammar. The body of the procedure may contain:

- Statements that match each of the terminals in the right-hand side of the production for N.
- Statements that call procedures corresponding to each of the nonterminals in the right-hand side of the production for N.
- Semantic actions.

Example 8.8
Consider the production $A \rightarrow aB$, where A and B are nonterminals and a is a terminal. The procedure corresponding to A must first match the next input symbol with the character a, and then call the procedure B. If the next input character does not match a, then the procedure corresponding to A does not accept the input. The procedure has the following appearance:

```
void A(void)
{
  if (look_ahead == a) {
    next_token();
    B();
  } else
    accept = false;
}
```

Note that the procedure uses the procedure *next_token* to place the next input character into the global variable *look_ahead* (see also Chapter 1 and 3). The above procedure will set *accept* to false if there is no match.   ◇

Let us now look behind the scenes of a recursive-descent parser. When we construct a recursive-descent parser, we convert the context-free grammar into a program that consists of a procedure for each nonterminal symbol in the context-free grammar. During parsing, then, each time a nonterminal is encountered, a procedure call is made. When we call a procedure, the procedure that we are in (corresponding to the nonterminal on the left-hand side of the production in which we are working) and our current position in the procedure are placed on the run-time stack in the form of an activation record. This is done automatically by the operating system. When we reach the end of a procedure (production), the operating system reinstates the procedure that was last placed onto the run-time stack. In other words, we go back to the previous production in which we were working. Note that the "current position" stored in the activation record determines precisely where we need to re-continue parsing. In this process, therefore, the operating system uses its run-time stack to keep a history of unfinished procedures (productions). In the following example we illustrate this process.

Example 8.9
The following grammar describes the language consisting only of the sentence *abc*.

p_1 S → A c
p_2 A → B b
p_3 B → a

A recursive-descent parser derived from this grammar executes the following steps when parsing the string *abc*. The actions that the operating system carries out are shown between parentheses. For the sake of brevity, we have not placed the current position onto the run-time stack, and when we say that we place a procedure on the stack, we actually mean its activation record.

1. Call procedure S.
2. In procedure S, call A. (S is pushed onto the run-time stack.)
3. In procedure A, call B. (A is pushed onto the run-time stack.)
4. In procedure B, match symbol a. (B terminates. A is popped.)
5. In procedure A, match symbol b. (A terminates. S is popped.)
6. In procedure S, match symbol c. (Procedure S terminates.)

Note that at the beginning of step 4, we are about to match the terminal symbol a in production p_3. Future matches, namely b and c, are part of the procedures A and S (respectively) that are stored on the stack.   ◇

8.2.2   Table-driven

An alternative method of top-down parsing makes the usage of a stack explicit. In this method, we must define our own stack, and operations on the stack such as initialisation, pushing and popping.

In the previous chapter we showed that a lexical analyser is based on a finite automaton. We now generalise the concept of a finite automaton, and add "memory" in the form of a stack. The resulting automaton, called a *stack automaton*, forms the basis, or model, of a syntax analyser (parser). Note that a language is context-free if and only if it is accepted by a stack automaton.

We define a stack automaton by extending the definition of a context-free grammar. A stack automaton is defined as a quintuple (Q, Z, F, G, V), where

   Q is a finite, non-empty set of states
   $Z \in Q$ is the start state
   $F \subseteq Q$ is a set of accept states
   $G = (N, T, P, S)$ is the underlying context-free grammar
   $V = N \cup T$ is the set of stack symbols

A state in Q is given by the pair (X, Y), where $X \in V^*$ represents the contents of the stack (the top of the stack is on the left-hand side), and $Y \in T^*$ is the input string (we read from left to right). We show a schematic of a stack automaton in Figure 8.1. In this automaton, the symbols $a_1 \ldots a_i \ldots a_n \in T$, and $X_1 \ldots X_m \in V$.

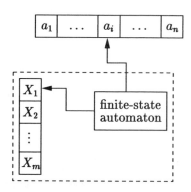

Figure 8.1 A schematic of a stack automaton.

Initially, the stack automaton is in the state $Z = (S, a_1 \ldots a_n)$, where S is the start symbol of G, and $a_1 \ldots a_n$ is the input string. A transition from one state to another is a mapping from $Q \times (T \cup \{\epsilon\}) \times V$ to $Q \times V^*$. There are 4 possible actions:

1. If we are in the state $(A\beta, a_i \ldots a_n)$ and $A \to \alpha$ is a production in G (in Figure 8.1, $X_1 = A$ and $X_2 \ldots X_m = \beta$), then we move to state $(\alpha\beta, a_i \ldots a_n)$.

```
#define false 0
#define true 1
STACK = ∅;
push(S, STACK);
look_ahead = read(input);
accept = true;
while (accept && (look_ahead != $ || STACK != ∅)) {
  top_of_stack = pop(STACK);
  if (top_of_stack ∈ T) {
      if (top_of_stack != look_ahead)
          accept = false;
      else
          look_ahead = read(input);
  }
  else if (top_of_stack ∈ N) { /* assume top_of_stack = A */
          select some production A→X₁ ... Xₙ;
          push(X₁ ... Xₙ, STACK); /* X₁ is on top of the STACK */
  }
  else
      accept = false;
}
output(accept);
```

Figure 8.2 A top-down parse algorithm.

Here $A \in N$ and $\alpha, \beta \in V^*$.

2. If we are in the state $(b\beta, a_i \ldots a_n)$ and $b = a_i \in T$ (in Figure 8.1, $X_1 = b$ and $X_2 \ldots X_m = \beta$), then we move to state $(\beta, a_{i+1} \ldots a_n)$.

3. If we are in the state (ϵ, ϵ), i.e. both the stack and the input are empty, then we are in an accept state, and we stop.

4. In all other cases we report an error.

Stack automata, like finite-state automata, can be deterministic and non-deterministic. The state automaton defined above is non-deterministic because there may be more than 1 production with the same left-hand side nonterminal. In the first state change above, for example, we may go to more than 1 state. Note also that if the context-free grammar is left recursive, then the first state change above may cause the automaton to loop. In this loop, no input is read and the stack may grow infinitely large.

In Figure 8.2 we present an algorithm that implements the stack automaton above. We assume in this algorithm that the input string is terminated by the symbol $. The algorithm begins by initialising the stack (for which we use the symbol ∅). The start symbol S is then pushed onto the stack, a character is read, and the Boolean *accept* is set to true. We then enter a loop in which we pop a symbol from the stack. If this symbol is a terminal, and it matches the look-ahead symbol, then another symbol is read. Alternatively, if the symbol is a nonterminal, then the symbols on the right-hand side of a production corresponding to this nonterminal are pushed onto the stack. We use the routine *push* to place a symbol on top of the stack and *pop* to deliver the symbol from the top of the stack. The instruction $push(X_1 \ldots X_n, \text{STACK})$, where X_i is a symbol in the grammar, is short for $push(X_n, \text{STACK}), \ldots, push(X_1, \text{STACK})$. After the execution of this instruction, the symbol X_1 is on top of the stack. If the stack is empty then *pop* returns something other than a terminal or nonterminal. Like a stack automaton, the algorithm cannot handle a left-recursive context-free grammar.

We now briefly consider error detection in the algorithm. If the look-ahead symbol does not match the top symbol on the stack then *accept* is set to false. There are 2 other cases of interest:

- The stack is empty but the input is not. This means that there is more input than expected. If STACK is empty then *pop* does not return either a terminal or a nonterminal symbol, and hence *accept* is set to false.
- The input is empty (i.e. we have reached $) but the stack is not. If there are only nonterminals on the stack, and they all derive ϵ, then there is no error and the input will be accepted. If at least 1 of these nonterminals does not derive ϵ, then we will ultimately find a terminal symbol on top of the stack. If there is a terminal symbol on the stack, then we have run out of input before parsing was complete. This terminal symbol will result in a mismatch with the look-ahead symbol (which equals $), hence *accept* is set to false.

The parse tree is not constructed by the algorithm in Figure 8.2—it is implicit. However, if we concatenate the input that we have read and the contents of the stack, then we produce a sentential form in a left-derivation of the sentence. We illustrate this in the following example.

Example 8.10
Consider the following grammar.

$S \rightarrow A \ B \ C$
$A \rightarrow a \ C$
$B \rightarrow b \ C$
$C \rightarrow c$

We use the algorithm in Figure 8.2 to parse the input string *acbcc*$. The contents of the stack after initialisation, and at the end of each iteration is shown in Figure 8.3. The number of the iteration is shown below the stack, and the character that is read, above the stack. The corresponding left-derivation of the string *acbcc*$ is the following:

$$S \Rightarrow ABC \Rightarrow aCBC \Rightarrow acBC \Rightarrow acbCC \Rightarrow acbcC \Rightarrow acbcc \qquad \diamond$$

If we were to implement the algorithm in Figure 8.2, then we need to declare a stack, and functions that initialise the stack, push and pop symbols on and off

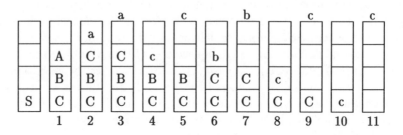

Figure 8.3 The changing contents of the stack for the input string *acbcc$*.

the stack, and test whether the stack is empty. We also need a mechanism to select a production that corresponds to a particular nonterminal. To do this we transform the context-free grammar into a table, which is referred to as the *parse table*. Together, the algorithm in Figure 8.2 and the parse table form a *table-driven top-down parser*.

The entries in the parse table are the symbols on the right-hand sides of the productions, and the indices are the nonterminals on the left-hand side. The 2 components in our table-driven top-down parser (namely, the algorithm and table) can be generated by a program, called a parser generator. A parser generator simply emits the code that implements the algorithm (the algorithm is the same for all grammars), and transforms the textual representation of the productions into a table and emits the result. The input of a parser generator is a context-free grammar, the output is a parser.

What does the generated parser do with incorrect input? The parser stops reading the input as soon as it has found a character that is not correct. If it stops while processing character a_i, then $a_1 \ldots a_{i-1}$ is a prefix of a correct input sentence. This is called the *correct prefix property*. Good error-recovery is, of course, an important part of a parser. We do not treat error-recovery techniques here, however.

Note that the recursive-descent and top-down table-driven parsers are equivalent. Both methods use a stack to store the yet-to-be-processed symbols. In the table-driven parser, these symbols are placed manually on the stack. In the recursive-descent parser, these symbols are automatically "placed" on the run-time stack as a consequence of the procedure-call convention. (In reality, a return address to an instance of the procedure is placed on the stack.) Of course, a recursive-descent parser involves a lot more program text than a table-driven parser. However, the recursive-descent parser is easier to extend with other kinds of actions that are not part of the parsing, but are controlled by it, such as checking the context constraints, and the generation of target code.

Let us now consider the nature of the parse table. At first glance, it would seem possible to use a 1-dimensional table in which each left-hand side nonterminal indexes a row, and in the only column we store the symbols on the right-hand sides of the productions. We illustrate such a table in the following example.

Example 8.11
The parse table corresponding to the context-free grammar in Example 8.10 is:

index	entry
S	A B C
A	a C
B	b C
C	c

          ◇

Referring back to the algorithm in Figure 8.2, to access the production that corresponds to the nonterminal *top_of_stack*, we simply need $M(top\_of\_stack)$, where M is the name of the parse table. To push the right-hand side of *top_of_stack* onto the stack, therefore, we use the statement $push(M(top\_of\_stack), STACK)$.

The table, as we have defined it, works fine in the example above. However, it does not work in the general case. It fails because the algorithm is non-deterministic—a nonterminal may occur on the left-hand side of more than 1 production. The context-free grammar $S \Rightarrow aS \mid b$, for example, fails.

How, then, do we choose between different productions with the same nonterminal symbol on the left-hand side? We can do this in 2 ways:

- We can modify the top-down algorithm to incorporate a backtracking scheme. Whenever we are faced with a choice, we select "randomly". If we find at a later date that our choice was incorrect, we backtrack and select another production. The resulting parser is said to be *non-predictive*.
- Alternatively, we can modify the top-down algorithm by adding a *look-ahead* capability, and restrict the class of context-free grammars that the algorithm can accept. For a restricted class of context-free grammars, the modified algorithm will always choose the correct production. This is called *predictive*.

Modifying the parser with a backtracking scheme is messy, and in the worst case (if we try all the "incorrect" productions before we find the "correct" one) the algorithm has poor performance. We therefore reject this approach.

Adding a look-ahead capability requires a trivial modification to be made to the algorithm. In the modified algorithm, we use a nonterminal and the next symbol in the input string to index the parse table. The next symbol in the input string is referred to as the *look-ahead* symbol. The performance of the parser is not significantly affected by this modification. We must also place restrictions on the context-free grammar. The restricted class of context-free grammars, called LL(1), and the modified parsing algorithm are discussed in detail in the next section.

8.3   LL(1) grammars

In this section we will modify the top-down parsing algorithm in Figure 8.2 to make
it deterministic. The basic idea is that by looking at the top-most symbol on the
stack and the next input symbol, the parser should be able to uniquely determine
which production it should select. We shall see that this is possible if the context-
free grammar is LL(k), for some value of k. LL(k) stands for L̲eft-to-right (scan
of the input string), and L̲eft (derivation of the input string), using k symbols of
look-ahead.

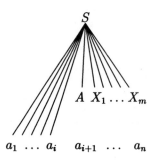

Figure 8.4 A partial parse tree that corresponds to the sentential form
$a_1 \ldots a_i A X_1 \ldots X_m$.

We can intuitively explain what an LL(k) grammar is in the following way.
Assume that we are given some context-free grammar $G = (N, T, P, S)$ and sentence $a_1 \ldots a_n$. Assume also that we have already parsed the first part of the
sentence, namely $a_1 \ldots a_i$, $i < n$, and that we want to select a production for some
nonterminal A. (Remember that A may be on the left-hand side of any number of productions.) At this point, therefore, our derivation has the general form
$S \Rightarrow^* a_1 \ldots a_i A X_1 \ldots X_m$. On the right of A there are still more terminals and
nonterminals, $X_1 \ldots X_m$, that have not yet been processed. The (partial) parse
tree corresponding to this derivation is shown in Figure 8.4. From the sentential
form $a_1 \ldots a_i A X_1 \ldots X_m$ we must derive the required input string $a_1 \ldots a_n$. This
means that $A X_1 \ldots X_m$ must derive $a_{i+1} \ldots a_n$. If the grammar G is (strong) LL(k)
then we can do this deterministically by examining the first k symbols of the input $a_{i+1} \ldots a_n$. We can rephrase this and say that, given a sentential form $uA\gamma$,
the (strong) LL(k) property states that the next k input symbols following u will
uniquely determine which production is to be used to expand A.

In the next section we define (strong) LL(k) grammars formally. In Section 8.3.2
we show how a parse table for an LL(1) grammar can be constructed from a
context-free grammar. The actual parse-table construction algorithm is given in
Section 8.3.3. Finally, in Section 8.3.4, we consider how grammars that are not
LL(1) can be transformed into LL(1) form. We assume at the outset that any given

grammar is reduced. That is, every nonterminal occurs in at least one production, and every nonterminal must generate a (possibly empty) string of terminals.

8.3.1 Strong LL(k) grammars

We begin by defining the *prefix* of length k of a string.

Definition 8.1
Let $a_1 \ldots a_n$ be a string of n symbols, $n \geq 0$. Then for $k \geq 1$:

$$\text{prefix}_k(a_1 \ldots a_n) = \begin{cases} a_1 \ldots a_k, & \text{if } k \leq n \\ a_1 \ldots a_n, & \text{otherwise} \end{cases}$$

$\diamond$

Notice that $\text{prefix}_k(\epsilon)=\epsilon$. We can now define strong LL(k) grammars.

Definition 8.2
Let $G = (N, T, P, S)$ be a context-free grammar, and $A \rightarrow \alpha$ and $A \rightarrow \beta$ be productions in G. G is strong LL(k) if, whenever there are 2 left derivations:

$$S \underset{1}{\Rightarrow}^* u_1 A \gamma_1 \Rightarrow u_1 \alpha \gamma_1 \underset{1}{\Rightarrow}^* u_1 v_1$$
$$S \underset{1}{\Rightarrow}^* u_2 A \gamma_2 \Rightarrow u_2 \beta \gamma_2 \underset{1}{\Rightarrow}^* u_2 v_2$$

such that $\text{prefix}_k(v_1) = \text{prefix}_k(v_2)$, then it follows that $\alpha = \beta$. In this definition $A \in N$, $\alpha, \beta, \gamma_1, \gamma_2 \in V^*$ and $u_1, u_2, v_1, v_2 \in T^*$. $\diamond$

This definition says that if the first k symbols in v_1 and v_2 are the same in the 2 derivations, then the 2 derivations are, in fact, the same. In other words, only the first k symbols in v_1 and v_2 are needed to choose the correct production to expand the nonterminal A.

This "strong" condition can be relaxed slightly by letting more of the string be used. This leads to a definition of a (non-strong) LL(k) grammar. The distinction between an LL(k) and a strong LL(k) grammar is that if a grammar is LL(k), then as well as the next k symbols in the input, that part of the input string that has already been read (namely, u_1 or u_2 in the definition above) can also be used to choose the correct production. Because extra information is available to choose a production in an LL(k) grammar, the class of LL(k) grammars is a superset of the class of strong LL(k) grammars. In the special case that $k = 1$, the class of LL(k) and strong LL(k) grammars are the same, however. (This can be quite easily proved.)

If a grammar is a strong LL(k) grammar then its strong LL(k) parser is deterministic. A language over an alphabet T is a strong LL(k) language if it is generated by some strong LL(k) grammar with terminal alphabet T. If a grammar is strong LL(k) then it cannot be ambiguous or left recursive, and vice versa, a left-recursive or ambiguous grammar cannot be strong LL(k). The larger the value of k, the larger is the class of grammars. This means that there are strong LL($k + 1$) languages that are not strong LL(k).

Example 8.12
Context-free grammars that contain the productions:

$$A \quad \rightarrow \quad a^n \alpha$$
$$| \quad a^n \beta$$

where $n \geq 1$, $\alpha, \beta \in V^*$ and $\alpha \neq \beta$, are not strong LL(n), but are strong LL($n+1$).

Consider the case $n = 1$, $\alpha = A$ and $\beta = \epsilon$, which corresponds to the grammar $A \rightarrow aA \mid a$. Consulting the definition above, the grammar is not strong LL(1) because we have the derivations $A \Rightarrow aA \Rightarrow aa$ and $A \Rightarrow a$. Intuitively, with a lookahead of only 1, we do not know which of the 2 productions to choose because the leading terminal in both right-hand sides is the same. However, if $n = 2$, then we can see that the first production should always be chosen as long as there are at least 2 a's in the input, and the second production if there is only 1 left.   ◇

While one would expect that a strong LL(k) grammar, where k is large, to be quite powerful (if k is large, then we can look a long way ahead to see which production should be applied next), there are many quite simple, useful grammars that are not strong LL(k), for any value of k.

Example 8.13
The following context-free grammar is not strong LL(k), for any value of k:

$$A \quad \rightarrow \quad B \mid C$$
$$B \quad \rightarrow \quad b \mid (A)$$
$$C \quad \rightarrow \quad c \mid (A)$$

Examples of sentences generated by this grammar are (b), (c) and $((((((b))))))$. Notice that there can be an arbitrary number of opening parentheses before a b or c. Looking k symbols ahead, therefore, may not be enough.   ◇

Unfortunately, the definition of strong LL(k) grammars above is inappropriate for deciding whether a grammar is strong LL(k). In order to give a more useful definition of LL(k) grammars, we define sets called FIRST and FOLLOW. We informally discussed these sets in Section 3.2.1. Here we treat them more formally. The first and follow sets are defined in the following way:

$$\text{FIRST}_k(\alpha) \quad = \quad \{u \mid \alpha \Rightarrow^* w \text{ and } u = \text{prefix}_k(w), \text{ for some } w \in T^*\}$$
$$\text{FOLLOW}_k(A) \quad = \quad \{u \mid S \Rightarrow^* \beta A \gamma \text{ and } u \in \text{FIRST}_k(\gamma), \text{ for some } \beta, \gamma \in V^*\}$$

for some context-free grammar G, with $\alpha \in V^*$, $A \in N$, $k \geq 1$. Notice that both sets contain strings of length at most k. We can now use the first and follow sets to provide an alternative definition of strong LL(k) grammars.

Definition 8.3
A context-free grammar is strong LL(k) if and only if, for each pair of distinct productions $A \rightarrow \alpha$ and $A \rightarrow \beta$, the following condition holds.

$$\text{FIRST}_k(\alpha \, \text{FOLLOW}_k(A)) \cap \text{FIRST}_k(\beta \, \text{FOLLOW}_k(A)) = \emptyset$$ ◇

In practice, "top-down" languages are generally specified using LL(k) grammars for $k = 1$. These grammars are sufficient to describe most programming constructs, although not always equally well. Because LL(k) and strong LL(k) grammars are equivalent if $k = 1$, we can use the definition of strong LL(k) grammars above for LL(1) grammars. In the next section we use the above definition to determine whether a given context-free grammar is LL(1), and we generate the corresponding parse table.

8.3.2 Constructing the parse table

We now concentrate on context-free grammars that are LL(1). If we let $k = 1$ in the definitions above of FIRST and FOLLOW, then we can write:

$$\text{FIRST}(\alpha) \quad = \quad \{a \mid \alpha \Rightarrow^* w \text{ and } a=\text{prefix}(w), \text{ for some } w \in T^*\}$$
$$\text{FOLLOW}(A) \quad = \quad \{a \mid S \Rightarrow^* \beta A\gamma \text{ and } a \in \text{FIRST}(\gamma), \text{ for some } \beta, \gamma \in V^*\}$$

where we have dropped the use of subscripts. (From now on, $k = 1$ unless stated otherwise.) FIRST(α) is therefore the set of terminals that begin the strings derived from the string α. Note that since prefix(ϵ)=ϵ, if $\alpha \Rightarrow^* \epsilon$ then $\epsilon \in$ FIRST(α).

FOLLOW(A) is the set of terminals that can follow the nonterminal A in some sentential form. Note that if $\gamma \Rightarrow^* \epsilon$ then, as the definition stands, $\epsilon \in$ FOLLOW(A). Conventionally, however, the input sentence is terminated by a special end-of-input symbol \$, where \$$\notin T$. In that case, if $\epsilon \in$ FIRST(γ) then \$$\in$FOLLOW($A$).

We also define a Boolean function EMPTY that determines whether a string α can derive ϵ:

$$\text{EMPTY}(\alpha) = \begin{cases} \text{true}, & \text{if } \alpha \Rightarrow^* \epsilon \\ \text{false}, & \text{otherwise} \end{cases}$$

Let us now reconsider Definition 8.3. Letting $k = 1$, the LL(1) condition becomes:

$$\text{FIRST}(\alpha\,\text{FOLLOW}(A)) \cap \text{FIRST}(\beta\,\text{FOLLOW}(A)) = \emptyset$$

This equality can be expressed in a more convenient form. Quite obviously, given some production $A \rightarrow \alpha$, if α cannot generate ϵ then the elements (terminals) in FIRST($\alpha\,$FOLLOW(A)) must come from FIRST(α). Alternatively, if α can generate ϵ, they will come from either FIRST(α) or FOLLOW(A). Similarly for β. We now define a set, called the *director set*, of a production $A \rightarrow \alpha$, with precisely this behaviour. The director set DIRSET of a production is defined as follows:

$$\text{DIRSET}(A \rightarrow \alpha) = \begin{cases} \text{FIRST}(\alpha), & \text{if } \neg\text{EMPTY}(\alpha) \\ \text{FIRST}(\alpha) \cup \text{FOLLOW}(A), & \text{otherwise} \end{cases}$$

Using these director sets, we can reformulate the definition of an LL(1) context-free grammar.

Definition 8.4
A context-free grammar is LL(1) if and only if, for each pair of distinct productions

$A \rightarrow \alpha$ and $A \rightarrow \beta$, the following condition holds:

$$\mathrm{DIRSET}(A \rightarrow \alpha) \cap \mathrm{DIRSET}(A \rightarrow \beta) = \emptyset \qquad \diamond$$

Given a context-free grammar G, this definition says that if the director sets of productions with the same left-hand side nonterminal are disjoint, then the grammar is LL(1). Let us now consider 2 examples in which we use the director sets to determine whether a grammar is LL(1).

Example 8.14
Consider the grammar with $N = \{expr, mterms, term, mfactors, factor\}$, $T = \{+, *, (,), digit\}$, start symbol *expr*, and the following productions:

p_1: *expr* → *term mterms* p_2: *mterms*→ + *term mterms*
p_3: *mterms*→ ϵ p_4: *term* → *factor mfactors*
p_5: *mfactors*→ * *factor mfactors* p_6: *mfactors*→ ϵ
p_7: *factor* → (*expr*) p_8: *factor* → *digit*

This right-recursive grammar describes constant arithmetic expressions that consist of the operators multiplication and addition, parenthesised expressions, and digits. This grammar defines the same language as the grammar in Example 8.1 (overlooking the fact that we have treated *digit* as a terminal here). We compute the empty, first and follow sets of the nonterminals in this grammar.

empty EMPTY(*mterms*) and EMPTY(*mfactors*) are true because of p_3 and p_6. The rest of EMPTY is false.

first From productions p_7 and p_8 we see that FIRST(*factor*)={(,*digit*}. Further, FIRST(*expr*)=FIRST(*term*)=FIRST(*factor*) because of productions p_1 and p_4. From p_2 and p_3 we see that FIRST(*mterms*)={+, ϵ}, and from p_5 and p_6, that FIRST(*mfactors*)={*, ϵ}.

follow Because the nonterminal *expr* is a sentential form, and using p_1 and p_4, and noting that *mterms* and *mfactors* can generate ϵ, we can say that \$ is in the follow set of all nonterminals. The string (*expr*) can also occur in sentential forms, hence ")" is also in every follow set. From p_2, p_4 and p_6 we deduce that + is in the follow sets of *term*, *mfactors* and *factor*. Finally, from p_5 we deduce that * is in FOLLOW(*factor*).

A table showing the results of these computations is shown below:

	FIRST	FOLLOW	EMPTY
expr	{(, *digit*}	{), \$}	false
mterms	{+, ϵ}	{), \$}	true
term	{(, *digit*}	{+,), \$}	false
mfactors	{*, ϵ}	{+,), \$}	true
factor	{(, *digit*}	{+, *,), \$}	false

To compute the director sets, we first need to compute the first sets of all the right-hand sides in the grammar. In the productions p_2, p_5, p_7 and p_8, these (singleton) sets can be read from the grammar. (Each of these productions begins with a terminal.) The right-hand sides of p_1 and p_4 begin with a nonterminal; the first sets of these nonterminals are shown in the table above. This only leaves productions p_3 and p_6. Because these productions are empty, we need FIRST(ϵ), which is ϵ, of course, and the follow sets of the left-hand side nonterminals, *mterms* and *mfactors*. These values are also shown in the table above. The results of these computations are shown below:

p_1: $\{(, digit\}$ p_2: $\{+\}$ p_3: $\{), \$, \epsilon\}$ p_4: $\{(, digit\}$
p_5: $\{*\}$ p_6: $\{+,), \$, \epsilon\}$ p_7: $\{(\}$ p_8: $\{digit\}$

We can now easily see if the grammar is LL(1) by checking Definition 8.4. Productions p_2 and p_3 have the same left-hand side nonterminal, as do p_5 and p_6. Both pairs have disjoint director sets, hence the grammar is LL(1).   ◇

Example 8.15
Consider again the grammar shown in Example 8.1. The director sets for the productions in this grammar are shown below:

$expr \rightarrow expr + term$: $\{(,0,\ldots,9\}$ $expr \rightarrow term$: $\{(,0,\ldots,9\}$
$term \rightarrow term * factor$: $\{(,0,\ldots,9\}$ $term \rightarrow factor$: $\{(,0,\ldots,9\}$
$factor \rightarrow (expr)$: $\{(\}$ $factor \rightarrow digit$: $\{0,\ldots,9\}$
$digit \rightarrow 0$: $\{0\}$ $digit \rightarrow 1$: $\{1\}$
$\ldots$

Note that, as there are no ϵ-productions, the director sets are simply the first sets. Checking Definition 8.4, we see that the director sets of the productions for *expr* and *term* are not disjoint (they are, in fact, the same). The grammar is therefore not LL(1).   ◇

The director sets are not only used to test whether a grammar is LL(1); they can also be used to construct the parse table for a given LL(1) grammar. If the director sets of productions with the same left-hand side nonterminal are indeed disjoint, then the elements (terminals) in the director sets can be used to select between alternative productions during a top-down parse. The correct production is the one whose director set contains the current look-ahead symbol. It is this role that the terminals in the director sets play that gives rise to their name: they direct the parse. The LL(1) parse table is defined in terms of the director sets in the following way.

Definition 8.5
Given a context-free grammar, for each $A \in N$ and $a \in T \cup \{\$\}$, the parse table $M(A, a)$ is defined by

$$M(A,a) = \begin{cases} A \rightarrow \alpha, & \text{if } a \in \text{DIRSET}(A \rightarrow \alpha) \\ \text{error}, & \text{otherwise} \end{cases}$$

◇

If the entry $M(A, a)$ is production $A \rightarrow \alpha$, then the parser chooses this production whenever A is on top of the parse stack and the look-ahead symbol is a. If this entry is not defined then the parser has recognised an error in the input. Note that if the director sets are not disjoint, then constructing the parse table will result in a table containing multiple entries.

Example 8.16

We construct the parse table M for the context-free grammar shown in Example 8.14 by using the director sets. For example, the director set of p_1, computed in Example 8.14, is $\{(, digit\}$. The corresponding entries in the parse table, therefore, are $M(expr, "(")=p_1$ and $M(expr, digit)=p_1$. Similarly for the other entries. The completed table is shown below.

	digit	+	*	(	)	$
expr	p_1			p_1		
mterms		p_2			p_3	p_3
term	p_4			p_4		
mfactors		p_6	p_5		p_6	p_6
factor	p_8			p_7		

$\diamond$

Now that we know how to construct the parse table for an LL(1) grammar, we can modify the (non-predictive) top-down parse algorithm in Figure 8.2 to make it predictive. Given a parse table M, a start symbol S, and an alphabet T of an LL(1) grammar, the predictive algorithm will parse an input string that is terminated by an end-of-input symbol $. The predictive algorithm is shown in Figure 8.5. If the string is correct then the output is the value true.

8.3.3   The LL(1) test

Let us now look more closely at the procedure for testing whether a given grammar is LL(1). In the previous section, we computed the empty, first, follow and director sets by inspecting the grammar. This is not good enough, however, if we wish to automate the process of generating a parser (i.e. build a parser generator). In that case, we need a rigorous procedure to compute the required sets. This requires more precise definitions of the above sets. In this section we define the new set-valued functions LEADING and TRAILING, and using these definitions, we re-define FOLLOW and DIRSET. From these definitions we derive algorithms to compute the sets.

Definitions of the leading, trailing, follow and director sets. We define the *leading set* of a nonterminal A, LEADING (A), to be the set of terminals and nonterminals X such that X is the leftmost symbol in some string derived from A. In other words, we define LEADING $(A) = \{X \mid A \Rightarrow^+ X\alpha\}$, where $A \in N$,

```
#define false 0
#define true 1
STACK = ∅;
push(S, STACK);
look_ahead = read(input);
accept = true;
while (accept && (look_ahead != $ || STACK != ∅)) {
  top_of_stack = pop(STACK);
  if (top_of_stack ∈ T) {
      if (top_of_stack != look_ahead)
          accept = false;
      else
          look_ahead = read(input);
  }
  else if (top_of_stack ∈ N) {   /* assume top_of_stack = A */
      if (M(top_of_stack, look_ahead) == A→α)
          push(α, STACK);
      else   /* no entry in the table */
          accept = false;
  }
  else
      accept = false;
}
output(accept);
```

Figure 8.5 A predictive top-down parse algorithm for LL(1) grammars.

$X \in V$ and $\alpha \in V^*$. Note that the only difference between this definition, and the definition of the set FIRST, is that here X can be either a terminal or a nonterminal symbol. That is, the terminals in the leading set of a nonterminal constitute the first set for that nonterminal.

If we have a production $A \rightarrow X\alpha$, then, by definition, $X \in \text{LEADING}(A)$. In general, if we have a production $A \rightarrow \eta X\alpha$, and $\eta \Rightarrow^* \epsilon$, then, by definition, $X \in \text{LEADING}(A)$. Note that $\eta \in N^*$. We call a symbol X satisfying this condition a *direct* leader of nonterminal A because it can be read directly from the production.

Symbols can also be in the leading set of a nonterminal as the result of a derivation (or indirection). Consider, for example, the production $A \rightarrow B\alpha$, where $B \Rightarrow^+ X\beta$. Such an X is also in the leading set of nonterminal A, and is called an *indirect* leader of A. This case can also be generalised. If we have a production $A \rightarrow \eta B\alpha$, $\eta \Rightarrow^* \epsilon$, and $B \Rightarrow^* \mu X\beta$, $\mu \Rightarrow^* \epsilon$, then $X \in \text{LEADING}(A)$. Notice that the second half of this formulation (i.e. $B \Rightarrow^* \mu X\beta$, $\mu \Rightarrow^* \epsilon$) is simply the requirement that $X \in \text{LEADING}(B)$. Here $\eta, \mu \in N^*$; $A, B \in N$; and $\alpha, \beta \in V^*$.

We can use the above direct and indirect cases to define the leading set of a nonterminal.

Definition 8.6

The leading set of a nonterminal **A** is defined as:

$$\text{LEADING}(A) = \{X \mid (A \to \eta X \alpha \ \wedge \ \eta \Rightarrow^* \epsilon) \ \vee$$
$$(A \to \eta B \alpha \ \wedge \ \eta \Rightarrow^* \epsilon \ \wedge \ X \in \text{LEADING}(B))\}$$

where $X \in V$; $A, B \in N$; $\eta \in N^*$; and $\alpha \in V^*$.   ◇

Further, we define the leading set of a terminal a, LEADING(a), to be the terminal itself. In other words, LEADING$(a) = \{a\}$, where $a \in T$. We can now use the definitions of the leading set of a terminal and nonterminal to define the leading set of a string α.

Definition 8.7

The leading set of the empty string, LEADING(ϵ), is $\emptyset$. The leading set of a string α that is of the form $X\beta$, is defined as:

$$\text{LEADING}(X\beta) = \begin{cases} \text{LEADING}(X), & \text{if } \neg\text{EMPTY}(X) \\ \text{LEADING}(X) \cup \text{LEADING}(\beta), & \text{otherwise} \end{cases}$$

Here $X, Y \in V$ and $\alpha, \beta \in V^*$.   ◇

We define the *trailing set* of a nonterminal A, TRAILING(A), to be the set of terminals and nonterminals Y such that Y is the rightmost symbol in some string derived from A. In other words, we define TRAILING$(A) = \{Y \mid A \Rightarrow^+ \alpha Y\}$, where $A \in N$, $Y \in V$ and $\alpha \in V^*$. Using precisely the same reasoning as above for the leading sets results in an analogous definition of the trailing sets. This is shown below.

Definition 8.8

The trailing set of a nonterminal A is defined as:

$$\text{TRAILING}(A) = \{Y \mid (A \to \alpha Y \eta \ \wedge \ \eta \Rightarrow^* \epsilon) \ \vee$$
$$(A \to \alpha B \eta \ \wedge \ \eta \Rightarrow^* \epsilon \ \wedge \ Y \in \text{TRAILING}(B))\}$$

where $Y \in V$; $A, B \in N$; $\eta \in N^*$; and $\alpha \in V^*$.   ◇

The leading and trailing sets can now be used to define the *follow sets*. We said in the previous section that FOLLOW(A), where A is a nonterminal, is the set of all terminals that can follow A in some sentential form. This means, for example, that if we have a production $B \to \alpha A a \beta$, then quite obviously, $a \in$FOLLOW(A). Generalising, we can write that if we have a production $B \to \alpha A \eta a \beta$, where $\eta \Rightarrow^* \epsilon$, then $a \in$FOLLOW(A). The terminal a here is called a direct follower of the nonterminal A.

Terminals can also be in the follow set of a nonterminal as the result of a derivation. Consider, for example, the production $B \to \alpha A \eta C \beta$, where $\eta \Rightarrow^* \epsilon$. If $a \in$LEADING(C), then $a \in$FOLLOW(A). Terminals that satisfy this condition are called indirect followers of the nonterminal A.

One other situation can arise that will contribute to the follow sets. Consider the production $D \rightarrow \alpha B \eta a \beta$, and the production $D \rightarrow \alpha B \eta C \beta$, where $a \in$ LEADING (C) and $\eta \Rightarrow^* \epsilon$. If $A \in$ TRAILING (B), then we have an analogous situation to the direct and indirect cases above, with the difference that B plays the role of A. In other words, we have $a \in$ FOLLOW(A).

We can now formally define the follow sets.

Definition 8.9

The follow set of a nonterminal A is defined as:

$$\text{FOLLOW}(A) = \{a \mid (B \rightarrow \alpha A \eta a \beta \wedge \eta \Rightarrow^* \epsilon) \vee$$
$$(B \rightarrow \alpha A \eta C \beta \wedge \eta \Rightarrow^* \epsilon \wedge a \in \text{LEADING}(C)) \vee$$
$$(A \in \text{TRAILING}(B) \wedge a \in \text{FOLLOW}(B))\}$$

where $a \in T$; $A, B, C \in N$; $\eta \in N^*$; and $\alpha, \beta \in V^*$.   ◇

The *director sets* are defined in terms of the leading and follow sets.

Definition 8.10

The director set of a production $A \rightarrow \alpha$ is defined as:

$$\text{DIRSET}(A \rightarrow \alpha) = \{a \mid (a \in \text{LEADING}(\alpha) \wedge a \in T) \vee$$
$$(a \in \text{FOLLOW}(A) \wedge \alpha \Rightarrow^* \epsilon)\}$$

where $A \in N$ and $\alpha \in V^*$.   ◇

LL(1)-test algorithm. Having defined the leading, trailing, follow and director sets, we can now present an algorithm that will test whether a grammar is LL(1). We begin by computing the function EMPTY. Once we have these values, we can compute the leading and trailing sets. The empty values and the leading and trailing sets are then used to compute the follow sets. Finally, the empty values and the leading and follow sets are used to compute the director sets. The precise order of evaluation is depicted in Figure 8.6.

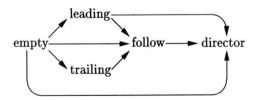

Figure 8.6 The order of computing the empty, leading, trailing, follow and director sets.

empty The following algorithm computes the set EMPTY for each nonterminal in a grammar $G = (N, T, P, S)$.

1. $\forall A \in N$, set EMPTY(A) to false.

2. $\forall p \in P$, if $p : A \rightarrow \alpha a \beta$ then remove production p from G. Here $a \in T$, $A \in N$ and $\alpha, \beta \in V^*$.

3. $\forall p \in P$, if $p : A \rightarrow \epsilon$ then set EMPTY(A) to true and remove all productions $A \rightarrow \alpha$.

4. $\forall p \in P$, if $p : A \rightarrow B_1 \ldots B_n \wedge$ EMPTY(B_i), $\forall i\,(1 \leq i \leq n)$, then set EMPTY($A$) to true and remove all productions $A \rightarrow \alpha$. Here, $B_i \in N$, $1 \leq i \leq n$.

5. Repeat the previous step until no more productions can be removed.

leading We can now compute the set LEADING for each nonterminal in the grammar.

1. $\forall A \in N$, set LEADING (A) to $\emptyset$.

2. $\forall p \in P$, if $p : A \rightarrow \eta X \alpha$ and $\eta \Rightarrow^* \epsilon$ then add X to LEADING (A). Here $A \in N$, $X \in V$, $\eta \in N^*$ and $\alpha \in V^*$. Note that η can be ϵ. This step computes the direct leaders of nonterminal A.

3. $\forall X \in$ LEADING (A), if $A \in$ LEADING (B) then add X to LEADING (B). This computes the indirect leaders of nonterminal A.

4. Repeat the previous step until no more symbols can be added. This computes the transitive closure of the leading sets.

We also need the set LEADING for strings α that are the right-hand sides of productions.

1. if $\alpha = \epsilon$ then set LEADING (α) to $\emptyset$.

2. if $\alpha = X \beta$ then set LEADING (α) to LEADING (X).

3. if $\alpha = X \beta$ and EMPTY(X) then add LEADING (β) to LEADING (α).

trailing Computing the TRAILING sets of nonterminals is analogous to computing the LEADING sets.

1. $\forall A \in N$, set TRAILING (A) to $\emptyset$.

2. $\forall p \in P$, if $p : A \rightarrow \alpha Y \eta$ and $\eta \Rightarrow^* \epsilon$ then add Y to TRAILING (A). Here $A \in N$, $Y \in V$, $\eta \in N^*$ and $\alpha \in V^*$. Note that η can be ϵ. This step computes the direct trailers of nonterminal A.

3. $\forall Y \in$ TRAILING (A), if $A \in$ TRAILING (B) then add Y to TRAILING (B). This computes the indirect trailers of nonterminal A.

4. Repeat the previous step until no more symbols can be added. This computes the transitive closure of the trailing sets.

follow   We can now compute the set FOLLOW for each nonterminal in the grammar.

1. $\forall A \in N$, set FOLLOW(A) to $\emptyset$.

2. $\forall p \in P$, if $p : B \rightarrow \alpha A \eta a \beta$ and $\eta \Rightarrow^* \epsilon$ then add a to FOLLOW(A). Here, $A, B \in N$, $a \in T$, $\eta \in N^*$ and $\alpha, \beta \in V^*$. Note that η can be ϵ. This step computes the direct followers of nonterminal A.

3. $\forall p \in P$, if $p : B \rightarrow \alpha A \eta C \beta$, $\eta \Rightarrow^* \epsilon$ and $a \in$ LEADING (C), then add a to FOLLOW(A). Here, $A, B, C \in N$, $a \in T$, $\eta \in N^*$ and $\alpha, \beta \in V^*$. Note that η can be ϵ. This step computes some of the indirect followers of nonterminal A.

4. $\forall B \in N$, if $A \in$ TRAILING (B) and $a \in$ FOLLOW(B), then add a to FOLLOW(A). This computes the rest of the indirect followers of nonterminal A.

5. Repeat the previous step until no more symbols can be added.

director   The director sets can be simply computed by using the leading and follow sets.

1. $\forall A \rightarrow \alpha \in P$, set DIRSET($A \rightarrow \alpha$) to $\emptyset$.

2. $\forall A \rightarrow \alpha \in P$, if $a \in$ LEADING (α) and $a \in T$, then add the terminal a to DIRSET($A \rightarrow \alpha$).

3. $\forall A \rightarrow \alpha \in P$, if $\alpha \Rightarrow^* \epsilon$ then add terminals from FOLLOW(A) to DIRSET($A \rightarrow \alpha$).

Note in the last step that if a grammar has no ϵ-productions, then EMPTY(α) is always false, and we do not need the follow sets.

LL(1) test   A grammar G is LL(1) if $\forall p_1, p_2 \in P$, if $p_1 : A \rightarrow \alpha$ and $p_2 : A \rightarrow \beta$ and $\alpha \neq \beta$ then DIRSET($A \rightarrow \alpha$) $\cap$ DIRSET($A \rightarrow \beta$) $= \emptyset$.

Example 8.17
We extend the LL(1) grammar shown in Example 8.14 by adding a unary operator $-$, and a multiple assignment statement. We also dispense with digits, and use identifiers instead.

p_1: *assn* $\rightarrow$ *id* := *assn*	p_2: *assn* $\rightarrow$ *expr*
p_3: *expr* $\rightarrow$ *term mterms*	p_4: *mterms* $\rightarrow$ + *term mterms*
p_5: *mterms* $\rightarrow \epsilon$	p_6: *term* $\rightarrow$ *sign factor mfactors*
p_7: *mfactors* $\rightarrow$ * *sign factor mfactors*	p_8: *mfactors* $\rightarrow \epsilon$
p_9: *sign* $\rightarrow -$	p_{10}: *sign* $\rightarrow \epsilon$
p_{11}: *factor* $\rightarrow$ *id*	p_{12}: *factor* $\rightarrow$ (*expr*)

This grammar can generate the string $a := b := -c + d * e$, where the identifiers are understood to be instances of the nonterminal *id*. Is this grammar LL(1)? To answer this question, we apply the LL(1)-test algorithm above.

empty In step 1 of the empty algorithm we set all of EMPTY to false. In step 2, we remove productions that contain a terminal (i.e. p_1, p_4, p_7, p_9, p_{11} and p_{12}). The ϵ-productions are p_5, p_8 and p_{10}. Hence, in step 3, we set EMPTY(*mterms*), EMPTY(*mfactors*) and EMPTY(*sign*) to true, and the corresponding productions are removed. None of the remaining productions satisfies the condition in step 4.

leading In step 1, we initialise by setting all of LEADING to the empty set. The direct leaders (step 2) of all nonterminals except for *term* are simply the first symbols of their respective productions. In the case of *term*, because *sign* can be empty in p_6, *factor* can also be a direct leader of *term*. The indirect leaders (step 3) are added by applying transitive closure. The leading sets of nonterminals *mterms*, *mfactors*, *sign* and *factor* contain no nonterminals, so there are no indirect leaders. Because *sign* and *factor* are in the leading set of *term*, their leaders ($-$, "(", *id*) are also in the leading set of *term*. Similarly for *expr* and *assn*. Notice that if we evaluate the indirect leaders bottom-up, then the computation can be carried out in one pass.

trailing The direct trailers (step 2) of *assn*, *sign* and *factor* are the last symbols of their respective productions. In the other cases, because the last symbol can be empty, the penultimate symbol must also be included. In step 3, because the nonterminal *factor* is in the trailing set of *mfactors* and *term*, the trailing set of *factor* is also in the trailing set of *mfactors* and *term*. Similarly for *mterms*, *expr* and *assn*.

follow We initialise by setting all of FOLLOW to the empty set. The production p_{12} satisfies the condition in step 2; hence we deduce that the symbol ")" is in FOLLOW(*expr*). In step 3, we look for right-hand sides of the form $\alpha A \eta C \beta$, where $\eta \Rightarrow^* \epsilon$. We deduce from productions p_3 and p_4 that the terminals in LEADING (*mterms*) are also in FOLLOW(*term*); and from p_6 and p_7, that the terminals in LEADING (*factor*) are in FOLLOW(*sign*), and the terminals in LEADING (*mfactors*) are in FOLLOW(*factor*). Finally, in step 4, for each nonterminal B, all terminals in FOLLOW(B) are placed in the follow set of the trailers of B. The symbol \$, for example, is in FOLLOW(*assn*), hence \$ is in each of the follow sets of the trailers of *assn*, namely *assn*, *expr*, *term*, *mterms*, *factor* and *mfactors*. Similarly, we find that ")", which is in FOLLOW(*expr*), is in the follow set of *term*, *mterms*, *factor* and *mfactors*, and we find that +, which is in FOLLOW(*term*), is in the follow set of *factor* and *mfactors*.

director We initialise by setting DIRSET of each production to the empty set. Using step 2, the terminals of the leading set of the right-hand side of each production are placed in the director set of the production. Because each of the productions p_1, p_4, p_7, p_9, p_{11} and p_{12} begins with a terminal, in each case the terminal is placed in the corresponding director set. The leading sets of the right-hand sides of productions p_2, p_3 and p_6 all contain the terminals $-$, "(" and *id*; so these terminals are placed in the corresponding director sets. Finally, using step 3, we add the follow sets of *mterms*, *mfactors* and *sign* to

	empty	leaders: direct and indirect	
assn	false	{*id,expr*}	{−,(,*term,sign,factor,id*}
expr	false	{*term*}	{−,(,*id,sign,factor*}
term	false	{*sign,factor*}	{−,(,*id*}
mterms	true	{+}	{}
factor	false	{(,*id*}	{}
mfactors	true	{∗}	{}
sign	true	{−}	{}

	trailers: direct and indirect		followers
assn	{*assn,expr*}	{*term,mterms,factor,mfactors,id*,)}	{$}
expr	{*term,mterms*}	{*factor,mfactors,id*,)}	{$,)}
term	{*factor,mfactors*}	{*id*,)}	{$,+,)}
mterms	{*term,mterms*}	{*factor,mfactors,id*,)}	{$,)}
factor	{*id*,)}	{}	{$,+,),∗}
mfactors	{*factor,mfactors*}	{*id*,)}	{$,+,)}
sign	{−}	{}	{(,*id*}

directors			
p_1: {*id*}	p_2: {−,(,*id*}	p_3: {−,(,*id*}	p_4: {+}
p_5: {$,)}	p_6: {−,(,*id*}	p_7: {∗}	p_8: {$,+,)}
p_9: {−}	p_{10}: {(,*id*}	p_{11}: {*id*}	p_{12}: {(}

Figure 8.7 The empty, leading, trailing, follow and director sets computed in Example 8.17.

the director sets of the ϵ-productions p_5, p_8 and p_{10}, respectively.

LL(1) test If a grammar is LL(1), then all productions with the same left-hand side will have disjoint director sets. We notice that *id* is common to both DIRSET(p_1) and DIRSET(p_2), hence the grammar is not LL(1).

In Figure 8.7 we summarise these computations. ◇

Implementation. In the above algorithm, we have expressed the leading, trailing and follow functions in terms of sets. We can compute these sets more efficiently in practice if we represent them as two-dimensional Boolean matrices. Consider the function LEADING, for example. We define a matrix IM (short for incidence matrix) as follows:

$$\mathrm{IM}\,[A,\,X] = \begin{cases} 1, & \text{if } X \in \mathrm{LEADING}\,(A) \\ 0, & \text{otherwise} \end{cases}$$

for $A \in N$ and $X \in V$. To compute this matrix, we begin as in the leading algorithm, by initialising (in this case setting all elements in IM to 0), and computing the direct leaders (if $A \to \eta X \alpha$ and $\eta \Rightarrow^* \epsilon$ then $\text{IM}\,[A,\,X\,] = 1$). To compute the indirect leaders, we can now apply Warshall's algorithm. This algorithm allows us to determine, in one pass, the transitive closure of a relation that is represented as an incidence matrix. If we denote the terminals and nonterminals of a grammar G by X_i, $1 \leq i \leq n$, then we can express Warshall's algorithm in the following way:

```
for (c = 1; c ≤ n; c++)
    for (r = 1; r ≤ n; r++)
        if (Xr,Xc ∈ N && IM[Xr][Xc] = 1)
            for (i = 1; i ≤ n; i++)
                if (IM[Xc][Xi] == 1) IM[Xr][Xi] = 1;
```

Notice that only the rows in IM corresponding to nonterminals are used (as one would expect), and that the matrix IM is processed column-wise. Warshall's algorithm can also be used to compute the trailing and follow sets.

8.3.4   Transformations

We have seen that it is possible (via Definition 8.4) to decide whether a given grammar is LL(1). If a context-free grammar is not LL(1), it is <u>sometimes</u> possible to make an equivalent grammar that is LL(1). In this section we consider two transformations that can be used to construct an LL(1) grammar starting from a non-LL(1) grammar that generates an LL(1) language. These transformations are left factorisation and the elimination of direct left recursion. Note, however, that it is *not decidable* whether a grammar that is not LL(1) can be transformed into one that is. In other words, it is not decidable whether a given language is LL(1) or not.

In this section we follow convention and let A, B, C, D and E be nonterminals, a and b be terminals, and α, β, γ and δ be strings of nonterminals and terminals.

Left factorisation. Suppose that a context-free grammar contains the productions:

$$A \to \alpha\beta$$
$$A \to \alpha\gamma$$

where α is not the empty string. These productions prevent the context-free grammar from being LL(1). To solve this LL(1) conflict, we left factor these productions, and introduce a new nonterminal. This results in the following productions:

$$A \to \alpha B \qquad B \to \beta$$
$$B \to \gamma$$

The new grammar is, of course, equivalent to the original one.

It is not always obvious that left factorisation can be used. Some substitutions may first need to be carried out. Consider, for example:

$$A \to B\alpha \qquad B \to b\gamma \qquad C \to b\delta$$
$$A \to C\beta$$

Substituting for B and C we find:

$$A \to b\gamma\alpha$$
$$A \to b\delta\beta$$

Left factorisation can now be applied to these productions. However, care must be taken, as this process can result in an infinite loop. Consider, for example, the following grammar:

$$A \to B \qquad B \to DB \qquad C \to DC$$
$$A \to C \qquad B \to \alpha \qquad C \to \beta$$

If we substitute for B and C in the productions for A, then we generate the following grammar:

$$A \to DB \qquad B \to DB \qquad C \to DC$$
$$A \to DC \qquad B \to \alpha \qquad C \to \beta$$
$$A \to \alpha$$
$$A \to \beta$$

We now factor out the D in the productions for A:

$$A \to DE \qquad E \to B \qquad B \to DB \qquad C \to DC$$
$$A \to \alpha \qquad E \to C \qquad B \to \alpha \qquad C \to \beta$$
$$A \to \beta$$

The reader will notice that we have come full circle—the nonterminal E now assumes the role of the original A.

Left recursion. Left recursion often occurs in the syntax specification of (programming) languages. Consider, for example, the following productions:

$$A \to AB$$
$$A \to \epsilon$$

Here, the nonterminal A is direct left recursive. A nonterminal A is *direct left recursive* if there is production of the form $A \to A\alpha$. Notice that left recursion is more general than direct left recursion. A context-free grammar given by the productions $A \to B$, $B \to A$ and $B \to a$ is left recursive but not direct left recursive. There is a method to transform a grammar containing direct left-recursive productions into an equivalent grammar that contains right recursion. Suppose that we have the following left-recursive productions for nonterminal A:

$$A \to A\alpha$$
$$A \to \beta$$

These productions can be replaced by the following set of (right-recursive) productions:

$$A \to BC \qquad B \to \beta \qquad C \to \alpha C$$
$$C \to \epsilon$$

Example 8.18

Consider the above left and right-recursive grammars, and let α=a and β=b. The equivalence of these grammars can easily be seen in Figure 8.8, where we show the corresponding parse trees for the sentence *baaa*.   ◇

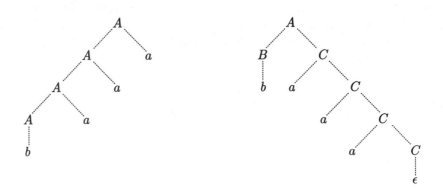

Figure 8.8 Parse trees for the sentence *baaa* using left and right recursion.

8.4   Extended context-free grammars

We have seen that the productions of a context-free grammar have the form $A \rightarrow X_1 X_2 \ldots X_n$. The symbol A on the left-hand side of the production is a nonterminal symbol, and the symbols X_1 through X_n on the right-hand side are terminal or nonterminal symbols. The same nonterminal may appear on the left-hand side of more than 1 production.

We now describe *extended* context-free grammars. An extended context-free grammar is a context-free grammar in which each nonterminal may appear on the left-hand side of only 1 production, and regular expressions are allowed on the right-hand sides of productions. Extended context-free grammars are sometimes referred to as *regular right-part grammars*.

Instead of the traditional regular-expression operators concatenation, choice and closure, however, a new, more comprehensive and useful set of operators will be used. In Section 8.4.1 we revise the regular-expression formalism and define these operators. We then use these operators to define extended context-free grammars. In Section 8.4.2 we show that an extended context-free grammar can always be transformed into a context-free grammar. Analogously to context-free grammars, we can restrict the class of extended context-free grammars to extended LL(1). In Section 8.4.3 we show the conditions that an extended context-free grammar must satisfy to be extended LL(1). Recursive-descent and table-driven parsers for an extended LL(1) grammar are discussed in Section 8.4.4.

8.4.1 Regular expressions revisited

The regular expressions in the productions of an extended context-free grammar are built up from a basic set of symbols, namely the terminal and nonterminal symbols of the grammar, the symbol ϵ, and a set of operator symbols. Each production of an extended context-free grammar has the form $A \rightarrow E$, where A is a nonterminal and E a regular expression.

Let T be the set of terminal symbols and N the set of nonterminal symbols of a grammar. If $E \in T$ or $E \in N$ then E is a regular expression. Moreover, ϵ is a regular expression. If E, E_1 and E_2 are regular expressions then the following are regular expressions:

$E_1 \,|\, E_2$ (choice)
$E_1 E_2$ (concatenation)
E^* (closure)
$\{E\}$ (bracketing)

In an extended context-free grammar, as well as choice, concatenation and bracketing, we define the following operators:

E **option**	meaning $E \,|\, \epsilon$
E **clos**	meaning E^*
E **seq**	meaning $E E^*$
E_1 **chain** E_2	meaning $E_1 \{E_2 E_1\}^*$
E **list**	meaning $E \, \{\text{list\_token } E\}^*$
E **pack**	meaning open_token E close_token

In the last two productions list_token, open_token and close_token typically stand for the terminal symbols "," , "(" and ")", respectively. These symbols should occur in the set T.

The language $L(E)$ is a set of strings over the alphabet of the grammar. If E is a terminal or nonterminal symbol, then $L(E)$ is the set of strings $\{E\}$. The language $L(\epsilon)$ is the set of strings $\{\epsilon\}$ that only contains the empty string. Note that we use the same symbol (ϵ) to denote an empty regular expression, an empty string and the right-hand side of an ϵ-production.

We define the language of the different constructs (expressions) in terms of the languages of their constituents (subexpressions).

$L(E_1 \,|\, E_2)$	$= L(E_1) \cup L(E_2)$	(choice)
$L(E_1 E_2)$	$= L(E_1) L(E_2)$	(concatenation)
$L(E^*)$	$= \cup_{i=0}^{\infty} (L(E)^i)$	(closure)
$L(\{E\})$	$= L(E)$	(bracketing)

Braces are used to mark the operands of the operators in a regular expression. For instance, in the expression $E_1 \{E_2 \,|\, E_3\}$ **pack**, the operand of **pack** is the expression $E_2 \,|\, E_3$. To reduce the number of braces in an expression, we assume that all operators are left associative. Hence, E_1 **chain** E_2 **chain** E_3 means

$\{E_1 \text{ chain } E_2\}$ **chain** E_3 and not E_1 **chain** $\{E_2 \text{ chain } E_3\}$. If the second expression is required, then braces must be used.

The operators for concatenation and choice are associative. Hence, $\{E_1 E_2\} E_3 = E_1 \{E_2 E_3\} = E_1 E_2 E_3$, and, $\{E_1 \mid E_2\} \mid E_3 = E_1 \mid \{E_2 \mid E_3\} = E_1 \mid E_2 \mid E_3$. We can omit braces in expressions of these forms. Notice, however, that there is a difference between $E_1 \{E_2 \mid E_3\}$ and $\{E_1 E_2\} \mid E_3$.

We also stipulate an order of priority for the operators. From highest to lowest, they are:

1. **option, seq, clos, list, pack**
2. **chain**
3. concatenation
4. |

Since concatenation has higher priority than |, we can omit the braces in $\{E_1 E_2\} \mid E_3$ without affecting its meaning, but not in $E_1 \{E_2 \mid E_3\}$.

An extended context-free grammar G is a 4-tuple (N, T, P, S), in which N is the set of nonterminals, T the set of terminals, S the start symbol and P a set of productions. The left-hand side of a production is a nonterminal symbol, the right-hand side is a regular expression, as defined above. For each nonterminal A in N there is exactly one production with left-hand side A. If a nonterminal symbol A occurs in a sentential form of a grammar, and $A \rightarrow E$ is a production in G, then A may be replaced by a string in $L(E)$. The language $L(G)$ generated by the extended context-free grammar G is the set of all sentential forms generated by G that only contain symbols from the terminal alphabet T.

Example 8.19
The following 4 extended context-free grammars all generate the same language consisting of a comma-separated list of identifiers.

$G_1 :$ $S \rightarrow id \{ \text{list\_token } id \} \textbf{clos}$
$G_2 :$ $S \rightarrow id \textbf{ chain } \text{list\_token}$
$G_3 :$ $S \rightarrow id \textbf{ list}$
$G_4 :$ $S \rightarrow id \ A$
           $A \rightarrow A \text{ list\_token } id \mid \epsilon$

Each grammar has a start symbol S and terminal symbols id and list_token. The terminal list_token is implicit in grammar G_3. Note that G_4 is also a context-free grammar, but because it is left recursive, it is not LL(1).   ◇

8.4.2   Transforming an extended context-free grammar

Every context-free grammar can be transformed into an extended context-free grammar, and vice versa. The transformation from a context-free grammar to an equivalent extended context-free grammar goes as follows. Let a context-free grammar contain more than one production for A. We can make one production for A by using the choice operator. For instance, the context-free productions $A \to \alpha$ and $A \to \beta$ can be written as one production $A \to \alpha \,|\, \beta$ in an extended context-free grammar. If we do this for all nonterminals and all the productions in a context-free grammar, we obtain an extended context-free grammar that generates the same language as the original context-free grammar.

The transformation from an extended context-free grammar G to an equivalent context-free grammar is, as one would expect, more complicated. An expression E is called *basic* if E is a sequence in V^* (i.e. a, possibly empty, sequence consisting of terminal symbols and nonterminal symbols only). Expressions that are not basic are called *compound* expressions. The transformation proceeds in a step-wise fashion.

step 1 Replace each production of the form $A \to E_1 \,|\, \ldots \,|\, E_n$ by n different productions, each with A as left-hand side: $A \to E_1, \ldots, A \to E_n$.

step 2 Rewrite all compound expressions in which the operators **option**, **clos**, **seq**, **chain**, **list** and **pack** occur by their equivalent expressions using the definitions of these operators.

step 3 Replace each production of the form $A \to E^*$ by the productions $A \to E A$ and $A \to \epsilon$.

step 4 For each compound expression E, introduce a new nonterminal symbol B. Replace all occurrences of the compound expression E by B, and add the production $B \to E$. Moreover, if a production has the form $A \to \{E\}$, then we replace it with the production $A \to E$.

The 4 steps are repeated as long as the resulting grammar is not context-free. Each step leads to an intermediate "grammar", equivalent to G. It should be clear from this construction that the resulting context-free grammar is equivalent to G.

Example 8.20
Consider the following extended context-free grammar:

p_1: *body*$\to b$ *decls* **option** *stmts e* p_2: *decls*$\to$ $\{decl\ s\}$ **seq**
p_3: *stmts*$\to$ *stmt* **chain** s p_4: *decl*$\to \alpha$
p_5: *stmt*$\to \beta$

This grammar specifies the body of a procedure of some programming language. The body of a procedure consists of an optional sequence of declarations, followed by a "chain" of statements. For the sake of clarity we leave the right-hand sides of the nonterminals *decl* and *stmt* unspecified, and we use the abbreviations b, e and s for the terminals *begin_token*, *end_token* and *separator_token*, respectively. We wish to transform this extended context-free grammar into a context-free grammar. The following steps are carried out.

Step 1 is not applicable. In step 2, we remove the operators **option**, **seq** and **chain** by rewriting their corresponding productions p_1, p_2 and p_3. The resulting grammar is then:

p_1: *body*→ *b* {*decls* | ϵ} *stmts e* p_2: *decls*→ *decl s* {*decl s*}*
p_3: *stmts*→ *stmt* {*s stmt*}* p_4: *decl*→ α
p_5: *stmt*→ β

Step 3 is not applicable. In step 4, we give compound expressions their own production. This requires us to rewrite p_1, p_2 and p_3, and add corresponding productions p_6, p_7 and p_8. We can also remove the extraneous parentheses in p_6.

p_1: *body*→ *b decls_opt stmts e* p_2: *decls*→ *decl s decls_clos*
p_3: *stmts*→ *stmt stmts_clos* p_4: *decl*→ α
p_5: *stmt*→ β p_6: *decls_opt*→ *decls* | ϵ
p_7: *decls_clos*→ {*decl s*}* p_8: *stmts_clos*→ {*s stmt*}*

Because we are not yet finished, we loop back to step 1 again, and rewrite p_6, and add ϵ-production p_9. Step 2 is not applicable. Step 3 removes the closure operators in p_7 and p_8, and adds productions p_{10} and p_{11}. There are no more compound expressions. The final context-free grammar is shown below:

p_1: *body*→ *b decls_opt stmts e* p_2: *decls*→ *decl s decls_clos*
p_3: *stmts*→ *stmt stmts_clos* p_4: *decl*→ α
p_5: *stmt*→ β p_6: *decls_opt*→ *decls*
p_7: *decls_clos*→ *decl s decls_clos* p_8: *stmts_clos*→ *s stmt stmts_clos*
p_9: *decls_opt*→ ϵ p_{10}: *decls_clos*→ ϵ
p_{11}: *stmts_clos*→ ϵ

$\diamond$

It follows from the existence of these transformations that the generating powers of context-free grammars and extended context-free grammars are the same. Thus, every context-free language can be specified by both a context-free grammar and an extended context-free grammar. The advantage of extended context-free grammars is that the notation using regular expressions is more concise, convenient and readable.

8.4.3   Extended LL(1) grammars

In Section 8.3.2 we saw how the first, follow and director sets can be used to determine whether a given context-free grammar is LL(1). In this section we show how these same sets can be used to determine whether a given extended context-free grammar is extended LL(1). Instead of terminals and nonterminals, however, we need to compute these sets for regular expressions. To a certain extent, we have already done this in the previous chapter (Section 7.3.2) as part of the element-construction method, but this was for a largely different set of operators. We are now interested in computing the above sets for the (new) operators **option**, **clos**, **seq** and **chain**. The operators **list** and **pack** are not included because these operators contain the tokens list_token, open_token and close_token. The **list** and **pack** operators are rewritten in the following way:

Reg. exp.	EMPTY
ϵ	true
$a \in T$	false
A where $A \to E \in P$	EMPTY(E)
$\{E\}$	EMPTY(E)
$E \mid E'$	EMPTY(E)$\vee$EMPTY(E')
$E\,E'$	EMPTY(E)$\wedge$EMPTY(E')
E **option**	true
E **clos**	true
E **seq**	EMPTY(E)
E **chain** E'	EMPTY(E)

Figure 8.9 Basic rules to compute the function EMPTY of a regular expression.

E **list**   : E **chain** list_token
E **pack** :   open_token E close_token

We begin as before by computing the Boolean function EMPTY.

Empty function. Let $G = (N, T, P, S)$ be an extended context-free grammar, with T and N the sets of terminal and nonterminal symbols, P the set of productions and S the start symbol. The function EMPTY(E) is true if and only if $\epsilon \in L(E)$. We can compute EMPTY for a given regular expression by using the basic rules shown in Figure 8.9.

Example 8.21
Consider the production $A \to a$ **option** $\mid b$ **seq** $\mid c$ **clos**. Applying the basic rules in Figure 8.9 to this production results in the following computation:

$$
\begin{aligned}
\text{EMPTY}(A) &= \text{EMPTY}(a \text{ **option** } \mid b \text{ **seq** } \mid c \text{ **clos**}) \\
&= (\text{EMPTY}(a \text{ **option**}) \vee \text{EMPTY}(b \text{ **seq**})) \vee \text{EMPTY}(c \text{ **clos**}) \\
&= (\text{true} \vee \text{EMPTY}(b)) \vee \text{true} \\
&= \text{true}
\end{aligned}
$$

$\diamond$

We must be careful, however, because in a recursive production, the basic rules in Figure 8.9 can generate cycles. We demonstrate this in the following example.

Example 8.22
The left-recursive production $A \to A$ **seq** $\mid a$ is not an elegant way of describing a string of a's. Applying the rules in Figure 8.9 to this production yields the following computation:

$$
\begin{aligned}
\text{EMPTY}(A) &= \text{EMPTY}(A \text{ **seq** } \mid a) \\
&= \text{EMPTY}(A \text{ **seq**}) \vee \text{EMPTY}(a) \\
&= \text{EMPTY}(A) \vee \text{false}
\end{aligned}
$$

Both EMPTY(A) = true <u>and</u> EMPTY(A) = false satisfy this equality. Logically, however, because the production describes a string of 1 or more a's, we expect that EMPTY(A) = false.   ◇

To circumvent this problem of circularity, we initialise the empty function to false for each nonterminal, and argue that a nonterminal can be empty only as a result of the application of a basic rule. In a (left or right) recursive grammar, this can involve an iterative process in which the values of EMPTY converge to their correct values. The number of iterations required will depend on the depth of the recursion.

Example 8.23
Consider the following context-free grammar:

$A \rightarrow B \mid AB$
$B \rightarrow a \mid \epsilon$

Initialising EMPTY(A) and EMPTY(B) to false, we recompute these functions using the rules in Figure 8.9.

$$
\begin{aligned}
\text{EMPTY}(A) \quad &= \quad \text{EMPTY}(B \mid AB) \\
&= \quad \text{EMPTY}(B) \vee \text{EMPTY}(AB) \\
&= \quad \text{EMPTY}(B) \vee (\text{EMPTY}(A) \wedge \text{EMPTY}(B)) \\
&= \quad \text{false} \vee (\text{false} \wedge \text{false}) \\
&= \quad \text{false}
\end{aligned}
$$

$$
\begin{aligned}
\text{EMPTY}(B) \quad &= \quad \text{EMPTY}(a \mid \epsilon) \\
&= \quad \text{false} \vee \text{true} \\
&= \quad \text{true}
\end{aligned}
$$

We find above that EMPTY(B) is, in fact, true. Recomputing EMPTY(A) we find:

$$
\begin{aligned}
\text{EMPTY}(A) \quad &= \quad \text{EMPTY}(B \mid AB) \\
&= \quad \text{EMPTY}(B) \vee \text{EMPTY}(AB) \\
&= \quad \text{EMPTY}(B) \vee (\text{EMPTY}(A) \wedge \text{EMPTY}(B)) \\
&= \quad \text{true} \vee (\text{false} \wedge \text{true}) \\
&= \quad \text{true}
\end{aligned}
$$

Hence EMPTY(A) is also true. If we again recompute the function EMPTY, then the values will not change. So, after 2 iterations the values of EMPTY(A) and EMPTY(B) have converged.   ◇

First sets. Having computed the empty function, we are now in a position to compute the first sets. The set FIRST(E) is the set of terminals that occur first in the strings of $L(E)$. We can compute FIRST for a regular expression by using the basic rules shown in Figure 8.10.

Reg. exp.	FIRST
ϵ	$\emptyset$
$a \in T$	$\{a\}$
A where $A \to E \in P$	FIRST(E)
$\{E\}$	FIRST(E)
$E \mid E'$	FIRST(E) $\cup$ FIRST(E')
$E\,E'$	$\begin{cases} \text{FIRST}(E), & \text{if } \neg\text{EMPTY}(E) \\ \text{FIRST}(E) \cup \text{FIRST}(E'), & \text{otherwise} \end{cases}$
E **option**	FIRST(E)
E **clos**	FIRST(E)
E **seq**	FIRST(E)
E **chain** E'	$\begin{cases} \text{FIRST}(E), & \text{if } \neg\text{EMPTY}(E) \\ \text{FIRST}(E) \cup \text{FIRST}(E'), & \text{otherwise} \end{cases}$

Figure 8.10 Basic rules to compute the set FIRST of a regular expression.

As with the computation of the empty function, recursive productions can lead to circular definitions. The circularity is broken by initialising the first set of each nonterminal to $\emptyset$.

Example 8.24
Let us consider the production from Example 8.22 that led to a circularity, namely $A \to A$ **seq** $\mid a$, and compute its first set. We expect that the first set consists of the symbol a. Applying the basic rules in Figure 8.10 results in the following computation:

$$
\begin{aligned}
\text{FIRST}(A) &= \text{FIRST}(A \text{ **seq** } \mid a) \\
&= \text{FIRST}(A \text{ **seq**}) \cup \text{FIRST}(a) \\
&= \text{FIRST}(A) \cup \{a\} \\
&= \emptyset \cup \{a\} \\
&= \{a\}
\end{aligned}
$$

Note that we have used the fact that, initially, FIRST(A) $= \emptyset$. ◇

Follow sets. We have computed the empty function and first sets bottom-up by breaking a regular expression down into its constituent subexpressions. Given the first sets of E and E', for example, we could compute the first set of $E\,E'$. The follow sets, however, require a top-down approach because we need to know the context of a regular sub-expression to determine its follow set. The follow set of E is the set of symbols that can follow a string derivable from E.

Example 8.25
Consider the extended context-free grammar:

$$G_1: \quad A \rightarrow B\ c$$
$$B \rightarrow a\ \textbf{chain}\ b$$

Examples of sentences specified by this grammar are *ac*, *abac* and *ababac*. By inspection we see that the follow set of *a* is {*b,c*}, and the follow set of *b* is {*a*}. Note also that the follow set of the nonterminal *B* is *c*, and that the follow set of the regular expression *a* **chain** *b* is *c*.   ⋄

Example 8.26
Consider the extended context-free grammars:

$$G_2: \quad A \rightarrow B\ c \qquad\qquad G_3: \quad A \rightarrow B\ c$$
$$B \rightarrow a\ b \qquad\qquad\qquad\quad\ B \rightarrow a\ b\ \textbf{option}$$

The follow set of the regular expression *a* in G_2 is {b}, but in G_3, it is {b,c}. We can generalise and say that if we have a regular expression *E E'*, then the follow set of *E* consists of the symbols in the first set of *E'*. However, if *E'* may be empty (*b* **option** in G_3 for example), then the follow set of *E E'* (*c* in G_3) must also be included. In other words, we have the following rule for *E E'*:

$$\text{FOLLOW}(E) = \begin{cases} \text{FIRST}(E'), & \text{if } \neg\text{EMPTY}(E') \\ \text{FIRST}(E') \cup \text{FOLLOW}(E'), & \text{otherwise} \end{cases}$$

We can also say that the follow set of *E'* is (obviously) the same as the follow set of *E E'*. That is:

$$\text{FOLLOW}(E') = \text{FOLLOW}(E\ E')$$

Notice that these equalities relate the follow set of a regular expression to the follow set of a subexpression, in top-down fashion.   ⋄

If we have a production $A \rightarrow E$, then FOLLOW(*E*)=FOLLOW(*A*) because everything that can follow *A*, can also follow *E* in some sentential form. In fact, this is how we pass follow-set information down the parse tree. If we have another production $B \rightarrow E$, for the same *E*, then in this instance FOLLOW(*E*)=FOLLOW(*B*). There is no conflict here—there are 2 different instances in the parse tree of the same regular expression *E*.

This is not the case, however, for nonterminals, as a nonterminal is "defined" in only 1 production, but may be "used" any number of times on the right-hand sides of productions. Each occurrence of a nonterminal *A* on the right-hand side will contribute to the follow set of the nonterminal *A*. Consider the following example.

Example 8.27
In the first extended context-free grammar below the nonterminal *C* occurs twice on the right-hand side of a production. In the second grammar, the regular expression *b* | *c* occurs twice.

$$G_4: \quad A \rightarrow C\ a\ B \qquad\qquad G_5: \quad A \rightarrow B\ C\ a$$
$$B \rightarrow C\ c \qquad\qquad\qquad\qquad B \rightarrow b\ |\ c$$
$$C \rightarrow b \qquad\qquad\qquad\qquad\ C \rightarrow b\ |\ c$$

Reg. exp.	FOLLOW
$A \rightarrow E \in P$	$\text{FOLLOW}(E) = \text{FOLLOW}(A)$
A_o	$\text{FOLLOW}(A) = \text{FOLLOW}(A) \cup \text{FOLLOW}(A_o)$
$\{E\}$	$\text{FOLLOW}(E) = \text{FOLLOW}(\{E\})$
$E \mid E'$	$\text{FOLLOW}(E) = \text{FOLLOW}(E \mid E')$
	$\text{FOLLOW}(E') = \text{FOLLOW}(E \mid E')$
$E\,E'$	$\text{FOLLOW}(E) = \begin{cases} \text{FIRST}(E'), \\ \quad \text{if } \neg\text{EMPTY}(E') \\ \text{FIRST}(E') \cup \text{FOLLOW}(E'), \\ \quad \text{otherwise} \end{cases}$
	$\text{FOLLOW}(E') = \text{FOLLOW}(E\,E')$
E **option**	$\text{FOLLOW}(E) = \text{FOLLOW}(E \text{ option})$
E **clos**	$\text{FOLLOW}(E) = \text{FIRST}(E) \cup \text{FOLLOW}(E \text{ clos})$
E **seq**	$\text{FOLLOW}(E) = \text{FIRST}(E) \cup \text{FOLLOW}(E \text{ seq})$
E **chain** E'	$\text{FOLLOW}(E) = \begin{cases} \text{FIRST}(E') \cup \text{FOLLOW}(E \text{ chain } E'), \\ \quad \text{if } \neg\text{EMPTY}(E') \\ \text{FIRST}(E) \cup \text{FIRST}(E') \cup \\ \quad\quad \text{FOLLOW}(E \text{ chain } E'), \\ \quad \text{otherwise} \end{cases}$
	$\text{FOLLOW}(E') = \begin{cases} \text{FIRST}(E), \\ \quad \text{if } \neg\text{EMPTY}(E) \\ \text{FIRST}(E) \cup \text{FIRST}(E') \cup \\ \quad\quad \text{FOLLOW}(E \text{ chain } E'), \\ \quad \text{otherwise} \end{cases}$

Figure 8.11 The rules to compute the set FOLLOW for regular expressions.

In grammar G_4, the 2 instances of C in the first and second productions mean that $\text{FOLLOW}(C)=\{a,c\}$. In contrast, in G_5, from production $B \rightarrow b \mid c$ we deduce that $\text{FOLLOW}(b \mid c)=\text{FOLLOW}(B)=\{b,c\}$, and from $C \rightarrow b \mid c$, that $\text{FOLLOW}(b \mid c)=\text{FOLLOW}(C)=\{a\}$. ◇

A list of rules to compute the follow sets of nonterminals and regular expressions is shown in Figure 8.11. In this figure, we denote an occurrence of a nonterminal on the right-hand side of a production by A_o. The follow sets of nonterminals are initialised to $\emptyset$.

Director sets. We could now use the first and follow sets to write down the condition(s) that an extended context-free grammar must satisfy to be extended LL(1). For convenience, however, we first define the director sets. The symbols in the director sets are used to select the correct part of a regular expression in the event of a choice (consider $E \mid E'$ for example) during the parse of an input string. The rules to compute the director sets are shown in Figure 8.12.

Reg. exp.	DIRSET
$E\,\|\,E'$	$\text{DIRSET}(E) = \begin{cases} \text{FIRST}(E), \\ \quad \text{if } \neg\text{EMPTY}(E) \\ \text{FIRST}(E) \cup \text{FOLLOW}(E\,\|\,E'), \\ \quad \text{otherwise} \end{cases}$
	$\text{DIRSET}(E') = \begin{cases} \text{FIRST}(E'), \\ \quad \text{if } \neg\text{EMPTY}(E') \\ \text{FIRST}(E') \cup \text{FOLLOW}(E\,\|\,E'), \\ \quad \text{otherwise} \end{cases}$
$E \textbf{ chain } E'$	$\text{DIRSET}(E') = \begin{cases} \text{FIRST}(E'), \\ \quad \text{if } \neg\text{EMPTY}(E') \\ \text{FIRST}(E) \cup \text{FIRST}(E'), \\ \quad \text{if } \neg\text{EMPTY}(E) \wedge \text{EMPTY}(E') \\ \text{FIRST}(E) \cup \text{FIRST}(E') \cup \\ \quad\quad \text{FOLLOW}(E \textbf{ chain } E'), \\ \quad \text{otherwise} \end{cases}$

Figure 8.12 The rules to compute the set DIRSET for regular expressions.

	Reg. exp.	Condition
1	$E\,\|\,E'$	$\text{DIRSET}(E) \cap \text{DIRSET}(E') = \emptyset$
2	$E \textbf{ chain } E'$	$\text{DIRSET}(E') \cap \text{FOLLOW}(E \textbf{ chain } E') = \emptyset$
3	$E \textbf{ option}$	$\neg\text{EMPTY}(E) \wedge (\text{FIRST}(E) \cap \text{FOLLOW}(E \textbf{ option}) = \emptyset)$
4	$E \textbf{ clos}$	$\neg\text{EMPTY}(E) \wedge (\text{FIRST}(E) \cap \text{FOLLOW}(E \textbf{ clos}) = \emptyset)$
5	$E \textbf{ seq}$	$\neg\text{EMPTY}(E) \wedge (\text{FIRST}(E) \cap \text{FOLLOW}(E \textbf{ seq}) = \emptyset)$

Figure 8.13 The conditions that regular expressions in an extended context-free grammar must satisfy.

Finally, we can present the definition of an extended LL(1) grammar.

Definition 8.11
An extended context-free grammar is *extended LL(1)* (or ELL(1)) if the conditions shown in Figure 8.13 are satisfied. ◇

Given the empty function and the first, follow and director sets, we can use this definition to determine whether an extended context-free grammar is ELL(1).

Example 8.28
Consider the following extended context-free grammar:

p_1: *prog* $\rightarrow$ *decl* **option** *expr* **chain** ;

p_2: *decl* $\rightarrow$ { { *int* | *real* } *id* **list** ;} **seq**

p_3: *expr* $\rightarrow$ *term* **chain** +

p_4: *term* $\rightarrow$ *factor* **chain** *

p_5: *factor* $\rightarrow$ { + | − } **clos** *id* | *expr* **pack**

The start symbol is *prog*, and the terminal symbols are +, −, *, ;, *id*, *int*, *real*, list_token, open_token and close_token. The symbols list_token, open_token and close_token are implicit in the **list** and **pack** operators. We assume that the input string is terminated by an end-of-input symbol $. The above grammar specifies a language consisting of declarations and expressions. An example of a sentence in this language is:

```
int a, b; real c; +-a++b; (a+b)*-c
```

Here we assume that "," represents list_token, "(" represents open_token and ")" represents close_token.

To determine whether the grammar is ELL(1), we need to check whether each production satisfies the conditions shown in Figure 8.13.

The production p_1 contains an **option** and a **chain** expression. We check the **option** expression with condition 3. Since EMPTY(*decl*) is false, we need to compute:

$$\text{FIRST}(decl) \cap \text{FOLLOW}(decl\ \textbf{option}) \quad = \quad \{int, real\} \cap \{+, -, \text{open\_token}, id\}$$
$$= \quad \emptyset$$

The **chain** expression in p_1 is checked with condition 2:

$$\text{DIRSET}(;) \cap \text{FOLLOW}(expr\ \textbf{chain}\ ;) \quad = \quad \{;\} \cap \{\$\}$$
$$= \quad \emptyset$$

The production p_2 contains a | expression, a **list** expression and a **seq** expression. Checking *int*|*real* with condition 1 is trivial and is not shown. We transform the expression *id* **list** into *id* **chain** list_token and check condition 2:

$$\text{DIRSET}(\text{list\_token}) \cap \text{FOLLOW}(id\ \textbf{chain}\ \text{list\_token}) \quad = \quad \{\text{list\_token}\} \cap \{;\}$$
$$= \quad \emptyset$$

Since EMPTY({{*int*|*real*}*id* **list** ;}) is false, checking the **seq** expression in production p_2 with condition 5 yields:

$$\text{FIRST}(\{\{int|real\}id\ \textbf{list}\ ;\}) \cap \text{FOLLOW}(decl)$$
$$= \quad \{int, real\} \cap \{+, -, \text{open\_token}, id\}$$
$$= \quad \emptyset$$

We check the **chain** expressions in productions p_3 and p_4 with condition 2. We show only the computation for p_3:

$$\text{DIRSET}(+) \cap \text{FOLLOW}(expr) \quad = \quad \{+\} \cap \{\$, \text{close\_token}, ;\}$$
$$= \quad \emptyset$$

The expressions + | − and {+ | −} **clos** in production p_5 are trivial to check, and are not shown. The expression *expr* **pack** in p_5 is transformed into open_token *expr* close_token, and need not be checked. Finally, we check the second | expression in p_5 with condition 1:

$$\text{DIRSET}(\{+ \mid -\} \textbf{ clos } id\,) \cap \text{DIRSET}(expr \textbf{ pack}\,)$$
$$= \{+,-,id\} \cap \{\text{open\_token}\}$$
$$= \emptyset$$

We find that all conditions are satisfied, hence the grammar is ELL(1). ⋄

8.4.4 ELL(1) parser generation

An ELL(1) parser can be either recursive-descent or table-driven.

Recursive-descent. In a recursive-descent parser, there is a procedure corresponding to each nonterminal. If $A \rightarrow E$ is the production for A in G, then the body of the procedure corresponding to A is constructed from the regular expression E. The statements in the body of the procedure associated with a regular expression E are determined by using a *syntax-directed* construction process, as shown in the table in Figure 3.13 in Chapter 3, for example. This process begins by generating a parser module $\Pi(E)$ for each production $A \rightarrow E$. The parser module may contain sub-expressions for which we can generate new parser modules. This top-down process continues until we reach the level of terminals and nonterminals in the specification. The procedure *next_token* is used to read the next input character from the input, and place it into the global variable *look_ahead*. The procedure *report_error* signals that there is an error.

The main program of the parser for G consists of a call to the procedure corresponding to the start symbol. If no errors are reported in processing the string w then w is a sentence generated by G. If an extended context-free grammar G is ELL(1) and has start symbol S then $\Pi(S)$ is a correct parser for G. It follows from the conditions in the ELL(1) definition that the parser constructed in this way is a deterministic program.

An ELL(1) parser generator parses the specification of the extended context-free grammar (the input grammar) and generates for each expression E in the productions of the grammar the associated parser text $\Pi(E)$. Before generating the text of the parser, it has to compute the empty function and the first, follow and director sets in order to determine whether it is able to generate a parser for the input grammar. If the grammar is not ELL(1), the parser generator will report an error.

Table-driven. In Section 8.3.2 we showed how the empty function and the first and follow sets are used to compute the director sets, and how the director sets can then be used to generate a parse table for an LL(1) context-free grammar. This parse table together with a predictive top-down algorithm (shown in Figure 8.5) constitutes an LL(1) parser.

A parser for an ELL(1) grammar also consists of a parse table and a predictive algorithm. There are 2 main differences between an ELL(1) and an LL(1) parser: first, the ELL(1) algorithm must handle regular expressions instead of terminals and nonterminals, and second, as well as the director sets, the ELL(1) algorithm needs the first sets for possibly all subexpressions in the regular expressions.

In the LL(1) parse algorithm (Figure 8.5), when we pop a nonterminal off the top of the stack, we use the director sets to select a production. The right-hand side of this production is then pushed onto the stack. In an ELL(1) grammar, the right-hand sides of productions consist of regular expressions. The ELL(1) parse algorithm must therefore be able to push and pop regular expressions consisting of operators like **option**, **clos** etc., together with their operands, on and off the stack. The first and director sets are then used in the algorithm to select the part of the regular expression that matches the current input (look-ahead) symbol. If we have, for example, the production $A \to a \,|\, b$ and the look-ahead symbol b, then we must match the second part of the regular expression with the look-ahead symbol (and "throw away" the first part). In practice this means that we pop the expression $a \,|\, b$ off the stack and push b back on if the look-ahead symbol is b.

We see how this works in practice in the ELL(1) parse algorithm shown in Figure 8.14. The preamble of this algorithm (i.e. initialising the stack and reading the initial look-ahead symbol) is the same as the preamble of both the LL(1) algorithm shown in Figure 8.5 and the non-deterministic algorithm shown in Figure 8.2. As before, in the main loop we pop the top element off the stack. If this element is a terminal, and if it matches the look-ahead symbol, then we read a new input symbol, and repeat the loop. If this element is a nonterminal, then we simply push its right-hand side onto the stack (remember there can only be 1 production for each nonterminal in an ELL(1) grammar) and repeat the loop. If the expression $E_1 \,|\, E_2$ is on top of the stack, then we push either E_1 or E_2 onto the stack depending on whether the look-ahead symbol is in the director set of E_1 or E_2.

The regular expression E **clos** is slightly more complex. Here we must "remember" (on the stack) that we are busy with a **clos** operator as long as there are look-ahead symbols that match E. We can express this recursively by replacing an expression E **clos** on the stack by $E\,E$ **clos** if the look-ahead symbol is in the first set of E. The first look-ahead symbol(s) are "consumed" by E, and the subsequent input symbols by the expression E **clos**. Note that because the grammar is ELL(1), we know that the first look-ahead symbol that is <u>not</u> in the first set of E marks the end of the part of the input that the **clos** matches. Further note that the instruction $push(E_1 \ldots E_n, \text{STACK})$, where E_i is a regular expression, is short for $push(E_n, \text{STACK}), \ldots, push(E_1, \text{STACK})$, and that after execution of this instruction, the symbol E_1 is on top of the stack.

The above technique of handling the **clos** operator can also be applied to the other iterative operators. If we find the regular expression E **seq** on the stack, then because we must match E at least once, we can treat E **seq** simply as $E\,E$ **clos**. Similarly, the regular expression E_1 **chain** E_2 can be treated as $E_1 \,\{E_2\,E_1\}$ **clos**. Eventually, each of the iterative operators will reduce to either a terminal symbol (which will be matched by the look-ahead symbol if the input is correct) or a nonterminal. The algorithm terminates successfully if all the input symbols are matched and the stack is empty.

```
while (accept && (look_ahead != $ || STACK != ∅)) {
    top_of_stack = pop(STACK);
    if (top_of_stack ∈ T) {
        if (top_of_stack != look_ahead)
            accept = false;
        else
            look_ahead = read(input);
    }
    else if (top_of_stack ∈ N || top_of_stack == {E})
        push(E, STACK);
    else if (top_of_stack == E₁E₂)
        push(E₁E₂, STACK);
        push(E, STACK);
    else if (top_of_stack == E₁|E₂) {
        if (look_ahead ∈ DIRSET{E₁})
            push(E₁, STACK);
        else if (look_ahead ∈ DIRSET{E₂})
            push(E₂, STACK);
        else
            accept = false;
    }
    else if (top_of_stack == E option) {
        if (look_ahead ∈ FIRST{E})
            push(E, STACK);
    }
    else if (top_of_stack == E clos) {
        if (look_ahead ∈ FIRST{E})
            push(E E clos, STACK);
    }
    else if (top_of_stack == E seq)
        push(E E clos, STACK);
    else if (top_of_stack == E₁ chain E₂)
        push(E₁{E₂E₁} clos, STACK);
    else
        accept = false;
}
output(accept);
```

Figure 8.14 A predictive top-down parse algorithm for ELL(1) grammars.

Example 8.29
Consider the following production:

$decl \rightarrow \{int \,|\, real\} \; id \; \textbf{chain} \; ,$

and the input string *real id,id* $ where $ is the end-of-input symbol. We will parse

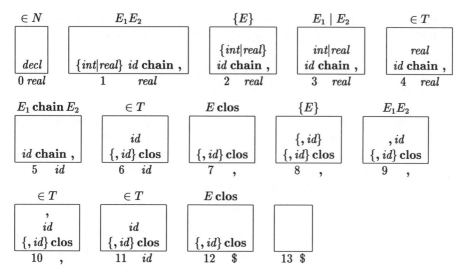

Figure 8.15   The changing contents of the the stack for the production *decl* →
{*int* | *real*} *id* **chain** ,.

this input string with the ELL(1) parse algorithm. The main stack operations
that occur during the parse are shown pictorially in Figure 8.15. Each diagram
in the figure represents 1 iteration of the loop. The value of *top_of_stack* is shown
above each stack, and the iteration number and the value of the look-ahead symbol
below.

We first initialise the stack with the start symbol *decl*, and read the first input
symbol, *look_ahead=real*. This is shown in the first stack. In the second stack we
have completed 1 iteration of the main loop. We have popped *decl*, and because
decl is a nonterminal, we have pushed the right-hand side of its production onto
the stack. In iteration 3 we must choose between the operands *int* and *real* of the
| operator. Since the look-ahead symbol is *real* we choose the latter. In iteration
4 we match the terminal symbol *real*. The next input symbol *id* is matched in
iteration 6. This leaves "," as the next input symbol. We expand the expression
{, *id*} **clos** in iteration 7 because the input symbol "," is in FIRST({,,*id*}). The
input symbols "," and *id* are matched in iterations 10 and 11. Only the symbol
$ now remains in the input. In iteration 12, we find that this symbol is not in
FIRST({,,*id*}), hence the stack becomes empty. As we have reached the end of the
input, we have successfully parsed the input string.   ◇

Implementing the ELL(1) parse algorithm is more difficult than the LL(1) algorithm because the elements in the stack are regular expressions, and these regular
expressions contain a mixture of infix operators (**chain** and |) and postfix oper-
ators (**clos**, **seq** and **option**). Ideally we require all the operators to be prefix
operators. In a regular expression made up of prefix operators, the operator with

the highest priority comes first. Knowing where the next operator is makes the implementation of the main loop in the algorithm straightforward.

8.5   Bottom-up shift/reduce parsing

Ideally, language constructs should be expressed as productions in a context-free grammar in a natural way. This is important for understandability and maintainability, but also for error handling and code generation, which may rely on the fact that the productions reflect the intention of a language construct. Naturalness of expression, therefore, is an important aspect of any class of context-free grammar.

The major disadvantage of the LL (or ELL) technique is that it is sometimes difficult to rewrite a given context-free grammar in LL (or ELL) form in a natural way. Factorisation in particular can make a grammar difficult to understand, and can make it difficult to generate code. A particular terminal symbol, for example, may be used in a number of quite different ways. When we factorise, all these uses are merged into 1 production.

A more powerful parsing technique that largely overcomes this problem is called *bottom-up parsing*. A particular bottom-up parsing technique called LR parsing is in fact the most powerful parsing technique known that does not use backtracking. This comes at some cost, however, as the technique is more complex and less intuitive than top-down parsing.

In Section 8.1 we saw that in a (left or right) derivation, we begin with the start symbol, and at each step, we replace the left-most or right-most nonterminal (respectively) by the right-hand side of its corresponding production in the given context-free grammar. This process continues until we have a sentence in the language. If we reverse the order of a derivation, then instead of deriving a sentence from the start symbol, we *reduce* a sentence *to* the start symbol. Each reduction step is a derivation step in reverse in which we replace a string that matches the right-hand side of a production by the corresponding left-hand side nonterminal.

Example 8.30
Consider the following context-free grammar:

p_1: $A \rightarrow B\,B$
p_2: $A \rightarrow a$
p_3: $B \rightarrow a\,B$
p_4: $B \rightarrow b$

and the string *abab*. A right-derivation of this string is the following:

$A \Rightarrow BB \Rightarrow BaB \Rightarrow Bab \Rightarrow aBab \Rightarrow abab$

Note that we have expanded the right-most nonterminal at each step. If we reverse this derivation, we generate a reduction of the string *abab*, as follows:

$abab \Rightarrow aBab \Rightarrow Bab \Rightarrow BaB \Rightarrow BB \Rightarrow A$ ◇

Reducing a sentence (the leaves of a parse tree) to the start symbol (the top of the parse tree) characterises bottom-up parsing. Like the top-down technique LL(k), the bottom-up technique LR(k) processes the input from left to right (hence the letter "L"), but using a right-derivation in reverse (the letter "R"). The look-ahead is k of course. All LL(k) grammars are LR(k), but there are many LR(k) grammars that are not LL(k). The grammar in Example 8.30 is LR(1), for example, but not LL(1) because the symbol a is in the director set of productions p_1 and p_2.

It is important to note in the reduction in the above example that we have carefully chosen the string that should be reduced at each step. In the first step, for example, we used production p_4 to reduce b to B. If, instead, our first step had been to use p_2 to reduce a to A, then we would not have successfully reduced the sentence. At each step in a reduction, the parser must be able to determine which string, if any, to reduce.

Like an LL parser, an LR parser consists of a driver (algorithm) and a parse table. The LR algorithm uses the parse table, and a stack, to reduce an input string to the start symbol. The elements on the stack are not symbols as with LL parsing, nor are they regular expressions as with ELL parsing; they are state numbers. A state is an abstraction of the input that has been read. There are only a finite number of states. The LR parser will always take the same action for a given state and look-ahead. The state transitions are stored in a table called *statetab*. By identifying all the states of the parser, we can determine which action the parser should take. There are 4 kinds of actions: *shift, reduce-by, accept* and *error*. The *shift* action involves reading an input symbol, the *reduce-by* action involves removing the top elements (that constitute the right-hand side of a production) from the stack, and the once-only actions *accept* and *error* signify that the parse was successful and unsuccessful (respectively). The actions for each state and input symbol are stored in a table called *actiontab*. Together, *statetab* and *actiontab* form the parse table.

Example 8.31
The parse table for the grammar in Example 8.30 is shown in Figure 8.16. In the action table in this figure, the letter "s" stands for *shift*, "rn" for reduce by production p_n and "a" for accept. Empty entries are error actions. The numbers in the state table represent states. ◇

The LR parse algorithm is shown in Figure 8.17. The algorithm begins by initialising the stack with state 0, reading an input symbol (look-ahead) and setting the Booleans to false. In the loop we set the current state to the state number on top of the stack. We define 3 stack functions: *push* to place a state (number) on top of the stack, *top* to inspect (but not pop) the top of the stack, and *chop* to remove the top element of the stack. The action *actiontab* with elements *current_state* and *look_ahead* must be one of the following:

shift A new current state determined by *statetab*[*current_state,look_ahead*] is pushed onto the stack, and a new look-ahead symbol is read.

state	actiontab			statetab			
	a	b	$\$$	a	b	A	B
0	s	s		3	4	1	2
1			a				
2	s	s		6	4		5
3	s	s	r2	6	4		7
4	r4	r4	r4				
5			r1				
6	s	s		6	4		7
7	r3	r3	r3				

Figure 8.16 A parse table for an LR parser.

reduce-by $A \rightarrow X_1 \ldots X_n$ The top n states on the stack (corresponding to the symbols $X_1 \ldots X_n$) are first removed. The state that is left on top of the stack, and the nonterminal A, are then used to compute the new current state. This state is pushed onto the stack.

accept Parsing is completed, and the input is accepted.

error The input contains an error.

Note that 1 symbol of look-ahead is used, hence the method is LR(1).

Example 8.32
Let us use the LR parse algorithm, and the parse table shown in Figure 8.16, to parse the string *abab*$. In the table shown in Figure 8.18 we show the sequence of actions carried out by the parser, and at each step, the contents of the stack (the top of the stack is on the left) and input. Each action, or line in the table, corresponds to an iteration of the loop in the algorithm. We briefly describe the sequence of actions below:

line 1 State 0 is on top of the stack, and the first input symbol (look-ahead) is a, so we must *shift*, and push state 3 onto the stack.

line 2 We are in state 3, with look-ahead b. We *shift* state 4 onto the stack.

line 3 In state 4, with look-ahead a, we reduce by p_4. The production p_4 is $B \rightarrow b$. The top state on the stack, corresponding to b, is removed, leaving state 3 on top. Since *statetab*[3,B] is 7, we push state 7 onto the stack.

line 4 In state 7, with look-ahead a, we reduce by p_3. The production p_3 is $B \rightarrow aB$. The top 2 states on the stack, corresponding to a and B, are removed, leaving state 0 on top. Since *statetab*[0,B] is 2, we push state 2 onto the stack. Skipping a number of actions, we go to line 9.

```
#define false 0
#define true 1
STACK = ∅;
current_state = 0;
push(current_state, STACK);
look_ahead = read(input);
error = false;
accept = false;
while (!error && !accept) {
    current_state = top(STACK);
    if (actiontab[current_state][look_ahead] == shift) {
        current_state = statetab[current_state][look_ahead];
        push(current_state, STACK);
        look_ahead = read(input);
    }
    else if (actiontab[current_state][look_ahead] == reduce-by A→X₁ ... Xₙ) {
        for (i=1; i≤n; i++)
            chop(STACK);
        current_state = statetab[top(STACK)][A];
        push(current_state, STACK);
    }
    else if (actiontab[current_state][look_ahead] == accept)
        accept = true;
    else
        error = true;
}
output(accept);
```

Figure 8.17 An LR parse algorithm.

line 9 In state 5, with look-ahead $, we reduce by p_1. The production p_1 is $A \rightarrow B\,B$. The top 2 states on the stack, both corresponding to a B, are removed, leaving state 0 on top. Since $statetab[0,A]$ is 1, we push state 1 onto the stack.

line 10 In state 1, with look-ahead $, we accept the input.   ◇

Note that a state is pushed onto the stack for every input symbol that is read, and that when we *reduce-by* a particular production, we remove the states from the stack corresponding to the symbols on the right-hand side of the production, and push a state onto the stack corresponding to the nonterminal on the left-hand side. Given the LR parse table corresponding to a context-free grammar, and the LR parse algorithm, we can parse a given input string. It is beyond the scope of this book to describe how the LR parse table is constructed. It suffices to say that it

	stack	input	action
1	0	abab$	s
2	30	bab$	s
3	430	ab$	r4
4	730	ab$	r3
5	20	ab$	s
6	620	b$	s
7	4620	$	r4
8	7620	$	r3
9	520	$	r1
10	10	$	a

Figure 8.18 The sequence of actions that are used to parse the string $abab\$$.

is, in general, too tedious a procedure to do by hand—an LR parse-table (parser) generator is essential.

8.6 Exercises

1. Write down the context-free grammars corresponding to each of the following languages.

   - $L_1' = \{wcw^r \mid w \text{ is in } (a|b)^*\}$, where w^r stands for w reversed

   - $L_2' = \{a^n b^m c^m d^n \mid n \geq 1 \text{ and } m \geq 1\}$

   - $L_3' = \{a^n b^n \mid n \geq 1\}$

2. A regular expression consists of the operators "*", "|", "(" en ")", and symbols from an alphabet. There is also (implicit) concatenation. The operator "*" has the highest priority, and "|" the lowest. Assume that the alphabet consists only of the letters "a" until "z".

   Write a context-free grammar for regular expressions.

3. Roman numerals are formed from the set of letters {I,V,X,L,C,D,M}. The Roman numeral for 999 is, for example, written CMXCIX. The relation between Roman numerals and (our) Arabic numerals is shown in the table below. Specify Roman numerals with a context-free grammar.

1	I	10	X	100	C	1000	M
2	II	20	XX	200	CC	2000	MM
3	III	30	XXX	300	CCC	3000	MMM
4	IV	40	XL	400	CD	4000	MMMM
5	V	50	L	500	D	5000	MMMMM
6	VI	60	LX	600	DC	6000	MMMMMM
7	VII	70	LXX	700	DCC	7000	MMMMMMM
8	VIII	80	LXXX	800	DCCC	8000	MMMMMMMM
9	IX	90	XC	900	CM	9000	MMMMMMMMM

4. Say why each of the following statements is true or false.

   (a) If a grammar is LL(k), then it is also LL($k + 1$).

   (b) If a grammar is LL($k + 1$), then it is also LL(k).

   (c) An LL(0) grammar can only generate a finite language.

5. Consider the following grammar:

   S → E
   E → T **chain** +
   T → F **chain** *
   F → (E) | ident_token

   (a) Carry out the ELL(1) test on this grammar.

   (b) By first transforming the grammar to remove the **chain** operator, carry out the LL(1) test on this grammar.

   Note that the input is terminated by the end-of-input symbol $.

6. Consider the following grammar:

program	→	begin_token declaration ; statement **chain** ; end_token
declaration	→	var_token ident_token **list**
statement	→	conditional
	|	assignment
conditional	→	if_token relation then_token statement **chain** ;
		else_token statement **chain** ; fi_token
relation	→	factor = factor
assignment	→	variable := expression
expression	→	term **chain** +
term	→	factor **chain** *
factor	→	variable
	|	num_token
	|	expression **pack**
variable	→	ident_token

   Note that the symbol ";" is a terminal.
   Compute the leading and trailing sets of each of the nonterminals.

7. Compute the empty function, and the first and follow sets for each nonterminal in the following grammars:

(a) S → A B c
    A → a | ϵ
    B → b | ϵ

(b) S → A B B A
    A → a | ϵ
    B → b | ϵ

(c) E → − E
    | (E)
    | V R
    V → **id** T
    R → − E
    | ϵ
    T → (E)
    | ϵ

Which of the above grammars is LL(1), and which is not?

8.7   Bibliographic notes

Although compiler builders have been using recursive-descent parsers since the
early 1960s, LL(k) grammars were only defined and developed at the end of the
1960s by Lewis and Stearns [99], and by Rosenkrantz and Stearns [127].

Almost all current compiler texts treat top-down, and LL(1), parsing. Some
texts are light in their treatment (of the theory at least): Bennett [22], Elder [39],
Lemone [94], Waite and Carter [141] and Watt [143] fall into this category. Elder
builds a recursive-descent parser from a BNF; Waite and Carter build a recursive-
descent parser from syntax diagrams; and Watt builds a recursive-descent parser
from an extended BNF. Because Bennett builds a compiler using YACC, his book
concentrates on bottom-up parsing.

Parsons [110] is an introductory text that the compiler novice will find highly
readable. For a (serious) implementor's viewpoint of top-down parsing, particularly
table-driven, the reader is referred to Holub [78].

The very well-known compendiums of compiler techniques Aho *et al.* [3], and
Tremblay and Sorenson [138], are useful references for top-down parsing. Other
texts, for example, Fischer and LeBlanc [45], Gough [60], Pittman and Peters [115],
and particularly Backhouse [18], provide more depth, however, treating theoretical
issues like strong and weak LL(k) grammars. The most extensive treatment of
top-down parsing, and also the most theoretical and daunting, can be found in
Aho and Ullman [4, 5].

A simple LL(1) grammar, also called an *s-grammar*, is an LL(1) grammar without ϵ-rules. This grammar was first investigated by Korenjak and Hopcroft [92]
(see also [4, 138]).

A thorough treatment of the implementation, but not the theory, of extended
BNF notation can be found in Watt [143]; and shorter descriptions in Backhouse [18], Pittman and Peters [115] and Tremblay and Sorenson [138]. The true
top-down extended-BNF enthusiast is directed to Lewi *et al.* [98], who describe the
LILA system. This system generates an ELL(1) parser.

An extensive discussion of error handling and repair in table-driven LL(1) and recursive-descent parsers can be found in Backhouse [18] and Tremblay and Sorenson [138]. Error handling in ELL(1) parsers is treated by Lewi *et al.* [98]. Other texts that address error handling are Aho *et al.* [3], Elder [39], Gough [60] and Waite and Carter [141]. See also the bibliographic notes in Chapter 3.

Chapter 9

Attribute evaluation

In Chapter 4 we informally introduced attribute grammars. We used attributes to solve the type-determination problem for arithmetic expressions, and we discussed the role of attribute evaluation in top-down parsing. In this chapter we more formally define attribute grammars, and reconsider attribute evaluation. We begin with the *one-pass scheme*, and go from there to the *multi-pass scheme*. We end this chapter with a more general and flexible attribute-evaluation scheme used for a class of attribute grammars called *ordered*.

9.1 Definition of attribute grammars

We start with a definition of an attribute grammar, which is an extension of the context-free grammar framework. We do not consider extended context-free grammars.

Definition 9.1
An *attribute grammar* is a five-tuple $AG = (G, SD, AD, R, C)$ defined as follows:

1. $G = (N, T, P, S)$ is the underlying *context-free grammar*. N is the set of nonterminal symbols, and T is the set of terminal symbols. The set $N \cup T$ is denoted by V, the alphabet of G. P is the set of productions. A production $p \in P$ will be denoted as $p: X_{p0} \rightarrow X_{p1} \ldots X_{pn_p}$, where $n_p \geq 0$, $X_{p0} \in N$, and $X_{pk} \in V$ for $1 \leq k \leq n_p$. $S \in N$ is the start symbol of the grammar. The grammar G is assumed to be reduced in the sense that every nonterminal is accessible from the start symbol and can generate a string that contains no nonterminal symbols.

2. $SD = (TYPE\text{-}SET, FUNC\text{-}SET)$ is a *semantic domain*. $TYPE\text{-}SET$ is a finite set of sets and $FUNC\text{-}SET$ is a finite set of total functions of type $type_1 \times \ldots \times type_n \rightarrow type_0$, where $n \geq 0$ and $type_i \in TYPE\text{-}SET$ $(0 \leq i \leq n)$.

384

3. $AD = (A, I, S, TYPE)$ is a *description of attributes*. Each symbol $X \in V$ has a set of *attributes* $A(X)$, which can be partitioned into 2 disjoint subsets $I(X)$ and $S(X)$ of *inherited* and *synthesised* attributes, respectively. The set of all attributes will be denoted by A, i.e. $A = \bigcup_{X \in V} A(X)$. I and S are the sets of all inherited and synthesised attributes, respectively. In other words $I = \bigcup_{X \in V} I(X)$ and $S = \bigcup_{X \in V} S(X)$. Attributes associated with different symbols are considered to be different, i.e. $A(X) \cap A(Y) = \emptyset$ if $X \neq Y$. If necessary an attribute a of symbol X will be denoted by a **of** X. For $a \in A$, $TYPE(a) \in TYPE\text{-}SET$ is the set of possible values of a.

4. $R(p)$ is the finite set of *attribute-evaluation rules* associated with production $p \in P$. $R = \bigcup_{p \in P} R(p)$. Production p: $X_{p0} \to X_{p1} \ldots X_{pn_p}$ is said to have the *attribute occurrence* (a, p, k) if $a \in A(X_{pk})$. The set of all attribute occurrences of production p will be denoted by $AO(p)$. This set can be partitioned into 2 disjoint subsets of *defined occurrences* and *used occurrences* denoted by $DO(p)$ and $UO(p)$, respectively. These subsets are defined as follows:

$$DO(p) = \{(s, p, 0) \mid s \in S(X_{p0})\} \cup \{(i, p, k) \mid i \in I(X_{pk}) \wedge 1 \leq k \leq n_p\}$$
$$UO(p) = \{(i, p, 0) \mid i \in I(X_{p0})\} \cup \{(s, p, k) \mid s \in S(X_{pk}) \wedge 1 \leq k \leq n_p\}$$

The attribute-evaluation rules of $R(p)$ specify how to compute the values of the attribute occurrences in $DO(p)$ as a function of the values of certain other attribute occurrences in $AO(p)$. The evaluation rule defining attribute occurrence (a, p, k) has the form

$$(a, p, k) = f((a_1, p, k_1), \ldots, (a_m, p, k_m));$$

where $(a, p, k) \in DO(p)$, $f : TYPE(a_1) \times \ldots \times TYPE(a_m) \to TYPE(a)$, $f \in FUNC\text{-}SET$ and $(a_i, p, k_i) \in AO(p)$ for $1 \leq i \leq m$. We say that (a, p, k) *depends on* (a_i, p, k_i) for $1 \leq i \leq m$. An attribute grammar is said to be in *normal form* if the extra condition $(a_i, p, k_i) \in UO(p)$ holds for $1 \leq i \leq m$, for every evaluation rule. Observe that it is easy to transform every attribute-evaluation rule (by a sequence of substitutions) so that only attribute occurrences in $UO(p)$ appear as arguments of f. We will assume our attribute grammars are in normal form.

5. $C(p)$ is a finite set of *semantic conditions* associated with production p. $C = \bigcup_{p \in P} C(p)$. These conditions are predicates of the form

$$f((a_1, p, k_1), \ldots, (a_m, p, k_m));$$

where $f : TYPE(a_1) \times \ldots \times TYPE(a_m) \to \{\text{true,false}\}$, $f \in FUNC\text{-}SET$ and $(a_i, p, k_i) \in AO(p)$ for $1 \leq i \leq m$.

$\diamond$

Semantic (and context) conditions allow the specification of a subset of the language defined by the underlying context-free grammar. A sentence that is generated by G is a sentence of the language specified by AG if the semantic conditions yield true.

We have so far only considered the syntax of attribute grammars. Now we discuss their semantics. A non-ambiguous context-free grammar assigns a single parse tree to each of its sentences. The nodes of a parse tree are labelled with symbols from V. For each interior node there is a production $X_{p0} \rightarrow X_{p1} \ldots X_{pn_p}$, such that the node is labelled with X_{p0} and its n_p children are labelled with $X_{p1}, \ldots, X_{pn_p}$, respectively. We say that p is the production (*applied*) *at* that node.

Given a parse tree, instances of attributes are attached to the nodes in the following way: if node N is labelled with grammar symbol X, then for each attribute $a \in A(X)$ an instance of a is attached to node N. We say that the parse tree has *attribute instance* $N.a$ (also written as a **of** N). Let N_0 be a node, p the production at N_0 and $N_1, \ldots, N_{n_p}$ the children of N_0 from left to right, respectively. An *attribute-evaluation instruction*

$$N_k.a = f(N_{k_1}.a_1, \ldots, N_{k_m}.a_m);$$

is associated with attribute instance $N_k.a$ if the attribute-evaluation rule

$$(a, p, k) = f((a_1, p, k_1), \ldots, (a_m, p, k_m));$$

is associated with production p. We say that attribute instance $N_k.a$ *depends on* attribute instance $N_{k_i}.a_i$ for $1 \leq i \leq m$. An *attributed parse tree* is a parse tree in which all attribute instances have a value. A *consistently attributed parse tree* is a parse tree in which all attribute instances are defined according to their associated attribute-evaluation instructions, i.e. the execution of any evaluation instruction does not change the values of the attribute instances. A well-defined attribute grammar assigns a single value to every attribute associated with a tree node. In this way, an attribute grammar assigns a consistently attributed parse tree to each of its sentences. Some applications concentrate on the result of the semantic conditions that determine whether a sentence is semantically correct or not. Other applications are only interested in an attributed parse tree as an intermediate result of the compilation process. For these applications semantic conditions are not used.

9.2   Attribute-evaluation methods

The task of an *attribute evaluator* is to compute the values of all attribute instances attached to a parse tree. In general, the order of evaluation is unimportant, with the only constraint being that an evaluation rule cannot be executed before the values of its arguments are available. Initially the values of all attribute instances attached to the tree are undefined, with the exception of the synthesised attribute instances attached to the leaves. These are determined by the scanner. In this scheme, the evaluator chooses at each step an attribute instance whose value can be computed. The evaluation process continues until all attribute instances are defined or until none of the remaining attribute instances can be evaluated.

The constraint that an evaluation rule can only be executed when the values of its arguments are available naturally leads to the concept of a dependency graph, in the following way. For every attributed parse tree, a *dependency graph* can be defined by taking the attribute instances of the parse tree as its vertices. For every pair of attribute instances $N_i.a$ and $N_j.b$, a directed arc $(N_i.a, N_j.b)$ is contained in the graph if and only if $N_j.b$ depends on $N_i.a$, i.e. if $N_i.a$ is an argument in the evaluation rule for $N_j.b$. Thus, the existence of arc $(N_i.a, N_j.b)$ indicates that the value of $N_i.a$ must be available before $N_j.b$ can be computed. A path in a dependency graph is called a *dependency path*. An attribute grammar is *circular* if it can produce an attributed parse tree whose dependency graph contains a circular dependency path. For a traditional attribute-evaluation scheme as described above, it is clearly impossible to evaluate the attribute instances involved in a circular dependency path.

Evaluators for non-circular attribute grammars can be divided into 2 categories: *dynamic* and *static* evaluators. Given a source program and its associated parse tree, a *dynamic evaluator* constructs a dependency graph, and performs a topological sort of its nodes to determine an evaluation order of the attribute instances in the tree. This occurs at attribute-evaluation time (compile time). A *static evaluator*, on the other hand, does not construct the dependency graph. Instead, the evaluation order is based on the dependencies between the attribute occurrences in the productions of the grammar. As a result, a static evaluator can be used for any parse tree of the grammar. The evaluation order is determined when the evaluator is generated (at compiler-construction time).

Here we do not consider the dynamic construction of attribute evaluators, and restrict ourselves to the static construction of attribute evaluators.

In order to choose a *tree-walk scheme* for a static evaluator, one could analyse the dependency relations between the attribute occurrences in the evaluation rules of the grammar. Such a scheme is *flexible* in the sense that the walk along the nodes of the parse tree is determined by the dependencies of the attribute occurrences in the grammar. In contrast to such a flexible scheme, in a *rigid* scheme the visiting order of the nodes is chosen *a priori*, i.e. independent of the attribute dependencies. An example of such a rigid scheme is to make a single pass (e.g. during parsing) or a number of passes of the parse tree, where a *pass* is defined as a depth-first left-to-right (or right-to-left) traversal of the parse tree. We call this approach "pass-oriented".

In this section we first reconsider the 1-pass evaluation scheme, which we have already discussed in Section 4.1.2, where we combined attribute evaluation with top-down parsing. We then introduce a block-structured language in which a variable need not be declared before it is used. This requires a 2-pass evaluation scheme, which can be easily generalised to a multi-pass scheme. We then reformulate the attribute grammar so that there is no upper-bound to the number of passes, i.e. the multi-pass scheme fails. This naturally leads us to the more flexible evaluation scheme of ordered attribute grammars.

9.2.1 1-pass evaluation

In Section 4.1.2 we explained that attribute instances can be evaluated during top-down parsing if the attribute instances can be evaluated during a single left-to-right pass of the parse tree.

For the "1-pass left-to-right" property the term "L-attributed" is often used. An attribute grammar is *L-attributed* if there are no right-to-left dependencies between the attribute occurrences of its productions.

Definition 9.2

An attribute grammar is *L-attributed* if for each production p: $X_{p0} \rightarrow X_{p1} \ldots X_{pn_p}$ with an attribute occurrence (b, p, k) that depends on an attribute occurrence (a, p, j), the following condition is satisfied: if $1 \le k \le n_p$ then $j < k$. ⋄

Figure 9.1 shows the 6 basic attribute dependencies. Note that the second and the third dependencies result in the attribute grammar not being L-attributed, whereas the others allow attributes to be evaluated in depth-first left-to-right order. The reader is invited to confirm that the attribute grammars in Examples 4.6, 4.8 and 4.9 are L-attributed, and that the attribute grammar in Example 4.7 is not.

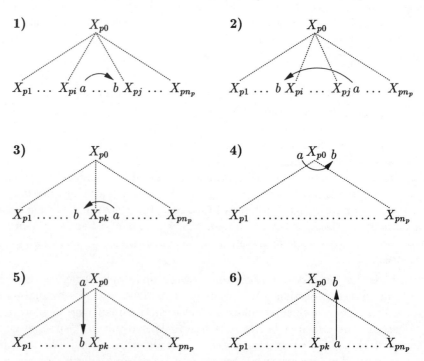

Figure 9.1 Attribute dependencies of a production.

9.2.2 Multi-pass evaluation

If an attribute grammar is not L-attributed, then evaluation in a single left-to-right pass is not possible. In that case one could try an evaluation scheme where a number of passes of the parse tree are made. It is, however, time-consuming if we must check at each pass and for each attribute instance whether the instance already has a value, and if not, to check whether the arguments of its evaluation instruction are defined so that the value of the instance under consideration can be computed. For practical purposes, preference must be given to a scheme that associates a fixed pass number with each attribute, so that the evaluation of all instances of that attribute in any parse tree can be performed during that pass. Consider, for example, an attribute *type* **of** *expr*. The above restriction means that all instances of attribute *type* **of** *expr* in any parse tree are evaluated during the same pass of the tree.

If pass numbers are known in advance, then it is also known that there is an upper-bound on the number of passes, i.e. the number of passes to be made is fixed for any parse tree of the attribute grammar.

The following example demonstrates the 2-pass evaluation scheme. It describes the scope rules of a language, and, in this sense, it is similar to the language presented in Example 4.8 in Section 4.1.2, with the difference that variables need not be declared before use. For productions and evaluation rules we will use the same notation as in Example 4.8.

The language has again a block structure. A *block* is built up out of statements, and a *statement* can be a *variable_declaration*, *simple_statement* or *block*. The grammar therefore allows the use of variable declarations and simple statements in any order. A *variable_declaration* specifies the declaration of a single identifier, e.g. **var** *a*, and a *simple_statement* specifies the use of a single identifier, e.g. **use** *a*.

As in Example 4.8, the attributes *or*, *up* and *us* (short for *original*, *updated* and *used*, respectively) represent symbol tables. The attributes *or* and *up*, associated with *statement_part* and *statement* are used to collect declaration information to be used in simple statements. The updated symbol table of *statement* is identical to the original one, except that it contains a new declaration if the statement is a variable declaration. Similarly, the updated symbol table of *statement_part* contains the information of the original table plus the declarations that are part of *statement_part*. The attribute *decl*, associated with *variable_declaration*, represents a single declaration. The attribute *us*, associated with *block*, *statement_part*, *statement* and *simple_statement*, is a symbol table that contains all identifiers that are valid for the grammar symbol concerned.

Example 9.1
The attribute grammar in which the scope rules of the language are implemented using a 2-pass attribute-evaluation scheme. Variables need not be declared before use.

grammar symbols:
  nonterminals: *program_declaration, block, statement_part, statement,*
                      variable_declaration, simple_statement.
  terminals: begin_token, end_token, var_token, use_token, ident_token.
  start symbol: *program_declaration.*

attribute types:
  { the definition of type symbol_table is not shown. }

description of attributes:
  or   :   symbol_table   **inh of** *statement_part, statement;*
  up   :   symbol_table   **syn of** *statement_part, statement;*
  us   :   symbol_table   **inh of** *block, statement_part, statement,*
                                          simple_statement;
  decl   :   declaration   **syn of** *variable_declaration;*
  lexeme :   string   **syn of** ident_token.

functions:
  symbol_table
  new_table(**void**)
  {   /*creates an empty table */
  }

  symbol_table
  append(string *decl*, /* **to** */ symbol_table *table*)
  {   /*adds a new declaration to the table,
            reporting an error, if a double declaration is found */
  }

  symbol_table
  concatenate (symbol_table *local_table*, symbol_table *global_table*)
  {   /*returns a symbol table by concatenating the local and the global
            table; in the case of identical names the declaration from the local
            table will be found first */
  }

  void check_declaration(string *name*, symbol_table *table*)
  {   /*reports an error if the name is not in the table */
  }

productions and attribute-evaluation rules:

  program_declaration   :   *block.*
        [*us* **of** *block* = new_table;]

block : begin_token *statement_part* end_token.
　　[*or* **of** *statement_part* = new_table;
　　us **of** *statement_part* =
　　　　concatenate (*up* **of** *statement_part*, *us* **of** *block*);
　　]

statement_part$_0$: *statement_part*$_1$ *statement*.
　　[*or* **of** *statement_part*$_1$ = *or* **of** *statement_part*$_0$;
　　or **of** *statement* = *up* **of** *statement_part*$_1$;
　　up **of** *statement_part*$_0$ = *up* **of** *statement*;
　　us **of** *statement_part*$_1$ = *us* **of** *statement_part*$_0$;
　　us **of** *statement* = *us* **of** *statement_part*$_0$;
　　]

statement_part : *statement*.
　　[*or* **of** *statement* = *or* **of** *statement_part*;
　　up **of** *statement_part* = *up* **of** *statement*;
　　us **of** *statement* = *us* **of** *statement_part*;
　　]

statement : *variable_declaration*.
　　[*up* **of** *statement* =
　　　　append (*decl* **of** *variable_declaration*, /*to*/ *or* **of** *statement*);
　　]

statement : *simple_statement*.
　　[*up* **of** *statement* = *or* **of** *statement*;
　　us **of** *simple_statement* = *us* **of** *statement*;
　　]

statement : *block*.
　　[*up* **of** *statement* = *or* **of** *statement*;
　　us **of** *block* = *us* **of** *statement*;
　　]

variable_declaration : var_token ident_token.
　　[*decl* **of** *variable_declaration* = *lexeme* **of** ident_token;]

simple_statement : use_token ident_token.
　　[check_declaration (*lexeme* **of** ident_token, *us* **of** *simple_statement*);]

◇

Figure 9.2 shows an attributed parse tree for the program

begin
　var a
　use a
　begin
　　use b
　　var b
　end
end

The dependencies between the attribute instances show that the instances of attributes *or* and *up* can be evaluated during the first pass, whereas the evaluation of the instances of attribute *us* must be postponed. The evaluation of the latter can be done during the second pass.

Below we present an implementation of the 2-pass evaluator by means of a set of recursive procedures. For each nonterminal X and each pass number i a procedure Xi is constructed. The body of such a procedure contains a case-statement if there is more than 1 production with the same left-hand side. The case-statement determines the production applied at the node being visited, which results in the selection of a sequence of actions associated with the production concerned (i.e. the evaluation of attributes, visits to child nodes, and finally a return to the parent node).

In the following procedures a parent node N is denoted by either "$N.0$" or "N", and the kth child of N by "$N.k$". Attribute instance a of node $N.k$ is written as "a **of** $N.k$". A call of procedure X is denoted by "**call** X".

```
void program_declaration1(node N)
{ call block1(N.1); }

void program_declaration2(node N)
{
    us of N.1 = new_table;
    call block2(N.1);
}

void block1(node N)
{
    or of N.2 = new_table;
    call statement_part1(N.2);
}

void block2(node N)
{
    us of N.2 = concatenate(up of N.2, us of N.0);
    call statement_part2(N.2);
}

void statement_part1(node N)
{
    switch (production at node N) {
    case statement_part0 : statement_part1 statement :
        or of N.1 = or of N.0;
        call statement_part1(N.1);
        or of N.2 = up of N.1;
        call statement1(N.2);
        up of N.0 = up of N.2;
        break;
    case statement_part : statement :
        or of N.1 = or of N.0;
```

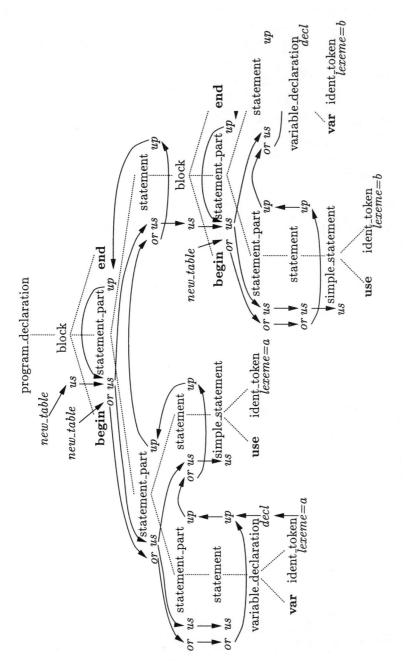

Figure 9.2 Attribute evaluation in 2 passes.

```
      call  statement1(N.1);
      up of N.0 = up of N.1;
      break;
  }
}


void statement_part2(node N)
{
  switch (production at node N) {
  case statement_part0 : statement_part1 statement :
    us of N.1 = us of N.0;
    call statement_part2(N.1);
    us of N.2 = us of N.0;
    call statement2(N.2);
    break;
  case statement_part : statement :
    us of N.1 = us of N.0;
    call statement2(N.1);
    break;
  }
}


void statement1(node N)
{
  switch (production at node N) {
  case statement : variable_declaration :
    call variable_declaration(N.1);
    up of N.0 = append(decl of N.1, /* to */ or of N.0);
    break;
  case statement : simple_statement :
    up of N.0 = or of N.0;
    break;
  case statement : block :
    call block1(N.1);
    up of N.0 = or of N.0;
    break;
  }
}


void statement2(node N)
{
  switch (production at node N) {
  case statement : variable_declaration :
    /* skip */
    break;
  case statement : simple_statement :
    us of N.1 = us of N.0;
    call simple_statement(N.1);
    break;
  case statement : block :
    us of N.1 = us of N.0;
    call block2(N.1);
```

```
      break;
   }
}

void variable_declaration(node  N)
{
   decl of N.0 = lexeme of N.1;
}

void simple_statement(node  N)
{
   check_declaration(lexeme of N.1, us of N.0);
}
```

The main program is:

```
call program_declaration1(rootnode);
call program_declaration2(rootnode);
```

9.2.3   Multi-visit evaluation

The extra requirement of the pass-oriented approach that every instance of the same attribute be evaluated during the same pass allows a simple evaluation algorithm. The method is therefore referred to as *simple multi-pass*. This extra requirement may, however, be too restrictive, as is shown in the following example.

Example 9.2
The following attribute grammar is not simple multi-pass.

grammar symbols:
   nonterminals: S, E.
   terminals: t.
   start symbol: S.

description of attributes:
   in : integer **inh of** E;
   out : integer **syn of** E;
   $result$: integer **syn of** S.

productions and attribute-evaluation rules:
   $S \rightarrow E_1 \ E_2$
      [in **of** $E_2 = 1$;
         in **of** $E_1 = out$ **of** E_2;
         $result$ **of** $S = out$ **of** E_1;
      ]
   $E \rightarrow$ t
      [out **of** $E = in$ **of** E];

◇

Figure 9.3 shows the parse tree with attribute instances and their dependencies of the only possible sentence of the attribute grammar in Example 9.2. Observe that the attribute grammar is not simple multi-pass as the 2 instances of *in* **of** E cannot be evaluated during the same pass. The same holds for the 2 instances of *out* **of** E.

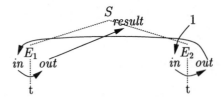

Figure 9.3 Attributed parse tree of the sentence **tt**.

If we drop the requirement that different instances of the same attribute be evaluated during the same pass, then the instances *in* **of** E_1 and *out* **of** E_1 should be evaluated during the first pass, and *in* **of** E_2 and *out* **of** E_2 during the second pass. This pass-oriented evaluation method, where no fixed pass number is associated with the attributes, is called *pure multi-pass*. The pure multi-pass method is characterised by the fact that the evaluation of attribute instances is performed during passes of the parse tree, and that the number of passes for a given attribute grammar has a fixed (known) upper-bound. The last requirement may, however, also be too restrictive, as is shown in the following example.

Example 9.3
The following attribute grammar is not pure multi-pass.

grammar symbols:
   nonterminals: S, A, B.
   terminals: a, b.
   start symbol: S.

description of attributes:
   in   : integer **inh of** A, B;
   out   : integer **syn of** A, B;
   result : integer **syn of** S.

productions and attribute-evaluation rules:
   $S \rightarrow A$
      [*in* **of** $A = 1$;
         result **of** S = *out* **of** A;
      ]
   $A_0 \rightarrow A_1 B$
      [*in* **of** B = *in* **of** A_0;
         in **of** A_1 = *out* **of** B;

$$out \text{ of } A_0 = out \text{ of } A_1;$$
$$]$$
$A \rightarrow a$
$$[\quad out \text{ of } A = in \text{ of } A;]$$
$B \rightarrow b$
$$[\quad out \text{ of } B = in \text{ of } B;]$$

◇

The possible sentences of the attribute grammar in Example 9.3 are ab^n $(n \geq 0)$. For sentence *abb* the parse tree is shown in Figure 9.4. Notice that the number of left-to-right passes needed to evaluate all the attribute instances depends on the depth of the recursion. There is therefore no fixed upper-bound on the number of left-to-right passes and hence the grammar is not pure multi-pass.

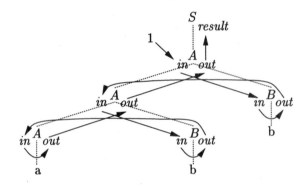

Figure 9.4 Attributed parse tree of the sentence abb.

Let us finally return to the attribute grammar of Example 9.1, where we change the attribution of the second production into

block : begin_token *statement_part* end_token.
    [*or* **of** *statement_part* = *us* **of** *block*;
        us **of** *statement_part* = *up* **of** *statement_part*;
    ]

Figure 9.5 shows the attributed parse tree of the sentence that we earlier considered in Figure 9.2. Notice that now the number of passes depends on the depth of the recursion. Hence, the grammar is not pure and certainly not simple multi-pass.

The attributed trees in Figures 9.2 and 9.5 show that an attribute grammar must sometimes be reformulated to allow a certain evaluation method to be applied. If the rigid method of passes fails, then we could use a more flexible tree-walk scheme that follows the dependencies between the attribute occurrences in the productions. An example of such a flexible scheme is that based on *ordered attribute grammars*.

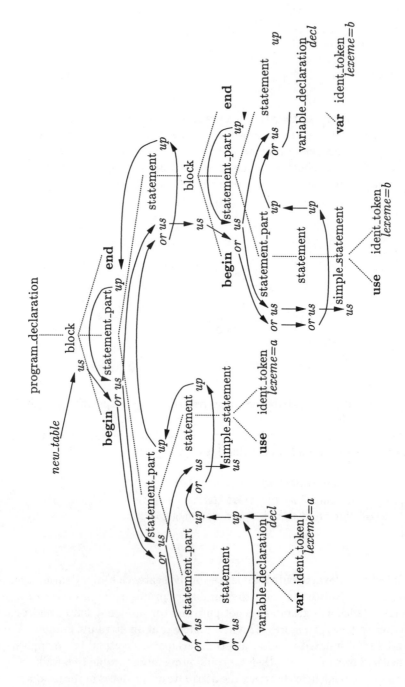

Figure 9.5 No fixed upper-bound on the number of passes.

An attribute grammar *AG* is *ordered* if for each grammar symbol a linear order of its attributes exists, such that the attribute instances for every node of a parse tree of *AG* can be evaluated in the prescribed order. For the attribute instances in Figure 9.5 the linear order of the attributes associated with the nonterminals is as follows:

> **block:** 1 visit: *us* at the downward visit and nothing at the upward visit
>
> **statement_part:** 2 visits: *or* at the first downward visit, *up* at the first upward visit; *us* at the second downward visit and nothing at the second upward visit.
>
> **statement:** 2 visits: *or* at the first downward visit, *up* at the first upward visit; *us* at the second downward visit and nothing at the second upward visit.
>
> **variable_declaration:** 1 visit: nothing at the downward visit and *decl* at the upward visit.
>
> **simple_statement:** 1 visit: *us* at the downward visit and nothing at the upward visit.

Note that the attribute instances no longer have *pass numbers*, but *visit numbers*. Taking into account the visit numbers and the attribute dependencies of the productions, the following implementation by means of recursive procedures can be derived. For each nonterminal X and each visit number i a procedure Xi is constructed. The visit number is deleted if there is only 1 visit.

```
void program_declaration(node N)
{
  us of N.1 = new_table;
  call block(N.1);
}

void block(node N)
{
  or of N.2 = us of N.0;
  call statement_part1(N.2);
  us of N.2 = up of N.2;
  call statement_part2(N.2);
}

void statement_part1(node N)
{
  switch (production at node N) {
  case statement_part0 : statement_part1 statement :
    or of N.1 = or of N.0;
    call statement_part1(N.1);
    or of N.2 = up of N.1;
    call statement1(N.2);
    up of N.0 = up of N.2;
    break;
```

```
      case statement_part : statement :
        or of N.1 = or of N.0;
        call statement1(N.1);
        up of N.0 = up of N.1;
        break;
      }
}


void statement_part2(node N)
{
  switch (production at node N) {
  case statement_part0 : statement_part1 statement :
    us of N.1 = us of N.0;
    call statement_part2(N.1);
    us of N.2 = us of N.0;
    call statement2(N.2);
    break;
  case statement_part : statement :
    us of N.1 = us of N.0;
    call statement2(N.1);
    break;
  }
}


void statement1(node N)
{
  switch (production at node N) {
  case statement : variable_declaration :
    call variable_declaration(N.1);
    up of N.0 = append(decl of N.1, /* to */ or of N.0);
    break;
  case statement : simple_statement :
    up of N.0 = or of N.0;
    break;
  case statement : block :
    up of N.0 = or of N.0;
    break;
  }
}


void statement2(node N)
{
  switch (production at node N) {
  case statement : variable_declaration :
    /* skip */
    break;
  case statement : simple_statement :
    us of N.1 = us of N.0;
    call simple_statement(N.1);
    break;
  case statement : block :
    us of N.1 = us of N.0;
```

```
    call  block(N.1);
    break;
  }
}

void  variable_declaration(node  N)
{
  decl of N.0 = lexeme of N.1;
}

void  simple_statement(node  N)
{
  check_declaration(lexeme of N.1, us of N.0);
}
```

The main program is:

```
call  program_declaration(rootnode);
```

Note that first 2 "passes" of the block at the first level are made, followed by 2 "passes" of the block at the second level, and so on. This is different from the approach in Section 9.2.2, where passes of the total tree are made.

9.3   Exercises

1. Consider the underlying context-free grammar of the attribute grammar shown in Example 9.1, where variable declarations and simple statements may occur in any order, and variables need not be declared before use. Assume, in contrast to the attribute grammar in Example 9.1, that variables must be declared before use. Augment the context-free grammar with attributes and attribute-evaluation rules so that evaluation is possible in 1 pass.

2. Consider the attribute grammar of Example 9.2. Rename the different occurrences of nonterminal E in the first production (e.g. replace E_1 by $E1$ and E_2 by $E2$, where $E1$ and $E2$ are different nonterminals). Show that the new attribute grammar is simple 2-pass.

3. The attribute grammar in Example 9.3 is not pur multi-pass and certainly not simple mult-pass. Show that the attribute grammar is ordered, and give an implementation of the ordered evaluator by means of recursive procedures.

4. Show that the following attribute grammar is not ordered.

grammar symbols:
   nonterminals: S, A.
   terminals: t.
   start symbol: S.

description of attributes:
   r : integer **inh of** S;
   a, b : integer **syn of** A;
   x, y : integer **syn of** A.

productions and attribute-evaluation rules:
   $S \rightarrow A$.
      [a **of** $A = 1$;
         b **of** $A = x$ **of** A;
         r **of** $S = y$ **of** A;
      ]
   $A_0 \rightarrow A_1\ t$.
      [x **of** $A_0 = a$ **of** A_0;
         b **of** $A_1 = b$ **of** A_0;
         a **of** $A_1 = y$ **of** A_1;
         y **of** $A_0 = x$ **of** A_1;
      ]
   $A \rightarrow t$.
      [x **of** $A = a$ **of** A;
         y **of** $A = b$ **of** A;
      ]

9.4   Bibliographic notes

Attribute grammars are used for specifying the context-sensitive syntax of programming languages, as well as for implementing syntax-directed editors, compilers, compiler writing systems, and, more generally, any application that has a strong syntactic basis. A large amount of literature on attribute grammars has appeared since Knuth [90, 91] introduced the basic concepts in the late 1960s. The ideas have recently been brought together in a number of publications. In 1988 a 3-part survey was published by Deransart *et al.* [37]. Part 1 presents main results on attribute grammars, including their classification, evaluators, space requirements and expressive power. Part 2 offers a review of existing systems, and Part 3 is a classified bibliography of about 600 references. In 1990 the International Conference WAGA (Workshop on Attribute Grammars and their Applications) [36] was held in Paris. The workshop covered all aspects of attribute grammars, with an emphasis on practical results and applications. In 1991 the International Summer School SAGA (Summer school on Attribute Grammars, Applications and systems) [15] was held in Prague. The course aimed at teaching the state of the art in attribute grammars, and their relation to other language specification methods. The emphasis was both on theory and applications. In 1995 Paakki [108] surveyed attribute-grammar-based specification languages and methods.

Over the years much attention has been paid to attribute-evaluation methods. The methods addressed in this chapter are the pass-oriented and ordered approach. The pass-oriented approach was first suggested by Bochmann [24] and further characterised by Alblas [8]. The ordered approach was invented by Kastens [89] and fully characterised by Engelfriet and Filé [42]. Other evaluation methods are described in an overview by Alblas [13]. The combination of attribute evaluation and parsing is surveyed by op den Akker *et al.* [6, 7].

Exploiting parallelism in attribute evaluation can speed up the compilation process. Most practical attribute grammars exhibit much parallelism. A review of the various methods that have appeared in the literature is given by Jourdan [86].

A number of extensions to attribute grammars have been proposed, including attribute-coupled grammars, higher-order attribute grammars, and attributed tree transformations.

The idea behind attribute-coupled grammars, as suggested by Ganzinger and Giegerich [52, 54], is that there is a designated synthesised attribute at the root of the derivation tree. An attribute grammar is then viewed as the mapping of the derivation tree to the value of the designated root attribute. If this value is again a tree, then a translation has been defined from the original tree to a new tree. This supports the mapping between intermediate representations (i.e. trees). In higher-order attribute grammars, introduced by Vogt *et al.* [139], an attribute can be a tree that is subsequently decorated with attributes and evaluated. The term higher-order is used because of the analogy with higher-order functions, where a function can be the result or parameter of another function.

Compiler optimisations and (context-sensitive) syntax-directed editing can be described by tree transformations. To specify optimising tree transformations, the classical attribute grammar framework has to be extended with conditional tree-transformation rules, where predicates on attribute values (carrying context information) may enable the application of a transformation (see e.g. Wilhelm [147]). A tree transformation may make attribute instances in a tree incorrect, not only in the restructured part of the tree but also elsewhere in the tree. To make the attribution of the tree consistent again a re-evaluation of the entire tree could be applied. However, a repeated computation of all the attribute instances after each transformation is inefficient and needs to be avoided. The only attribute instances that need to be re-evaluated are the attribute instances having an incorrect value (and the attribute instances directly depending on these attribute instances). Algorithms exist that minimise the number of visits to tree nodes and the number of re-evaluations. Evaluators employing such algorithms are called incremental evaluators. A simple pass-oriented approach is explained in Alblas [11]. For an overview we refer to Alblas [14]. The Synthesizer Generator, due to Reps, Teitelbaum and Demers, is the best-known system, based on incremental attribute evaluation, that supports syntax-directed editing [35, 119, 121, 122, 123, 124, 134]. The system has been the source of inspiration of several research topics, such as multiple subtree replacements [43, 112], remote attribute updating [120], bypassing of copy rule chains during re-evaluation [79], and evaluation of aggregate values [80]. Attribute re-evaluation in combination with optimising tree transformations is the goal of the OPTRAN system, due to Wilhelm and coworkers [100]. Criteria that permit a delay in calling the re-evaluator are considered by Alblas [9, 10]. Concurrent incremental attribute evaluation in distributed language environments is discussed by Alblas [12] and Kaplan and Kaiser [88].

References

[1] A. V. Aho, M. Ganapathi, and S. W. K. Tjiang. Code generation using tree matching and dynamic programming. *ACM Transactions on Programming Languages and Systems*, 11(4):491–516, October 1989.

[2] A. V. Aho and S. C. Johnson. Optimal code generation for expression trees. *Journal of the ACM*, 23(3):488–501, 1976.

[3] A. V. Aho, R. Sethi, and J. D. Ullman. *Compilers: Principles, Techniques and Tools*. Addison-Wesley, Reading, MA, 1986.

[4] A. V. Aho and J. D. Ullman. *The Theory of Parsing, Translation, and Compiling, Volume I: Parsing*. Prentice-Hall, Englewood Cliffs, NJ, 1972.

[5] A. V. Aho and J. D. Ullman. *The Theory of Parsing, Translation, and Compiling, Volume II: Compiling*. Prentice-Hall, Englewood Cliffs, NJ, 1973.

[6] R. op den Akker, B. Melichar, and J. Tarhio. The hierarchy of LR-attributed grammars. In P. Deransart and M. Jourdan, editors, *Proceedings of the International Conference WAGA: Attribute Grammars and their Applications*, volume 461 of *Lecture Notes in Computer Science*, pages 13–28. Springer-Verlag, New York–Heidelberg–Berlin, 1990.

[7] R. op den Akker, B. Melichar, and J. Tarhio. Attribute evaluation and parsing. In H. Alblas and B. Melichar, editors, *Proceedings of the International Summer School SAGA: Attribute Grammars, Applications and Systems*, volume 545 of *Lecture Notes in Computer Science*, pages 187–214. Springer-Verlag, New York–Heidelberg–Berlin, 1991.

[8] H. Alblas. A characterization of attribute evaluation in passes. *Acta Informatica*, 16:427–464, 1981.

[9] H. Alblas. Attributed tree transformations with delayed and smart evaluation. In D. Hammer, editor, *Proceedings of the 2nd Workshop Compiler Compilers and High Speed Compilation*, volume 371 of *Lecture Notes in Computer Science*, pages 160–174. Springer-Verlag, New York–Heidelberg–Berlin, 1989.

[10] H. Alblas. Iteration of transformation passes over attributed program trees. *Acta Informatica*, 27:1–40, 1989.

[11] H. Alblas. Optimal incremental simple multi-pass attribute evaluation. *Information Processing Letters*, 32:289–295, 1989.

[12] H. Alblas. Concurrent incremental attribute evaluation. In P. Deransart and M. Jourdan, editors, *Proceedings of the International Conference WAGA: Attribute Grammars and their Applications*, volume 461 of *Lecture Notes in Computer Science*, pages 343–358. Springer-Verlag, New York–Heidelberg–Berlin, 1990.

[13] H. Alblas. Attribute evaluation methods. In H. Alblas and B. Melichar, editors, *Proceedings of the International Summer School SAGA: Attribute Grammars, Applications and Systems*, volume 545 of *Lecture Notes in Computer Science*, pages 48–113. Springer-Verlag, New York–Heidelberg–Berlin, 1991.

[14] H. Alblas. Incremental attribute evaluation. In H. Alblas and B. Melichar, editors, *Proceedings of the International Summer School SAGA: Attribute Grammars, Applications and Systems*, volume 545 of *Lecture Notes in Computer Science*, pages 215–233. Springer-Verlag, New York–Heidelberg–Berlin, 1991.

[15] H. Alblas and B. Melichar, editors. *Proceedings of the International Summer School SAGA: Attribute Grammars, Applications and Systems*, volume 545 of *Lecture Notes in Computer Science*. Springer-Verlag, New York–Heidelberg–Berlin, 1991.

[16] H. Alblas and J. P. Schaap-Kruseman. An attributed ELL(1)-parser generator. In D. Hammer, editor, *Proceedings of the Workshop Compiler Compilers*, pages 77–91, Schwerin, Germany, 1990.

[17] H. Alblas and J. P. Schaap-Kruseman. An attributed ELL(1)-parser generator (abstract). In D. Hammer, editor, *Proceedings of the Workshop Compiler Compilers*, volume 477 of *Lecture Notes in Computer Science*, pages 208–209. Springer-Verlag, New York–Heidelberg–Berlin, 1991.

[18] R. C. Backhouse. *Syntax of Programming Languages*. Prentice-Hall, Englewood Cliffs, NJ, 1979.

[19] A. Balachandran, D. M. Dhamdhere, and S. Biswas. Efficient retargetable code generation using bottom-up tree pattern matching. *Computer Languages*, 15(3):127–140, 1990.

[20] D. W. Barron, editor. *Pascal—The Language and its Implementation*. John Wiley & Sons, New York, 1981.

[21] M. E. Benitez and J. W. Davidson. A portable global optimizer and linker. *Proceedings of the ACM SIGPLAN '88 Conference on Programming Language Design and Implementation, SIGPLAN Notices*, 23(7):329–338, July 1988.

[22] J. P. Bennett. *Introduction to Compiling Techniques, A First Course using ANSI C, Lex and YACC*. McGraw-Hill, New York, 1990.

[23] G. Berry and R. Sethi. From regular expressions to deterministic automata. Technical report 649, INRIA, Rocquencourt, France, March 1987.

[24] G. V. Bochmann. Semantic evaluation from left to right. *Communications of the ACM*, 19(2):55–62, February 1976.

[25] G. V. Bochmann and P. Ward. A compiler writing system for attribute grammars. *The Computer Journal*, 21(2):144–148, 1978.

[26] B. B. Brey. *The Intel 32-bit microprocessors: 80386, 80486 and Pentium*. Prentice-Hall, Englewood Cliffs, NJ, 1995.

[27] M. G. Burke and G.A. Fisher. A practical method for LR and LL syntactic error diagnosis and recovery. *ACM Transactions on Programming Languages and Systems*, 9(2):164–197, April 1987.

[28] J. Cai, R. Paige, and R. Tarjan. More efficient bottom-up multi-pattern matching in trees. *Theoretical Computer Science*, 106:21–60, 1992.

[29] R. G. G. Cattell. *Formalization and Automatic Derivation of Code Generators*. UMI Research Press, Ann Arbor, Michigan, 1982.

[30] D. R. Chase. An improvement to bottom-up tree pattern matching. In *Proceedings of the Fourteenth Annual ACM Symposium on Principles of Programming Languages*, pages 168–177, Munich, Germany, January 1987.

[31] N. Chomsky. Three models for the description of language. *IRE Transactions on Information Theory*, 2(3):113–124, 1956.

[32] N. Chomsky. On certain formal properties of grammars. *Information and Control*, 2(2):137–167, 1959.

[33] J. W. Davidson. *Simplifying Code Generation Through Peephole Optimization*. PhD thesis, Computer Science Department, University of Virginia, Charlottesville, Virginia, January 1987.

[34] J. W. Davidson and C. W. Fraser. Automatic inference and fast interpretation of peephole optimisation rules. *Software—Practice and Experience*, 17(11):801–812, November 1987.

[35] A. Demers, T. Reps, and T. Teitelbaum. Incremental evaluation for attribute grammars with application to syntax-directed editors. In *Conference Record of the Eighth Annual ACM Symposium on Principles of Programming Languages*, pages 105–116, Williamsburg, Virginia, January 1981.

[36] P. Deransart and M. Jourdan, editors. *Proceedings of the International Conference WAGA: Attribute Grammars and their Applications*, volume 461 of *Lecture Notes in Computer Science*. Springer-Verlag, New York–Heidelberg–Berlin, 1990.

[37] P. Deransart, M. Jourdan, and B. Lorho, editors. *Attribute Grammars, Definitions, Systems and Bibliography*, volume 323 of *Lecture Notes in Computer Science*. Springer-Verlag, New York–Heidelberg–Berlin, 1988.

[38] P. Naur (Ed.). Revised report on the algorithmic language ALGOL 60. *Communications of the ACM*, 6(1):1–17, January 1963.

[39] J. Elder. *Compiler Construction: A Recursive-descent Model.* Prentice-Hall, Englewood Cliffs, NJ, 1994.

[40] H. Emmelmann. Code selection by regularly controlled term rewriting. In R. Giegerich and S. L. Graham, editors, *Code generation—concepts, tools, techniques*, Workshops in Computing Series, pages 3–29. Springer-Verlag, New York–Heidelberg–Berlin, 1991.

[41] H. Emmelmann, F. W. Schröer, and R. Landwehr. BEG—a generator for efficient back ends. *ACM SIGPLAN Notices*, 24(7):246–257, July 1989.

[42] J. Engelfriet and G. Filé. Simple multi-visit attribute grammars. *Journal of Computer and System Sciences*, 24:283–314, 1982.

[43] A. Feng, T. Kikuno, and K. Torii. Incremental attribute evaluation for multiple subtree replacements in structure-oriented environments. In P. Deransart and M. Jourdan, editors, *Proceedings of the International Conference WAGA: Attribute Grammars and their Applications*, volume 461 of *Lecture Notes in Computer Science*, pages 192–206. Springer-Verlag, New York–Heidelberg–Berlin, 1990.

[44] C. Ferdinand, H. Seidl, and R. Wilhelm. Tree automata for code selection. *Acta Informatica*, 31(8):741–760, 1994.

[45] C. N. Fischer and R. J. LeBlanc. *Crafting a Compiler.* Benjamin/Cummings, Menlo Park, CA, 1988.

[46] C. N. Fischer, D. R. Milton, and S. B. Quiring. LR parsing for affix grammars. *Acta Informatica*, 13:141–154, 1980.

[47] C. W. Fraser, D. R. Hanson, and T. A. Proebsting. Engineering a simple, efficient code-generator generator. *ACM Letters on Programming Languages and Systems*, 1(3):213–226, September 1992.

[48] C. W. Fraser, R. R. Henry, and T. A. Proebsting. BURG—fast optimal instruction selection and tree parsing. *ACM SIGPLAN Notices*, 27(4):68–76, July 1992.

[49] C. W. Fraser and A. L. Wendt. Automatic generation of fast optimising code generators. *Proceedings of the ACM SIGPLAN '88 Conference on Programming Language Design and Implementation, SIGPLAN Notices*, 23(7):79–84, July 1988.

[50] M. Ganapathi and C. N. Fischer. Semantic attributes integrate code generation and optimisation. In *Proceedings of the Twentieth Annual Hawaii International Conference on System Sciences*, pages 307–317, Kailua-Kona, Hawaii, January 1987.

[51] M. Ganapathi and C. N. Fischer. Integrating code generation and peephole optimisation. *Acta Informatica*, 25(1):85–109, 1988.

[52] H. Ganzinger and R. Giegerich. Attribute coupled grammars. *Proceedings of the ACM SIGPLAN 1984 Symposium on Compiler Construction, ACM SIGPLAN Notices*, 19(6):157–170, June 1984.

[53] C. Ghezzi and M. Jazayeri. *Programming Language Concepts*. John Wiley & Sons, New York, 1987.

[54] R. Giegerich. Composition and evaluation of attribute coupled grammars. *Acta Informatica*, 25:355–423, 1988.

[55] R. Giegerich. Code selection by inversion of order-sorted derivors. *Theoretical Computer Science*, 73:177–211, 1990.

[56] R. Giegerich and K. Schmal. Code selection techniques: pattern matching, tree parsing, and inversion of derivors. In H. Ganzinger, editor, *Proc. 2nd European Symp. on Programming*, volume 300 of *Lecture Notes in Computer Science*, pages 247–268. Springer-Verlag, New York–Heidelberg–Berlin, 1988.

[57] R. S. Glanville. *A Machine Independent Algorithm for Code Generation and its Use in Retargetable Compilers*. PhD thesis, University of California, Berkeley, December 1977.

[58] R. S. Glanville and S. L. Graham. A new method for compiler code generation. In *Conference Record of the Fifth Annual ACM Symposium on Principles of Programming Languages*, pages 231–240, Tucson, Arizona, January 1978.

[59] M. J. C. Gordon. *The Denotational Definition of Programming Languages: An Introduction*. Springer-Verlag, New York–Heidelberg–Berlin, 1979.

[60] K. J. Gough. *Syntax Analysis and Software Tools*. Addison-Wesley, Reading, MA, 1988.

[61] J. H. Groen and W. J. M. Schepers. *Twente Compiler-Generator System, User's manual, version 2.5*. Enschede, The Netherlands, 1995.

[62] J. Grosch. Efficient generation of lexical analysers. *Software—Practice and Experience*, 19(11):1089–1103, November 1989.

[63] J. Grosch. Generators for high-speed front-ends. In D. Hammer, editor, *Proceedings of the 2nd Workshop Compiler Compilers and High Speed Compilation*, volume 371 of *Lecture Notes in Computer Science*, pages 81–92. Springer-Verlag, New York–Heidelberg–Berlin, 1989.

[64] J. Grosch. Efficient and comfortable error recovery in recursive descent parsers. *Structured Programming*, 11:129–140, 1990.

[65] K. Hammond and V. J. Rayward Smith. A survey of syntactic error recovery and repair. *Computer Languages*, 9(1):51–67, 1984.

[66] P. J. Hatcher and T. W. Christopher. High-quality code generation via bottom-up tree pattern matching. In *Proceedings of the Thirteenth Annual ACM Symposium on Principles of Programming Languages*, pages 119–130, Tampa Bay, Florida, January 1986.

[67] R. Heckmann. An efficient ELL(1)–parser generator. *Acta Informatica*, 23:127–148, 1986.

[68] J. Heering, P.Klint, and J. Rekers. Incremental generation of lexical scanners. *ACM Transactions on Programming Languages and Systems*, 14(4):490–520, October 1992.

[69] J. Heering, P.Klint, and J. Rekers. Lazy and incremental program generation. *ACM Transactions on Programming Languages and Systems*, 16(3):1010–1023, May 1994.

[70] C. Hemerik and J.-P. Katoen. Bottom-up tree acceptors. *Science of Computer Programming*, 13:51–72, January 1990.

[71] R. R. Henry. The CODEGEN user's manual. Technical report 87-08-04, Computer Science Department, University of Washington, Seattle, Washington, October 1988.

[72] R. R. Henry. Encoding optimal pattern selection in a table-driven bottom-up tree-pattern matcher. Technical report 89-02-04, Computer Science Department, University of Washington, Seattle, Washington, February 1989.

[73] R. R. Henry and P. C. Damron. Algorithms for table-driven generators using tree-pattern matching. Technical report 89-02-03, Computer Science Department, University of Washington, Seattle, Washington, February 1989.

[74] R. R. Henry and P. C. Damron. Performance of table-driven code generators using tree-pattern matching. Technical report 89-02-02, Computer Science Department, University of Washington, Seattle, Washington, February 1989.

[75] C. A. R. Hoare. An axiomatic basis for computer programming. *Communications of the ACM*, 12(10):576–583, October 1969.

[76] C. A. R. Hoare and N. Wirth. An axiomatic definition of the programming language PASCAL. *Acta Informatica*, 3:335–355, 1973.

[77] C. M. Hoffmann and M. J. O'Donnell. Pattern matching in trees. *Journal of the ACM*, 29(1):68–95, January 1982.

[78] A. I. Holub. *Compiler Design in C*. Prentice-Hall, Englewood Cliffs, NJ, 1990.

[79] R. Hoover. Dynamically bypassing copy rule chains in attribute grammars. In *Proceedings of the Thirteenth Annual ACM Symposium on Principles of Programming Languages*, pages 14–25, Tampa Bay, Florida, January 1986.

[80] R. Hoover and T. Teitelbaum. Efficient incremental evaluation of aggregate values in attribute grammars. *Proceedings of the ACM SIGPLAN 1986 Symposium on Compiler Construction, ACM SIGPLAN Notices*, 21(7):39–50, June 1986.

[81] J. E. Hopcroft and J. D. Ullman. *Introduction to Automata Theory, Languages, and Computation*. Addison-Wesley, Reading, MA, 1979.

[82] R. N. Horspool. An alternative to the Graham–Glanville code generation scheme. *IEEE Software*, 4(3):33–39, May 1987.

[83] E. T. Irons. A syntax-directed compiler for ALGOL 60. *Communications of the ACM*, 4(1):51–55, January 1961.

[84] H. Jansohn. *Automated Generation of Optimised Code*. PhD thesis, University of Karlsruhe, Germany, 1984.

[85] S. C. Johnson. A portable compiler: Theory and practice. In *Conference Record of the Fifth Annual ACM Symposium on Principles of Programming Languages*, pages 97–104, Tucson, Arizona, January 1978.

[86] M. Jourdan. A survey of parallel attribute evaluation methods. In H. Alblas and B. Melichar, editors, *Proceedings of the International Summer School SAGA: Attribute Grammars, Applications and Systems*, volume 545 of *Lecture Notes in Computer Science*, pages 234–255. Springer-Verlag, New York–Heidelberg–Berlin, 1991.

[87] E. Kantorowitz and H. Laor. Automatic generation of useful syntax error messages. *Software—Practice and Experience*, 16(7):627–640, July 1986.

[88] S. M. Kaplan and G. E. Kaiser. Incremental attribute evaluation in distributed language environments. In *Fifth Annual ACM Symposium on Principles of Distributed Computing*, pages 121–130, 1986.

[89] U. Kastens. Ordered attribute grammars. *Acta Informatica*, 13:229–256, 1980.

[90] D. E. Knuth. Semantics of context-free languages. *Mathematical Systems Theory*, 2(2):127–145, 1968.

[91] D. E. Knuth. Semantics of context-free languages, correction. *Mathematical Systems Theory*, 5(1):95–96, 1971.

[92] A. J. Korenjak and J. E. Hopcroft. Simple deterministic languages. In *IEEE Conference Record of the 7th Annual Symposium on Switching and Automata Theory*, pages 36–46, 1966.

[93] H. Kron. *Tree Templates and Subtree Transformational Grammars*. PhD thesis, Information Sciences Department, University of California, Santa Cruz, CA, 1975.

[94] K. A. Lemone. *Design of compilers: Techniques of programming language translation*. CRC Press, Boca Raton–Ann Arbor–London–Tokyo, 1992.

[95] M. E. Lesk. Lex—a lexical analyser generator. Technical report 39, Bell Telephone Laboratories, Murray Hill, NJ, 1975.

[96] J. Lewi, K. de Vlaminck, J. Huens, and M. Huybrechts. The ELL(1) parser generator and the error recovery mechanism. *Acta Informatica*, 10:209–228, 1978.

[97] J. Lewi, K. de Vlaminck, J. Huens, and M. Huybrechts. *A Programming Methodology in Compiler Construction, Part 1: Concepts*. North-Holland, Amsterdam–New York–Oxford, 1979.

[98] J. Lewi, K. de Vlaminck, J. Huens, and E. Steegmans. *A Programming Methodology in Compiler Construction, Part 2: Implementation.* North-Holland, Amsterdam–New York–Oxford, 1982.

[99] P. M. Lewis, II, and R. E. Stearns. Syntax directed translation. *Journal of the ACM*, 15(3):464–488, 1968.

[100] P. Lipps, U. Möncke, and R. Wilhelm. Attribute (re)evaluation in OPTRAN. *Acta Informatica*, 26:213–239, 1988.

[101] J. Mauney and C. N. Fischer. Determining the extent of lookahead in syntactic error repair. *ACM Transactions on Programming Languages and Systems*, 10(3):456–469, July 1988.

[102] W. M. McKeeman. Symbol table access. In F.L. Bauser and J. Eickel, editors, *Compiler Construction, An Advanced Course*, volume 21 of *Lecture Notes in Computer Science*, pages 253–301. Springer-Verlag, New York–Heidelberg–Berlin, 1974.

[103] H. Mössenböck. Alex—a simple and efficient scanner generator. *ACM SIGPLAN Notices*, 21:139–148, 1986.

[104] K. Nori, U. Ammann, H. H. Nagel, and Ch. Jacobi. Pascal P implementation notes. In D. W. Barron, editor, *Pascal—The Language and its Implementation*, pages 125–170. John Wiley & Sons, New York, 1981.

[105] A. Nymeyer. Review of the Graham–Glanville code-generation scheme. Technical report INF-88-61, Department of Computer Science, University of Twente, Enschede, The Netherlands, December 1988.

[106] A. Nymeyer. Backtracking non-deterministic recognizers. *Journal of Programming Languages*, 3:231–253, 1995.

[107] A. Nymeyer, J.-P. Katoen, Y. Westra, and H. Alblas. Code generation = A* + BURS. In *International Conference on Compiler Construction*, Linköping, Sweden, April 1996. To be published in Lecture Notes in Computer Science.

[108] J. Paakki. Attribute grammar paradigms—a high-level methodology in language implementation. *ACM Computer Surveys*, 27(2):196–255, June 1995.

[109] A. B. Pai and R. B. Kieburtz. Global context recovery: A new strategy for syntactic error recovery by table-driven parsers. *ACM Transactions on Programming Languages and Systems*, 2(1):18–41, January 1980.

[110] T. W. Parsons. *Introduction to Compiler Construction.* Computer Science Press, New York, 1992.

[111] V. Paxson. *Flex—Manual Pages.* Lawrence Berkeley Laboratory, 1988. Public domain software.

[112] S. B. Peckham. Globally partitionally attribute grammars. In P. Deransart and M. Jourdan, editors, *Proceedings of the International Conference WAGA: Attribute Grammars and their Applications*, volume 461 of *Lecture Notes in Computer Science*, pages 327–342. Springer-Verlag, New York–Heidelberg–Berlin, 1990.

[113] E. Pelegrí-Llopart. *Rewrite Systems, Pattern Matching, and Code Generation.* PhD thesis, University of California, Berkeley, December 1987. Also as Technical Report CSD-88-423.

[114] E. Pelegrí-Llopart and S. L. Graham. Optimal code generation for expression trees: An application of BURS theory. In *Proceedings of the Fifteenth Annual ACM Symposium on Principles of Programming Languages*, pages 294–308, San Diego, CA, January 1988.

[115] T. Pittman and J. Peters. *The Art of Compiler Design, Theory and Practice.* Prentice-Hall, Englewood Cliffs, NJ, 1992.

[116] T. W. Pratt. *Programming Languages: Design and Implementation.* Prentice-Hall, Englewood Cliffs, NJ, 1984.

[117] T. A. Proebsting. BURS automata generation. *ACM Transactions on Programming Languages and Systems*, 3(17):461–486, 1995.

[118] P. Rechenberg and H. Mössenböck. *A Compiler Generator for Microcomputers.* Prentice-Hall, Englewood Cliffs, NJ, 1989.

[119] T. Reps. *Generating Language-based Environments.* MIT Press, Cambridge, MA, 1984.

[120] T. Reps, C. Marceau, and T. Teitelbaum. Remote attribute updating for language-based editors. In *Proceedings of the Thirteenth Annual ACM Symposium on Principles of Programming Languages*, pages 1–13, Tampa Bay, Florida, January 1986.

[121] T. Reps and T. Teitelbaum. The Synthesizer Generator. *Proceedings of the ACM SIGSOFT/SIGPLAN Software Engineering Symposium on Practical Software Development Environments, ACM SIGPLAN Notices*, 9(3):41–48, April 1984.

[122] T. Reps and T. Teitelbaum. *The Synthesizer Generator: A System for Constructing Language-Based Editors.* Springer-Verlag, New York–Heidelberg–Berlin, 1989.

[123] T. Reps and T. Teitelbaum. *The Synthesizer Generator Reference Manual.* Springer-Verlag, New York–Heidelberg–Berlin, 1989.

[124] T. Reps, T. Teitelbaum, and A. Demers. Incremental context-dependent analysis for language-based editors. *ACM Transactions on Programming Languages and Systems*, 5(3):449–477, July 1983.

[125] H. Richter. Noncorrecting syntax error recovery. *ACM Transactions on Programming Languages and Systems*, 7(3):478–489, July 1985.

[126] J. Röhrich. Methods for the automatic construction of error correcting parsers. *Acta Informatica*, 13:115–139, 1980.

[127] D. J. Rosenkrantz and R. E. Stearns. Properties of deterministic top-down grammars. *Information and Control*, 17(3):226–256, 1970.

[128] J. van de Snepscheut. The design of a SATHE translator on the B 7700. Masters thesis, Department of Electrical Engineering, University of Eindhoven, Eindhoven, The Netherlands, April 1976.

[129] M. W. Spenke, M. Mühlenbein, M. Mevenkamp, F. Mattern, and C. Beilke. A language independent error recovery method for LL(1) parsers. *Software—Practice and Experience*, 14(11):1095–1107, November 1984.

[130] C. P. Stirling. Follow set error recovery. *Software—Practice and Experience*, 15(3):239–257, March 1985.

[131] J. Strong, J. Wegstein, A. Tritter, J. Olsztyn, O. Mock, and T. Steel. The problem of programming communication with changing machines, Part 1. *Communications of the ACM*, 1(8):12–18, August 1958.

[132] J. Strong, J. Wegstein, A. Tritter, J. Olsztyn, O. Mock, and T. Steel. The problem of programming communication with changing machines, Part 2. *Communications of the ACM*, 1(9):9–15, September 1958.

[133] D. Szafron and R. Ng. LexAGen: an interactive incremental scanner generator. *Software—Practice and Experience*, 20:459–483, 1990.

[134] T. Teitelbaum and T. Reps. The Cornell Program Synthesizer: A syntax-directed programming environment. *Communications of the ACM*, 24(9):563–573, September 1981.

[135] R. D. Tennent. The denotational semantics of programming languages. *Communications of the ACM*, 19(8):437–453, August 1976.

[136] R. D. Tennent. *Principles of Programming Languages*. Prentice-Hall, Englewood Cliffs, NJ, 1981.

[137] K. Thompson. Regular expression search algorithm. *Communications of the ACM*, 11(6):419–422, June 1968.

[138] J. Tremblay and P. G. Sorenson. *The Theory and Practice of Compiler Writing*. McGraw-Hill, New York, 1985.

[139] H. H. Vogt, S. D. Swierstra, and M. F. Kuiper. Higher order attribute grammars. *Proceedings of the ACM SIGPLAN '89 Conference on Programming Language Design and Implementation, SIGPLAN Notices*, 24(7):157–170, July 1989.

[140] W. M. Waite. The cost of lexical analysis. *Software—Practice and Experience*, 16(5):473–488, May 1984.

[141] W. M. Waite and L. C. Carter. *An Introduction to Compiler Construction*. Harper-Collins College Publishers, New York, 1993.

[142] W. M. Waite and G. Goos. *Compiler Construction*. Springer-Verlag, New York–Heidelberg–Berlin, 1984.

[143] D. A. Watt. *Programming Language Processors.* Prentice-Hall, Englewood Cliffs, NJ, 1993.

[144] B. Weisgerber and R. Wilhelm. Two tree pattern matchers for code selection. In D. Hammer, editor, *Proceedings of the 2nd Workshop Compiler Compilers and High Speed Compilation*, volume 371 of *Lecture Notes in Computer Science*, pages 215–229. Springer-Verlag, New York–Heidelberg–Berlin, 1989.

[145] C. Wetherell. Why automatic error correctors fail. *Computer Languages*, 2(4):179–186, 1984.

[146] R. Wilhelm. Attributierte Grammatiken. *Informatik Spektrum*, 2:123–130, 1979.

[147] R. Wilhelm. Computation and use of data flow information in optimizing compilers. *Acta Informatica*, 12:308–320, 1979.

[148] R. Wilhelm and D. Maurer. *Compiler Construction.* Addison-Wesley, Reading, MA, 1995.

[149] N. Wirth. *Algorithms + Data Structures = Programs.* Prentice-Hall, Englewood Cliffs, NJ, 1976.

[150] W. A. Wulf, B. W. Leverett, R. G. G. Cattell, S. O. Hobbs, J. M. Newcomer, A. H. Reiner, and B. R. Schatz. An overview of the Production-quality Compiler Compiler project. *IEEE Computer*, 13(8):38–49, August 1980.

Index